D0426261

More Praise for A CURIOUS MAN

"Brilliant . . . What's truly unbelievable is that it's taken us so long to get a full-fledged biography of this great American character. . . . **It was worth the wait."**

—A. J. JACOBS, *NEW YORK TIMES* BESTSELLING AUTHOR OF
THE KNOW-IT-ALL AND *THE YEAR OF LIVING BIBLICALLY*

"Neal Thompson has written the book many writers dream of—the great American rags-to-riches story—and has done it in an intoxicating way. The story of the man who created Ripley's *Believe It or Not!* is a rip-roaring tale of head-shaking amazement."

—MARC J. SEIFER, AUTHOR OF *WIZARD: THE LIFE AND TIMES OF NIKOLA TESLA*

"Robert Ripley was curious in both senses: first, his life was unbelievable to himself; and second, he couldn't feel life as a real thing, so he endlessly collected unbelievable bits of ephemera to make clear to himself that the world was as strange as he was, and also that he was equal to the world. In a way that I'm not sure I was expecting, the book builds real sadness into the considerable momentum of its narrative. **Neal Thompson constructs an elegant argument: the world Ripley created is the world in which we now live."**

—DAVID SHIELDS, *NEW YORK TIMES* BESTSELLING AUTHOR OF
THE THING ABOUT LIFE IS THAT ONE DAY YOU'LL BE DEAD

"*A Curious Man* is a work of real beauty and fun and emotion—and intense readability. It is a single-session book, one of those that takes your clock and renders it mute until the book has had its say. **Thompson is the genuine article: smart and witty, empathetic and a pleasure to read."**

—DARIN STRAUSS, BESTSELLING AUTHOR OF *HALF A LIFE* AND *CHANG AND ENG*

"Like Robert Ripley, Neal Thompson has a nose for the strange and wonderful. *A Curious Man* **is a rich, compelling read for fans of the exotic and uncanny."**

—STEWART O'NAN, BESTSELLING AUTHOR OF *THE ODDS*

"A biography of a man who was as unusual as the items he collected for his *Believe It or Not!* **cartoons . . . An outstanding work . . . I couldn't pull myself away."**

—FRANK BRADY, BESTSELLING AUTHOR OF *ENDGAME: BOBBY FISCHER'S REMARKABLE
RISE AND FALL—FROM AMERICA'S BRIGHTEST PRODIGY TO THE EDGE OF MADNESS*

"Most of my childhood I wondered, 'Who is this person Ripley, and why does he keep demanding to know if I believe his bizarre-seeming claims?' Finally Neal Thompson has given us the man's story, and Ripley's life turns out to have been as weird as his facts. **A fun but also compelling read that lingers in an unexpected way."**

—JOHN JEREMIAH SULLIVAN, AUTHOR OF *PULPHEAD*

"Believe it! Neal Thompson has written the definitive biography of the larger-than-life Robert L. Ripley, the father of our minutiae-mad modern society."

—KEN JENNINGS, ALL-TIME *JEOPARDY!* CHAMP AND BESTSELLING
AUTHOR OF *MAPHEAD* AND *BECAUSE I SAID SO!*

ALSO BY NEAL THOMPSON

Light This Candle:
The Life & Times of Alan Shepard,
America's First Spaceman

Driving with the Devil:
Southern Moonshine, Detroit Wheels,
and the Birth of NASCAR

Hurricane Season:
A Coach, His Team, and Their Triumph
in the Time of Katrina

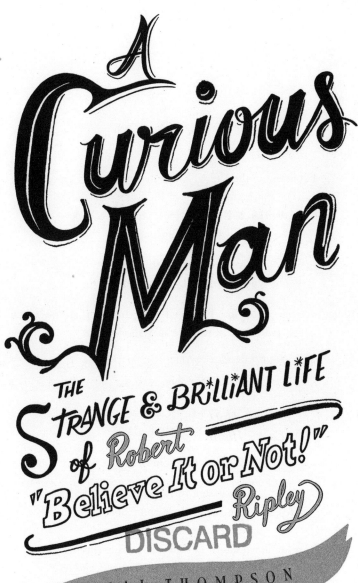

A Curious Man

THE STRANGE & BRILLIANT LIFE of Robert "Believe It or Not!" Ripley

NEAL THOMPSON

CROWN
ARCHETYPE
NEW YORK

SANTA CLARA PUBLIC LIBRARY
2635 Homestead Road
Santa Clara, CA 95051

DISCARD

Copyright © 2013 by Neal Thompson

All rights reserved.
Published in the United States by Crown Archetype,
an imprint of the Crown Publishing Group,
a division of Random House, Inc., New York.
www.crownpublishing.com

Crown Archetype with colophon
is a trademark of Random House, Inc.

Ripley's, Believe It or Not!, Ripley's Believe It or Not! are registered
trademarks of Ripley Entertainment Inc.

Library of Congress Cataloging-in-Publication Data
is available upon request.

ISBN 978-0-7704-3620-9
eISBN 978-0-7704-3621-6

Printed in the United States of America

Book design by Jaclyn Reyes
Jacket layout by Joel Holland and Nupoor Gordon
Jacket typography by Joel Holland
Jacket illustrations: © Ripley Entertainment Inc.
Jacket photograph: © Triff/Shutterstock
Author photograph: Charis Brice

All interior photographs copyright © Ripley Entertainment Inc.

1 3 5 7 9 10 8 6 4 2

First Edition

For Mary, always

For Sean and Leo

Ripley's Rambles

ADEN
Afghanistan
Ajmer-Merwara* ALASKA Albania ALGERIA
Andorra ANTIGUA Arabia ARGENTINA
Armenia AUSTRALIA Austria AZERBAIJAN
Azores BAHAMAS Bahawalpur* BALI
Baluchistan BARBADOS Baroda* BASQUE
Bechuanaland BELGIUM Bengal* BERMUDA
Bihar & Orissa* BOLIVIA Bombay Presidency* BOSNIA
Brazil BRITISH GUIANA* British Honduras* BULGARIA
Burma Canada CAPE ZONE Cape Colony* CELEBES*
Central Provinces (Africa)* CEYLON Channel Islands
CHILE China COLOMBIA Corsica COSTA RICA Croatia
CUBA Curaçao CYRENAICA* Czechoslovakia*
DALMATIA Danzig* DELHI Denmark DJEBEL DRUZE*
Djerba DOMINICAN REPUBLIC Dutch East Indies*
EAST PRUSSIA* Ecuador EGYPT El Salvador ENGLAND
Er Rif* ESTONIA Finland FIJI ISLANDS Formosa* FRANCE
French Guiana FRONTIER PROVINCES (IRAQ)
Garden of Eden* GEORGIA Germany GIBRALTAR
Greece GUADELOUPE Guatemala HAITI Hawaiian
Islands HERZEGOVINA Holland HONDURAS Hong
Kong HUNGARY Iceland ININI TERRITORY* Iraq
IRISH FREE STATE* Isle of Man ITALY Jamaica
JAPAN Java JEHOL* Johore KARELIA*
Kashmir-Jammu* KENYA COLONY* Khairpur* KOREA*

* No longer exists or has been renamed

Kurdistan **KWANTUNG*** *Lapland* LATVIA *Lebanon*
LIECHTENSTEIN *Lithuania* LLÍVIA *Luxembourg* MACAO
Madeira MADOERA *Madras* **MALLORCA** *Malta*
MANCHUKUO* *Martinique* MEXICO *Mombasa*
MONACO *Montenegro* MOROCCO *Mozambique*
NATAL* *Newfoundland* **NEW ZEALAND** *Nicaragua*
NORTH CAUCASUS *Northern Ireland* NORTHERN
RHODESIA* *Norway* **ORANGE FREE STATE*** *Orkney*
Islands PALESTINE *Panama* PAPUA*
Paraguay **PERSIA*** *Peru* PHILIPPINE ISLANDS*
Poland PORTUGAL *Puerto Rico* **PUNJAB** *Quelimane*
RAJPUTANA *Rhodes* SAAR *Sahara (French)* *
ST. CROIX *St. Lucia* **ST. PIERRE-MIQUELON** *St. Thomas*
Samoa SAN BLAS *San Marino* SARDINIA *Sark*
SCOTLAND *Serbia* SHETLAND ISLANDS *Siam** SICILY
Sinai **SINDH** *Southern Rhodesia** SOVIET RUSSIA* *Spain*
STRAITS SETTLEMENTS* *Sudan* SUMATRA *Suriname*
SWAZILAND *Sweden* SWITZERLAND *Syria*
TONGA ISLANDS *Tanganyika** **TANGIER** *Tchad**
TRANSJORDAN* *Transvaal** TRINIDAD
*Tripolitania** **TUNISIA** *Turkey* UGANDA
Ukraine UNITED PROVINCES *United States*
URUGUAY *Vatican City State*
VENEZUELA *Virgin Islands*
WALES *Württemberg** **YUCATÁN**
*Yugoslavia** ZANZIBAR *Zara*

**PASSPORT
OFFICE**

Dear Reader,

Want to see archival footage of Ripley in China? At sea? On stage? Want to see a man stick a spoke through his tongue, or get shot in the gut with a cannonball and survive? Unlock exclusive content hidden in the photo section of this book—including rare videos and images, audio of Ripley's radio shows, and dozens of original Ripley's *Believe It or Not!* cartoons—by downloading the free Ripley's *Believe It or Not!* app and activating the oddSCAN™ feature. Select "Ripley Bio" and look for the oddSCAN logos in the photo section of this book. Scan the *full page* with your smartphone to reveal the hidden content. For more information, visit www.nealthompson.com/books/curiousman.

The freakish breaks all rules; it seems beyond belief because it fails to make any sense; it upsets comforting notions. The freakish is the ultimate avant-garde, a finger in the eye of the buttoned-up bourgeois vision of ordered life, like a tattoo parlor in the midst of a holistic spa.

—"O, BELIEVERS, PREPARE TO BE AMAZED!"
EDWARD ROTHSTEIN, *NEW YORK TIMES*

Our daily life is so cut and dried that we get relief from fairy tales. Except Ripley's fairy tales are true, and this excites people. They like to learn that nature makes exceptions. These are fairy tales for grown-ups.

—NORBERT PEARLROTH

In the middle of the Syrian Desert, halfway between Damascus and Baghdad, the half-breed vehicle with twelve sand-surfing balloon tires came to a stop at an indistinct pile of rocks bordered by a scrawny stand of palm trees. It was time for lunch.

Passengers stepped off the car-bus into the brutal heat, including two Americans, one of them more portly and distinctly American than the other.

Robert L. Ripley was dressed in his preferred global traveler's outfit—black-and-white wing tips, knee-high socks, white shorts, and a short-sleeved shirt. Atop his head sat a wide-brimmed pith helmet. As the tour bus staff handed out bagged sandwiches, Ripley withdrew his own lunch: a thermos of scotch and soda. He turned and offered a swig to his traveling partner, an earnest young Mormon from Utah named Joe Simpson, who worked for Ripley's boss.

Newspaperman William Randolph Hearst had hired Ripley in 1929, paying him more than $100,000 a year and making Ripley one of the best-paid journalists in all of newspapers. Simpson's job was to protect and serve the famed and famously erratic cartoonist, a role that veered from traveling secretary to photographer to drinking partner. That night, Ripley's caravan stopped at the sprawling fortress compound called Rutbah Wells, whose gates lifted as a small crowd gathered to greet the new arrivals. Ripley emerged from his vehicle to hear the distinct drawl of his friend, Will Rogers: "Hi, Bob. Where d'you think you're goin'?"

Rogers was headed the opposite way, toward Damascus, while Ripley was trying to add two new countries to his list, Iraq and Persia, part of his relentless search for material for his increasingly popular cartoon and its lucrative offshoots: books, films, radio shows and, currently on display at the Chicago World's Fair, a kooky museum and performance hall called the Odditorium.

After a three-hour stopover at the bustling Rutbah encampment, Ripley said good-bye to Rogers and reboarded his bus, which drove on through the sweltering night. At dawn, 250 miles later, Ripley spotted the sun-sparkled minarets of Baghdad's mosques.

* * *

RIPLEY HAD BEEN TRAVELING the world ever since moving to New York as a skittish rookie newspaper cartoonist in 1912. In recent years, thanks to his six-figure salary from Hearst and even more income from other ventures, he'd ramped up his travels, accumulating more than 130,000 miles in the past two years alone—more than half the distance to the moon— ranging from South America to North Africa, Fiji to Singapore, Indian holy cities to war-wracked China. His current journey had routed him through Naples, Alexandria, Tel Aviv, Jerusalem, Haifa, and then Damascus. His real goal was the Garden of Eden, in Iraq, then on to Persia and, finally, forbidden *Russia*.

At the Tigris Palace Hotel in Baghdad, Ripley washed away

two days of Syrian Desert dust and walked among the ancient city's coffeehouses, jotting his first impressions of Iraq in a journal: "never see women. men everywhere, talking and drinking–smoking . . . they talk constantly . . . they are talking about nothing at all."

Ripley had been warned that Iraqis didn't always appreciate the arrival of "unbelievers" in their towns, that visitors were sometimes injured for failing to respect local customs and protocols. Despite such warnings, Ripley and Simpson pointed their cameras at everything, which usually drew curious and sometimes angry crowds, especially in poor and remote villages. At a school in Najaf, where cross-legged men studied the Koran, a group of locals surrounded them, gesturing urgently at Simpson's camera and shouting at Ripley, who later called them "a strange mixture of humanity, paralytic, half-blind, dirty, ragged, and altogether unfriendly."

In the city of Ur, he and Simpson found a secret canteen that sold cold beer and, despite a sign warning NO DRINKING ON THE PREMISES, tossed back twenty-one bottles between them, then fell asleep on an overnight train ride to Basra, where they finally reached the purported site of the Garden of Eden. An unfaithful husband and Prohibition violator, Ripley was both familiar with and fascinated by sin, which he once called "the curse of the human race—although it is very popular."

He was disappointed not to find an intact version of the biblical garden where man's first sin allegedly occurred. "NO APPLES. NO FIG LEAVES," he complained. Instead of the Tree of Knowledge of Good and Evil, from which Eve had plucked the forbidden fruit, Ripley found only a dead stump.

Still, before getting back on the road, he was sufficiently inspired to strip naked and have Simpson take pictures of him posing, Adam-esque, behind a palm tree.

Back in Baghdad, Ripley drank German beers at a café near Maude Bridge, then dressed in the white robe and *keffiyeh* head-dress he'd purchased, to the amusement of a nearby crowd. An overnight train ride delivered him to Persia, his 153rd country, where he drank beer for breakfast and began mapping a route home.

✳   ✳   ✳

DURING THE DEPRESSION, as Americans in a pre-television era sought affordable means of escape and entertainment, Ripley the traveling cartoonist provided both.

A connoisseur of mosts and bests, of fastest and farthest, of the weirdest and freakiest that the world could offer, his cartoons and essays appeared in hundreds of newspapers around the globe, in dozens of languages, and were read by many millions. His life's mission was to prove to readers that veracity and reality were elusive—King George I of England never spoke English; Aesop did not write Aesop's Fables; Buffalo Bill never once shot a buffalo; Lindbergh wasn't the first man to fly the Atlantic—and that sometimes you can't recognize truth until someone shines a light.

"I think mine is the only business in which the customer is never right," Ripley once said. "Being called untruthful is, to me, a compliment. And as long as I continue to receive the lion's share of this odd form of flattery, I don't worry about a wolf being at my door."

Fans yearned to see their own strange accomplishments, their disfigurements, and their curious misfortunes reimagined inside a *Believe It or Not* rectangle. But Ripley, never content to rely on volunteers, roamed constantly, always searching for strange facts and exotic faces for his cartoons. He met beggars and bedouins, headhunters and heads of state, royal highnesses and holy men, most of these forays funded by Hearst, whose publicists dubbed Ripley the Modern Marco Polo.

An insecure and effete kid named LeRoy, with terrible buckteeth and no shoes, Ripley had grown into an athletic and self-assured young man who always seemed to have luck and an influential patron in his corner. Once he stumbled onto his Believe It or Not concept (on the verge of age thirty), he was smart enough to parlay it into more than a newspaper cartoon, transforming and expanding himself from artist to radio and film star, to museum curator, to unlikely playboy-millionaire.

His goofy everyman perception of the world, his limited education and simplistic worldview, his naiveté . . . turns out, it all meshed with that of his core readership.

The shy, awkward misfit-loner had become champion of the freakishness of others. By celebrating weirdness, he made it mainstream, becoming one of the most widely read and influential syndicated cartoonists of his day—and among the best-traveled men in history.

More than entertainment, his global dispatches gave readers hope.

＊　＊　＊

DURING THE SEVENTEEN-HOUR DRIVE from the Iraq border to Tehran, Ripley was stopped nearly every hour by police. He complained bitterly about the "deadly barrenness and dryness" of the police-controlled country.

Ripley had hoped to escape Tehran by plane and fly into the Soviet Republic of Georgia, anxious to slip into the USSR and finally witness the collectivist, communist regime that Stalin had recently formed. Unable to secure a flight, he and Simpson decided to drive to the Persian-Soviet border, where they would walk across into Azerbaijan and then drive to Georgia—an ambitious and potentially hazardous route that would require passage through the snow-packed Caucasus Mountains.

When Ripley and Simpson finally reached the Aras River Bridge, across which lay Soviet territory, they waited two hours for the Persian border patrol to arrive and awaken their sleeping chief. Sullen officials took their time searching each piece of Ripley's luggage, which had multiplied to more than a dozen pieces in recent weeks with a surging accumulation of trinkets, carvings, and artwork.

When the guards finished with each bag, they'd carry it to the middle of the bridge and drop it in a growing heap. Ripley and Simpson were finally allowed to cross to the middle of the bridge, where they were ordered to "Halt!" Persian soldiers told them to wait while they finished their tea.

Across the bridge, young and twitchy Soviet soldiers stared coldly, aiming their bayonets as if primed for attack. Already Ripley had been at the border for more than four hours, the longest crossing in his two decades of travel. The sky grew dark as he and Simpson, hungry and cold, tired and angry, stood beside their rumpled pile of bags, hour after hour, in no-man's-land. Just thirty yards away sat their unreachable transportation: a donkey-pulled wooden carriage and its bored-looking driver.

Meanwhile, editors back in New York waited for their well-paid, peripatetic cartoonist to *please* send another batch of popular and profitable *Believe It or Not*s.

CHAPTER

1

Isaac Davis Ripley, whose son would one day explore all corners of the earth, fled his dead-end Appalachian home at age fourteen and headed west. He didn't get far before the Ohio River blocked his path. Unable to pay for a ferry crossing, Isaac swam solo across the turbulent river, eventually making his way to Northern California, seeking gold but instead finding work as a carpenter and cabinetmaker. By 1889, having settled in Santa Rosa, he fell in love with a woman fourteen years younger.

Lillie Belle Yocka's family made their own risky journey toward dreams of a sunnier California life. The Yocka clan left Westport Landing (later called Kansas City) in the late 1860s, joining a straggly crowd along the Santa Fe Trail. During the westward journey, Lillie Belle was born in the back of a covered wagon, and she spent her childhood in a Northern California encampment on the banks of the Russian River.

On October 3, 1889, Lillie Belle—twenty-one and pregnant—married thirty-five-year-old Isaac Ripley, their union earning a brief mention in the *Sonoma Democrat*. Isaac built a cottage on a postage-stamp lot on Glenn Street, with intricate wood trim that looked like icicles.

A son arrived five months later, although the exact year and date of birth would remain a lingering mystery. Possibly to prevent profilers from revealing his mother's premarital pregnancy, LeRoy Robert Ripley would never admit to being born on February 22, 1890; on passport applications and other documents he'd declare 1891, 1892, 1893, or 1894 as his birth year. He'd also later claim to have been born on Christmas Day or Christmas Eve.

Isaac and Lillie named him LeRoy but usually called him Roy. Only later in life would he adopt his middle name. A daughter, Ethel, arrived three years later and the family moved into a two-story bungalow Isaac built on Orchard Street, in a quiet grid of streets, home to saloon keepers and dentists, milliners and hops brokers.

LEROY WAS LEAN and slight, socially timid but full of energy. He had a ball-shaped head and high forehead, a tousled mop of hair above comically jutted-out ears, a freckled and often-dirty face. His most notable feature was an unfortunate set of protruding and misaligned front teeth, a crooked jumble that practically tumbled from his mouth. When he smiled, it looked like he was wearing novelty teeth. He usually kept his mouth closed, lips stretched to hide his dental deformity.

He suffered from a debilitating shyness, caused largely by his disfigured smile, and by a stutter that filled his speech with *uhs,* *ums,* and frozen words. Ripley carried himself in ways meant to shield his smile and stutter from others: hunched inward, chin tucked down, shoulders drawn forward, a protective stance. He seemed fragile, almost effeminate, and years later would admit to feeling embarrassed about his "backwardness."

Though thin, he grew to be fast and fit. A tireless neighborhood explorer, he ventured into the orchards north of town and probed south into the beckoning city. Mostly, he preferred to be alone. Barefoot, wearing carpenter's overalls or knickerbocker pants and a ragged straw hat, the curious, dreamy boy roved and reconnoitered, collecting bottle caps, cigar bands, and the baseball cards that came inside cigarette packs. He amassed a set of nails bent in the shape of each letter of the alphabet, keeping them in a cigar box under his bed.

At the one-room Lewis School, he was forced to wear shoes. He owned a single beat-up pair and would stuff newspaper into the holes and gloss them over with shoe polish. Once, he actually made a pair of shoes from folded-up newspapers, tied together with string and caked black with polish. "He wasn't fooling anyone," said one classmate. When his clothes began to fray and tear, his mother crafted new outfits by recycling old dresses and leftovers from her laundry jobs. In his flower-print pants and shirts, LeRoy was cruelly mocked. *Hey kid, why are you wearing a dress?*

At lunchtime, while the other boys chased girls around the water pump and outhouse, Ripley sat beneath a tree, drawing pictures or reading books about pirates or explorers. In class, students were required to stand and recite poems or essays, but Ripley's stutter made this an excruciating nightmare. Hunched over at his desk, he constantly scribbled and sketched in his notebooks. One teacher would smack him upside the head whenever she caught him copying scenes out of his history book instead of paying attention to the lessons.

"Everyone at school picked on him because he was so different," a classmate would later say. "Not one of the guys," said another.

After a bad day at school he'd escape to the attic of his house to draw or carve letters into the roof beams. Other early artistic inclinations included defacing his bedroom wall and chewing on pencils.

* * *

THOUGH IT WOULD become an epicurean mecca, the land of Ripley's youth—known by the Pomo and Miwok Indians as *Sonoma,* or Valley of the Moon—was more Wild West than wine country. A few years past its cowboy-and-Indian days, Santa Rosa and nearby Sonoma and Napa could be dangerous and deadly. When Ripley was a toddler, the *Sonoma Democrat* reported in breathless detail how Indians had looted a winery, adding: "The red-skins have been on a wild debauch."

Also full of debauch were the newspapers. LeRoy learned to read in a lively two-paper town whose editors practiced what would soon be called yellow journalism. The *Democrat* and its rival, the *Santa Rosa Republican,* cackled with stories of murderous deeds and accidental deaths, divorces, suicides, and all variety of lunacy, a daily "news of the weird." People plunged off railroad trestles, lost limbs beneath train wheels, became mangled by farm machines. They shot each other over card games, stole horses, robbed banks. The *Democrat* was especially poetic in its depictions of death, offering vivid descriptions of "putrescent" bodies "lying in pools of blood."

Santa Rosa's children were kept close to home and warned to stay away from the streets of downtown, especially Chinatown and its alleged opium dens. With his parents working—Dad as a carpenter, Mom taking in laundry and sewing jobs—Ripley had the freedom to ramble. A shoeless ragamuffin, he scampered through streets and alleys, avoiding the train and trolley traffic but irresistibly lured to Chinatown, where he'd peek into the laundries, restaurants, and shops. The proprietors, all men, puffed on long bamboo pipes and beckoned the curious kid, offering peculiar treats like lychee nuts.

Ripley found Santa Rosa's small Chinese community exotic and bizarre. He was awed by the strange clothes, the spicy food smells, and the hand-lettered signs whose symbols looked like hieroglyphs. On the few occasions his parents took him to San Francisco, the highlight was always a brief glimpse of shambling Chinatown.

By 1900, Santa Rosa was home to six thousand farmers, timbermen, miners, vintners, and railroad workers—a vibrant downtown of dusty roads clotted by horse-drawn carts, bicycles, and livestock. The region had attracted a variegated mix of romantic eccentrics, including Thomas Lake Harris, charismatic leader of an alternative-lifestyle "Brotherhood of the New Life" commune, who extolled the virtues of wine, tobacco, and sexuality. As one Sonoma County historian put it, Santa Rosa and its environs was a land of "explorers, rancheros, vintners, artists, writers, athletes, movers & shakers & dreamers."

Among the dreamers was famed horticulturalist Luther Burbank, who created hundreds of fruit, flower, and vegetable varieties at his agricultural laboratory—a thornless cactus, a white blackberry, a "New Seedling Cherry," the result of grafting two hundred cherry varieties onto one tree. Burbank considered California an unconquered land, a new world where a man who avoided alcohol and tobacco "has ten thousand chances of success."

↶ BELIEVE IT! ↷

Burbank's prized creation, the perky perennial he named the
Shasta Daisy, took seventeen years of trial and error.

✳ ✳ ✳

THE SANTA ROSA of his childhood taught Ripley many things, not least of which was to appreciate off-kilter hobbyists, obsessives, and fanatics, the kind who would years later become targets of his own journalistic curiosity. Ripley's hometown confirmed that you could be both odd and fascinating, obsessive and successful.

Even Ripley's mother's church had an appealingly curious backstory. In 1873, congregants of the First Baptist Church, having outgrown their place of worship, felled a 275-foot redwood; sawed and sliced it into studs, beams, and planks; hauled it to town; and assembled a new church from the single tree. Isaac Ripley had been among the builders of the structure that earned headlines as "The Church Built of One Tree."

Evidence that a town of death and debauchery could also be a place of magic and wonder was found on the city's stages, too. The Athenaeum Theatre hosted a unique medley of entertainment, from Shakespeare to vaudeville to minstrel shows. Newspaper ads hawked the "world's greatest cornetist" and the "world's most marvelous dancer." The nearby Novelty Theatre hosted lowlier acts: a midget show, a bone-playing musician, a boxing kangaroo.

Santa Rosa was also a regular stop on the circus circuit, visited by Tom Thumb's "Smallest Human Beings in the World" and Buffalo Bill's "Wild West Show." The Ringling Brothers Circus visited annually, and when Barnum & Bailey's "Greatest Show on Earth" arrived in town, the *Democrat* described its "troupe of wonderful midgets [and] a giant who stands nearly eight feet tall—All these curious people . . . living wonders."

For a kid who was mocked and teased for his funny looks and shabby clothes, his balky speech and his pathological dread of girls, Santa Rosa proved to be an ideal hometown, a place where the unusual was acceptable, where a person could be a bit peculiar and still succeed.

"Anybody who is born in Santa Rosa must turn out to be either an artist or a poet, for the spirit of the hills gets into your blood out there," Ripley would say years later, calling his home "the quaintest little town in the United States."

BY THE FALL OF 1904, when he entered Santa Rosa High, Ripley had grown taller and stronger, filling out his scrawny frame and showing signs of athletic prowess. In the spring of his freshman year he joined the baseball team, though he remained an awkward, eye-averting doodler. "No one thought he would amount to much of anything," said a classmate.

In the presence of female classmates, he showed a laughable insecurity. Teachers recalled seeing him run when girls came near and classmates would later remember him as "not much of a ladies' man." His one true female friend, who had roamed with him through downtown and among Chinatown's alleys, was Nell "Nellie Bell" Griffith. By high school, Nell had grown into a dark-haired beauty, a poet and basketball standout. Though she'd tell classmates that she and LeRoy were just "very close friends," Ripley clearly thought it was more than that.

Nell never seemed bothered by Ripley's gawky looks. She knew he was "awkward," but also funny, smart, and artistic. Nell's parents owned an orchard, where she and Ripley often played among the rows of trees. Ripley once upset a bees' nest and ran away screaming—a scene that he captured in a pencil drawing, which he presented to Nell.

In class, Ripley began letting classmates lean over his shoulder to watch him draw amusing caricatures of peers and teachers. Among his popular sketches were those of the balding, bespectacled history teacher, Charles T. Conger, despised by students and teachers alike, whom Ripley posed in what he called "some of his favorite attitudes": sitting at his desk with arms spread wide; sitting on a stool pointing a long ruler at the blackboard. Conger didn't appreciate the likenesses, but others did, and classmates' reactions to his drawings marked the first time Ripley stood out for reasons other than his crooked teeth and stammer.

Notebooks, textbooks, sheets of scrap paper—no empty space was safe from Ripley's eager pencil. His happiest, purest school moments were with a pencil in his right hand, a clean white space before him. His family couldn't afford art supplies, so he hoarded butcher paper and used a cutting board as an easel. Though he never took drawing lessons, he practiced relentlessly, sitting in front of a mirror to study his own lips, eyes, and facial muscles, then drawing his own expressions on crumpled scraps of butcher paper, smiling, scowling, frowning.

He once splurged on a five-cent postcard featuring a painting called *The Wedding Feast,* and practiced copying the scene, over and over. He would follow his sister and mother around, sketching them as they cleaned dishes, washed clothes, or hung laundry, pleading with Ethel or Lillie Belle to sit or stand still for just a few minutes. "Pose for me just a little while, will you?" he'd ask, and they usually gave in.

As he prepared to enter his second year of high school, in mid-1905, Ripley seemed to be settling into a comfortable routine. He'd started making a few friends, and had begun making a less-than-negative impression on classmates. The bucktoothed young misfit was beginning to feel *normal.*

That's when everything changed.

ISAAC RIPLEY WAS A GLUM, gruff, and serious man, judging by the scant few surviving photographs: the corners of his mustachioed mouth were pulled low and his deep, dark eyes were typically pinched into a scowl. He must have seemed especially forlorn that Friday night in September of 1905.

Ripley's grandmother, who had recently moved to Santa Rosa, had died of a lung hemorrhage that summer, and Isaac was still mourning his mother's death. After dinner on the night of September 15, he felt a crushing pain in his chest. Lillie Belle summoned the local physician, Dr. Jesse, who gave Isaac some medicine to ease his discomfort. A few hours later, just before midnight, Isaac was beset by another attack. Within thirty minutes he was dead, his wife and children by his side.

Ten days shy of his fifty-first birthday, Isaac was buried at the Odd Fellows Cemetery, just blocks from his home. A choral quartet sang as Isaac's brethren from the carpenters' union and the Woodmen of the World lowered his casket into the ground. LeRoy and sister, Ethel, stood beside their mother, who held in her arms the newest family member, sixteen-month-old Douglas.

Alone with three children, Lillie had no apparent skills with which to find a decent job. She began renting out a room to tenants, baking bread, continuing to take on needlework and the laundry of others while looking for a nursing job. Somehow, she was determined to keep her fragile household intact.

Short, tough, and attractive, she had always been the dominant parent, quick-witted and sharp-tongued. With a pouty mouth, dark skin and eyes, narrow waist, and shapely hips, even Ripley's classmates thought his mother was "quite attractive." Though he'd later speak adoringly of Lillie, Ripley "never spoke much about his father," according to one longtime friend. "And the impression is left, somehow, that he did not think too much of him."

Ripley tried to continue in the pose of a typical high school kid, joining the yearbook and school newsletter staffs in his sophomore year. His first credited drawings were published in *The Porcupine* just weeks after his father's death, including a caricature of the football team's fullback. His mother thought little of her son's drawings, though. Without a family breadwinner, she needed her son to find a job. He reluctantly started delivering newspapers before school but quickly decided that early-morning newspaper delivery wasn't for him, and by early 1906 he had quit.

Leaving his newspaper job kept Ripley safely in bed the morning of April 18, 1906, the deadly and historic day that he'd rarely talk about as an adult.

CHAPTER

2

In downtown Santa Rosa, the Fourth Street trolley was preparing for its morning runs and Chinatown's laundrymen began washing the day's clothes. On that otherwise normal morning, paperboys were among the few people outside before dawn, loading up copies of the *Press Democrat* to hurl onto steps and stoops. Among the headline-wielding delivery boys were Charles Shepard and brothers George and Willie Bluth. They would be the first to die.

As the deadliest earthquake in US history began to inflict its devastating wrath, sixteen-year-old ex-paperboy LeRoy Ripley was asleep at his Orchard Street home.

Just past five a.m., miles to the west and deep beneath the Pacific, slabs of earth began to wrench and buck, sending shivers along the San Andreas Fault, the recently discovered jagged crack in the planet. Estimated between 7.9 and 8.3 on the Richter scale, the quake ripped up and down America's western shoreline, heaving earthen grumbles that began rocking Northern California and sending quivers as far north as Oregon and as far south as Los Angeles.

The timbers of the Ripley house twisted and bowed, and the cottage that Isaac had built seemed about to implode into splinters. Pictures popped off walls, beds and furniture danced, dishes fell and shattered. Ripley and his family sprinted out the front door, across the small front yard and onto the dirt-paved street, which undulated as if liquefied. No place felt safe.

Santa Rosans were used to occasional seismic episodes; Ripley had experienced dozens and older residents had survived hundreds. But this felt different. Houses jumped, swayed, and moaned. During an excruciating sixty seconds of tremors, Ripley's town was torn apart. Local plant king Luther Burbank would later describe how everything moved in all directions at once, the "violent vertical and horizontal vibrations . . . a twisting back and forth . . . all this tipping from side to side."

Trees jumped like pogo sticks, streets rose and fell like ocean swells. Seemingly indestructible brick-and-mortar buildings imploded. The courthouse, the Athenaeum, department stores, and banks wiggled and fell, crushing or trapping occupants. One witness later described scenes of sheer chaos: "With fires advancing unchecked, people were crawling out through the rubbish, bleeding and half-dressed, covered from head to foot with lime and sickening dust."

Downed electrical wires crackled and sparked, a broken gas line caught fire, and eight people died when Haven Hardware exploded. A blaze at Rochdale's grocery store swept through downtown, killing Eli Loeb, whose wife's legs had to be amputated to save her from the fire. One man found himself trapped beneath a large timber and with flames prowling nearer begged someone to shoot him, but no one could get close.

Flames raged unchecked all morning. The Occidental, Saint Rose, and Grand hotels all "fell as if constructed of playing cards, and in the heaps were buried the hundreds of lodgers," the *San Francisco Bulletin* would report the next day.

The *Press Democrat* would describe its own losses. During the first rumblings, employees had rushed from the building. A press operator named W. S. Lindley was last to reach the exit, and as he got to the door the outer wall collapsed, falling away from him and onto three paperboys and Lindley's fellow pressman, Milo Fish, who left behind a wife and six children. A fourth paperboy burned to death.

As the terrible day came to a solemn close, Santa Rosans could see a deep glow to the south. They weren't the only ones to experience death and destruction.

* * *

DAYS AFTER THE FIRES had been doused, Ripley visited San Francisco by train to see the destruction for himself, climbing atop Nob Hill to look out at a heartbreaking panorama that he'd one day describe as "a mass of smoking ruins as far as the eye could see."

While it would historically be known as the Great San Francisco Earthquake, Santa Rosa sustained proportionally more damage than any other city and, with at least a hundred dead, a higher per-capita death toll. The headline in a joint earthquake edition of San Francisco's newspapers declared, SANTA ROSA IS A TOTAL WRECK.

⟡ BELIEVE IT! ⟡

Millions of gallons of wine, stored in casks in warehouses, ruptured and spilled, turning Santa Rosa's streets into red rivers of wine, whose bouquet attracted the discerning noses of farm animals. Residents soon found drunken pigs and dogs staggering in the streets.

When the smoke cleared, the heart of Santa Rosa was revealed to have been churned into absolute carnage. The dome above the stately courthouse, as one writer put it, had "collapsed like a fallen wedding cake." City Hall was gone. The hotels, the beloved theaters, and even Chinatown, all gone. The children of Santa Rosa would weep to learn that even Reed's candy store was now ash and rubble.

It was suddenly a busy time for carpenters, and Santa Rosa could have used the skills of a man like Isaac Ripley, who had been dead now for half a year.

The earthquake would remain a dark scar on Ripley's childhood—second in a double dose of tragedy. In less than a year, his otherwise comfortable life had been unmade by the dual cataclysms of his father's death and the quake, the defining events of his youth. With streets still littered with debris, schools reopened within a month. But the earthquake ignited in Ripley a far-fetched goal: to leave his busted-up hometown, just as Isaac had done.

At Santa Rosa High, he got help toward that goal from an unlikely patron.

* * *

FRANCES LOUISE "FANNY" O'MEARA, daughter of a feisty Oregon newspaperman, started teaching English in the late 1880s and would dedicate her entire life to Santa Rosa High. "Beloved" is how most graduates would describe her, as well as "tenacious" and "strict." Said one: "She saturated us with poetry and filled every day with such lively imagination." Ripley adored O'Meara, often addressing her as "Mother."

Six months after the earthquake, in the fall of Ripley's junior year, O'Meara assigned an essay about John Greenleaf Whittier's poem "Snowbound." Ripley hated writing compositions and, especially, reading them aloud. O'Meara would cringe at Ripley's stuttering attempts to recite for his classmates. Knowing that he liked to draw—the evidence was all over his notebooks—she decided to allow him to turn in his assignment in the form of a drawing.

The next day, Ripley handed in a sketch entitled "The Coming of the Snowstorm Told." In black-and-white, it conveyed the mood of Whittier's whiteout: *No cloud above, no earth below / a universe of sky and snow!* The next day, Ripley arrived early to class and handed O'Meara another drawing, a living-room scene drawn in pencil of Whittier's snowbound family.

The drawing had "so much feeling" that O'Meara declared it "a masterpiece" and posted it prominently at the front of the classroom. O'Meara realized she could spare Ripley the mortifying experience of reciting his essays aloud. "You like to draw," she told him. "Now, when I assign a paper to the class, if you would rather draw a picture, I'll take the picture as a paper."

Ripley would turn in dozens of drawings, from Shakespearean scenes to Longfellow's village smithy. O'Meara considered Ripley's art more than just boyish efforts at avoiding essays. He took each assignment seriously, researching the historical details. She'd hang them above the blackboard to use as teaching aids and kept them stacked and numbered in a closet. (The drawings would be lost in a 1921 fire that leveled the school.)

MEANWHILE, Ripley had begun spending more and more time on the baseball diamond, having discovered an agile, loose-limbed adaptability that earned him time at left field, second base, and even the pitcher's mound. "He was one of the best ballplayers we ever had," said a classmate.

Ripley started playing for local semi-professional "bush league" teams, and let himself dream of one day playing for his favorite team, the New York Giants. But Lillie Belle told her son he was too smart to waste time on art and baseball and encouraged him to choose a trade to pursue after high school—if not sooner. "Get a *real* job," she'd say. He earned some money drawing posters and advertisements for one ball team while working various odd jobs—loading fruit and vegetable wagons, painting neighbors' porches, doing yard work. Some weeks he took home as much as $15.

By his senior year, he'd found part-time work polishing headstones at Fisher & Kinslow Marble Works, which had crafted the tombstone atop his father's grave. Old man Fisher, a jolly man in a solemn profession, even let Ripley create a couple of tombstone designs. But Ripley soon quit, rejecting tombstones as "too gloomy." His mother suggested he consider the ministry while warning that if he insisted on becoming an athlete or an artist he faced the "thoroughly enjoyable prospect of slowly expiring at an early age of starvation."

Ripley tried convincing his mother there was money to be made in the popular new phenomenon called *comics*. The success of *Hogan's Alley*, introduced in Joseph Pulitzer's *New York World* in 1895 and featuring a bucktoothed, barefoot immigrant known as the Yellow Kid, had ignited a fierce competition for dominance in the new world of the funnies. Comics had since become newspaper staples, luring a new generation of boys toward the newspaper business.

Santa Rosa's papers weren't yet carrying regular comic strips; the *Press Democrat* lost its cartoonist years earlier. But down in San Francisco, the *Bulletin, Chronicle, Call,* and *Examiner* all

employed staff artists and illustrators, some earning $1,000 a
year or more—*drawing pictures for a living.*

With that kind of money in comics, Ripley decided to give it
a shot. In late 1907 he mailed a one-panel cartoon to *LIFE* magazine in New York. The sketch showed a pretty woman standing beside a wooden washtub, steam curling up from the water
as she wrings clothes through hand-cranked twin rollers. She
wears a thin hint of a contented smile, her hair drawn back in
a tight bun, sleeves rolled up, her dress draped to her ankles.

Playing with homonyms—*belle/bell, wringing/ringing*—his
caption read: "The Village Bell Was Slowly Ringing." In the
bottom right corner he signed "Ripley '07."

WHILE WAITING for *LIFE*'s reply, Ripley continued drawing
cartoons for the school newsletter, *The Porcupine,* where he had
been named "staff artist." In early 1908, he began working on
drawings for his commencement program. Graduation was now
less than six months away.

As high school drew to a close, Ripley posed with the rest
of the yearbook staff wearing a new suit and tie his mother had
saved for. In this and other photos, it was apparent that Ripley
had matured into an oddly striking specimen. With his stuck-
out teeth and jutting ears, his long nose and greased-back hair,
he had a vaguely Dracula-like appearance. Instead of grotesque,
though, he now looked almost menacing. Other high school
photos show him with expressions that look variously as if he's
about to snicker, or has a barely contained secret, or is crazy or
scared—as though he *knows* something about you.

Such facial expressions were often the result of attempting to hide his buckteeth behind constantly pulled-shut lips.
But a mouth like Ripley's simply refused to be hidden. When

he laughed or smiled, spoke or ate, teeth spilled out, especially when he stuttered. Letters *b*, *f*, and *p* were particular nuisances, and Ripley frequently wrestled with the choices facing someone who couldn't afford expensive dentistry. He could avoid the world, crawl into a hole, become a monk or a hermit. Or he could create a defiant "I am who I am" persona. Buoyed by the confidence gained from his artwork and athleticism, he chose the latter.

It showed in his emerging style of dress and his dimpled and unabashedly toothy smiles in certain photos. No longer a barefoot street rat in overalls, he often wore a white shirt and thin black tie with his new graduation suit. Later, as his income allowed, he would complement the suit with bow ties, hats, and nice shoes—efforts to distract people's attention, to stand out and be noticed for something other than his catastrophe of teeth.

One person had seen this self-assured side of Ripley all along. After their childhood days of romping around Santa Rosa, Nell Griffith had watched the real LeRoy Ripley slowly emerge through high school. For his part, Ripley considered Nell his best friend. But in the love letters he'd begun writing he made it clear he was now ready for more.

✻ ✻ ✻

SANTA ROSA HIGH'S CLASS of 1908 commencement was held on a warm June night, an overflow crowd spilling out of the auditorium as graduates received their diplomas. It was, as the newspaper put it, "a happy event in the lives of their fathers and mothers," who clutched copies of the commencement program, its cover featuring a boy in cap and gown, diploma in his hand, drawn and signed "By LeRoy Ripley."

Ripley, however, was not among the twenty-eight graduates that night. Despite Miss O'Meara's best efforts to help him after his father's death, he had left school that spring. The story he'd tell years later was that it was time to find a job and help his family. One problem with that story is the lack of evidence of gainful employment. Instead, there's much evidence of baseball playing, with Ripley's name appearing regularly on the local sports pages through 1908.

Rumors tittered among classmates. *Did he get kicked out? Did he just get bored with it all?* Among the nastier rumors was that Ripley was so poor his mother had turned to prostitution. He'd been a mysterious presence in their school. Other kids liked him fine, they just didn't understand him. Maybe they'd never been able to get past the discomfort of seeing those terrible teeth up close. Maybe they judged him, unable to dispel memories of the stammering elementary school misfit. Or maybe Ripley was the one who pulled back, not letting others get close.

"He was modest and shy, but he couldn't be pushed around," one classmate said.

The timid boy had grown into a young man who was far bolder, smarter, and more ambitious than he let on. Not wanting to be viewed as "a goofy kid from a farm town," as he once put it, he'd already decided to leave the farm town behind. However, even the nearest city seemed beyond his reach.

"San Francisco was where I wanted to go," he confessed many years later. "It wasn't fifty miles away, but it could have been Peking for all the hope I had for ever living there."

Yet, when he received good news from New York, those fifty miles suddenly seemed like less.

CHAPTER

3

LIFE's editors decided to publish Ripley's "Village Bell" cartoon, which ran in the June 18 issue of the magazine—five days after his classmates graduated without him. The poised and pretty "Bell," a dead ringer for Ripley's mother, appeared in the lower-left corner of page three. A letter soon arrived from New York containing his $8 payment. Amazed that his hobby was worth $8 per drawing, he realized that cartooning might indeed be his way out.

That summer, Ripley earned the attentions of a patron who would help him leave Santa Rosa, introducing him to the newsman's life, a life beyond all dreams.

"A high and narrow string bean of a boy" was Carol Read Ennis's first impression of LeRoy Ripley. An attractive freelance writer, she visited Santa Rosa in the summer of 1908 to profile Luther Burbank for the *San Francisco Call*. While renting a room at the Ripley home, Ennis often saw her landlady's son curled beneath a tree, scribbling in beat-up sketch pads when he was supposed to be weeding the garden.

But she felt the bucktoothed high-school dropout had "a

terrific dynamo of unharnessed energy" and decided to make him her pet project. Just as O'Meara had perceived something special in Ripley, Carol Ennis saw a talent where others saw a fantasist, promise where others saw indolence.

"Do you know anything about politics, Roy?" Ennis asked him.

"Not a thing," he admitted, confessing that what he really cared about was baseball.

Ennis suggested he work up a series of cartoon panels about the upcoming presidential race. Ripley drew a few political and sports sketches, which Ennis took to San Francisco and began peddling to friends and colleagues.

By fall, Ripley's portfolio had reached the desk of Fremont Older, the man who had turned the moribund *San Francisco Bulletin* into one of the largest papers west of Chicago. Older handed Ripley's drawings over to his brother-in-law, Hiland L. "Hy" Baggerly, the paper's sports editor, and in February of 1909 Ripley received a letter. "Just came back in time to receive your cartoons, which are very good," Baggerly wrote. "They are so good I have decided to give you a trial, providing we can agree upon a salary." Baggerly offered $8 a week and the promise of a $2 raise "if you make good."

"I think you have a great future," said the editor who helped launch the careers of such pioneering cartoonists as Rube Goldberg and Thomas "Tad" Dorgan.

Though he'd later claim to have started his newspaper career at age sixteen, Ripley was about to turn nineteen. Lacking a diploma or any prospects, he willingly hung up his baseball mitt and wrote to tell Baggerly he was "tickled." He would save Baggerly's letter the rest of his days, and Ennis would remain a lifelong friend.

The *Press Democrat* soon published a brief item, headlined

ROY RIPLEY IS A STAFF ARTIST NOW. He would never live in Santa Rosa again.

✦ ✳ ✳

WHEN SANTA ROSANS visited San Francisco, though traveling fifty miles south, they called it "going up to the city." When Ripley went up to the city in 1909, he wore his best clothes— his graduation suit, a huge bow tie, a straw hat perched high atop his head—but still felt like "a gawky youth . . . a wistful rube."

After a Northwest Pacific train ride to Sausalito, he took the ferry past Alcatraz and across the bay to the Embarcadero. From there, walking up Market Street, he stopped at the Block Mercantile Co., a curio shop filled with antique weapons, stuffed mermaids, Asian tools, and a life-size, eerily realistic wooden statue of a Japanese man, which Ripley coveted. Atop Nob Hill, where he had stood dumbstruck three years earlier watching the ruined city smolder, he looked out from the steps of the elegant Fairmont Hotel onto a resurrected San Francisco.

Since the earthquake and fire, the resilient city by the bay had surged ahead, a new stone-and-brick metropolis replacing the wooden city that had burned to cinders. Even Chinatown had rebuilt, with an effort toward pagoda roofs, paper lanterns, and Oriental architecture, looking more exotic and colorful than before.

Ripley loved what he saw, even though the only affordable lodging he could find was *beneath* the city, in a one-room basement apartment on McAllister. The $5 weekly rent would leave just a few dollars a week for food and other basics. He adapted quickly, learning to hop on and off cable cars, wandering through Chinatown, just as he had in Santa Rosa. Though he considered city life to be "thrilling and daring," his lone fear was losing Nell. She'd worried the big city would change him, but Ripley assured her by letter that he'd only change for the better.

When he arrived at the three-year-old Bulletin Building off Market Street and reached the top-floor art room, Ripley was told his job was simple: a cartoon a day, if not more. His first professional cartoon ran on his birthday, February 22, 1909: a bucktoothed baseball fan's head emerges from a flower-shaped baseball. The caption: "A Spring Blossom." The signature: "Rip '09." During his first weeks, he worked tirelessly, producing more than three dozen full-size cartoons and scores of smaller illustrations.

He even wrote his first article—"By Rip," said the byline— about a fighter who had caused a stir in New York by breathing pure oxygen between rounds. In sticking to familiar territory, he mostly focused on baseball. When the minor-league San Francisco Seals prevailed in a twenty-four-inning battle against the Oakland Oaks, Ripley sketched Father Time writing in his "Baseball History" book, "This is the greatest yet."

Six months into his new job, however, his lack of training as either journalist or artist began to show. His drawings still resembled his high school newsletter work and Ripley worried that his limited knowledge of sports "made the job doubly difficult." He hadn't even found his signature yet, still experimenting with "Rip," "Ripley," occasionally "R" or "R2." Coworkers tried to encourage him, but Ripley could tell that his boss, Baggerly, might be having second thoughts.

AS A CHILD, Ripley's exposure to art had been limited to the illustrations in his adventure and history books. He received little encouragement at home or at school, and would later say that his youthful art training consisted of teething on a pencil as an infant, drawing on his bedroom walls, and scrawling on his schoolbooks. "Who did I study under?" he'd say when asked who taught him to draw. "I studied under the stars in Santa Rosa."

In San Francisco, Ripley was suddenly working alongside—or in the shadow of—cartoonists who were taking the concept of illustrated newspaper entertainment to new levels. At the time, sports photography was still an imperfect format, with photos playing a secondary (and blurry) role to cartoons. Sports cartoonists gave readers a visual summary of last night's game or a preview of tomorrow's. Relying heavily on caricature, they also gave intimate portrayals of the personalities of sport.

Cartoons had migrated to all sections of the newspaper, and a golden era for cartooning was under way. In fact, Ripley arrived in San Francisco shortly after the nation's first daily "comic strip" had appeared in print. While working in the *San Francisco Chronicle*'s sports department, Bud Fisher drew a tall, chinless, mustachioed gambler called Mr. A. Mutt. A year later he paired Mutt with a short, bald guy named Jeff. Though it wasn't yet called *Mutt and Jeff,* the cartoon was hugely popular and Fisher was soon earning an unheard-of $45 a week at William Randolph Hearst's *San Francisco Examiner.*

Two of Ripley's predecessors had been lured to New York by larger salaries and readerships. Thomas Aloysius Dorgan, known as "Tad," had started at the *Bulletin* at age fourteen, only a year after losing three fingers on his right hand in a freak accident. He now worked for Hearst's *Evening Journal* in New York. Tad's successor at the *Bulletin*, Rube Goldberg, had also moved to New York, where he earned $50 a week drawing his popular *Foolish Questions* cartoon. (Example: A father asks his pipe-smoking son, "Son, are you smoking that pipe again?" The son's reply, "No, Dad, this is a portable kitchenette and I'm frying smelt for dinner.")

ᘓ BELIEVE IT! ᘐ
*Through the early 1900s Tad coined dozens of American slang
terms, including "for crying out loud," the "cat's meow,"
the "cat's pajamas," "hard-boiled," "drugstore cowboy,"
"Yes, we have no bananas," "twenty-three, Skidoo," and
"as busy as a one-armed paperhanger."*

San Francisco had become an important training ground for anyone hoping to actually make a *living* drawing pictures for newspapers. Goldberg later said San Francisco was where he honed his craft, borrowing ideas from others and learning to trust his personality. "Personality is all-important in any creative art," said the man who would later create *Mike and Ike* and *Boob McNutt*. "If you have personality, it will show in your drawing."

Ripley worked among other pioneering cartoonists at the *Bulletin*—Herb Roth, Hype Igoe, and Paul Terry, soon to be household names. Like many cartoonists, Ripley borrowed heavily from techniques that had evolved over the previous decade. Characters "spoke" in overhead balloons; exclamation points meant surprise; question marks meant confusion. Puffs of dust behind someone's feet meant motion, buzzing z's meant sleep. Such pioneering devices had become universal by 1909. Still, there was plenty of room for innovation, yet Ripley struggled to find his own ideas and to trust his own sheepish personality.

His recently honed self-confidence now weakened, Ripley was learning that a talented artist wasn't automatically a talented cartoonist.

Many of his early efforts suffered from clutter and cliché, a hodgepodge of recycled techniques. His drawings were top-notch and his talent shined bright when he sketched realistic portraits of sports stars, especially facial close-ups. But his cartoony cartoons just weren't that funny, distinguished, or sophisticated. Ripley struggled with a nagging feeling that he didn't quite belong. "It was a hard grind," he'd later confess.

His boss seemed to agree. Four months after hiring him, he changed his mind.

* * *

RIPLEY WASN'T ANGRY about getting fired in June of 1909. Like Miss O'Meara and Carol Ennis, Hy Baggerly had taken a chance on him, and Ripley would remain "everlastingly in debt." He would similarly dote on O'Meara and Ennis, one day lavishing them with gifts, flowers, and limousine rides, signing letters "ever devotedly." Still, losing his job confirmed the feeling that had gnawed at Ripley during his early months in San Francisco, that he was still just an "uncultured" boob.

"My fellow workers felt sorry for me . . . and did everything possible to help me along," he'd later say. "But my work was poor. I was too young."

Maybe his mother had been right—with no art training, he had been unequipped for an artistic career and should have kept working with tombstones. He remained a fatherless kid from the country, thrown into the sophisticated big city whose societal rules he'd yet to master.

"I'm as yet a stranger in a strange world," he wrote to Nell. "And such a strange world, too!"

He had hoped to convince Nell to join him in San Francisco, suggesting by letter that they could be together "forever." Now he was jobless.

After his firing, he wandered the narrow, spice-scented streets and alleys of Chinatown, where he could mingle unselfconsciously, slurping cheap noodles and listening to shopkeepers tell stories of the old country in chopped-up English while puffing on their bamboo pipes. Just as Santa Rosa's small Chinatown had been an enticement, he was fascinated by the exotic people in their long gowns, the shops and aromas of the nation's liveliest Chinatown. At a time of loneliness and near poverty, having lost his first real job, with a $5 weekly rent to cover and a widowed mother counting on his contributions, he found the Chinese to be kind and generous, a "truly civilized people."

"When I was hungry, they fed me," he'd say years later when asked about the origins of his love of all things Oriental.

He would soon meet men who had actually visited the places he learned about in Chinatown—Peking and Nanking, Shanghai and Canton—further stoking a passion for Asia that would slowly grow into an obsession. But before he could even dream of visiting China, he needed a job.

He had made it to San Francisco, but it might as well be Peking without an income.

CHAPTER

4

Three years after the earthquake, San Francisco had rebounded beautifully, as had its journalism—the *Call, News, Post, Chronicle, Examiner,* and *Bulletin* all thriving in modern new buildings. The city that launched the careers of Mark Twain (the *Call*) and Sinclair Lewis (the *Bulletin*) continued to bolster its reputation as a lively literary town whose competitive cluster of publications vied for the attentions of more than half a million readers.

Determined to remain a San Francisco newsman and not skulk back to Santa Rosa, Ripley gathered a portfolio of drawings and one foggy June morning slipped through the front doors of the *Chronicle,* whose post-quake headquarters was just a block up Market Street from the *Bulletin.* His timing was just right. The *Chronicle*'s sports cartoonist, Harry Hershfield, had injured his eye and was unable to keep up with his assignments. When Ripley arrived—admittedly scared and "mute as a dumbwaiter"—Hershfield suggested, *Let this young fellow do it.*

"The boy is good," Hershfield told sports editor Harry B. Smith, after looking at Ripley's work. "Give him a chance."

Smith offered Ripley a trial run at $10 a week, two dollars

more than he'd been making at the *Bulletin.* Barely two weeks after his final cartoon had run in the *Bulletin,* his work was suddenly appearing in the pages of his former competitor, sometimes on the front page.

This time, Ripley wasn't taking any chances. Immediately after starting at the *Chronicle,* he signed up for his first-ever art classes.

Five mornings a week he studied in a downtown classroom, learning about the proper size of an ear, proper head-to-body proportions (an eight-to-one ratio), and the best materials (Gillott's pens and Bristol or Ross board). After class, he'd report to the *Chronicle*'s art room and toil "like a madman," drawing hundreds of cartoons and seeking advice from anyone willing to critique him. Most nights, he stayed until ten—long after the others had left. He ate cheap Chinatown meals, collapsed in his basement apartment, and was back at art school by eight thirty a.m.

Within a few months, Ripley felt he had finally become "a passable artist."

✳ ✳ ✳

RIPLEY HAD LEARNED a valuable lesson about his new profession: fear and uncertainty were the side effects of being paid to do what he loved. "An artist is a natural coward," he'd tell an interviewer years later. "He's always afraid of losing his job."

That fear inspired him to draw constantly, obsessively: editorial-page cartoons, slice-of-life scenes, political rallies, car shows, dog shows. He caricatured theater stars and businessmen, no topic too insignificant that it couldn't be rendered by his pen. For a short article about a drunk cat that jumped to its death, he offered *two* sketches. (Said the cat, midair: "Farewell cruel woild.") He sketched actors, comedians, acrobats, magicians, and once, a man who could "walk" up and down stairs on his head.

"The Chronicle is an excellent place to work," he wrote to Nell Griffith late that summer of 1909. "And everything is most agreeable."

Editors loved his enthusiastic productivity and rewarded him with steady raises that would lift his weekly salary to $20. He had been sending money home to his family but now decided he was making enough to invite his mother and brother to join him in the big city. When his sixteen-year-old sister, Ethel, got married and left home, Lillie and Doug moved into the small McAllister Street apartment. Ripley reported to Nell that Santa Rosa now "seems well rid of the Ripleys."

By letter, he repeatedly urged Nell to visit too. "I tell you it is hell to live so apart!" he wrote.

In the fall of 1909, Nell finally gave in. She stayed at his apartment for two days and toured the city with Ripley, his mother, and his brother. Before heading back to Santa Rosa, she gave him a sultry picture of herself. Ripley soon wrote to tell her the photo had become "a stimulant to my imagination of you."

In increasingly romantic letters, calling her "honey girl" and "dearest friend in the world," he practically begged her to move to San Francisco. "I don't know of anything more pleasing or beautiful than that friendship in which each one trusts the other, and where frankness is enjoyed by both!" Ripley wrote. "I hope ours is, or will be of that kind. Do you?"

But Nell soon began backing away, telling him they lived too far apart. Then, when Ripley visited Santa Rosa that Christmas, Nell broke his heart. She didn't envision a future as Mrs. LeRoy Ripley, she said. In fact, she'd begun dating another ex-classmate, a handsome Santa Rosa High football star.

Ripley kept writing letters—"I want to see you!"—but in time he reluctantly accepted that he might become nothing more than a warm memory of Nell's youth, "something to look back upon, maybe to think about sometimes," he told her.

In one of his final letters to Nell, he somewhat pathetically told her that he hoped his own life mate would appear "in the misty distance of the future," and that she and Nell might become friends. But so far, "that girlie of the future is not in sight yet," he wrote. "If she was, I would be too busy to look."

Fortunately, after the breakup, Ripley found himself distracted by the assignment of a lifetime.

✻ ✳ ✻

AFTER LESS THAN A YEAR at the *Chronicle*, Ripley was picked as lead cartoonist to cover the upcoming fight between retired champion Jim Jeffries and Jack Johnson, the first black heavyweight champ. Under pressure from sportswriters and cartoonists, including Ripley, Jeffries had agreed to emerge from retirement. Scheduled for July 4, 1910, the highly anticipated and racially charged battle—"The Great White Hope" versus "The Big Black Menace"—had grown into one of the biggest sporting events in US history. A few *Chronicle* old-timers grumbled about the new kid getting such a plum assignment, but sports editor Harry B. Smith insisted the job was Ripley's.

He spent a few weeks at Jeffries's training camp north of Santa Cruz, drawing daily cartoons of the aging boxer's workouts. At night, Ripley and the other journalists would gather for drinks on the hotel's front porch or around a campfire. A newsman's uniform at the time was typically a slouchy gray suit, wrinkled white shirt, dark tie, and fedora. Ripley stood out in his straw hat and knickers, sitting awkwardly among rumpled older men. He kept his head down and legs tucked beneath him in the humble, protective pose he often struck in the face of intimidation or embarrassment.

Photos of Ripley at Jeffries's camp show a clean-shaven man-boy among mustachioed men, a timid child who'd been allowed to stay up late with the grown-ups.

Yet, when the old-timers got him talking, they found Ripley to be an oddly funny fellow, and a bit of a perky smart aleck. They particularly liked one of Ripley's cartoons that showed a huddle of sportswriters rolling dice outside Jeffries's gym. ("Seven! Come eleven!")

He'd been assigned plenty of sports events during his first year as a cartoonist, and had used those opportunities to study the habits and language of more experienced artists and writers. Having lost his father at such a young age, Ripley looked to other men for lessons on how to be manly. He was savvy enough to know that the upcoming fight loomed larger than any event he'd covered. If he played it right, it could be a turning point in his journalistic apprenticeship.

* * *

THREE WEEKS BEFORE the big day, the fight was moved from San Francisco to Reno, Nevada. Writers, celebrities, and fans stormed the lawless desert city, conquering its saloons and gambling houses. Ripley considered Reno "a riot—a seething cauldron of the sporting clan."

He was soon mingling with the biggest names in newspapers. At dinner one night, he met two of his *Bulletin* predecessors, Rube Goldberg and Tad Dorgan. Also sitting at the table was the famous and famously troubled *Call of the Wild* author, Jack London, who had been hired as part of the *Chronicle's* "fight team"—making Ripley, for the moment, colleagues with America's most famous writer.

Full-page *Chronicle* ads touting its "corps of experts" showed a pubescent-looking LeRoy Ripley, who would be stationed ringside with London. When London learned that Ripley was from Santa Rosa, just a few miles from his estate at Glen Ellen, he offered to take a look at Ripley's drawings, which had taken on a grittier, moodier quality during the weeks leading up to the fight. Despite the many racist depictions of Johnson—big lips and an apelike head—Ripley had drawn one serious portrait, a near-perfect likeness titled "The Dusky Champion—And His Golden Smile." London was impressed by Ripley's work and encouraged him to keep at it.

Ripley became so "overawed" by his encounters with London and others that he almost missed the fight, nearly sick with nervous indigestion. On fight day, more than 16,000 spectators gathered to watch "The Battle of the Century," scheduled for *forty-five* rounds. Sitting a few feet from center ring in the journalists' section with London, Ripley watched as Johnson slowly ripped Jeffries apart.

In Ripley's post-fight cartoon, Jeffries is depicted lying on his side as a wide-eyed crowd looks on.

"When the old champion went down and out," reads the caption, "there was not one cheer for the victor!"

✳ ✳ ✳

THE FIGHT HAD been an exhilarating chance for Ripley to meet the top men in his field, including journalist and author Peter B. Kyne, a California newsman turned novelist who advised Ripley to take his talents to a bigger stage. "If I was a kid your age, you know what I'd do?" Kyne said. "I'd go to New York."

Others, including London, also suggested that Ripley leave San Francisco behind. Noted *New York World* columnist Ned

Brown even offered a letter of introduction if Ripley made it to Manhattan. "You should be in New York with Tad and Goldberg," said Brown.

By the time he'd returned to San Francisco, Ripley was fixated on the idea, even though New York was "a long way off—almost out of the question." Plus, with his mother and brother now living with him, and the whole family dependent upon his income, Lillie would never comprehend his need to ditch a steady job for the hope of a better life nearly three thousand miles away. Yet, from Reno onward, he dreamed about nothing else.

The theme of Ripley's tenure in Nevada could be distilled into two words: *go east*. Meeting London, a model of masculinity to Ripley's generation, had a particularly lasting effect. In fact, London's success story—a poor California kid who succeeded in his art form and became an adventurer-traveler and a wealthy but sad-drunk celebrity—would echo throughout Ripley's life.

He told Nell Griffith by mail that while he was still "getting along swimmingly" at the *Chronicle*, "I hope to be in New York in a while—and from there to Europe!"

* * *

IT HAD BEEN nice to come home to McAllister Street each night and serve as a father figure to brother Doug, who never knew his dad. For Ripley, his own father figures had become newsmen like London and Kyne, whose influence far outweighed Ripley's mother's view of a sensible future. Ripley *loved* the work of a sports cartoonist, loved being around elite athletes and cheering/jeering crowds and important journalists, especially people who might help advance his career.

The encouragement from men he'd met in Reno and the maturing of his cartoons emboldened Ripley to finally take a chance and ask for a raise. Ripley walked into the office of the *Chronicle*'s bulldog managing editor, John Young, and asked for another $2.50 per week.

"Who are you?" Young demanded of the cartoonist whose name appeared daily in the man's paper. "And in which department do you work?"

Ripley later heard that Young often played dumb when he suspected someone was looking for money. The editor told him he'd "look into the matter," but each time Ripley renewed his request, he got the same *Who are you?* brush-off.

Finally, he boldly told Young one day that if he didn't start getting $25 a week, he would quit.

"Very well, Mr. Ripley," Young said. "We're a happy family here, and we don't want any dissatisfied employees on this newspaper. You are free to leave immediately."

Realizing too late that he'd accidentally quit, Ripley did what he often did to clear his head.

He walked through Chinatown.

* * *

UNABLE TO FACE his mother with the bad news, and barely able to breathe, he wandered for hours and finally stopped at the San Francisco Press Club, where he planned to throw back his last drinks as a member and then resign. Fortunately, just hours after losing his job, Ripley found Peter Kyne at the bar.

"I'm in a fine fix," he told Kyne. "I've been fired from two papers here in two years. I'm a failure even before I start."

Kyne told Ripley the same thing he'd told him in Reno.

"Take a chance, kid. Go to New York," he said. "You'll never get anywhere unless you start somewhere."

Kyne also told Ripley not to panic about his sudden lack of employment. "We'll try to get you something," he said.

Something appeared quickly in the form of an aging actor, singer, and self-proclaimed womanizing brawler looking for someone to illustrate his autobiography.

As a child, Joe Taylor had crisscrossed America with a minstrel show, then ventured in his teens to Hawaii. In his twenties, he joined a troupe touring Shanghai, Hong Kong, and Singapore, surviving knife-slashing pirates and killer typhoons. In China he witnessed twelve prisoners beheaded by a sword-wielding executioner.

Ripley was enthralled by Taylor's tales, such as getting a shave in Manila from a barber using a butcher's cleaver. Ripley chose that particular scene as one of twenty-five he illustrated for Taylor's memoir. The result of the unlikely collaboration between eighty-three-year-old Taylor and young Ripley was a 250-page book, *Joe Taylor: Barnstormer.* Taylor gave Ripley a much-needed dose of cash—$100—and a book credit: "Illustrated by Ripley."

"Accidents have always been a boon to me," Ripley would later say, counting Taylor's memoir among the turning points of his charmed post-quake career.

Equally important, Taylor had stoked Ripley's curiosity about the great wide world beyond California, especially the Orient.

* * *

ALTHOUGH SAN FRANCISCO was just a three-year stint, a way station between Santa Rosa and his soon-to-be-real home of New York, Ripley's time in the reborn city had been transformative, a period he would come to view as more educational than any college.

As Ripley grew from tentative teen into cocksure young adult, San Francisco had exposed him to the competitive world of newspaper cartooning and the riskier world of *possibility*. He met men who had traveled the globe, hedonists and self-indulgers who had tasted the fruits and women of exotic lands, men who wrote books and drank whiskey, smoked opium, got divorced and made lots of money, men who knew how to live large.

Though Ripley would become one of the great global travelers of his day, he had thus far never ventured beyond Northern California, except for the head-spinning visit to the Babylonian streets of Reno. He considered San Francisco "my hometown" and referred to himself as "a westerner at heart."

Setting course for New York, then—with little money, no confirmed job, lugging just a portfolio of drawings and the names of a few contacts—was not only Ripley's first gutsy adventure, but would forever loom as the boldest. He was twenty-one.

He said good-bye to his family, boarded an eastbound train, then dozed in his wooden seat as one American panorama linked with another: San Francisco to Sacramento, Ogden to Cheyenne, Kansas City to St. Louis, Louisville to Nashville to Cincinnati, where he felt snowflakes touch his face for the first time.

During the dirty two-week crossing he imagined himself enacting a modern version of his parents' cross-country journey, but in reverse. Eating from butcher carts and warming himself near the coal stove, he rolled farther north and east toward an uncertain future.

CHAPTER

5

After safely making his way across the country, Ripley got off the train lugging a battered trunk containing all of his possessions: some clothes, an extra suit, his baseball glove, and a flat-pack portfolio of drawings. Tucked deep in his pants pocket was $15, the last of his cash.

One look around told him that he was *not* in New York. He had accidentally disembarked one stop too soon, in New Jersey. It was cold, it was nighttime, and he had no idea how to cross the Hudson River. Swimming as his father had during his cross-country journey was no option—Ripley couldn't swim. Looking confused and lost, he caught the attention of a man who offered to guide Ripley into Manhattan via the newly opened train tunnel that ran beneath the Hudson.

"You're a real westerner, and I like your style," the man said.

Emerging from the subterranean tube onto the streets of midtown Manhattan, Ripley gawked at the skyscraper forest and the humming, starlit city. Ripley's new buddy helped him find a cheap, closet-sized hotel room to stash his trunk, and at dinner introduced him to two friends. One claimed to be an insurance man, the other a judge. Ripley thought the judge's gnarled, cauliflower ear looked suspiciously like the ear of a boxer.

When the insurance man pulled out a pair of dice and suggested they shoot a friendly game, it finally dawned on Ripley that the yokel was being scammed. He explained that he couldn't play—"All my m-money is in ch-checks," he stammered—but offered to meet them again at nine o'clock the next morning. He excused himself and scurried back to his hotel, where he propped a chair against the door and hardly slept. At seven a.m., he arose and checked out—a precarious entry to a new life.

WITH INCOMING SHIPLOADS of immigrants and a rising literacy rate, New York journalism was thriving, sustained by dozens of news publications. Atop the heap loomed Joseph Pulitzer's *New York World*, an innovative and cartoon-friendly newspaper that was the first stop in Ripley's job search. At the domed Pulitzer building—among the tallest of New York's sky pokers—he sought out Ned Brown, who in Reno had offered to help him find a job.

⌐ BELIEVE IT! ¬

In 1895, the World *launched the seminal* Hogan's Alley *cartoon, whose barefooted star character in an oversized yellow shirt earned him the nickname "The Yellow Kid." In his* New York Journal, *William Randolph Hearst created his own yellow-kid cartoon, a blatant knockoff that stoked the feud between him and Pulitzer. Their subsequent attempts to outsensationalize each other in print birthed the term "yellow journalism."*

But the *World* had been in turmoil since Pulitzer's death a few months earlier, and wasn't hiring. For days, Ripley visited other newspapers, struggling with his portfolio on slushy, snow-slick sidewalks but unwilling to trust himself to the decade-old subways. Feeling as low as he could remember, he began wondering if he'd made a mistake. It didn't help that he had no overcoat.

Ripley finally asked a street-corner newsboy for directions to the *Globe and Commercial Advertiser,* and was soon lost in the street maze of Greenwich Village, yet another complication in his already sloppy introduction to the streets of New York.

One of the city's oldest papers, founded in 1797 by Alexander Hamilton and first edited by Noah Webster (of dictionary renown), the *Globe and Commercial Advertiser* had sunk into relative obscurity, a quaint, thin rag sometimes called "the old-time *Globe.*" Editor Henry J. Wright and his staff were struggling to change that perception, in part with eye-grabbing cartoons meant to offer the immigrant and working class a more exciting alternative to the dull-gray text that remained the dominant style of the city's papers.

When Ripley arrived at the *Globe*'s front door, daily circulation had been hovering for years around 100,000; the *World* reached six times as many readers. But *Globe* readership was growing fast, thanks largely to the front-page political cartoons of its popular and populist new artist, J. N. "Ding" Darling.

Ripley was eventually led to the office of sports editor Walter St. Denis, a short-tempered Canadian who had been seeking a new style for his sports pages. St. Denis left Ripley waiting for more than an hour, but when Ripley finally got the chance to spread out his drawings, St. Denis liked what he saw, the mix of art and humanity. He called in Ding Darling for a second opinion.

Darling's initial opinion was that the lean, anxious, and disheveled young Ripley was dressed more for gardening than a job interview. Ripley wore a thick woolen army shirt and, due to the snow, had rolled up his trouser legs, exposing scuffed and worn-out shoes. Darling felt sorry for Ripley but was impressed by his cartoons and smitten by his innocence and eagerness.

"The boy's got something," Darling finally told St. Denis. "Hire him for six months, and if he doesn't make good, I'll be responsible for his salary."

* * *

RIPLEY STARTED AT THE *GLOBE*, in the chilly first days of 1912, at $25 a week. He found a small room in a boarding-house on West Sixtieth Street, a short walk to Central Park. Though *Globe* headquarters was at Globe Square in Greenwich Village, Ripley's office would be in lower Manhattan atop the new Singer Building, built by the sewing-machine company in 1908 and briefly reigning as the world's tallest building.

In addition to Ding Darling (who would later win two Pulitzer prizes), Ripley's new colleagues were an elite clan. The paper had recently hired such recognizable artists as H. T. Webster and H. A. MacGill, and would soon hire Carl "Bunny" Schultze, each of whom developed America's earliest serialized daily comic strips. As in San Francisco, Ripley's coworkers would be some of the most innovative artists in the business. The timing of his assimilation into this rare gathering couldn't have been better.

The *Globe* had recently partnered with Associated Newspapers, a newly formed syndicate (housed in the Singer Building) that distributed stories and cartoons to dozens of midsize papers. Syndication had proved to be a boon to newspapers and their cartoonists. Bigger papers got extra mileage from their cartoons by selling them to smaller papers, which in turn published cartoons that their staffs couldn't otherwise produce. The upside for cartoonists was having their work exposed to a nationwide audience, and some of them were becoming the country's first media celebrities. For Ripley, this meant his cartoons would be distributed nationally by Associated Newspapers and seen by hundreds of thousands of newspaper readers across the United States.

So when Ripley's name first appeared in the *Globe*'s pages—atop a cartoon about the boxer Abe Attell, on January 18, 1912—in a nicely poetic twist, it also appeared three thousand miles away, in the *San Francisco Bulletin*.

* * *

THE *GLOBE* BILLED ITSELF as "New York's Oldest Newspaper" but had lately begun acting like a scrappy upstart. Its editors had been hiring new talent and investing in new printing presses. It sold for a penny and most days devoted two full pages to sports. Ripley quickly became a steady presence on those pages, his cartoons appearing at least every other day, sometimes daily, always in the top center, swallowing the top fourth or more of the sports pages.

In addition to drawing, Ripley began writing in earnest. He launched a series of illustrated stories about Olympic athletes headed to Sweden that summer. In a series called Hardest Battles of Ring Stars as Told by Them to Ripley, he interviewed boxers about their most grueling fights. He created a recurring cartoon character, Demon Dug, named for his brother but clearly based on his younger self. A mop-topped, dirty-faced, mischievous kid in knickers, Dug couldn't stay away from the baseball diamond, lost his schoolbooks, played hooky, broke windows, and got dragged home by the ear by his mother.

As a writer, Ripley developed an ease with the tough-guy language of the pugilist, describing one boxer as "a cold-blooded proposition [who] fought cruelly and unceasingly." He also showed signs of wit. After winning a fight, one hard-drinking fighter was "in the best of spirits (and the best of spirits were in him)." It was no small achievement for an unproven newsman to hold his own among the *Globe*'s sports scribes, who ranked among New York's best.

✌ BELIEVE IT! ✌

One of Ripley's colleagues, Mark Roth, was sometimes credited with coining a new name for the New York Highlanders baseball team—the Yankees.

Globe veterans were impressed by Ripley's prolific output, even if they found him quiet and a little odd. Sportswriter Sid Mercer considered him "a plain lad" and columnist Herb Corey called him the "trembling artist." But Ripley attracted a loyal patron in Associated Newspapers' founder, George Matthew Adams, a minister's son from Michigan who felt Ripley was "unspoiled . . . a modest chap."

Baseball continued to dominate his cartoons, his arrival in New York coinciding with the start of the preseason. His apartment was close to the Ninth Avenue El, which delivered him to the northern tip of Manhattan, home to the Polo Grounds and the New York Giants, whose pugnacious fireplug of a manager, John McGraw, was now part of Ripley's sports beat. Instead of just drawing cartoons and portraits of McGraw, though, what Ripley really wanted was to play for him.

* * *

AN ENDURING HIGHLIGHT of Ripley's pre-celebrity legacy was that after his modest success in California's bush leagues he came within striking distance of a professional baseball career.

Ripley would perpetually claim that after arriving in New York he immediately went chasing that *other* life dream.

The story goes like this: In February of 1912, Ripley joined the Giants for a train ride to Marlin, Texas, to cover spring training workouts for the *Globe*. When coaches learned Ripley had played semi-pro ball, they invited him to work out with the team. One coach thought Ripley showed "considerable promise and ability," and McGraw allegedly told Ripley that with a few years in the minors he might become a big-league prospect. During a scrimmage, Ripley was called in to pitch, and in one reporter's retelling McGraw called Ripley "the best curve-ball pitcher I've seen in a long, long time."

The story continues: Ripley reared into his windup, whipped his arm forward, and felt a sharp snap. His arm had broken in a ninety-degree fracture, a jagged edge of bone actually poking through the skin. In less gruesome versions, his arm "shattered," though sometimes it was just a broken finger. Later reports would claim that Ripley signed a minor-league contract with the Giants, *then* broke his arm. Yet, while there is an impressive picture of Ripley wearing a Giants uniform and swinging a bat, his name doesn't appear in any Giants statistics or record books, or in any news stories about spring training from 1912 to 1914. The writer Damon Runyon saw Ripley at the Giants' training camp in Texas one year and remembered him more as a poker player than a pitcher.

Ripley loved the story of his flirtation with pro ball—as would future PR men, honing the Ripley legend—even if they all overreached in the retelling. Regardless of the true version, the results were the same. Ripley viewed the injury as "a godsend" and "a great thing" because it forced him to choose between competing career paths. "It ruined me as a baseball player," he'd say. "And it made me a cartoonist."

✳ ✳ ✳

SOMETIME DURING HIS first year at the *Globe*, Ripley's editors decided it was time for their young artist—who had continued to sign his cartoons "Rip" or "Ripley"—to have a real first name. "We can't have a 'LeRoy' in the sporting department," Walter St. Denis said.

"LeRoy" apparently wasn't masculine enough for a sports cartoonist/reporter, so Ripley willingly adopted his middle name, Robert. He became Bob or Rip to his new East Coast friends, still Roy to his mother and siblings, who must have been shocked to receive a letter containing the first "By Robert Ripley" clipping. He'd soon reclaim LeRoy for his middle initial, becoming Robert L. Ripley.

Soon after adopting his new name, Ripley was given an unexpectedly plum assignment, which the *Globe* announced in January of 1913 in a large headline across the top of the sports page: RIPLEY IS OFF FOR EUROPE TODAY. Beneath that appeared a six-column Ripley self-portrait, with slightly underexaggerated buckteeth, wearing a plaid cap and striding across the ocean, a pencil in one hand and sketch pad in the other. In a balloon, Ripley asks Europe, "Well, whatcha got?"

At the time, overseas travel was rare, expensive, and risky. Crossing the Atlantic was an astonishing perk for a rookie staffer and an inexperienced traveler. It was also a reflection of the editors' trust in Ripley's ability to turn his overseas travels into a series of entertaining stories and cartoons. Ripley was thrilled, and hoped his first taste of the world beyond America's shores would not only provide material for a unique new style of cartoon but also guide him toward his eventual big idea.

Instead of traveling directly to Europe, Ripley first sailed through the Mediterranean and visited Egypt. In Giza, he toured the ancient pyramids and in a nearby sandlot noticed a group of men in long gowns playing something like baseball. Using a skinny bat, they had modified the game: eight men per team; eight outs per inning; one strike and you're out. But they played as aggressively as any bush leaguer and were especially vocal in taunting opponents and umpires. Ripley pulled out his sketch pad and started working on a cartoon of Egyptian ball-players wearing "headache towels," as he called their turbans.

As he continued on to Europe, he kept his reporter's eye narrowly focused on sports. Either by habit or under editors' orders, he seemed unwilling to expand his curiosity and test his pen on non-sports topics, unsure of his footing outside the familiar comforts of an arena or stadium.

In Rome he visited the Coliseum, the alleged birthplace of professional boxing, where sixty thousand spectators once watched enslaved fighters pound each other with studded leather gloves called cesti. In Germany, he witnessed a bizarre sword-fighting contest called Mensur, in which duelers swiped at each other's faces. The goal wasn't so much to *win* as to suffer an opponent's blade without flinching. The inevitable scars were borne with pride, scabbed badges of honor. After witnessing a duel, Ripley watched in awe as a doctor stitched the loser's face together without eliciting a wince from the patient.

In France he attended an oddly collegial boxing match at the Cirque de Paris. With plush seats and carpeting, it seemed more opera than prizefight. Only once did he venture outside the pre-planned itinerary, putting his provincialism on full, unapologetic display. In Paris, he went looking for the boxer Georges Carpentier, whom he hoped to interview. "I wanta see Carpentier!" he told his taxi driver, certain that his request was delivered in "perfectly good English." When the confused taxi driver responded in rapid-fire French, Ripley grew flustered and then angry. He began repeating his instructions, but louder. *"CAR-pen-TEER!"* he finally shouted.

Eager to get back to English-speaking New York, he became emotional on the ship's deck as he spotted the faint outline of the Statue of Liberty, the gargoyled spires and peaks of Manhattan. When the ship docked at Hoboken, New Jersey, Ripley suddenly realized he had no money left. He offered to help another passenger with his luggage so he could earn a dollar for the ferry ride to New York.

* * *

THE *GLOBE* ANNOUNCED his return with another six-column cartoon of a caricatured Ripley hugging New York City and kissing the new Woolworth Building. Stacked behind him on the ship's deck was a pile of "sketches." Though the *Globe* offered no explanation for the bold overseas stint, a balloon quote above the cartooned *Globe* building suggested that his editors might have been eager to have their productive new artist back.

"Hey," it read. "Come on, get busy."

Ripley wasted no time, launching a months-long series of stories and cartoons that introduced readers to his take on Europe, and to his clever and curious mind.

His first cartoon was accompanied by a story about the Egyptians he'd watched playing the game they called *leep el tabe.* "What a spectacle it was—a baseball game at the base of the pyramids!" He called the Coliseum "the Madison Square Garden of the Roman days" and the Cirque de Paris "the Madison Square Garden of Paris." He described the pretty female ushers at the Parisian boxing match and the "terrible open gashes and streaming blood" of the Mensur fighters.

His style was casual, colloquial, even a bit irreverent. He admitted to drinking beer in Germany and relied heavily on slangy contractions—*y'know, dontcha, y'see.* He sang the praises of Parisian women but revealed an uneasy distrust of most foreigners and their strange ways. He was the perfect yokel American, never mentioning that King George of Greece had been assassinated during his time abroad.

It amounted to a remarkable series of global dispatches from a mere sports cartoonist, and an entertaining diversion for *Globe* readers. New York's sportswriters and illustrators typically covered baseball, boxing, and horse racing, with lesser sports relegated to an occasional inch of type at the bottom of the page. To read about Egyptian baseball and German Mensur was, in the view of many readers, fascinating.

In his first year and a half at the *Globe*, Ripley had developed a reputation as a cutting-edge journalist and a darn good read. He settled into a steady grind, scurrying across New York to cover games, scouring the city by foot and train, day and night, cranking out cartoons by the score. He averaged two dozen cartoons and/or columns a month through late 1913, expanding his scope to cover billiards, auto racing, horse racing, polo, tennis, and golf.

His work contributed to the *Globe's* upticking circulation, now above 130,000. Associated Newspapers acknowledged his contributions by offering a two-year contract and bumping his salary to $60 a week.

✷ ✳ ✸

IN EARLY 1914, Santa Rosa's *Press Democrat* published a story about the success of its homegrown dropout of an artist. His syndicated cartoons were being published in thirty papers and the *Press Democrat* boasted that Ripley, a proud "product of Santa Rosa," had become wildly popular back east. Later that year, just before the holidays, Ripley managed to return home for the first time in nearly three years. He hopscotched by train across to San Francisco, where he visited friends and former coworkers, including E. T. "Scoop" Gleeson, a sportswriter he'd first worked with at the *Bulletin*.

⌒ BELIEVE IT! ⌒

Gleeson is credited with coining the term "jazz." At the San Francisco Seals' spring training camp in 1913, players called the bubbly spring water "jazz water." When a few Seals began playing ragtime-style music with some local musicians, Gleeson said the tunes had "pep" and "jazz."

Gleeson decided to interview his former colleague and write a story about Ripley's blossoming career. Beneath the headline RIPLEY RETURNS TO SCENES OF HIS EARLY TRIUMPH, Gleeson's story described how his formerly shy friend had matured since leaving San Francisco, how Ripley "dresses quietly but with good taste . . . and converses with all the freedom of a campaign manager."

When Lillie Belle read the story, she felt proud of her son's surprising success. She'd managed to witness the planting of the seeds, the gestation of his career. But she would not enjoy her son's achievement for long, or see his burgeoning fame. In mid-1915, Ripley received word that his mother had become gravely ill, suffering from sudden heart failure. He immediately sent a telegraph.

Dear Mom, Hope you are recovered, Mom. I want you to be well and jolly when I come home. When you are unhappy then I am unhappy. So be of good heart, Mom, is the earnest wish of your loving son, Roy.

Ripley boarded the first westbound train. During a stopover in Chicago he received a Western Union wire from his sister. "All thought Mamma would die during the night," she wrote. "Heart stronger today." Two days later, in Colorado . . . "Another bad night," Ethel wired. A similar message reached Ripley in Nevada, and he wired back, urging his sister to "Do all possible" and telling Ethel he was on the "fastest train," due to arrive in Santa Rosa before noon the next day, a Monday.

A trackside shed fire near Truckee, California, delayed Ripley's train just before dawn on Monday. When he reached Sacramento, just hours from home, he learned he was too late. Lillie Belle had died during the night. Just forty-six, she was buried beside Isaac at Odd Fellows Cemetery. The *Press Democrat* praised her as "a well-known resident" with a "wide circle of friends." The paper also noted that, due to his train's delay, "the cartoonist who has made such a success of his profession" had been unable to say good-bye.

RIPLEY HAD PREVIOUSLY PROMISED his mother that he would always look after Ethel and Doug. Now he faced a difficult decision. Should he bring eleven-year-old Doug back to New York? Or stay in California and go back to the *Bulletin* or *Chronicle*? Either way, could he become a substitute *dad*?

As a boy, Ripley had always been on the outside, different from the other kids, unhandsome and goofy, picked on and mocked, a fatherless stutterer, a high school dropout. Even now, he often considered himself an overgrown adolescent and "just a boy," and if he returned to Santa Rosa he'd bear a new label: *orphan*. Yet, having traveled to Egypt and Europe, having crisscrossed America and made New York City his playground, he knew he had finally outgrown the awkward, solitary kid he'd been in Santa Rosa. Just as his pioneering parents and grand-parents had ventured into unknown lands in their day, he too had become a pioneer of a sort.

His upbringing had somehow instilled in him a desire to travel and explore. He had outgrown his childhood shyness and timid-ity to become the type of person who could appreciate a baseball game beneath the Egyptian pyramids. But as Doug's caretaker, further long-distance travels would be harder to come by.

So, despite the promise to his mother, he made his decision. Uncertain days loomed ahead, with the crescendo of artillery across the Atlantic. New York was no place for Doug. Rather than uproot him, he decided it'd be best for Doug to stay in California. Ethel and her husband, Fred Davis, now lived in Sacramento, where Fred made furniture and Ethel worked as a nurse. But living with his big sister was apparently not an op-tion for Doug—the two were not close. Family friends offered to let Doug live with them in Santa Rosa, and Ripley agreed to send money until Doug was old enough to come to New York.

Ripley then endured a contemplative train ride east, a somber commute between the two influential cities of his young-adult life. Though it had once loomed as an unthinkable destination, he now considered San Francisco just "a horse town" and would not return to Santa Rosa for fifteen years. Back in Manhattan, he plunged even deeper into the social and sporting circles of the city that was now his true home.

CHAPTER

6

Gaining confidence as a cartoonist and a New Yorker, Ripley began to dress the part. In a mid-teens photograph, he poses hands on hips beside a stone wall in Central Park, wearing a checked suit whose long-tailed coat is cinched at the breast by a single button. Narrow, cuffed pants terminate a few inches shy of the ankle, accentuating shiny two-tone shoes. His hair is shaved to a stubble on the sides, long and slicked back on top. He looks pleased with himself, smiling his deformed smile.

Though his misaligned and protruding teeth can't be ignored, in most photographs from this period Ripley looks somewhat stylish and almost handsome. In a city and a profession full of extroverts, the nerdy introvert was finding a middle place where he could fit in.

During his first years in New York, he'd stuck cautiously with San Francisco connections, socializing with former *Bulletin* and *Chronicle* colleagues Paul Terry and Herb Roth (who was now cartooning for the *New York World*). Through 1916, Ripley extended his range and befriended other ambitious young transplants, including a pretty young art school grad, Vyvyan Donner. She and Ripley would attend Sunday-night dinners at the Greenwich Village apartment of Helena Smith-Dayton, an ex-reporter turned artist and filmmaker. One magazine called Smith-Dayton's weekly dinners "a Washington Square institution at which the notables from all the professions gather." Donner would later recall the cocktails, dancing, and laughter of those "wonderful gatherings at Helena's."

Other nights found him playing pool at Jack Doyle's Billiards Academy in Times Square or sitting ringside with Tad Dorgan or Damon Runyon at Madison Square Garden, the world's largest indoor sports arena, which had become like Ripley's second office. Around this time (and most likely at a barroom), Ripley met the man who would become his closest male companion, a short, balding, crag-faced cartoonist who was as odd-looking as him but funny as hell—a real-life Jeff to Ripley's Mutt.

AS A SPORTS CARTOONIST in Philadelphia and Washington, DC, Arthur "Bugs" Baer had drawn insects with baseball bodies, calling his ball-shaped creatures "bugs" and earning himself a nickname. Now writing a humor column at the *New York World*, Baer was developing a reputation as a master of one-liners, having coined the quip "What this country needs is a good five-cent cigar." (Comedian Milton Berle would later confess to mimicking Baer's style.)

ᗡ BELIEVE IT! ᗡ
Baer would bestow upon George Herman "Babe" Ruth the nickname "Sultan of Swat."

This cigar-smoking, whiskey-drinking storyteller was the perfect sidekick for someone as shy and self-conscious as Ripley. A natural showman and entertaining social butterfly, Baer knew the best nightclubs and parties. He schooled Ripley in the subtleties of celebrity and the fine art of self-promotion. Soon after the two became friends, Baer and Ripley approached Jack Curley, the pudgy promoter who had helped broker the 1910 Johnson-Jeffries fight in Reno, with an idea.

Born and raised in San Francisco, Curley had run away from home to work as a reporter at the *Chronicle*—it was becoming a theme of Ripley's life, these links back to San Francisco. Curley was fired for fabricating stories and eventually took up sports promotion, which led to his role brokering the Reno fight. Ripley had gotten to know Curley fairly well since Reno and occasionally caricatured the tubby man in the *Globe*'s sports pages.

A likable yet shady character, Curley had recently turned to professional wrestling. The working class and the upper class alike thought it was a hoot to watch costumed men named "Americus" and "The Terrible Turk" scrum with each other. Ripley acknowledged in print that they might be "cheap press agent stunts," but he felt Curley had revived "a grand old game" and considered the Masked Marvel "one of the best wrestlers in the United States." Well-dressed and polite, Curley would claim with a straight face, "I have never promoted a wrestling match that was not absolutely honest."

The idea Ripley and Baer brought to the savvy promoter was a wrestling match in which the two minor celebrity cartoonists faced each other at the Lexington Opera House, as a warm-up act before the main event. Like George Plimpton would years later, they wanted to perform as athletes instead of journalists for a change, participants instead of spectators. They'd take home $150 apiece and Curley could pocket the rest.

Ripley and Baer decided they'd give the crowd a good show, then Ripley would flip Baer onto the mat for the win. But after ten minutes of insults and trash talk to amuse the crowd, Baer decided he didn't want to be the loser, and instead of taking the fall he threw Ripley hard on his back. Ripley squirmed free, but minutes later Baer—only 148 pounds, but squat and athletic—had Ripley on his back again, and kept him there.

When Ripley later tried to collect his $150 cut, Curley told him he'd given the full $300 to Baer. Curley similarly told Baer that he'd given the money to Ripley, and the two amateur wrestlers seethed for months before realizing Curley had scammed them both.

The stunt earned some publicity in a few papers, easing Ripley's disappointment over the lost paycheck. Fortunately, losing $150 would hardly break him. His salary had soared in the past four years to nearly $100 a week.

RIPLEY COULD FINALLY AFFORD to dress well and eat well—no more cheap Chinatown meals—but he remained thrifty. After paying $35 a month for his first apartment, he moved into a brownstone on Fiftieth Street with Paul Terry, his former *San Francisco Bulletin* colleague. They split the $40 rent and slept on cots in the small bedroom. Some weeks, the roommates hardly saw each other. Terry had recently left newspapers altogether, convinced that the future of cartoons was on the big screen. He had begun producing animated films and would soon form his own production company, Paul Terry Productions.

ꞔ BELIEVE IT! ꞔ

Terry would eventually produce more than 1,300
"Terry-Toons" cartoons, including Mighty Mouse *and*
Heckle and Jeckle.

Many of Ripley's peers were venturing into the uncharted waters of film, and all across New York innovative cartoonists were expanding their craft. Yet, while animated cartoons were making progress, they were still experimental. The public received the bulk of its information and entertainment from newspapers, and newsprint remained the primary medium of the cartoonist. In fact, due to a steep rise in literacy, circulation was flourishing, and some cartoonists were becoming fabulously wealthy. Bud Fisher was earning $78,000 a year from his syndicated *Mutt and Jeff* cartoons, and boys across the country were enrolling in mail-order art classes, hoping to become the next Tad Dorgan or Rube Goldberg, each making six-figure salaries.

⌒ BELIEVE IT! ⌒

In the late teens, an obsessive childhood doodler named Walt Disney began attending art classes, fascinated by newspaper cartoonists and "hoping that some day I, too, would be on the staff of a big newspaper." Rejected by the Kansas City Star *and other papers, he turned to animation.*

Ripley studied the work of artists who were pushing the boundaries of illustrated entertainment, particularly Tad, who was both artistic and prolific. "He had no restrictions or limitations," Ripley would later say. Still, Ripley worried that he spent too much time mimicking his heroes.

The mid-1910s were filled with rags-to-riches stories of cartoonists who toiled through multiple experiments before latching on to a clever concept that separated them from the pack.

Inside the black-and-white cardboard covers of schoolboy notebooks, Ripley collected articles about peculiar athletic feats and peculiar people. On slow news days, he'd flip through the notebooks and cobble together sketches about such achievements. One cartoon, entitled *The Iron Man,* featured men who walked or ran long distances, like John Ennis, who crossed America on foot in eighty days. Another, called *Some Famous Kicks,* profiled the longest field goal and the most kicks in a row. In *Some Jumps* he featured extreme skiing and ice-skating leaps, and in *Some Baseball Records* he offered hard-to-believe swings of the bat. Turning to football, *Gridiron Oddities* included a 105-yard touchdown by a player who hid the ball under his jersey and a game in which Harvard beat Exeter, 158–0.

Ripley's knack for locating and depicting odd facts proved especially useful during the winter lull, a dry period for athletes and the men employed to draw them. On one of those slow days in December 1916, the enterprising cartoonist skimmed through his scrapbook, pulled together a few notable feats of athletic endurance, and drew a sketch for each. One man had stayed under water for six minutes, another skipped rope 11,810 times, while another ran 623 miles in 142 hours, and two men once boxed to a draw after seven and a half hours. He called this cartoon *UNUSUAL RECORDS*—a harbinger of his eventual "big idea."

Other slack days, he'd whip up another sketch of Demon Dug, who ached all winter for baseball season. *Globe* readers would see Dug in bed, sulking: "No Baseball, an' no football, a-a-aw! Woe is me—I'm a woe!" Dug and his ragamuffin friends reflected Ripley's admiration for the outcast and the underdog. The cartoons featuring endurance and achievement, meanwhile, showed Ripley's appreciation for winners, people who were the best at something.

Readers seemed to appreciate the mix, especially this emerging focus on the off-the-wall accomplishments by those striving to be fastest, longest, farthest, and best. Said the *Globe* in a promotional ad: "If you really appreciate art and literature combined, you can't afford to miss Ripley."

He was onto something, but his progress—and the good-time New York parties—were soon interrupted by war.

WHEN THE FIGHTING in Europe first began, Ripley joked in print about America's apathy, possibly conveying his own. One cartoon showed a man at a ball game holding a newspaper covered with headlines about war. "War?" says the sports fan. "Who cares?" But as the United States committed itself to battle in the spring of 1917, World War I became the dominant theme of Ripley's cartoons, especially after he was exempted from military service.

The recently passed Selective Service Act required Ripley to fill out a draft registration card, on which he listed his age as twenty-five (he was really twenty-seven) and his occupation as "artist, writer, cartoonist." Asked whether he had any family members dependent on him for support, Ripley wrote that he was responsible for "two dependents," including a "brother under 12." (Doug was still living with family friends in Santa Rosa, and Ripley had continued to send money.) Ripley's request for an exemption was granted that summer of 1917, and his status as Doug's financial caregiver kept him stateside during the final sixteen months of the brutal conflict.

Though he never discussed his apparent willingness to avoid military service, it seems Ripley preferred being a fan rather than a participant. Intrigued by the idea of battle but not inclined to fight, he seemed content to cheer from the sidelines.

He tried to play his own wartime role, profiling athletes

at the Annapolis and West Point military academies. He visited military training bases, spent time aboard the USS *Texas,* promoted Liberty Loans and Red Cross donations. He turned sketches of sports contests into battlefield skirmishes, aerial dogfights, torpedo launches, and hand-to-hand combat. Team managers became "generals," players "soldiers." He even got Demon Dug and friends into the act, playing "war" instead of baseball or getting chased by a truant officer in a sketch titled "The Retreat of the Allies."

His patriotism was unabashed, as he doggedly portrayed American athletes as *the best:* "Englishmen are boxers; Americans are fighters." When a US athlete/soldier died, he gave them a sober sendoff. The death of a Yale track star resulted in a dramatic half-page sketch of Johnny Overton running on the track and, beneath that, being killed midstride on the battlefield. The title: "Johnny Overton's Greatest Race."

In Ripley's reverent view, which he repeated over and over, American soldiers were the best "in the world" because many of them were *athletes.* He frequently depicted Uncle Sam as a muscle-bound ballplayer or boxer. "Remember," he wrote at the time, "WAR is merely athletics." American ballplayers "make excellent grenade tossers," he said, while the throwing ability of the Germans was "on par with our schoolgirls."

Some of Ripley's wartime sketches were used as recruitment posters, as was James Montgomery Flagg's drawing of a finger-pointing Uncle Sam—"I Want You for U.S. Army"—which was reprinted millions of times during the war. Such posters were part of a massive domestic propaganda campaign run by the Committee on Public Information, which promoted patriotic newsreels, photos, and magazine and newspaper articles. The committee's Bureau of Cartoons supplied the nation's top cartoonists with suggestions and news tips via the weekly *Bulletin for Cartoonists*. George Creel, head of the Committee on Public Information, viewed the work of Ripley and other cartoonists as a "constructive force for shaping public opinion and winning the war."

His patriotic, pro-athlete cartoons earned approving letters to the editor. In response to one of Ripley's athlete/soldier profiles, a reader named Frank Seng wrote, "That kind of cartoon does more to mobilize the sentiments and feelings of the people than any number of stories. It gives us a victorious attitude, which is essential."

On November 11, 1918, Armistice Day arrived, and with it peace. Though he had avoided serving overseas, Ripley had loved the wartime assignments, traveling to Army bases and Navy ships, mingling with interesting new people and playing his part. World War I had stoked Ripley's competitive spirit (*war is athletics*) and presented a challenging artistic diversion. But in late 1918 he went back to being just a sports cartoonist. Compared to the real war, baseball and boxing seemed a tad boring.

WORLD WAR I had transformed the pages of American newspapers into daily adventure stories. Afterward, readers' hunger for drama and intrigue in their daily paper lingered. Readers also now wanted to know more about the world, particularly the strange-sounding places they'd heard about—obscure lands such as Luxembourg and Romania, the exotic corners of Europe, the Balkans, and the Ottoman Empire.

At the same time, soldiers returned home with a taste for the adrenaline and dangers they'd been exposed to in war. In pursuit of such thrills, some began attempting risky feats—scaling the world's peaks, flying airplanes long distances—striving to accomplish something bold, to be first, fastest, or best.

All of which provided Ripley with cartoon fodder. The aftermath of war would slowly alter the trajectory of his cartooning, and his life.

Before the war, he had experimented with various serials that celebrated impressive sports feats and the overlooked Everyman. Wartime took him in a different direction, allowing him to give readers dramatic life-and-death scenarios. Those cartoons felt more *thoughtful* than anything else he'd done. "The ability to think is perhaps a greater asset to the cartoonist than the ability to draw," he'd one day write, in a manuscript he titled *How to Draw*.

After the war, Ripley resumed his search for a niche cartoon that combined all of his skills and interests. The "unusual records" concept had been headed in the right direction, except that it focused almost exclusively on sports. What he really wanted was to indulge his desire to learn about the wonders of the world, to share that curiosity with readers, and to find a consistent and unique artistic style that would "please the great majority."

World War I had allowed him to abandon typical "cartoon" drawings and create newspaper *art*. In his *How to Draw* book (which was never published), Ripley revealed how much thought he gave during his early New York apprenticeship to the craft of pen-and-ink cartooning, to the importance of facial features and muscle and bone structure. Ripley also felt an obligation to get the details of his drawings just right. During the war, he made sure he put foreign soldiers in their correct uniforms, to avoid complaints from readers miffed by imperfections. If he couldn't conjure the details from memory, he'd call down to the *Globe*'s "morgue," the library where old articles and photos were stored. He relied heavily on those photos for accuracy, calling the morgue "an invaluable aid."

He also continued assembling his own morgue, pasting more clipped-out newspaper articles and magazine photos into his scrapbooks. During and after the war, these clippings began veering away from sports, becoming more reflective of the postwar fascination with dangerous places and extreme activities. He truly believed that this hodgepodge of quirky scraps might someday "prove of the utmost assistance." In other words: You never know when scraps will make a meal.

* * *

IN MOST VERSIONS of Ripley's breakthrough moment, the original *Believe It or Not* cartoon (which wouldn't adopt its exclamation point with any consistency until the 1930s) came about on a sluggish winter afternoon in late December 1918. With the war ended, football season over, and baseball season a few months away, Ripley allegedly found himself at a loss for a cartoon topic.

"I was bereft of ideas," he would later claim.

So he dug into his rainy-day notebook collection, sifting through clippings of ambitious athletic endeavors. He chose nine such feats and drew a miniature cartoon for each. Ripley would later claim that "Believe It or Not" was the original title idea. Other times he'd concede that his first idea for a title— "Champs and Chumps"—was not good enough and he offered editors "Believe It or Not" as an alternative title.

Years later, looking back on that day, he said he wasn't entirely sure whether his choice of those four words was "sudden inspiration" or "unconscious accident."

Either way, Ripley was not thrilled with the result and he

left the office that night "very disgusted." He considered the cartoon a throwaway and "a stinker." (In other retellings, he'd claim he was in a hurry to get out the door—he and Bugs Baer had a double date.)

Ripley's editor, Walter St. Denis, had different recollections, later insisting that not only were "believe it or not" *his* words, but the cartoon had been his idea in the first place, that *he* had thrown a stack of clips about odd sports feats onto Ripley's desk and instructed him to come up with a catchy compilation.

Neither recollection was quite right. The original "Believe It or Not" cartoon appeared in the December 19 *Globe,* and it was unequivocally titled "Champs and Chumps." It wasn't an entirely new concept, since it resembled the "unusual records" compilations Ripley had been experimenting with in recent years. Still, something about the layout, the choice of oddball feats, and the appreciative tone Ripley used in describing them seemed quirky and fresh.

Among the nine champs and chumps were J. Darby of England, who jumped backward twelve feet, eleven inches; M. Pauliquen of Paris, who stayed underwater for six and a half minutes; and an unnamed "chap" who walked backward across America. Three of the odd feats involved variations on the hundred-yard dash: one man ran it backward in fourteen seconds; another hopped it in eleven seconds; two men finished in eleven seconds in a three-legged race.

Regardless of who originated the idea, St. Denis agreed with Ripley that it wasn't one of his better cartoons, calling it "just guys who did some screwy athletic stunts." When a few readers wrote in to praise the cartoon, however, St. Denis told Ripley to keep collecting ideas and produce another champ-chump compilation once he had enough material.

According to subsequent legend, another "Believe It or Not"

appeared a week later, followed by another, and soon it was appearing twice a week, then a daily feature—*and the rest was history . . .*

In truth, Ripley's screwy-stunt cartoons were hardly an overnight success, and there was no sudden change in his fame, income, or prospects. He was still a sports cartoonist, covering fights, ball games, and dog shows. In fact, the second "Believe It or Not" cartoon—the first with that exact title—wouldn't appear for another ten months, in October of 1919. A third "Believe It or Not" wouldn't appear until 1920, and only sporadically after that.

Ripley had found his niche, he just didn't know it yet, and wouldn't fully realize what he had stumbled across for at least two more years. Until then, he would continue to view cartooning as a hard grind. "There is no shortcut to success in the field of cartooning," he wrote in his unpublished book. "It is only by hard work and constant practice that [the cartoonist] can hope to prepare himself to conquer the difficulties that will constantly besiege his path."

Indeed, such difficulties were coming, not least of which was an ill-advised marriage to a beautiful teenaged dancer.

CHAPTER 7

Orphaned by parents who died young—Isaac at fifty, Lillie at forty-six—Ripley, nearing thirty, thought constantly of his health.

As a child he used to read *Physical Culture* magazine, published by eccentric fitness guru Bernarr Macfadden, a flamboyant bodybuilder, nutritionist, and health advocate who could tear a deck of cards in half. Though some doctors branded Macfadden a fake and a kook, he railed against "pill-pushers" and processed foods, inspiring millions of acolytes with claims that exercise, fasting, and a heavy intake of milk could help a man live to 150.

⋲ BELIEVE IT! ⋟
Macfadden died at age eighty-seven after refusing treatment for a urinary tract infection.

Ripley considered himself "an ardent follower of the great health-preacher." Into his late twenties, he remained obsessed with "firm hard flesh, supple muscles, the alertness of health," as he once put it.

It wasn't mere vanity. A late bloomer, Ripley had begun dating. To make himself attractive to women, he had his work cut out for himself. There wasn't much he could do about his fanged teeth or jug ears, so he exploited what he had—dressing colorfully and maintaining a muscular physique.

Having spent the bulk of his adulthood among the nation's finest athletes, he had learned to emulate their workouts. After taking up boxing in San Francisco, he began sparring at the New York Athletic Club, occasionally entering the ring with his heroes, including Jack Dempsey and Georges Carpentier, both club regulars. He also visited the New Jersey health farm and gymnasium created by his boxer friend Freddie Welsh, another Bernarr Macfadden apostle.

⌁ BELIEVE IT! ⌁

One of Welsh's camp visitors was F. Scott Fitzgerald, and some historians believe Freddie Welsh (real name Frederick Thomas) was the model for Jay Gatsby (real name James Gatz). One clue is that a woman named Myrtle Wilson had been injured in a car accident with Welsh. In The Great Gatsby, *Myrtle Wilson is struck by Daisy Buchanan, driving Gatsby's car.*

Ripley also took up tennis and golf, partly because they relaxed him but also, judging by photographs, because they allowed him to wear knee pants, argyle socks, and wool caps. He wasn't much for running—"Laborious exercise, to my mind, is harmful," he once said—but he loved a good long walk. He'd often forgo buses and taxis and walk from event to event, at times covering five miles on foot.

Ripley found that when he wasn't exercising or walking, he became tense and grumpy. This renewed vigor for physical fitness led him to take his New York Athletic Club membership to a new level by joining the subset of members, the so-called confirmed bachelors, who actually lived there.

Known mostly by its acronym, the NYAC had been founded in 1868 by a group trying to promote amateur "manly sports" in America. Thirty years later it moved into a spectacular new headquarters on Central Park South. With a marble swimming pool, billiards and card rooms, a dark wood-paneled dining hall, full gymnasium, and handball courts on the roof, it was the ultimate boys' club.

Some of the world's top athletes called the NYAC home, including Olympic medalists whose success in the 1908 and 1912 Games contributed to its prestige. By the time Ripley moved in, around 1919, membership had reached an all-time high of roughly five thousand. George M. Cohan was a member and had introduced his World War I tune "Over There" at the NYAC; Teddy Roosevelt, who died earlier in 1919, had been an honorary member.

Ripley wasn't interested in the NYAC's more popular sports—trap shooting, swimming, water polo. Instead, he joined a small group known as the Killers' Club, devotees of handball, the sport that would captivate him to the point of obsession. He didn't have many hobbies, but when he found one he loved, he immersed himself.

IN CHOOSING THE NYAC as his new residence, Ripley joined nearly two hundred others who lived at the main headquarters. Ripley's room, number 59, was more like a large closet than an apartment. The low-ceilinged studio barely contained his bed and drawing table. He showered in a communal bathroom. But it cost just a dollar a day, as did dinner. Plus, he spent very little time in his room. After a day at the *Globe,* he'd pull on his sweatshirt and shorts, lace up his high-top sneakers, then head to the handball courts.

"It is the most natural thing in the world to slap a ball with the hand," he once said of his new favorite sport. "It quickens the eye. It refreshes the nervous system, it gives the body an electric vitality and resilience." The modern game was said to have originated in English prisons of the Middle Ages—inmates bounced balls against cell walls. In New York the sport took root on street corners, Irish immigrant kids hitting balls against tenement walls. As handball's popularity grew, NYAC members converted their roof into courts and shoveled off winter's snow to play year-round.

Ripley's first and most frequent opponent was his pal Bugs Baer, a competitive and testy foe who flung his pudgy little body heedlessly about the court, as if rubberized. Sometimes the two teamed up for doubles matches, winning so often they began entering citywide tournaments.

Over the next few years Ripley would play in dozens of tournaments, including the annual national championship tournament, traveling regularly to Milwaukee, Chicago, Detroit, and Cleveland. One newspaper would later refer to him as "one of the leading handball players of the country."

Ripley viewed handball as the perfect all-around athletic endeavor: "It polishes down my raw nerves after I've been working overtime." He would encourage anyone who'd listen to play handball "when you're emotionally wrought up . . . You simply cannot play this game hard and think of your troubles at the same time."

* * *

THE NYAC and its handball courts offered Ripley an invigorating male culture, a place where his buckteeth and stutter mattered less than his competitiveness and physical performance. Being an athlete made him feel special, just as being a talented high school artist had helped him feel less of a misfit.

In the same way that his loud clothes sought to draw attention away from his face and teeth, Ripley's athleticism offset his odd looks and mannerisms. Sportsmen were *supposed* to be eccentric, he'd learned after years of covering athletes. In fact, for a man who still felt like the only bumpkin in New York, the NYAC was a perfect home. Because, for all his insecurities, Ripley loved to be around people and *hated* to be alone. At the bustling club, with its meat-and-potatoes restaurant, its amply stocked bar ringed by a brass foot rail, its parties and sporting events, he had access to a built-in network of friends.

Ripley also learned, thanks to Bugs Baer, that being an athlete earned other privileges—mainly women. Baer had recently moved to the gossip-savvy *New York American*. William Randolph Hearst hired him after reading Baer's description of Yankees baseball player Frank Stephen "Ping" Bodie (whom Ripley had known in California's bush leagues) and Bodie's failed attempt to steal second base. "His head was full of larceny," Baer wrote. "But his feet were too honest."

With a hefty new salary from Hearst, and a growing reputation as a hard-drinking night owl who could crack wise on cue, Baer introduced Ripley to a repertoire of lively nightspots: Perry's Gluepot, the Times Gate, and Churchill's. They'd gorge on lobster at Rector's or head up to Columbus Circle to eat wild game at Tom Healy's Golden Glades Cafe, where ice-skaters performed on an indoor rink. Or they'd visit the stage doors of Broadway's theaters, waiting for actresses and dancers to emerge and invite them out for drinks. At times, his and Baer's saucy exploits were recounted in the gossip pages.

A favorite haunt was Jack Doyle's Billiard Academy, a renowned newspaper hangout. Doyle once hosted a pool tournament for journalism's elite, and Ripley beat one famous newsman or cartoonist after another to become co-champion.

Ripley found himself caught up in a giddy postwar euphoria, embracing a heady new lifestyle rich with athletic and social pursuits and hobnobbing with celebrities. He started taking dancing lessons. His taste in clothes grew incrementally flashier—three-piece suits with knicker-length pants, bow ties, two-tone shoes and spats. He sometimes wielded a walking stick. Baer liked to tell his friend that he looked like "a paint factory that got hit by lightning."

The idea was to prove that the bumpkin could fit in, that the big city wasn't too big for Roy Ripley. He had money in his pocket too, thanks to his cheap new living quarters and some cash earned from drawing illustrations for another book, a retired Army colonel's memoir, to be published later in 1919.

With his bachelor's lifestyle revolving around clubs, cafés, and bars, it was a great disappointment when America launched its nationwide experiment in abstinence. Ripley called the Eighteenth Amendment, which would prohibit alcohol consumption starting in 1920, a "foolish law."

Possibly inspired by the looming threat of limited access to legal drink, Ripley decided in the spring of 1919 to treat himself to a journey. On his passport application he wrote that he was traveling to Havana for "health and recreation." It would be his first departure from American soil since his 1913 travels to Egypt and Europe.

* * *

NOT LONG AFTER his return from Cuba, Ripley stunned Baer and other friends with the news that he was engaged to be married.

Ripley had previously expressed pride in his bachelorhood and, typical of the boys' club attitudes of the day, an immature understanding of the fairer sex. Maybe it was inevitable that amid so much testosterone Ripley would develop caveman-like views toward women. He swapped dirty jokes in the NYAC's locker room and at the Friars Club bar. In print, he would acknowledge a passion for the company of a shapely woman and a well-made cocktail. Yet, for someone who was mostly raised by his mother and who remained close to his sister, he revealed an astonishing lack of savvy about women.

In general, he felt women required too much time and effort—"Time to woo 'em, win 'em, and time to keep 'em," he'd grouse—and that women had become "spoiled with the gallantries of the ages." After losing his first love, Nell Griffith, he often professed doubts that he'd ever find the right woman. In more petulant moments, he'd disparage Manhattan's female office workers as "the most tragic sight in our cities."

Terrified of finding himself in a "matrimonial wreck," he had seemed happy to pursue the single life. Then again, his petite bride-to-be was no office girl.

SOME NEWSPAPER ACCOUNTS said Beatrice Roberts was born in Manhattan to a well-heeled Jewish family. Other accounts said she was a Texas-bred Italian from the cowboy flatlands outside Waco. In truth, she came from a blue-blood Boston family with lineage to the *Mayflower*. Born in Medford, Massachusetts, one of six kids, she had been a teen beauty queen before moving to New York, harboring dreams of a dancer's life.

Her first New York jobs were modeling. Curvy and dark-eyed, with pouty, twin-peaked lips, her face appeared on billboards and in magazines. Beatrice danced on Broadway and in shows directed by Ned Wayburn, a *Ziegfeld Follies* choreographer. She played piano and sang, but her most bankable talents were her high-kicking legs and a pretty face, talents recognized by a man who knew how to nurture young girls' dreams.

Florenz Ziegfeld had created his *Follies* in 1907 and launched many careers over the next quarter century, including W. C. Fields, the actress-singer Fanny Brice, and the singing Cherokee-American Will Rogers. Future Hollywood stars such as Lillian Gish and Bette Davis got their start as Follies Girls. The *Ziegfeld Follies* combined music, comedy, and dance, shot through with innuendo and sex appeal. One Ziegfeld biographer called the 1919 *Follies*, featuring a nude Lady Godiva character atop a horse, "a union of lovely music and lovely girlflesh."

Many *Follies* dancers found their way to an audition with Mr. Ziegfeld at age thirteen or fourteen, and were onstage soon after. Marrying one of Ziegfeld's teens was considered a badge of honor, as impressive as landing a young starlet would be years later. (Bugs Baer would marry a Follies Girl too.) Beatrice briefly danced alongside a Follies Girl named Marion Davies, soon to become William Randolph Hearst's infamously public mistress.

Ripley's first date with Beatrice had been the night he drew his "Champs and Chumps" cartoon in late 1918. She would have been a week past her eighteenth birthday at the time; Ripley was a decade older. They may have been introduced by Bugs Baer, who'd started performing comedy routines in vaudeville shows and would invite Ripley to parties with dancers and singers. Or maybe one of Ripley's NYAC pals—Ziegfeld comedian W. C. Fields or *Follies* composer Robert Baral—introduced them. One writer described her as "a prominent figure in the Ziegfeld Follies on account of her statuesque beauty."

Despite his affinity for the single life, Ripley was moved by her beauty. In a pattern that would later repeat itself regularly, Ripley fell in love quickly, poetically, and passionately. She called him Roy, he called her Bea. They played tennis, walked through Central Park, went to dinners and Broadway shows. In the summer of 1919, he posed for a portrait—his hair slicked back, wearing a bow tie and a suit—and gave her a framed copy: "To Beatrice, With Affection, Roy." She responded with a photograph of herself, posed in mid-pirouette: "To Roy—My Boy."

They married on October 23, 1919, in Newark, New Jersey, then honeymooned in Atlantic City, strolling along the boardwalk and posing for touristy photos. Ripley wore his NYAC handball uniform to the beach—a tank top and tight shorts that revealed his muscular limbs—while Beatrice wore a black bathing suit and a polka-dot sun hat. In photographs, Ripley seems truly happy. Possibly, after so many years of insecurity about his strange looks, he was elated to have landed a *model* and a *dancer.*

Back in New York, however, they both began to wonder if they'd been hasty.

✳ ✳ ✳

MAYBE HE'D HAD an inkling from the start, for when Ripley told friends about the end of his bachelorhood, he seemed uncomfortable with the news, and not particularly enthused. "We're married," he'd say, with no further explanation.

One sign of ambivalence was his unwillingness to give up his room at the NYAC. He told Beatrice he wasn't ready to cohabit, that he would be traveling too much and didn't want to commit to a house or apartment just yet. The newlyweds spent nights in midtown hotels—a suite at the Tavern Inn on West Forty-eighth Street or at the spectacular Hotel Marie Antoinette on Broadway. Though Beatrice didn't mind the nice hotels, she must have wondered what she'd gotten herself into.

Prior to wedlock, Ripley had dated other young women, and Beatrice apparently didn't trust her new husband to entirely give up his old lifestyle. It didn't help that Ripley, in addition to spending nights alone at the NYAC, would disappear for days at a time—on assignments or touring with boxer pals—while Beatrice remained in Manhattan. She phoned him constantly, suspicious that Ripley might be seeing other women, but he always insisted he was being faithful.

Still, the whole arrangement felt too bizarre for Beatrice, who had expected a more conventional union. She wanted to be doted on, and her husband's failure to meet her marital expectations triggered loud arguments on the nights they actually shared a room. She would accuse him of drinking too much or flirting with waitresses, and he'd argue that she had too much time on her hands and too vivid an imagination.

"There should be a law to compel suspended animation among wives during the afternoons," he once said. "A wife can get into more trouble to present her hardworking spouse on his return at night than a chorus of Pandoras."

In more introspective moments, Ripley would admit that for a devoted bachelor with limited knowledge of the female mind, an attempt at domestic stability was probably a bad idea. While he truly cared for Beatrice, he had gotten used to living simply and somewhat rootlessly. His NYAC apartment was more a locker room than a home, a sloppy place to change clothes or sleep before getting back to the clubs, the baseball stadiums, the handball courts. Regardless of whom was to blame, the marriage was on the rocks and coming apart fast. Ripley was relieved, then, when the *Globe* decided in mid-1920 to send him on the road.

* * *

THE FIRST CARTOON to actually carry the *Believe It or Not* title had appeared on October 16, 1919, a week before Ripley and Beatrice wed and ten months after the initial "Champs and Chumps" cartoon. After settling into his uneasy union with Beatrice, Ripley's interest in the year-old feature seemed suddenly rejuvenated.

Each of the *Believe It or Not* cartoons he produced in the first half of 1920 featured a medley of odd athletic feats—a wrestler who tested his neck strength by hanging himself (he survived); a pool shark who sank 23,000 balls; a Babe Ruth home run that flew 600 feet. Ripley also weaved random sketches that skewed from modern sports: Alexander the Great's courier, who ran 150 miles in a day, or Olympic hero Melancomas, who stood with arms outstretched for two days.

In response to this new energy, Ripley's editors decided to send him to cover the 1920 Olympic Games in Antwerp, Belgium, which would be one of the crowning journalistic achievements of his early career, placing him in the front row for another important moment in sports history, just like the Jeffries-Johnson fight. For Ripley, the Olympics also offered a much-needed escape from his marital woes and his disgruntled wife. But it wasn't the cushiest assignment.

In late July, he sailed to Europe with the US teams, including three dozen NYAC members. Athletes and newsmen complained about the bad food on the USS *Princess Matoika*, the cramped sleeping quarters, and the lack of training facilities. Ripley sketched athletes on the *Matoika*'s deck praying for land and complaining that the ship was just "a cattle boat." In Antwerp, events were scattered miles apart and frequent rains turned running tracks into muddy ruts. Water for swimming events was dank, dirty, and frigid. Ripley found Belgians to be rude, overweight, and uninterested in the Games.

ℰ BELIEVE IT! ℐ

Hawaiian swimmer Duke Kahanamoku (controversial, due to his darkish skin) won two of the forty-one gold medals taken by the United States: more than twice as many as the next most successful team, Sweden.

But the Games gave Ripley the chance to veer further from covering traditional sports and to stoke his curiosity about the history and oddities of sport. One dispatch described the origins of the marathon, the fabled run by a foot soldier from the Battle of Marathon to the city of Athens. After delivering his message, "Rejoice, we conquer!" the runner collapsed and died. In September, after a month away, Ripley sailed home on the SS *Imperator*. His spoiling marriage awaited.

* * *

RIPLEY AND BEATRICE passed their first wedding anniversary in the fall of 1920. Though they'd lived apart for most of that year, they were still husband and wife and they tried occasionally to reconcile, usually with terrible results. They once got into a marathon shouting match at the Hotel Marie Antoinette. Another night, beckoned by an anonymous caller, Beatrice found her husband dancing with another woman at a Broadway café. When she confronted him, he dragged her to the street and put her in a cab.

Over the next year, Ripley further distanced himself from his young bride, traveling to handball tournaments with Bugs Baer, his partner in sport and in drink. It's possible that the onset of Prohibition had contributed to Ripley's refusal to give up his NYAC apartment and settle down with Beatrice. He referred to his kind as "the great criminal element," so it helped to have a bed at the NYAC, just a few blocks north of the notorious stretch of speakeasies along Fifty-second Street, known to house more illegal pubs than anywhere in the city, where secret chutes were built into the walls to dump liquor during a bust.

Through 1921, Ripley began cranking out a steadier stream of *Believe It or Not* cartoons, averaging roughly two a month. Though they still largely contained sports feats, he'd begun featuring more non-sports vignettes, such as the man who ate sixty eggs a day for a week and a man named Martin Laurello who had a "revolving head." He scavenged gossip rags and stuffed his notebooks full of news clippings about hard-to-believe facts and feats, the stranger the better.

As his marriage dissolved and his personal life got messier, his cartoons seemed to grow incrementally weirder. He'd slip in a sketch of a man who never shaved, a man who ate glass and nails, a man who crossed the English Channel on a mattress, a man who stood on one leg for twelve hours, and a 147-year-old man who could lift two hundred pounds. He also presented to readers a billiards player with no hands who sank 799 straight balls, and another who sank 46 straight with his nose.

Signs of Ripley's marital strife sometimes slipped into print. In a mid-1921 essay titled "The Female of the Species," he derided America's female athletes as inferior to their European counterparts. "What is the matter with the American girl?" he asked in print, stating that European women excelled in "stage, opera, science, and letters . . . [and] how about beauty?" He felt American women suffered from "strained nerves" and too many soda-fountain lunches. In an unpublished article advocating physical fitness for women, he fretted that every beautiful woman inevitably "begins to fade."

> After that she begins her desperate fight with cosmetics to save the remnants of her girlishness; she develops a warped "office-girl" figure, spongy muscles, listless eyes . . . Then there's nothing left except bitter, lonely spinsterhood.

Despite Ripley's outbreaks of chauvinism, and his fights with and absences from Beatrice, she still loved him. She gave him a sultry photograph of herself that summer of 1921, signed "Your lover girl." But against so much competition—from nightclubs to baseball games, boxing matches to handball courts—she eventually realized there was nothing to salvage. In December of 1921 she filed papers requesting a formal separation, charging her husband with "cruel treatment," "excessive indulgence in intoxicants," and a "fondness for other young women." A judge granted the separation and awarded Beatrice a monthly alimony of $125, plus $750 in legal fees. Her attorney told the press he'd "made several appeals to Mr. Ripley to do the right thing by his wife," but Ripley's failure to do so had forced Beatrice to bring her complaints to the judge.

Ripley declined to publicly defend himself, allowing the accusations of womanizing, alcoholism, and physical abuse to stand.

Finally, the marriage went down in flames one night after

Beatrice followed him to the Great Northern Hotel and up to Room 304.

He and another woman had shared a quiet dinner and a few drinks, then returned to his room for a nightcap. One thing led to another. Clothes were removed.

The romantic mood was suddenly interrupted by urgent knocking at the door, and then shouting, then *pounding*. Somehow his spouse had found him. Ripley emerged, flustered and wearing only a bathrobe, to find Beatrice accompanied by two other men (an elevator operator and a shoe salesman, he'd later learn—in court). He tried to block them from seeing his companion, but Beatrice could tell the other woman was "scantily attired."

When the shouting died down, Beatrice announced that she was finally, completely through with him. She'd let a judge decide the details.

CHAPTER

8

Exactly one year after his noisy split from Beatrice, Ripley landed the assignment and the adventure of a lifetime.

"All my life I have waited for this day—the day when dreams come true," Ripley told readers in his first dispatch from afield, on December I, 1922. "To go 'round the world is a youthful dream. Now is the time, before it is too late . . . from the New York Athletic Club and back. Impossible to go further than that."

A decade after escaping San Francisco and landing a fruitful partnership with the *Globe*, Ripley ceased to be a mere sports cartoonist as he embarked on a journey that would change everything. Over the next four months, he would travel by train, steamship, army transport, rickshaw, sedan chair, elephant, horse, camel, and on foot. The journey would test his skills as an aspiring adventurer and offer readers a rare firsthand look into the non-Western world. It would provide rich new material for subsequent *Believe It or Not* cartoons, leading Ripley in a new artistic direction—more worldly, more weird.

The unexpected around-the-world expedition would also

introduce him to the country whose people and culture would transfix him for the rest of his life.

✳ ✳ ✳

TRANSGLOBAL TRAVEL REMAINED a rarity among the masses, such journeys typically undertaken only by the military, merchants, or true explorers. In recent years, attempts at luxury cruise travel had ended badly: the *Titanic* in 1912; the *Lusitania* in 1915.

↩ BELIEVE IT! ↪

Among the Titanic *victims were NYAC members whose bodies were identified by the leather key tabs imprinted with their membership numbers.*

The RMS *Laconia,* owned by pioneering British steamship operator Cunard, had been launched in late 1921 to replace the original *Laconia* (sunk off the Irish coast in 1917 by German U-boat torpedoes). The luxury ocean liner now sought the ambitious distinction of becoming the first passenger ship to circle the earth. Having his name on the passenger list made Ripley feel like some modern-day Magellan or Marco Polo, and Ripley proudly called the *Laconia* "my houseboat around the world."

Unlike previous assignments, confined by stadium walls and sports teams' schedules, the itinerary would be mostly in Ripley's hands. Instead of writing about others, as he had during World War I and at the Olympics, Ripley would be his own leading man. He was expected to file a dispatch every day or so, accompanied by a sketch or two, for the next four months. But where he went, whom he met, and the stories he told . . . that would all be largely up to him.

The *Globe* offered "Ripley's Ramble 'Round the World" series to dozens of newspapers who subscribed to the Associated Newspapers syndicate. The inaugural dispatch was accompanied by a logo of a caricatured Ripley in full stride, wearing a jaunty cap, bow tie, and knickers, a huge sketch pad under one arm, and wielding a pen like a sword in the other hand.

Ripley first boarded a Lake Shore Limited train bound for Chicago, then west on to Las Vegas, Los Angeles, and San Francisco, where he'd meet the *Laconia*. As the lights of New York faded, and the train window framed only darkness, Ripley lay back on the shelf-bed of his sleeper car, suddenly wondering if he was ready to leave his comfortably urban and urbane lifestyle behind. Now entirely on his own, away from friends and mentors, responsible for describing the world to millions of readers, he felt scared—a "fear that creeps toward your throat," he'd later call it—as he watched his hometown recede from view.

THE TRANSCONTINENTAL RAIL journey was his first return to California since his mother's death seven years earlier.

His solemnity fizzled upon reaching Los Angeles, where he toured Hollywood studios, watched Charlie Chaplin act in a few scenes, and joined up with three traveling companions who would make cameo appearances throughout the Ramble: Jack Davidson, an actor who had appeared in fifty films (including *The Winning of Beatrice* and *The Wild Girl*); May Allison, Davidson's costar in *The Winning of Beatrice*, also the star of nearly fifty films; and Allison's new husband, Robert Ellis, a prolific actor, screenwriter, and director, whose most recent film was *A Divorce of Convenience*. Ripley's otherwise extensive journal keeping offered no commentary on the eerie similarity between his Hollywood friends' films and his own life—*Beatrice, wild girl, divorce . . .*

The foursome traveled to San Francisco and Ripley played tour guide, showing his companions a few favorite haunts—the Barbary Coast, the Cliff House, Mission Delores, and the Hotel Fairmont, where he'd witnessed the smoldering city days after the earthquake—as well as his humble old basement apartment. He introduced them to Coffee Dan's, an underground speakeasy accessed through a hidden wall leading to a playground slide that deposited guests onto the barroom floor. Inside, they ordered "ham and eggs"—code for liquor. Ripley told Jack Davidson the place had the spirit of San Francisco "before the fire."

The ship left San Francisco the next morning, steaming through the burly shoulders surrounding Golden Gate Bay. Slightly hungover, Ripley grew woozy and melancholy watching San Francisco shrink in his wake. He had eagerly left for the East Coast a decade earlier, but still felt pangs of homesickness for Northern California.

"Once again I leave home," he wrote in an essay, revealing to *Globe* readers that his Ramble might become more than a mere travelogue.

> Why any one place should forever hold enchantment for the reason you are born there is a mystery. But like cats and birds we are pussy-footed and pigeon-toed and our footsteps lead toward home. . . . The Eskimo longs for his northern bleakness and his ice hut, the cowboy dreams of the wide open towns and prairies of the west, the old salt is looking out to sea . . . and down in the hold of many ships are dead Chinamen's bones going home to China.

In his sketch of the *Laconia* disappearing over the horizon, smoke from the stack spelled "Goodbye."

DURING HIS FIRST DAYS aboard the *Laconia*, Ripley met the other pioneering travelers who would visit remote parts of the world while also sipping martinis in the ship's saloons, perfectly legal since the *Laconia* sailed under the British flag. Among the passengers were ten honeymooning couples, five ministers, thirty widows, twelve millionaires, and, as Ripley told readers, "one of the best known prohibition enforcement officers New York ever had."

Ripley was soon taunting his Prohibition-restricted readers: "You folks at home have doubtless forgotten the saloon," he said. "Let me tell you . . ." The ship's most popular bar, unobtrusively called A Aft, was filled with "American law-breakers." A beer cost fifteen cents, a whiskey twenty cents, and a bottle of champagne $6. A sign on the wall gave helpful advice to wine buyers: WILL PASSENGERS KINDLY GIVE THEIR ORDERS FOR WINES IN ADVANCE, SO THAT THEY MAY INSURE THEM BEING SERVED AT THE PROPER TEMPERATURE.

Two weeks after leaving New York, Ripley spotted the shimmering Hawaiian archipelago. Onshore at Hilo, he was surrounded by slender, dark-skinned native girls who welcomed Ripley with effusive alohas and piled garlands around his neck. He was instantly smitten, calling the Big Island "an emerald jewel set in the sea."

Though the Prohibition officer searched passengers disembarking at Hilo, to prevent anyone from bringing alcohol ashore, Ripley had developed a knack for sniffing out liquor wherever he went. He and his friends found a local resident who offered some Hawaiian moonshine, *okolehao*, distilled from pineapple and the root of the Ti plant. Ripley bragged in print about the smile that *okolehao* put on his face. Paraphrasing Shakespeare and the Bible, he wrote: "Oh Mule! Where is thy sting?"

At the Moana Hotel on Waikiki Beach in Honolulu, Ripley reunited with Duke Kahanamoku, a local swimming and surfing legend whom he had met at the 1920 Antwerp Olympics. Kahanamoku introduced Ripley to "surf riding," which Ripley attempted to describe to readers: "These bronze-skinned natives paddle on a board . . . to a distance upward of a mile, where they catch a likable wave and then mount to their feet and stand upright."

Ripley tried surf-riding in an outrigger canoe and later enjoyed a tribal hula dance at midnight. He considered the Hawaiian Islands "a land of romance and happiness," although he worried that the Hawaiian race—"the most lovable and hospitable race on earth"—was being eradicated by disease and the influence of Japan, China, and America. He thought Honolulu was too full of US soldiers and sailors to be a novelty. Then again, he felt comforted by the strong military presence. "And that means that the outpost—the frontier, if you will, of America—is safe from foreign aggression," he wrote, nineteen years to the day before the Pearl Harbor attacks.

Reluctantly, he left Hawaii, worried that he'd never experience "such genuine, whole-hearted hospitality again." Then again, having earned a blistering red sunburn, he looked forward to the cold, legal beer aboard the ship.

✶ ✳ ✶

FOUR DAYS LATER, after roiling through a twelve-hour storm, Ripley spent a sullen Christmas at sea, thinking of Christmases gone by. His morose holiday worsened as the ship struck the edge of a violent typhoon, and Ripley hunkered in the A Aft saloon beside a snarling man from New Jersey named Sam. Ripley's drinking partner complained miserably about the weather, regretting his decision to spend a month at sea just to see "a lotta Chinks."

When the *Laconia* finally passed through the howling winds of the typhoon, the clouds broke and Ripley was able to leave the bar, walk onto the deck, and witness a spectacularly setting sun. It looked like a giant blood-red orange melting behind Japan's white-tipped Mount Fuji, the perfect welcome to Asia.

A month after leaving New York, Ripley began to find his travel-writer voice in Japan. Instead of focusing on Prohibition and saloons, he started to weave history lessons with cultural analyses, travelogue and random cogitations, weird facts and personal opinion, the type of wide-ranging commentary that would decades later be called *blogging*. He sometimes exposed his biases, sharing hints of racism and stereotyping that had previously made cringe-inducing appearances in his cartoons.

"The Japs and the Jews are the only civilized peoples with a fundamental religion of their own," he wrote in a dispatch on Shintoism. He called the Japanese religion a "strange faith," but was impressed that it preached "love of nature, patriotism, love of family, and filial reverence." He was equally impressed by the Japanese emphasis on ceremony, though he found it frustrating that it took so long to get a cup of tea. He toured temples and shrines, Tokyo's red-light district ("bizarre and brilliant"), and spent New Year's Eve amid the "kaleidoscopic throng" of the Ginza ("the busiest, noisiest, unhandsomest, and most flamboyant of all streets").

He found Japan to be "a hive of industry" where "everybody seems to be pushing or pulling something." As with his remarks about America's military presence in Hawaii, he presciently assessed Japan's military affairs, troubled by the ubiquity of naval vessels and the rampant construction of "massive and murderous" battleships.

Despite his passionate curiosity about the world, Ripley could be a lazy traveler, and sometimes a boor. Just as he seemed to relish opportunities to divulge his chauvinism (and possible alcoholism) in print, he rarely hesitated to put his provincialism on full display. He considered it too much work to learn even a few phrases of his host country's language, unabashedly speaking English at all times. As he'd done in Europe years earlier, when someone didn't understand him, he spoke *louder.*

"Rickshaw man!" he yelled at a driver in Kobe. "Do you speak English?"

"Darn near," the man replied.

In one dispatch he described the Japanese language as so complicated "the Japs can't learn it themselves." It was sometimes hard to tell whether his oafishness was tongue-in-cheek, but he insisted that he could travel anywhere speaking English alone: "Simply speak up and let the other fellow do the worrying."

He was equally unflinching with readers when he confessed, after reboarding the *Laconia* for the next leg of the journey, that he was surprised that he liked Japan so much. "I never thought I would, being born and raised in California and holding the western idea of the Jap," he said.

Folks back in New York must have gagged at a few comments from their otherwise civilized and sophisticated friend, remarks that would proliferate as the trip wore on. Ripley seemed to be trying out different traveler personas, waffling somewhere between small-town yokel and streetwise foreign correspondent.

* * *

AFTER A BRIEF STOP in Manchuria, the ship reached the ancient Chinese city of Tsingtao, and Ripley's first thought upon landing in the country he'd long dreamed of was that "human life is the cheapest thing in Asia." China was both beautiful and horrible, he quickly learned, an uneasy dichotomy that he'd confront in many future travels. He first witnessed the horrible. Along the wharves, he and the other tourists were beset by the local poor—clots of alms-seekers tugging at his sleeves and cuffs.

"I wonder what China is going to look like if this collection of deformities, rags, and leprosy is a sample," he wondered aloud.

After Tsingtao came Shanghai, which astonished him as "one of the most interesting and cosmopolitan places in the world." He and his actor friends dined on bird's nest soup and shark's fin. While touring the old city by rickshaw, he was again swarmed by beggars as he rolled through foul-smelling alleys "thronged with a noisy mass of humanity, the existence of such that I never would have believed." He saw crawling lepers with twisted limbs and at one point was chased down a cobbled alley by a man dragging another man strapped to a board, his hands and feet eaten away by leprosy.

"It is not pleasant to be chased by a thing like that," Ripley reported, heedless of his insensitivity. "Surely there is no lower form of life to be found than in this decayed old poverty-stricken spot."

Still, even in his disgust Ripley found his curiosity aroused by China and its people. Unlike his fellow first-class passengers, who shopped for trinkets and postcards, he frequently ventured off the itinerary in search of a more authentic experience, discovering in himself an unexpected facility with improvised exploration. In Hong Kong, he left the others for an impulse drive around Repulse Bay. On Formosa, he insisted on making a side train trip to see the headhunters he'd read about, though he was disappointed to find the men corralled behind barbed wire, looking "more like lounge lizards than blood-thirsty cannibals . . . I could lick them all myself."

At Formosa, the *Laconia* had anchored offshore and passengers were delivered from the pier to the ship by small shuttle boats. When a sudden storm kicked up, a dozen tourists were thrown overboard from the shuttle and had to be rescued by a Japanese warship. Laughing at their cuts and bruises, Ripley considered the rescue a thrilling highlight. Anytime the trip became ridiculous or dangerous, Ripley grew giddier, as if it were all a game.

In fact, he seemed surprisingly fearless at times, less afraid of gun-toting soldiers than alms-seeking beggars. When he learned about military skirmishes in Canton (as Guangzhou was then called), he asked the US consul for permission to visit. His request was denied, so he and Bob Ellis negotiated with local military leaders for passage on a midnight transport boat out of Hong Kong. Like a Boy Scout on his first campout, Ripley gushed with excitement: "They say it is very dangerous and we are strongly advised not to go," he said. "But I have always wanted to be a war correspondent like Herb Corey."

Squeezing through flotillas of houseboats, Ripley's boat arrived in Canton at dawn. He and Ellis then walked nervously among the soldiers of Sun Yat-Sen's revolutionary army, part of the Kuomintang, which battled Chinese warlords and regional armies in an effort to unite the fractured Chinese Republic. The soldiers must have been surprised and/or amused to see Ripley in town, wearing a herringbone suit, knicker pants, a bow tie, and boyish cap, his sketch pad always in hand. Among the uniformed soldiers and poorly clothed locals, he stood out like a clown at a funeral.

One soldier finally snatched Ripley's sketch pad and accused him of being a spy. "I no like strange soldiers," the man yelled before Ripley's guide came to the rescue. He and Ellis then climbed into sedan chairs, each borne on the shoulders of three men who plunged into the labyrinthine streets of the ancient city, into the "evil-looking alleys" and the "mystic, foul-smelling center" of what Ripley breathlessly discovered to be the *real* China.

After spending the night at the deserted Victoria Hotel, he and Ellis returned to Hong Kong the next day, and Ripley felt that in Canton he had experienced a more genuine taste of China than he would in a year in Hong Kong or Shanghai. Those cities, he scoffed, had been built mainly by Europeans.

As the *Laconia* steamed toward its next stop, Ripley was sorry to leave China, which had repulsed, appalled, and dazzled him. He worried that it would now be impossible for anyplace else to top "the vast, old decaying land of the Celestial."

✳ ✳ ✳

COASTING INTO MANILA, he thought about Magellan entering the same port four hundred years earlier. The bay, crammed with warships flapping with American flags, made Ripley swell with patriotism and pride. "Our Uncle Sam has done well with his most pretentious colonization effort," he wrote.

Halfway around the world at this point, he had come to fancy himself a far more adventurous traveler than his high-class compatriots, whom he mocked for their petty complaints about heat and food. He scorned those wearing Gallagher and Sheans—"the concrete helmet which distinguishes all tourists of tropical climes."

❧ BELIEVE IT! ❧

*Ed Gallagher and Al Shean were a popular vaudeville act,
earning $1,500 a week at the 1922 Ziegfeld Follies.
(Shean was uncle of the Marx Brothers; Gallagher married a
Follies Girl.) In their most famous skit, Gallagher parodied an
American tourist, wearing a white suit and
pith helmet.*

"Why a human being will wear such a human lid passeth all understanding," claimed Ripley, who would one day adopt the exact same traveling costume.

Again, he seemed embarrassed by the timidity of the parochial American traveler, even as he was clearly afflicted by the same backwater lack of international sophistication. One moment he could be the keen and curious observer, the next he'd be the insensitive doofus. He had been tickled by the "pidgin English" many Chinese used to converse with tourists, but also found Chinese merchants too shrewd and aggressive—"a Jap or a Jew hasn't a chance with him," he wrote.

And yet, emboldened by his adventures in China, he was now eager to leave the Philippines and reach India. Along the way he visited Java, Singapore, and Rangoon, but India beckoned loudly. "Can India offer more wonders than Japan or China, especially China?" he wrote one night in his journal. "It seems impossible . . ."

In the meantime, he was finding his rhythm as a correspondent—and having a blast. In playful dispatches home he teased his audience, a mischievous tool he'd wield in future cartoons. After visiting a beer garden in Java he declared, "I went to bed and slept with a Dutch wife." The next day he explained that a Dutch wife was an oblong pillow, and that the previous night was "not as romantic as it sounds." He kept razzing those suffering under Prohibition with stories of exotic drinks and taverns. When it got cold, he told readers, he "drank gin to keep warm." When it was hot, he drank beer. He discovered "Chota Peg" (whiskey and soda), and raved about noontime Gin Slings at John Little's Department Store in Singapore, the recipe for which he shared with readers: "Let me whisper . . ."

Upon reaching India, however, his tone shifted, from playful to shocked and somber, and Ripley's question about whether anything could top China was quickly, horrifically answered.

THROUGHOUT THE RAMBLE, he frequently declared, aloud and in print, often with unambiguous authority, that something he had witnessed was the best or worst or most or least *in the world*, which would become his pet three-word tic. Repulse Bay was "the most beautiful in the world"; the Javanese were "the cleanest people in the world"; Singapore "the most cosmopolitan city in the world"; the Hooghli River in India "the most dangerous in the world." Buddhists were "the happiest people on earth"; and a Chinaman was the "most virtuous and most honest man in the world," but also "the dirtiest."

He was blatant about these statements, and seemed to care little about redundancy or contradiction (or insult). If he felt it at the time, that was truth enough. But in the city of Benares—"the most remarkable in the world"—he discovered a place in no need of hyperbole.

"I have traveled 20,000 miles and have seen no place which so baffles description as this," he reported. "Here in India cows are sacred, little girls are married at the age of three, the dead are fed to vultures, holy men sleep on beds of nails, and a man may marry as many wives as he wants. What a motley mixture of mystery!"

India introduced Ripley to the devout Hindu ascetics and beggars known as fakirs. (He sometimes called them fanatics or "wretches.") These men performed inhumane, self-flagellating acts to prove their sanctity. One man had been sitting on a bed of nails for twelve years, while others kept their arms aloft all day—Ripley called them "up-arm men." Some never clipped their cuticles ("nail men") and others hung upside down from limbs like monkeys ("tree men").

The holy city of Benares seemed to be an epicenter for the extremes of Hindu spirituality, home to what Ripley called "the weirdest collection of humanity on the face of the earth—demented, delusioned, diseased, and devout." One of the few white faces, he roamed streets clotted with goats and sacred cows, gawking at the blood and bones scattered about, at the "insane worshippers" and wild-eyed beggars. Walking along the banks of the Ganges River, he watched in amazed horror as a woman, with no sign of emotion, set afire the body of her recently dead husband, using a long pole to make the fire burn faster as vultures circled overhead.

"Not a pleasant site [*sic*]," he wrote that night by kerosene lamp, concluding: "You are never so dead as when you die in India."

Similar "burning ghat" ceremonies were held all along the riverbanks, and Ripley returned three days in a row to witness numerous cremations. Meanwhile, orthodox Hindus bathed in—and drank—the same murky water in which human ashes were being scattered, in which dead bodies floated, and into which sewage seeped. Ripley worried whether leprosy was contagious, but seemed unable to turn away from the corpses and deformed beggars. In home-movie footage Ripley gapes as a man pierces his own tongue with a bicycle spoke; he gives coins to a gnarled beggar who walks on all fours; he walks among the half-clothed poor, skittish but agog.

"Nowhere on earth can you see such a weird cross-cut of human life," Ripley wrote. "All this pagan panorama."

In contrast to the horrible, Ripley also witnessed the sensational. At the Taj Mahal ("the most beautiful building in the world"), he was relieved to enjoy such dazzle after the squalor of Benares. In Jaipur ("a kaleidoscope"), he watched a rainbow-like wedding procession led by an elephant carrying the bridegroom through the streets. But death was never far away. The wedding party marched past a man carrying his dead son wrapped in thin red gauze.

"Funerals and weddings are continually passing each other," he wrote back to America. "Such is life."

India fascinated, revolted, beguiled, and *moved* him. His hotels were wretched, his mattresses festered with bedbugs. Still, he disparaged those who "travel for the sole purpose of mailing picture postcards back to envious home folks," and he continued to explore outside the safe bubble of the tour company's itinerary.

In Delhi, he and Jack Davidson bribed their way into the sacred Jama Masjid mosque during midday prayer. When they were spotted, furious elders dragged them out a side gate as worshippers shouted and jeered. In Calcutta, wanting to visit the famous Black Hole dungeon, he hailed a cab and yelled, "Black hole!" The driver nodded enthusiastically, and after an hour of meandering they stopped beside a miserable riverside structure. The driver pointed and said, "Black hole!" Ripley walked through a door and was hit by the sight and smell of partially cremated bodies. The driver had delivered him to a burning ghat, where Ripley watched a young boy attempting to burn his father's corpse. He left wondering if the boy's meager supply of wood would get the job done.

Back aboard the *Laconia*, Ripley confessed to readers the origins of his now-sated curiosity about India. He had once dated "a little blond sweetheart named Jean" who had lived in India and had given him a book of Kipling's poetry, in which she'd underlined her favorite verses. Among them:

> **If you've 'eard the East a-callin', why you won't 'eed nothin' else.**
> **No! you won't 'eed nothin' else, but them spicy garlic smells,**
> **an' the sunshine an' the palm-trees, an' the tinkly temple-bells.**

Ripley would pen eight dispatches from Benares alone, and a total of 26—out of roughly 120 total—from India, "that enchanting land of squalor and splendor." As the *Laconia* cruised west, he summed it all up: "A strange country is India. . . . It is a common thing to die here."

⁕　＊　⁕

AS HE HEADED toward the Middle East, his thoughts turned to God. Though his mother had been Christian and Ripley believed in a Christian version of God, he was hardly devout and sometimes admitted to having mixed feelings about Christianity. But in recent weeks he had been exposed to Shintoism, Buddhism, Hinduism, and witnessed the extreme and painful lengths to which people go to prove their devotion. So now, sailing toward Egypt, he found himself pondering the mysteries of Islam.

"For the life of me I cannot make up my mind whether the

vaunted power of the prophet is a myth or not," he admitted to readers. At the same time, he couldn't deny the anxiety that most Westerners felt for "the fanatical Muslim," with his robes, his daily prayers, his fierce piety. "Always it seems the European statesmen have lived in dread of the power of Islam," he wrote—once again, with eerie premonition. "The fear of Jehad has been upon the Christian world for ages."

At such moments, Ripley displayed a surprisingly well-calibrated cultural tuning fork. Ever the self-absorbed American, dark-skinned non-Westerners confused and unsettled him, eliciting insensitive commentary (similar to his chauvinistic remarks about women). Then again, he was capable of astute and prophetic observations—on Japan's aggressive military buildup and the threat of the "fanatical Muslim." Even so, he seemed at the same time able to find compassion and respect for the Other.

Ripley admired the restraint of Muslims, as well as Buddhists and Hindus. He reluctantly envied their ability to shun liquor and felt something close to shame that "the only people in the world who drink are Christians." He realized that, except for fellow passengers, he hadn't seen anyone drunk since Coffee Dan's in San Francisco.

In Jerusalem, however, he became downright enraptured at being at "the center of the world . . . my Holy City!" At St. John's Hotel, near the Church of the Holy Sepulchre, he couldn't believe he was near the spot where Christ died, the tomb where Jesus was briefly buried, the pathways "trodden by His feet." But he was also keenly aware of the ancient city's sizzling religious tensions. Rioting between Arabs and Jews had gone underreported in the American press, he realized. He learned that Palestinian Arabs were intent on preventing Zionists from controlling the Middle East, which he found not surprising since 90 percent of Palestine was Arab.

Still, he remained wary and distrustful of Islam, comparing the Mohammedan (as many Westerners then called Muslims) to the "Ku Klux Klan" for their head-to-toe white robes. Ultimately, he hoped that the potential dangers of Muslim fanaticism and threats of jihad were empty, that "the rising tide of his faith is only a ripple."

Again, the two sides of Ripley the traveler were on display— the ethnocentric American buffoon, and the curious anthropologist. He appreciated the "otherness" of the world but didn't necessarily want to get too close or, God forbid, shake its hand—an attitude that would change in time.

One thing he did admire about Islam was a man's ability to marry numerous women and to divorce them simply by repeating "Thou art divorced" three times.

He called their method of divorce "a great idea!"

CROSSING THE MEDITERRANEAN toward Europe, Ripley suddenly longed for home, his enthusiasm sapped. A Monaco casino looked beautiful on the outside, but inside was foul, smelly, and filled with American gamblers. In southern France, he thought Nice was "nice" and Marseilles was "quaint."

Though he'd sent eight dispatches from Benares, he would send just eight from Paris and Rome combined. The European stopover that intrigued him the most was Pompeii's ruins: "the deadest town I was ever in—and I am not excluding Philadelphia."

In Paris, he watched the funeral procession of actress Sarah Bernhardt and spent a day with Georges Carpentier, the boxer. He played tennis with Molla Mallory, one of the world's top-ranked female players, who had lost in the finals at Wimbledon six months earlier. When Mallory beat him 6–0, 6–0, Ripley blamed the previous night's drinking and smoking. "I didn't come over to play tennis, anyway," he griped.

One day he introduced himself to a stunning Peruvian woman named Carmela and they walked the gaslit streets and shared what he'd later coyly describe as "some wonderful moments." Ripley promised to visit her in Lima. "I'm a man of my word," he told Carmela, calling her "my little dark-eyed señorita."

Yet, after China and India, Europe seemed like an indulgence. Even while standing before Rodin's hunched-over *The Thinker*, he wondered aloud: "If he is thinking of man, he cannot think very much." Before sailing home, Ripley grew philosophical about his global odyssey, and shared some of his thoughts with readers: "Paris is all things to all people. You can find good and bad and indifferent here just the same as you can in Santa Rosa, California—my home town."

Ripley eagerly boarded the massive RMS *Aquitania*, bound for New York, then slipped into a glum reverie as the journey of a lifetime drew to an end. During the five-day westward crossing, completing his circle around the globe, he had plenty of time to look back on the strangest months of his life.

In his cabin one night, Ripley began cataloguing the world's cities of wonder. Benares ranked first, he decided, followed by Canton ("a vast rabbit warren of slant-eyed humanity"), then Jerusalem, Rome, Cairo, and Paris. Seventh on his top-seven list was New York, whose buildings were soon twiddling on the horizon.

"There is no city like Benares," he wrote in his Ramble's final dispatch. "But there is no place like home. . . . Columbus was right. The world is round."

Gliding into New York harbor at dusk, he felt exhausted and dejected, thinking back on Cairo ("a plundered land")

and Monaco ("Man is a gambling animal!"). He found himself wondering how so many could be starving in India and China—"Oriental millions wallowing in filth, ignorance and starvation"—while America was so full-fed. But he admitted that, whatever miseries he had witnessed, and whatever "waves of pessimism" he felt, he wasn't ready to reform the world.

"I can't reform myself!"

In his journal, which he did not share with readers, he wrote: "Why should the spirit of mortal be proud—ideals and actualities are far apart."

CHAPTER

9

Encircling the earth had rewired Ripley. The poverty and hunger he'd witnessed *haunted* him.

"If this world suffers from anything more than another it is malnutrition—malnutrition of brain and belly," he wrote in one of many stories that continued to appear for months after his Ramble. "What the world needs most is one God and one square meal!"

Certain sights and smells would linger forever, from the Chinese man with deformed hands like lobster claws to the smoke rising off burning corpses beside the Ganges to the man with two faces and one eye: "the most horrible living thing I have ever seen." It was now unavoidable that this uneasy fascination with the "demented, delusioned, diseased, and devout" of the world would alter the tone of his cartoon.

He had already come to realize that sports feats alone couldn't sustain his *Believe It or Not* series. After his Ramble, he grew even less interested in the strange things people did in the name of sport, and more fascinated by the inexplicable things people did for their gods. His cartoons began featuring oddities of a more freakish nature: the "Hanging Hindu," whom Ripley had seen dangling from a tree, a hook dug into his back; the "Hindu Sky-Facer," whom Ripley had watched stare directly at the sun with milky and withered eyes; the "Ever-Standing Man," who had been on his feet for twenty years, balanced on a crude wooden rack.

Gruesome became a new staple of Ripley's *Believe It or Not.* Friends and colleagues thought he seemed refreshed by his big adventure, liberated to finally be able to indulge his long-gestating desire to draw and write about something other than sports. From admirers who appreciated the eccentric new tenor of his work, requests trickled in . . . *Would Mr. Ripley speak to our organization? Write a story for our magazine? Donate a drawing to our charitable group? Cash to our orphans' home?*

Back at the *Globe,* he started hunting for a translator to help him mine even more believe-it-or-nots from the stacks of foreign books and magazines he'd collected from around the world. But just as he was getting back to work, he found his career jeopardized by a new employer, ominously known as "The Grocer."

FRANK A. MUNSEY owned three New York papers: the *Sun,* the *Evening Telegram,* and the *Herald.* In mid-1923, for $2 million, he added Ripley's *Globe* to his collection, boosting his overall circulation and putting him in league with William Randolph Hearst as one of the city's top newspapermen.

As a pioneer of inexpensive printing on untrimmed pulp paper, Munsey had helped create dime novels and "pulp" magazines in the early 1900s. Unlike Hearst, who spent money freely and recklessly to perfect his papers and expand his empire, Munsey was a penny-pinching horse trader with a reputation for selling, merging, or dismantling his possessions, earning such nicknames as "The Great Consolidator" and, because he also owned grocery stores, "The Grocer."

Since 1891, Munsey had purchased sixteen papers, sold six, consolidated or closed seven, and by 1923 owned just the three. As Munsey's biographer put it, he was like an engineer monomaniacally focused on building a huge dam, but indifferent to the homesteads that would be flooded—"No man in the newspaper field was more hated than Munsey."

As a cartoonist, Ripley had good reason to fear Munsey's purchase of the *Globe*. Back in 1920, when Munsey bought the revered *New York Herald*, he instructed the art director to fire cartoonist J. Norman Lynd, adding, "He'll know what it's for." It turned out that four years earlier, Lynd had drawn a caricature of Munsey as a gravedigger, knee-deep in a *Daily News* grave, the headstones of other dead newspapers behind him. Munsey never forgot a slight. A week after buying the *Herald* he shut it down, merging it with the *Sun* and putting hundreds out of work. On the *Herald*'s last night, employees met in the newsroom for drinks and toasts as a bugler played "Taps." One competitor said Munsey had "the talent of a meat-packer, the morals of a money changer, and the manner of an undertaker."

For Ripley, the *Globe*'s new ownership and uncertain future spoiled an otherwise happy return from abroad. Despite the success of his Ramble and the steady popularity of his cartoons, Ripley's future was suddenly as uncertain as it had been in a decade.

At such a tenuous time, it didn't help to get bad publicity.

RIPLEY'S GROWING RENOWN among New York journalists meant his personal life was subject to scrutiny. And the failing marriage of a world-traveling cartoonist and a high-kicking Follies Girl gave society writers a sordid story line. Ripley's as-yet-unresolved split with Beatrice became fair game for the *Globe's* gossip-hungry competitors, the type of story that up-and-coming columnist Walter Winchell liked to call "hot news." Various headlines began to appear through mid-1923:

FORMER 'FOLLIES' GIRL IN COURT AGAIN
EX–STAGE BEAUTY SUES CARTOONIST
CARTOONIST'S WIFE SUES FOR DIVORCE

Such stories were usually accompanied by photographs of Beatrice in a long gown, draped in furs, wearing a fashionable hat, and looking entirely pissed-off.

In her latest complaint, Beatrice wanted a judge to make their two-year-old separation permanent. She wanted a divorce. When her lawyer tipped off the press, writers responded with lurid stories about the couple's troubles, citing "new evidence" submitted by her lawyer, including a detailed account of the night in late 1922 when Beatrice found Ripley and his "scantily attired" friend at the Great Northern Hotel.

When the New York Supreme Court agreed to hear the case, Beatrice, now living on Madison Avenue, appeared at the hearing in "a costly fur-trimmed, hand-embroidered gown," as one columnist described it. The newspapers called Ripley her "stalwart, handsome husband." But the judge had harsher words, claiming that Ripley's poor husbanding skills and extramarital affairs were sufficient evidence to grant Beatrice the divorce.

Ripley's refusal to publicly deny Beatrice's accusations left an impression of guilt. At times, all he would say was that marriage had been a "rough voyage." Other times, he'd pretend the marriage never happened at all. In rare introspective moments, he would acknowledge that he was simply "too temperamental" to be a good husband. Losing his father at age fifteen had denied him a grown-up's perspective on love and marriage. And after leaving Santa Rosa, he had mostly lived and worked among newsmen and athletes who harbored manly views on women and wedlock.

His own chauvinistic views inevitably continued to appear in print. Women "are fast causing modern man to degenerate into a mechanical toy for their sole amusement," he declared in one article. Elsewhere he wrote: "The husband of today is little more than a slave with the divine gift of writing checks." America would be happier, he believed, "if husbands did not quarrel with their wives. And men were masters in their own houses."

RIPLEY HAD BEEN THRIFTY in his New York lifestyle, living for a dozen years in modest quarters and owning few possessions. Though his *Globe* salary had quadrupled to $100 a week, his savings began dwindling after the divorce.

In addition to $200 monthly payouts to Beatrice, plus legal fees, he had continued sending money to California. His brother, Doug, after living for years with his surrogate Santa Rosa family, had moved in with his older sister Ethel and her husband in Sacramento. Doug was a difficult young man, disinterested in school or work, and he'd sometimes disappear into the woods for days at a time. He declined his older brother's invitation to come live with him in New York, and Ripley felt bad that he couldn't do more for his family.

In a letter sent after the divorce became final, he complained to Ethel about the heavy price of his failed marriage. "I received my divorce on Friday 13—not so unlucky after all," he wrote. "It cost me a great deal more money than I had and leaves me in debt up to my neck. But I think the relief from worry will permit me to earn a little more." He promised to send Ethel more money "as soon as I get some—I am going to work hard."

He signed the letter "Lovingly, Roy," and then added, in reference to both his Ramble and his recent woes: "The world is round, but a little bumpy."

Unfortunately, Frank Munsey soon made good on his reputation as a newspaper killer.

✳ ✳ ✳

IN ANNOUNCING HIS PLANS to merge the *Globe* with the *New York Sun*, to create a "bigger and better newspaper," Munsey insisted he was doing New Yorkers a favor by pruning the "oversupply of evening newspapers." Munsey was unsentimental about such consolidations, claiming "there is no greater menace to society than newspapers that are struggling to keep alive."

Ripley's last cartoon appeared on May 31, 1923. Three days later, the *Globe* published its final issue, ending its reign as the nation's oldest paper. Among the five hundred employees to lose their jobs were "good men and women, for the *Globe*'s staff had been notable," wrote George Britt in a 1935 biography of Munsey.

Ripley landed on his feet, finding a spot at the *Evening Telegram*, which Munsey had purchased in 1920. But he felt unsettled by the recent tumult. He'd recently enjoyed the peak experience of his life on the Ramble, then became roiled in a painfully public divorce. That was followed by the premature end to his entrenched position at the *Globe* and a forced separation from longtime editors and colleagues. All of it threatened his shaky finances and his ability to support Doug.

So when he started at the *Evening Telegram,* he decided he needed a little help. At first, all he really wanted was someone to help him decipher the foreign-language publications he'd gathered during his Ramble, someone who could help breathe new life into *Believe It or Not.*

What he found was more than a mere translator. He found a business partner and ally, a man who similarly appreciated the eccentricities of the world.

NORBERT PEARLROTH WAS BORN in Tarnow, in the ancient Austrian section of Galicia. He was tall, handsome, and always the smartest in his class, possessing a near photographic memory of anything he read. In his youth, Pearlroth had devoured books of all types, and found at an early age that other languages came easily.

Before the war, he had attended the university in Krakow, where he breezed through his studies with plenty of time to earn extra money doing homework for classmates. One day he saw a newspaper ad for a series of encyclopedias printed in German called the *Library of Entertainment and Knowledge* and decided to buy it with his homework earnings. World War I upended his plans to become a lawyer, as Tarnow remained a dangerous battlefront throughout the war. (It became part of southern Poland after World War I.) So Pearlroth fled to America and by 1923 was married, living in the Bronx, and commuting into Manhattan to work at a bank.

Through a mutual friend, Pearlroth learned that a newspaper cartoonist was seeking a linguist and translator. Pearlroth was fluent in Italian, French, Russian, Polish, Yiddish, Hebrew, and more. He sometimes studied three languages at a time, and could quickly figure out the basics of any language.

"Tell me something odd," Ripley said to Pearlroth when the two first met, sometime in late 1923. Ripley had gotten into the habit of asking new acquaintances, *What's the strangest thing you know?* He'd figured: you never knew who might have a bizarro story that could be worked into a *Believe It or Not* cartoon. In recent years, his schoolboy notebooks had grown fatter with handwritten ideas added among the clipped-out articles, partly the result of asking questions of strangers.

Pearlroth served up a factoid that day about a California church built from the wood of a single redwood tree. At first, Ripley seemed confused. *Is this guy making fun of me?* Pearlroth later said he had no idea the First Baptist Church of Santa Rosa—the so-called Church Built of One Tree—was Ripley's parents' house of worship. When Pearlroth explained that he'd learned of the church from his *Library of Entertainment and Knowledge* encyclopedias, Ripley grew excited.

"*I'm* from Santa Rosa," he declared. "And I *know* that church."

On the spot, Ripley offered Pearlroth a part-time job. "I'll only need you for an hour a week," he said, suggesting payment of $25 a week.

To Pearlroth, the deal sounded too good to be true. Twenty-five bucks an *hour?* But working for Robert LeRoy Ripley, Pearlroth soon learned, would be more than an hour-a-week commitment.

Ripley must have known that he'd found a unique and potentially valuable assistant. The two men were kindred spirits in some ways, opposites in others. Ripley was the shy kid who'd found success based on his alleged knowledge of the world. Pearlroth was the handsome supergenius who'd found comfort in a private, solitary pursuit of scholarship. Ripley was athletic and social, a drinker and womanizer. Pearlroth was bookish, a faithful husband, and a devout Jew. Both shared a passion for oddball scraps of information, and Pearlroth was attracted to Ripley's enthusiastic, if naïve, quest for the mysterious arcana of humanity.

"Our daily life is so cut and dried that we get relief from fairy tales," Pearlroth said years later, in a rare interview about what drew him to Ripley in 1923. "Except his fairy tales are *true*, and this excites people. They like to learn that nature makes exceptions. These are fairy tales for grown-ups."

In time, Pearlroth would quit his bank job and commit himself to the most eager and enigmatic boss he could have imagined. Pearlroth would soon be exploiting, on a daily basis, his beloved *Library of Entertainment and Knowledge* collection, from which he would learn that birds had no sense of taste or smell, that a Brazilian butterfly had the fragrance and color of chocolate, that the dental nerve of an elephant weighed twelve pounds. Armed with such off-kilter curiosities, Pearlroth would help Ripley take *Believe It or Not* to unexpected new heights, and a rare and symbiotic relationship would bloom.

But not without some setbacks.

THOUGH RIPLEY HAD BEEN WELCOMED at the *Evening Telegram* in mid-1923, he soon became a twice-burned victim of Frank "The Grocer" Munsey's obsession with consolidation. Munsey merged the *Evening Telegram* with the *Evening Mail,* which he purchased in early 1924. Again, scores of employees lost their jobs.

Ripley was replaced by a sports cartoonist named Ed Hughes, whose sketches and columns seemed near replicas of his own, including assorted *Believe It or Not*–style bests and mosts in sporting achievements. Even Hughes's signature looked like Ripley's.

Ripley wasn't quite jobless, since Associated Newspapers agreed to keep him on its art staff. Still, for the first time he would not be affiliated with a local newspaper. Instead, his cartoons would be produced solely—and infrequently—by Associated Newspapers, appearing nationally, but *not* in New York.

Until now, he had worried little about imitators or competitors. But without a home at the *Globe,* his *Believe It or Not* concept began losing momentum, allowing Hughes and others to offer similar hard-to-believe-themed cartoons. *Believe It or Not* slowed to a trickle through 1924, the start of an awkward new career phase. During this period of semi-employment, weeks could go by with Ripley not being in print at all. He tried to stay busy writing and drawing on a freelance basis for magazines, including the NYAC's in-house newsletter. He pitched a book about his Ramble around the world, but couldn't find a publisher. Putting his love of handball into print, he authored *Spalding's Official Handball Guide,* which was published in late 1923. A year later he edited and illustrated *The Everlast Boxing Record,* a book of essays by well-known sportswriters.

Ripley sent copies of the handball and boxing books to his brother, but in an exchange of letters with his sister he learned that Ethel was struggling to help Doug finish high school. "Keep him at it and he will thank you some day," he wrote. He and Ethel then agreed by mail that, due to his financial woes and her troubles with Doug, they should sell the family house on Orchard Street. Ripley told his sister the house "seems to be a source of trouble and expense."

BY LATE 1924, Ripley was looking back gloomily on two volatile years. The end of his marriage, Doug's truancy, and the sale
of the Santa Rosa house had all combined with the lingering effects of the death of the *Globe* and his premature departure from
the *Telegram*. Signs of melancholy crept into his work. When
an earthquake leveled parts of Japan—including places he had
visited—Ripley drew a stunning visual commentary, an illustration of a Japanese man lying amid the ruins as an angel hovers
above. "Tokio and Yokohama will rise again," Ripley wrote in
the caption. "San Francisco rose again—greater than ever . . .
spirit never dies!" In that year's Christmas cartoon, he sketched
two raggedy orphans huddled beside a woodstove, from which
hang two socks. The caption: "Empty Stocking."

Later he would use words like "indolent," "disillusioned,"
and "easily annoyed" to describe the simmering depression that
vexed him through the mid-1920s. He felt his characteristic optimism replaced by despondency. He had worked hard during
more than ten years in New York and had proven himself to be
more than just a sports cartoonist. He was an athlete, an author,
a lecturer, a world traveler, and, as he liked to consider himself,
a circumnavigator. He had even been invited to join the prestigious Circumnavigators Club, whose membership included arctic explorers Richard Byrd and Robert Peary.

But now he was divorced and an orphan, an underemployed
cartoonist and not really a New York newsman. Though he'd
found an able assistant in Pearlroth, he felt unmoored and alone.
He'd lost his wife and, in the bloodbath of Frank Munsey layoffs, had lost his editor and mentor, Walter St. Denis.

In the past, others had come to Ripley's rescue at crucial moments, patrons who helped him survive school (Miss O'Meara),
escape Santa Rosa (Carol Ennis), and reach New York (Peter
Kyne). Now, facing the most difficult period of his adult life,

it was up to him to find a reserve of resilience and mettle for a comeback, to regroup and then regain his edge as America's purveyor of oddities. A firm believer in the restorative effects of a road trip, he began planning another big adventure.

* * *

A YEAR EARLIER, not long after his divorce was finalized, one of Ripley's few *Evening Telegram* cartoons had featured his brother/alter-ego, Demon Dug, hiding behind a tree, spying on a girl who is walking arm in arm with another boy. The cartoon was titled "A Bachelor's Decree."

From his hiding spot behind the tree, Dug mutters, "I'm off wimmen for LIFE!"

That's how Ripley initially felt after his divorce. In an interview with the "We Women" columnist Betty Brainerd, Ripley was asked why such a successful artist wasn't yet married. At first, he told Brainerd that he simply didn't have the time. Then he warmed to the topic and let loose a tirade on the virtues of bachelorhood: "I tremble when I look about at the matrimonial wrecks around me. Divorces grow more common every day and domestic squabbles fill the dockets of the courts and the pages of the newspapers. Ninety percent of the troubles that afflict us are due directly or indirectly to men and women fighting with each other."

Ripley had declared, to friends and in print, that he "never had a voyage as rough as that one on the sea of matrimony." But there was something unresolved about his drawn-out split from Beatrice, some emptiness that handball and boxing couldn't fulfill.

If he couldn't find what he needed in New York, he decided it was probably time once again to search abroad for what was lacking. His global Ramble had changed him. And when the world got bumpy and life became a torment, he now knew, the surest cure was to skedaddle.

Then again, with Prohibition soon to celebrate its fifth birthday, maybe all he really needed was a stiff drink in a less puritanical land.

CHAPTER

10

In the Peruvian town of Juliaca, twelve thousand feet above the Pacific, Ripley trudged through the rain toward his hotel, across a small plaza and past huddled groups of Peruvians who seemed "as joyless and sullen as this bleak and bare highland."

It had been a long day's train ride, followed by a soggy walk through town, and he was soaked and shivering. At the hotel, he asked the proprietor to start a fire so he could dry off. The proprietor refused: "No fire in Juliaca."

Stunned, Ripley asked how he was supposed to get warm.

"Go to bed," said the proprietor.

Ripley stormed off into the cold, rainy night, muttering that he was "not going to bed at seven o'clock in the afternoon if I can help it." Finding no bars or anything of interest except a windmill, he walked back to the hotel and went to bed in his dank, windowless room.

The next morning, after a chilly, sleepless night, Ripley walked back to the town plaza and stopped in front of the windmill. He started counting the windmill's revolutions, hopping from one foot to the other to stay warm, wondering why he'd again decided to roam so far from the comforts of home.

As if on cue, a stranger tapped him on the shoulder. His name was Miller. He was English, now living in Juliaca. Curious to see another Westerner in town, Miller invited Ripley to dinner that night, along with his wife and an American couple, also named Miller. "We're the only white people in this place," Miller said.

At dinner with the four Millers, Ripley huddled beside the kitchen stove, warming himself while describing to his hosts his latest adventure—a lengthy tour through South America. He described his sail through the Panama Canal and his recent visit to the corpse of Saint Rose, in Lima, casually mentioning that his California hometown was named for Saint Rose. The wife of the American Mr. Miller then jumped up, realizing the cartoonist was the former "LeRoy" Ripley.

"That's my home! I went to Santa Rosa High," she practically shouted. "I *remember* you. You used to play on the baseball team!"

And suddenly Ripley was reminded why he traveled. Because even in a place like Juliaca—"the most dreary, dismal spot on Earth"—life could surprise him.

Ripley laughed and reminisced with his new friends, joking that it really is "a small world after all."

HE HAD LEFT NEW YORK in late January of 1925 aboard the SS *Santa Luisa*, a remodeled World War I transport ship. Associated Newspapers announced Ripley's *Ramble 'Round South America* in a series of promotional ads, promising readers they'd "learn things about South America that are not found in books."

Though Ripley was toting stacks of research material supplied by Pearlroth—about Peruvian guano production, Chilean gauchos, Uruguayan silver mining, and the life of conquistador Francisco Pizarro—what readers would mostly learn about was Ripley's pursuit of women and wine.

Ripley made it clear from the start that he'd be taking this Ramble less seriously than his previous journey to Asia. He began this trip, thanks to a farewell party with friends, nursing a throbbing hangover. While passing through the Panama Canal, the ship stopped in Cristobal, a city straddling Prohibition-restricted American territory and unrestricted Panama. Ripley's first great South American discovery, therefore, was how quickly waiters at the Washington Hotel could scamper into Panamanian territory and return with cold champagne.

Freed from Prohibition's shackles, Ripley drank like an acquitted convict. One night he met Panama's president, Rodolfo Chiari, who spoke enthusiastically to Ripley in Spanish, while Ripley slurred right back—in English. Life aboard ship began too early for Ripley's tastes, a dilemma he solved by staying up all night. In Lima, he was invited to dinner with city officials, but his dress clothes had been sent ahead to the next city, and Ripley arrived in less-than-formal attire. In his eagerness to loosen up, he ignored the local custom of offering a toast before each sip of wine and began to drink at will. Every time he lifted his glass, the others scrambled to do the same. Sheepish and exhausted, woozy from a lack of sleep and too much wine, he topped off the night with an embarrassing bloody nose.

Such episodes did little to prompt an attempt at sobriety. During a stopover in Pisco, he walked off the ship, down the pier, and straight to the Gran Hotel in search of Pisco Punch, a cocktail made of the Peruvian-Chilean liquor *pisco*, which he'd first tasted in San Francisco. His drinking partner, an Italian count, called it *"agua ardiente"* (fire water) and Ripley called it "kerosene," then announced, "We're both correct!"

"Give me the tropics!" he crowed in print. "They suit my indolent nature well." At one point Ripley seemed to realize how his dispatches might be perceived by readers, and he soon admitted he had been on a quest. He never mentioned Beatrice or the recent divorce but made it clear he'd been looking for love.

* * *

BEFORE LEAVING NEW YORK, Ripley had sent a telegram to Carmela, the "dark-eyed señorita from Lima" he'd met in Paris. He had promised to visit her, never imagining he would ever reach Peru. Then came his divorce and an unexpected assignment to South America. He wired Carmela and apologized for the two-year lag, but reminded her that he was "a man of my word," and said he desperately hoped she'd be happy to see him.

Carmela never responded, but from the moment he left New York he had been praying she would be waiting at the pier. When he disembarked in Lima, Ripley anxiously scanned the crowds but never found Carmela's lovely face. He soon learned that his señorita was a *señora*, married with two children.

Unabashedly, Ripley confessed all this to his readers. "A woe is me," he wrote, sounding like a moody schoolboy with hurt feelings—like Demon Dug. "I am indeed a woe; I never did have any luck."

After the failed reunion, Ripley was determined to find another dark-eyed señorita. Like a romantic adolescent, he was back on the prowl.

In the southern Peruvian city of Arequipa, beneath the smoky pinnacle of the volcano El Misti, he stayed at a well-known boardinghouse run by Ana Bates, a salty-tongued woman who called everyone "Sonny Boy" and whom guests called Tia. The Quinta Bates boardinghouse was a favorite destination of movie stars, writers, and royalty. Clark Gable loved to visit and drink Pisco Sours; Noël Coward came for a two-day visit that turned into a month.

There, Ripley met Bates's stunning niece, Consuelo, which in Spanish means "consolation." At eighteen, she was half his age, shy and beautiful, and "chic and charming," Ripley wrote in his journal. "When she speaks Spanish it is like a rippling brook, and her English is sweet melody."

One night, he and Consuelo ascended to the roof garden and looked out at the moonlit El Misti. Ripley told Consuelo the volcano reminded him of Mount Fuji in Japan, and when she asked which was more beautiful, he confessed that he preferred Fuji.

"I could never lie to you," he told her. "And I am a pretty good liar, too, by the way."

Ripley later described the scene atop Misti in a dispatch home, telling readers things he should have told Consuelo: "She is modest and unspoiled and when she talks with you, tingling half-moons of guilt creep up your spine, although you have done nothing wrong; and you feel ashamed of the life you are leading, although it is nobody's business but your own."

Readers might have found it strange and even a bit creepy to read such confessional revelations from a newsman, but he seemed unable to hide his desperate and almost juvenile romantic pursuits—early signs of an earnestness, an unfiltered honesty, and naiveté that would endear him to readers.

✳ ✳ ✳

ACROSS LAKE TITICACA and into Bolivia, he found that a bruised heart could be healed by a stunning landscape and a fiery cocktail. When he first spotted the city of La Paz, tucked into a chasm between towering mountains, he was dumbstruck. It looked exactly like someone had flung the city of Reno into the

Grand Canyon and he declared the high-altitude city of clouds to be "the most startling sight I have ever seen!"

Inspired by La Paz, and shamed by his recent sullenness, Ripley did what he often did when he felt aflutter. He drank. As he had on his first Ramble, Ripley spilled much ink on the topic of drink, openly declaring himself a Prohibition violator by complaining that the Inca corn liquor *chicha* tasted "almost as bad as the stuff we get in New York." He described how the Incas attached bouquets of flowers to poles outside their saloons: "Beautiful, isn't it? Flowers instead of padlocks!" When he met drinking partners, he amiably introduced them to readers, who thus became acquainted with an Irishman named Heavy and a Scotsman named Ferguson, whom Ripley dubbed one of his three favorite Scots, along with Haig & Haig (a brand of scotch).

While descending from the jagged Bolivian highlands to the Pacific coast, a fourteen-thousand-foot drop in half a day, he visited a tribe that once decapitated enemies, skinned their heads, and shrank them to the size of a baseball—his first exposure to the shrunken heads that would become a *Believe It or Not* emblem. (He bought one for $100.)

Pearlroth had provided history books for Ripley to mine, but Ripley only dug into this cache when there wasn't a woman or a drinking partner worth mentioning. His favorite book was William H. Prescott's *Conquest of Peru,* which chronicled Spanish conquistador Francisco Pizarro's plunder of the Inca Empire. "I am traveling the same road Pizarro trod!" he boasted to readers. "How I admire that villainous old fellow."

For days, he remained fixated on Pizarro. Passing through once-great cities such as Cuzco, he was horrified to witness how completely the Spanish conqueror and his men had trashed Inca culture. Ripley felt Pizarro's greed for gold and his treatment of the Incas were black spots on "the darkest page in all Spanish history."

⚜ BELIEVE IT! ⚜

*In Cuzco, Pizarro had imprisoned Inca emperor Atahualpa
for refusing to cede control of Peru. Pizarro offered to spare the
emperor's life if he filled a room with gold, silver, and jewels.
Atahualpa complied. But instead of freeing the emperor,
Pizarro had Atahualpa executed.*

In between drinking bouts, he occasionally found his poetic travel-writer voice, vividly describing "Indians with burden-bent backs trudging silently and stolidly" and "little fields where grim-faced Indians are plowing the unwilling land with bent sticks." One day he could be lyrical—"bright ponchos gleamed through the twilight of the nave and a faint chant came from the cloister"—and the next philosophical: "The vanity of man grows weak before the majesty of the mountains."

But on this trip, with or without Pearlroth's well-intended research materials, Ripley was at his most entertaining as the goofball American traveler. While traversing the Andes toward Buenos Aires, his train stopped for the night and passengers swarmed the town's few hotels. Ripley had been drinking with a German named Hans, who spoke fluent Spanish and offered to get them each a room. Hans secured two rooms but then bumped into a fellow German and gave away Ripley's key.

When Ripley learned Hans had double-crossed him, he begged the hotel clerk for a room, but there were none. The clerk offered Ripley a bunk in a room with three Chilean men. Afraid to be alone with three dark-skinned strangers, Ripley sat in the lobby, writing in his journal by kerosene lamp, wishing he'd stayed in Santiago, where he'd briefly met a woman whose smile had warmed his "soft and vagrant heart," as he put it in his journal. When his roommates were asleep, he crept into the room, slept a few hours in his clothes, then left the "evil-looking hombres" before dawn.

BY NOW, Ripley had grown keenly aware of the typical American's unworldliness and national arrogance. He knew South Americans laughed at the ignorance of their northern neighbors. "We are too prone to think of South America as one country when as a matter of fact it is made up of a dozen different countries," he added, proving his point.

In Buenos Aires, he continued to play the bumbling gringo. Among stylish men and women in Parisian-influenced clothes, Ripley stood in the hundred-degree heat of a midday plaza wearing the cream-colored linen suit he'd bought in India. With his sweat-darkened armpits and his sunburned and peeling skin, he was not a pretty sight. He wondered why people seemed to be staring at him until he realized he was the only man wearing a light-colored (and sweat-stained) suit.

Ripley was hardly a typical yokel, even if it was becoming his shtick. He continued to boast that learning other languages was "more a pleasure than necessity" and that his California dialect had served him well. And while he enjoyed meeting new people from other lands, all conversations had to be conducted in English.

SIX WEEKS into his Ramble he had explored more of South America than an average American might see in a lifetime. After journeying by rail into the Andes and across the continent's belly, Ripley finally felt a weight lifting, relieved to be far from "the static and cross-word puzzles and the rest of the wrangling world," as he put it.

Still, on this particular trip, with the shadow of divorce still looming, what he yearned for more than natives and their culture was the company of a stiff drink and/or a fiery young woman. In Buenos Aires, he managed to coax an attractive Australian named Whupsie Strelitz to spend an afternoon with him. She agreed to meet the next morning in her hotel lobby, and Ripley arrived to find Whupsie's stern-looking mother standing beside her, wanting to know their destination.

"To the cemetery!" he told Whupsie's mother. For their date, Ripley took Whupsie to the "City of the Dead," as La Recoleta Cemetery was known. They strolled among the graves of Argentine presidents, poets, scientists, and soldiers.

Two days later, Ripley met Maggie, a New Yorker who had been living in Buenos Aires. Maggie agreed to spend a day with Ripley and they walked along the Rio Tigre, then drank champagne at the High Life café with another couple. But when Ripley invited Maggie to dinner, she said no, claiming she didn't want to send the wrong message to the locals that she was "a bad woman."

"You must remember that Buenos Aires is not the Bronx," she said.

The next morning he waved good-bye to Maggie, who grew smaller and smaller on the pier as Ripley sailed to Uruguay and then up the coast to Brazil. At sea, he reflected on his eight weeks on the southern continent, and somewhat morosely summarized his limited success with women, a failure he blamed partly on the women. The movies and musicals back in New

York had led him to expect streets filled with dancing Latinas wrapped in shawls, roses clenched in their teeth.

"I am beginning to believe that the famous Spanish señoritas are a myth," he said.

Playing the lovestruck Yankee was part of the woe-is-me persona he'd begun honing in print. And he reluctantly one day acknowledged to readers that maybe Latina women simply weren't interested in *him*. At the thought of it, Ripley spent a melancholy and reflective few days sailing toward Brazil.

The reason Ripley so desperately sought female companionship was that he hated being alone. And he wasn't much for drinking alone, either. His first stop in Rio was a beachside bar, where he met an American journalist, Dick Hyman, and happily agreed to let Hyman interview him for the *Brazilian American Weekly*. While watching a rainbow of locals stroll past. Ripley joked that the biracial couples "would make a Southern gentleman forget himself."

The following day, Ripley again sought out Dick Hyman (soon to become a business partner and a lifelong companion), who found Ripley to be nothing like the man he expected. Ripley was appealingly shy, thought Hyman, a man primarily interested in his work—and women. At dinner that night, Ripley couldn't take his eyes off Hyman's girlfriend, Helena, whom he described without chagrin as "beautiful, with black eyes and snowy teeth, a true Brazilian."

In a sign of Ripley's still-strong readership back home, Hyman's father read Ripley's "Ramble" in his local paper, the *Kansas City Star*. Ripley had incorrectly described Helena as Hyman's fiancée, and Hyman's father sent an urgent telegram begging his son to reconsider.

Helena thought Ripley was adorable, and even coaxed him into trying a few words of Portuguese.

"Luco! Luco!" she said.

Ripley agreed that he was a bit crazy, until Helena explained that *luco* meant "good," or at least that's what it sounded like to Ripley.

✶ ✳ ✳

ABOARD THE USMS *American Legion* for the two-week journey home, Ripley rejoined his Scottish friend Ferguson. He was happy to be at sea, sleeping late, roaming the decks, warming himself at night with cocktails. He considered a good ship on smooth seas to be "a floating paradise to lazy people."

During those last days, Ripley seemed to realize how often he had written about two particular topics. In the last of his South American dispatches he wrote:

> I have talked so much about South American drinks and women that I guess you think I am too fond of both . . . I admit that they have had their moments; and you must admit that they are interesting subjects. Or would you have rather heard about the "business opportunities of the Southland" or the "cattle-raising statistics for the fiscal year"?

He may not have found love, but Ripley returned to New York with a rekindled love of travel and a broader perception of the world. The seventy-two-day trip had cost $750—ten bucks a day. Ripley considered it a pittance, and felt that Americans were too stingy when it came to spending on travel.

"Traveling is easy. Traveling is cheap," he wrote. "People should travel more, but they put it off. Don't wait until you are too old . . . Travel will often show you the faults of our own country, but it will make you love it all the more!"

As he neared home, Ripley thought about what awaited him in New York. He didn't own a house or a car. His bank account was under assault by payments to Beatrice, his brother, and his sister. His personal possessions at the NYAC could fit in a steamer trunk. Yet, by traveling so far and wide, he hoped he was gaining something more valuable than material wealth. What he lacked in physical or monetary possessions was offset by what he called "a broader and more tolerant nature."

* * *

BACK IN NEW YORK, however, Ripley didn't always display tolerance.

South American women had large behinds and too many babies, he wrote, and their husbands—"little fellows" who talked too much but spoke no English—beat them weekly to keep them happy. The men were "dirty and coarse" and "sheiks of shirk!" They rarely smiled, he said, because theirs was "a short life and a weary one."

He meant for such comments to be taken lightly, but it was hard to disguise the sense that the continent had let him down. Having seen women torch their husbands' corpses and religious men hanging from trees, it now took a lot to wow Ripley. In the twelve years since his first overseas trip, he had explored more than two dozen countries, and in China and India had dug deep, taken risks, mixed with locals, and explored their politics and history, their gods and idols, their freaks and fanatics.

In South America, though, instead of aggressively pursuing temples and holy men and cannibals as he had in Asia, Ripley had mostly sought out the company of North Americans or other Westerners. Women and wine had been the journey's theme. South America, it turned out, simply wasn't peculiar enough for Ripley.

The only bit of history that invigorated him was the story of Pizarro, whose mummified body he'd visited in Lima and whose route of plunder he'd followed across the continent. "What a man he must have been!" Ripley wrote. "He destroyed a civilization of a continent and the nation of the Incas; and now he serves as a peep-show." But Ripley showed little empathy for the conquered, describing Peru's natives as having "strong backs and weak minds."

Some letter writers complained of Ripley's crass characterizations of Latin Americans, while others defended his casual style of foreign reportage, blaming the critics for having a "woeful lack of sense of humor." Some said they couldn't *wait* to visit the places Ripley so vividly rendered with his pen. "I have read few things that have given me more pleasure," said a writer named Charles Noonan. "Rip has revealed South America to us so alluringly that we all wish we could go there."

Just as Marco Polo's fantastic tales of Asia had incited awe and disbelief, Ripley's far-fetched travelogues and bold-ink cartoons, plus his likably odd personality, gave newspaper readers a new way of looking at the world. He was becoming a voice for the people, bringing the world's weirdness to their doorsteps each morning.

At the time, anti-immigrant forces were trying to shut America's doors to outsiders, a movement bolstered by a recent ban on Japanese immigration and by newly elected president Calvin Coolidge's declaration that "America must be kept American." Amid such nationalistic fervor, Ripley attempted to dispel misperceptions and suspicions about the strangers beyond America's borders. With radio still in its infancy, most people learned of other cultures from books or newspapers. Ripley's conversational reports from far-off lands differed greatly from the textbooks and tabloids. Reading about shrunken heads, señoritas, and strange drinking partners was like sitting barside with an avuncular tippler who slurs, "Let me tell you about the time . . ."

He was hardly a Marco Polo, and neither could he put himself in company with *real* adventurers like polar voyager Roald Amundsen or travel lecturer Burton Holmes. Ripley freely admitted that he liked nice hotel rooms and good bars, that he was terrified of speed and heights. He considered himself an explorer of a particular sort, but far more intrepid than a mere tourist, whom he held in contempt. "Most people I meet should not be allowed by law to travel," he once said. "They see as much in a subway."

While he dressed increasingly like the typical tourist—the Gallagher and Sheans pith helmet he once disparaged, plus khaki shorts, knee socks, and two-toned shoes, were becoming his trademark traveling outfit—Ripley's off-the-beaten-path approach to foreign travel carried its own brand of risk. He wasn't looking for new routes to the North Pole but for dark shadows, hidden deformities, and secret rites. He didn't necessarily seek physical adventure (preferring to keep his hands and shoes clean), but he did confront the people and their cultures. A self-taught ethnographer and anthropologist, what he sought most was *information*. He asked countries to show him their warts and sores, their maimed and poor, their crazy old uncles, their torture chambers, and their dead.

"The more I see of the world the more I like it," he had summed up in his final South American dispatch.

It's a pretty good little old place after all, and I have little time for the gloomers who are eternally shrieking that this old mud ball is rolling to the bow wows. I am satisfied to take my chances with this one, thank you, and not worry about the next . . .

You must carry along with you a lively imagination and plenty of romance in your soul. Some of the most wonderful things in the world will seem dull and drab unless you view them in the proper light.

CHAPTER

11

Frank "The Grocer" Munsey died from a ruptured appendix at his New York City home in late 1925. He was a lonely old man with few friends, no heirs, and a legacy as a newspaper killer. Said Baltimore's curmudgeon columnist H. L. Mencken: "I am glad Munsey is dead and I hope he is in hell!"

By selling, folding, and merging his newspapers he had personally put thousands out of work. Of the sixteen newspapers he'd bought over the course of twenty-five years, he died owning just two, the *Telegram* and the *Sun*. Neither would survive, sealing his legacy.

~ BELIEVE IT! ~
Munsey's estimated net worth was $40 million, most of which he left to the Metropolitan Museum of Art.

Munsey had been more than a little responsible for the two recent years Ripley spent in newspaper limbo. Walter Winchell would later describe in his column how Ripley, after the *Globe* shut down, had "faded from the Metropolitan scene," unable to find a job because an "army of imitators underbid him . . . pirating his style so well that editors hired them and told Rip he was too expensive."

But Ripley never slowed down or gave up. In fact, after his South American Ramble he dove back into an exhausting schedule of boxing matches, illegal cocktails with Bugs Baer at secret Midtown speakeasies, and daily games of rigorous handball. His NYAC room was often splashed with evidence of the bachelor's lifestyle: empty bottles, butt-filled ashtrays, scattered newspapers, art supplies, and sweat-stained workout clothes.

One benefit of his part-time employment was being able to spend more time on the NYAC's handball courts. A loud and aggressively competitive player, lunging for every shot, Ripley was soon back in peak physical shape, slapping the pink Spalding No. 101 handball better than ever.

Alone or with a partner, he traveled regularly to tournaments in the Midwest through 1925. In Chicago, he defeated the Chicago Athletic Club's best player, Avery Brundage, who had been a world champ. At the National Championships in Cleveland, Ripley lost to top-ranked Maynard Laswell, who went on to win the tournament. At the annual NYAC championship, he reached the finals and found himself facing Jim Kelly, an Irishman and former world champion, considered one of the best to play the game. Kelly had won his first world title in 1909 and in recent years had mentored Ripley, who in his handball book called Kelly "a master of the game."

Before a stunned and drunken crowd, Ripley upset the master to become the 1925 NYAC singles handball champ.

While he would continue to play in local and national tournaments over the next few years, Ripley's handball playing would begin tapering off in 1926, squeezed aside by the sudden demands of an unexpected job change. His period of limbo was about to end.

* * *

IN JUNE OF 1926, Ripley traveled to England to cover the prestigious horse race known as the Derby, as well as the Wimbledon tennis tournament and the British Open golf tournament. On that trip, Ripley decided to attempt a stunt: to wirelessly send his Derby cartoon from London to New York.

When jockey Joe Childs whipped the stallion Coronach to victory, Ripley quickly sketched the horse crossing the finish line. Then he rushed to the Ambassador Hotel, where his sketch paper was wrapped around a cylinder and, using radio facsimile technology—similar to the fax machines of the future—was transmitted line by line across radio waves to the United States. The cartoon was then delivered by airplane to newspapers across the country.

It was touted as the first transatlantic cartoon transmission, and in a few years the same technology would be used to transmit newspaper photographs by telephone. The feat caught the attention of editors at the creaky old *New York Evening Post*, who felt they could use a promising brand like *Believe It or Not* and its innovative creator.

Alexander Hamilton had founded the *Evening Post* in 1801 (four years after he'd launched the *Globe*). A century later, it was being run by Henry Villard and his son, Oswald, who had helped found the National Association for the Advancement of Colored People (NAACP) and the American Civil Liberties Union (ACLU). When pro-German accusations against Oswald Villard during World War I crippled circulation, he sold the *Post*, which suffered through several halfhearted ownerships.

The *Post* was briefly owned by a group of New York business leaders that included Franklin Delano Roosevelt. But the paper hemorrhaged money and circulation until Cyrus Curtis came to the rescue in 1924. Curtis published a handful of magazines, most profitably the *Ladies' Home Journal* and the *Saturday Evening Post,* two of the largest circulating publications in the world. With wealth rivaling J. P. Morgan's and Henry Ford's, Curtis had no problem meeting Ripley's salary request of $200 a week.

↜ BELIEVE IT! ↝

When income taxes were first made public in 1925,
Curtis reported earning $5 million, putting him fifteenth
on the list of America's wealthiest men, one slot ahead
of J. P. Morgan. In terms of relative wealth,
he remains one of the richest men in
world history.

The *Post* introduced Ripley on August 16, 1926: "Believe It or Not, Ripley's returned!" Days later, a subscriber named M. E. Farrington wrote, "I have been an admirer of Mr. Ripley for many years and have often wondered which of the New York newspapers would again treat the public to his fine work."

He'd be making ten times what he'd first earned at the *Globe* in 1912, but in terms of circulation Ripley was moving backward. The *Evening Post*'s readership was a measly 33,000—one of the lowest in the city, and laughable in comparison to the top-ranked *Daily News,* with 633,000 readers.

At the *Evening Post,* Ripley would still be affiliated with Associated Newspapers, which meant his syndicated readership would continue to extend far beyond New York City. He would be starting over with new editors and coworkers—the third job shift in three years—but he was relieved to be anchored to a

New York paper, even if the *Post*'s gray and serious pages desperately needed the levity Ripley was hired to bring.

Ripley introduced himself to readers with a short, enthusiastic article, promising that his *Believe It or Not* cartoons "are all true."

"I have traveled the world over searching for strange and unbelievable things," he wrote in his *Post* debut.

> I have seen white negroes, purple white men, and I know
> a man who was hanged but still lives . . . Believe me when
> I tell you about the man who died of old age before he was
> six years old; the river in Africa that runs backwards; oysters that grow on trees; flowers that eat mice; fish that walk
> and snakes that fly.

Ripley's perseverance during his time in Munsey-inflicted purgatory had finally paid off, as had hiring Norbert Pearlroth, who stuck by Ripley through the recent ups and downs. Ripley now decided to make a salesman's pitch to his new readership, a new guarantee: "If by chance any reader should doubt any of the facts depicted in my cartoons, I will be glad to explain and prove the truth of them if he will write me." Slowly, he was learning to be a showman.

WITH HIS NEW SALARY, Ripley could afford to rent more of Pearlroth's brain. In the three years since they'd met, Ripley had discovered that Pearlroth was far more useful than a mere translator. An autodidact and a "walking encyclopedia," as he'd later be described, Pearlroth seemed to possess a bottomless supply of curious and interesting facts, memorized from the books he read constantly. Ripley phoned Pearlroth daily at the bank where he still worked, hungry for more material.

Soon, with Pearlroth's help, Ripley was introducing readers to such characters as James Thompson of New Mexico, who crossed America by wheelchair; Mary Rosa, a Nantucket toddler who found her mother's ring on the beach twenty-one years after it had been lost; two Russian brothers who slapped each other's faces for thirty-six hours; and Haru Onuki, a Japanese prima donna he'd met (and begun dating), who required a full day to prepare her hair, which then stayed in place for a month.

With America growing more urban and urbane, newspaper readers had developed Jazz Age tastes in new forms of journalism, and publishers were tripping over themselves to accommodate. Cartoons, photographs, and color printing were more popular than ever, as were sexy, gossipy stories. Leading the way (up or down was a matter of debate) were the half-sized papers called tabloids. *The Daily News*, created in 1919 as the nation's first true tabloid, was followed in 1924 by the *Evening Graphic*, founded by Bernarr Macfadden, the fabulously wealthy health guru whose magazines Ripley had read as a boy and whose athletic lifestyle he'd emulated.

Macfadden's credo—"sex on every front page, big gobs of it"—had prompted Hearst in 1924 to enter the tabloid game by creating the *New York Daily Mirror*, which Hearst described as "90 percent entertainment, 10 percent information."

Critics likened tabloids to addictive drugs, fretting that they'd precipitate the demise of American culture. They quickly became the highest-circulation publications in New York, boosted by their pictures and the everyman reportage of gossip writers like Walter Winchell, the *Graphic*'s Broadway columnist. As Winchell's biographer later put it, readers had grown tired of dreary stories about "mice in China" and would rather read of celebrity indiscretions and peccadilloes.

Ripley wanted to give readers *all* if it—the mice in China, the pictures, the gossip and innuendo, the slang and the sex, the information and the entertainment. Ripley the salesman was finally ready to invest the bulk of his artistic talent, his peculiar personality, and his relentless energy solely in *Believe It or Not*.

He was finally ready for his high-wire act.

ON MAY 20, 1927, Charles Lindbergh departed from muddy Roosevelt Field on Long Island and aimed his fuel-stuffed *Spirit of St. Louis* eastward. Thirty-three treacherous hours later, the lanky aviator touched down at an airfield outside Paris and was swarmed by 150,000 spectators cheering his non-stop flight across the Atlantic. Only two dozen years past the Wright brothers' first flight, he had achieved the unachievable, the unbelievable—crossing an ocean in a day and a half, flying more than three thousand miles, alone through the night, through storms and without sleep. It was the most daring and astounding achievement of its day.

The feat captivated the world and made Lindbergh an instant international hero. He began touring the world in a relentless series of appearances and lectures.

Months later, Pearlroth was at the New York Public Library, conducting research for Ripley, when he picked up a British newspaper someone had left on a table. It carried a story about one of Lindbergh's speeches, in Liverpool, where he explained that a number of other aviators had previously flown across the Atlantic, though none had flown solo. Pearlroth felt "electrified" to discover how many others had crossed the Atlantic before

Lindbergh. He dug up more details and consulted with Ripley, who crafted a risky *Believe It or Not* shocker.

Ripley's sketch showed Lindbergh's *Spirit of St. Louis* flying through dark clouds, beneath which read this heretical caption: "Lindbergh Was the 67th Man to Make a Non-Stop Flight over the Atlantic Ocean!" The cartoon appeared on February 14, 1928, just one day after Lindbergh was feared to have been lost at sea during a flight from Cuba to St. Louis. Ripley's cartoon declared that not only was the famed aviator *not* the first to successfully cross the Atlantic, he wasn't even in the top *fifty.*

It sounded absurd, even anti-American, as some angrily claimed. It was as if someone recklessly asserted that George Washington wasn't the first president, that New Jersey wasn't really a state, that Pluto wasn't a planet. The reaction startled even Ripley, who was assailed by telegrams, phone calls, and many thousands of letters—some containing unprintable language. Three days after his Lindbergh cartoon, during a lecture to the Corps of Cadets at West Point, Ripley defended his statement, explaining how two English aviators, John Alcock and A. Whitton Brown, had flown nonstop from Newfoundland to Ireland in 1919, and that two dirigibles later made transatlantic crossings, carrying thirty-one and thirty-three men, respectively. By omitting the word "solo" from his statement, Ripley was able to justify ranking Lindbergh as sixty-seventh.

"His almost incredible statements are very often challenged by skeptical readers," reported West Point's newspaper. "And his remarks sometimes need a substantial argument to verify their truth."

A few weeks later Ripley spoke at a society luncheon in New York, where he introduced himself as the man who had been called a liar "more often than any other living person."

Seemingly overnight, Ripley found himself entering a new career phase, the moment when "unbelievable" and "liar" converged.

Instead of acting defensively, Ripley immediately struck the pose of the noble truth-teller who considered it high praise to be called a fibber. Being accused of lying by so many people, Ripley realized, was the best publicity he could have hoped for. If someone tagged him as a fabulist, he'd say, "I do not mind it a bit . . . I feel flattered!" He was becoming the embodiment of what H. L. Mencken once said about liars: "The men that American people admire most extravagantly are the most daring liars; the men they detest the most violently are those who try to tell them the truth."

✳ ✳ ✳

EVER SINCE CHILDHOOD, Ripley had displayed what an early profile writer called a "bottomless, off-kilter curiosity." Nothing was safe from the musings of a man whose mind was "uncluttered by culture," as one colleague put it: *"Everything was new to him."*

Indeed, inspiration could come from anywhere. One night a friend's casual use of "hi-ho" as a form of address got stuck in Ripley's brain and became spiced with remnants of his Chinese dinner, inspiring a vivid dream about the Chinese men he'd once seen carrying bundles and marching along the Bund singing, "Hi! Ho!" He awoke at dawn and sketched his dream. Days later, on April 5, 1928, the *Evening Post* published a cartoon entitled "The Marching Chinese," featuring seemingly endless rows of Chinese men. The caption declared that if all the Chinese people in the world were to march four abreast past a given point, "they would **never** finish passing though they marched forever and ever!"

Befuddled readers had to wait a week for Ripley's explanation. Based on the estimated Chinese population (600 million) and the estimated birth rate (10 percent), he calculated that each new generation of Chinese marchers would replace the previous one, which meant the Chinese could "march on and on, forever."

The Marching Chinese was a bigger hit than Lindbergh, and would remain one of Ripley's personal favorites.

With Pearlroth now in on the scheme, Ripley created more cartoons that seemed intentionally designed to earn skeptical if not outright angry letters. Napoleon crossed the Red Sea—on *dry land.* Buffalo Bill never shot a buffalo in his life. (He shot bison.) US naval hero John Paul Jones was not an American citizen, did not command a fleet of American ships, and his name wasn't Jones. Ripley even found a way to state that "George Washington was not the first president of the United States." The subsequent explanation was that John Hanson, when he signed the Articles of Confederation, was briefly "president of the United States in Congress assembled."

Ripley encouraged Pearlroth to help him find such startling statements, to engage and enrage readers. In short, Ripley loved to be called a liar because of the mischievous joy he took in proving his shockers true. One admiring writer said Ripley was "always waiting, with his authority in his hand, like a club."

By mid-1928, *Believe It or Not* was syndicated in a hundred papers in North America, and Associated Newspapers claimed that Ripley had ten million loyal readers. Other papers in the Associated Newspapers family began claiming Ripley as their own, crowing in print that he "worked" for them, with ads appearing in the *Kansas City Star, Chicago Daily News, Pittsburgh*

Chronicle-Telegraph, and even Ripley's former hometown paper, the *Santa Rosa Press Democrat.*

An editor at Louisville's *Courier-Journal* called Ripley "more than a sports cartoonist . . . He is a student, an artist and a popular psychologist."

WITH THIS NOTORIETY came speaking invitations, and Ripley discovered that a cupful of liquor could tame the stage fright that had dogged him since childhood. So when the Nomad Lecture Bureau asked him to talk on stage about his travels and draw a few sketches, Ripley agreed to take his *Believe It or Not* stories on the road.

He gave dozens of lectures—to schools and art clubs, to the Brooklyn Rotary Club, at the annual convention of the Kelvinator Corporation, and once sailed for a month aboard a Canadian cruise ship to perform as part of the nightly "Programme of Entertainment." At some lectures he was billed as the "World's Biggest Liar," and Ripley kept stoking the theme. In a speech to a group of athletes, he joked, "It makes no difference what I say, you won't believe me anyway." At most of his lectures, he was asked the same question: *Where do you find the things you draw about?* Speaking to the Advertising Club of New York, he explained that he got some ideas from readers, some from encyclopedias, and some, like the "Marching Chinese," in his dreams. Instead of thanking Pearlroth as a collaborator, Ripley claimed full credit, telling audiences that he found his material "here and there, day and night; through observation, conversation, and edification. I am constantly searching . . . Everywhere, all the time."

By mid-1928 he was receiving at least a hundred letters a day, many purporting to have found an error in Ripley's work, others gushing with praise. One *Evening Post* reader wrote, "My favorite article in your paper is 'Believe It or Not' by Ripley." A competing newspaper even praised Ripley's sports sketches as "better than photographs, because his pictures show the real action and the spirit of the contestants."

After just two years at the *Post,* he was becoming something of a celebrity. The *Post* hired an extra person just to read Ripley's mail, and offered to hire Pearlroth full-time. Thanks in large part to Ripley's sudden infamy, the *Post*'s circulation more than doubled between 1926 and 1928.

* * *

THE SCHOOLBOY NOTEBOOKS Ripley had started compiling years earlier were initially filled with clipped-out articles and handwritten notes about sports, with a particular preference for *endurance* and *going the distance:* the hundred-hour dance marathon, the seventy-four-day swim marathon, the man who ran two and a half miles every hour of every day for forty days, or the men (they were almost always men) who biked or walked or rode motorcycles from New York to Los Angeles.

After his Asian and South American travels, the notebooks became cluttered with freakier foreign entries—shocking or nauseating tidbits like the West African tribe that played rugby using a human skull instead of a ball. More recent notebook entries had grown playful and diverse, with fun facts and puzzles and unsolved mysteries, which Ripley called "queeriosities"— there is no lead in a lead pencil (it's graphite); a cuttlefish is not a fish (it's an octopus); it takes two years to make a billiard ball.

Armed with these notebooks, and fueled by Pearlroth's findings, Ripley continued to expand beyond sports and to explore the pull of his eccentric inquisitiveness.

He had always had an affinity for underdogs and outcasts,

since he often felt like one himself. Now he could more fully indulge his fascination with the characters that P. T. Barnum and his progeny had been exploiting for decades on the carny circuit. For the first time, Ripley gave sideshow freaks a place in the daily newspaper, introducing readers to a widening cast of oddballs: sword swallowers, people who ate glass, a man who nailed his tongue to a piece of wood, another who lifted weights with a hook sunk through his tongue, a woman missing the lower half of her body. Other notables included the one-armed paperhanger, the man who hypnotized fish, and the man burned by an electrical wire whose brain was permanently exposed. He sketched men with horns, a child cyclops, an armless golfer, a fork-tongued woman. There were fish that climbed trees, wing-less birds, four-legged chickens, peg-legged cows.

He also loved quirks of language, word puzzles, and palin-dromes. What was the longest curse word? *Forty letters.* How many four-letter words are there for God? *Thirty-seven.* Though he never finished high school, he had developed his own unique mathematical skills. One cartoon, featuring a man with a knife in his chest, said that if three witnesses to a midnight murder told two people, who told two more people, and so on, "everyone on earth would know about it by morning."

Everything had a *Believe It or Not* to offer—science, reli-gion, literature. A coin the size of a nickel made of star matter would weigh 200 pounds; a bundle of spiderwebs no larger than a pea, if untangled and straightened out, would reach 350 miles; a ship weighs less sailing east than sailing west. And the shortest letter ever mailed? That would be Victor Hugo's one-character missive to his publishers, inquiring about his *Les Mis-erables* manuscript. The letter: ? And the reply: !

Clearly, Ripley was no longer a sports cartoonist. A decade

past that December day when he'd stumbled into his first "Champs and Chumps" cartoon (and twenty years after his first cartoon in *LIFE*), *Believe It or Not* had become not only a regular feature in US newspapers, but a catchphrase that was seeping into the nation's consciousness.

The *Believe It or Not* concept was like some gold mine he'd been sitting atop, unsure of how to mine it or how deep to dig.

*　*　*

THE 1920s were evolving into a decade of the possible. New technologies—radio, moving pictures, vacuum cleaners, electric razors—had reached mainstream status. Recently unveiled mass-produced products were flying off shelves and influencing the nation's brand-conscious allegiances: Wonder Bread, Eskimo Pies, Kleenex, Wheaties, Butterfinger candy bars, and Chanel No. 5 perfume. Ripley's brand was that of a liar who always told the truth.

He now regularly provoked readers, *I dare you to prove me wrong.* That was his trademark. His cartoon now carried a new tagline: "Full proof and details on request." And the *Evening Post* helped market their "falsely accused liar" with advertisements promising, "Ripley Will Prove It" and "He Will Send You Proof."

In reality, he couldn't always prove it. In striving for a folksy style, he sometimes erred, and there were frequent efforts to trip him up. A man who signed his letter R. Van Winkle griped that in an effort to be "independent and funny" Ripley sometimes distorted history. The writer asked, "What is the use of writing nonsense instead of facts?" When one cartoon described how a Frenchman poured thirteen pints of wine into a vase and quaffed it in one breath, *Time* magazine consulted two doctors who declared it "impossible." Ripley was able to refer *Time* to the French history book in which Pearlroth had found the story.

Ripley tried to deliver it all with a wink, and most readers accepted the hint of charlatanism, knowing that some of Ripley's statements couldn't possibly be proven or disproven, that it was all for fun. Yet, while he loved being called a liar, he hated to be wrong, knowing it would damage the cartoon if he developed a reputation for sloppy reportage. More than ever, he needed Pearlroth to prove him right.

Pearlroth had by now quit his bank job to work full-time on Ripley's staff, which had grown to include a secretary and two assistants who handled Ripley's mail and checked facts. Pearlroth's official title was "linguist," his facility for multiple languages allowing Ripley to accurately publish oddities from places he didn't actually visit. As a stickler for accuracy, Pearlroth helped Ripley provoke with confidence, to push *Believe It or Not* to the brink of falsehood without tumbling over.

"When I first started to draw these cartoons, I wasn't so careful about details," Ripley admitted in a late-1920s interview. "But now I want things to be right. If a costume is to be of a certain period, I make it of that period. People write to me from Singapore, from Calcutta, from all over the world about my cartoons, and it gives me great satisfaction when they tell me, 'I've been there' or 'I've seen that fellow and your cartoon was right.'"

But for Ripley to remain the fact-wielding authority, he couldn't admit that his secret helper was a brainy ex-banker from Brooklyn.

They may have been partners, but they lived in very different worlds.

* * *

ONE OF RIPLEY'S favorite haunts was the 300 Club on West Fifty-fourth Street, the speakeasy run by Mary Louise "Texas" Guinan, an actress and chorus girl who had divorced her cartoonist husband and found her calling as a saloon keeper. With scantily clad dancers and free-flowing alcohol, Guinan's place became a favorite of such celebrities as Al Jolson, George Gershwin, Irving Berlin, and Walter Winchell, and Guinan's greeting to patrons—"Hello, suckers"—would enter the lexicon.

ᎯᏉ BELIEVE IT! ᏉᎦ

The most infamous of New York's Prohibition-era gin joints, Guinan's 300 Club netted $700,000 in 1926 alone. Each time she was arrested, Guinan swore she never sold an alcoholic drink in her life—patrons brought their own, she'd claim. And the dancers? The club was so small they had to dance in patrons' laps.

Other nights Ripley attended rowdy parties at Rube Goldberg's apartment with Bugs Baer and Damon Runyon, sharing cocktails with the Marx Brothers, George Gershwin, and Fanny Brice. One night, the petite shimmy-and-shake Ziegfeld star Anne Pennington performed a raucous dance on the hardwood floors while Harry Houdini swallowed sewing needles and pulled them out of his throat, all threaded on a string.

Pearlroth, meanwhile, didn't seem to mind toiling in the shadows, happy to be quietly contributing to Ripley's "fairy tales for grown-ups."

Early each morning Pearlroth rode the subway into Manhattan. Most days he'd go straight to the New York Public Library's main branch on Fifth Avenue, and he'd be one of the first to ascend the front steps between the twin lion statues. He'd grab a card catalogue tray, sift through it and select ten or more books, then find a spot in the cavernous third-floor reading room. He always turned off the reading lamps, preferring the natural light beneath the towering carved-wood ceiling.

Skipping lunch, he'd wander about, scanning shelves, collecting more books, scribbling notes until his eyesight grew blurry. He learned to make Photostat copies, so that Ripley had pictures to copy for his sketches. Librarians came to know Pearlroth by name and would often have to ask him to leave at closing time. He'd arrive home well past dinner, and rarely saw his wife and children during the week.

Though the hours he devoted to his employer caused friction within his family, Pearlroth felt he had found, somewhat remarkably, the dream job. Research and information had long been his hobby, but now he got paid to spend time among dusty history and reference books. What Pearlroth sought day in and day out were facts and truths that made his heart race, evidence that life wasn't "boringly uniform," that there were "glorious exceptions"—the Moroccan emperor who fathered 888 children; the Hindu who married his daughter to a tree; the Slovak who ate 150 hard-boiled eggs for dinner; the two German railroad workers who drank 352 glasses of beer in seventeen hours. "Curiosity is a fundamental human trait," Pearlroth would gush.

Even if they aren't aware of it, people hunger for the "astonishing but true." Pearlroth was proud to be contributing to cartoons that "satisfied a human urge to flee from the daily grind into the realm of the incredible."

By now, Ripley had also learned that what readers loved more than the elite celebrity athletes he'd spent his career featuring were pictures and stories of underdogs and misfits. They wanted the grotesques, the geeks, the goofballs—they wanted less *champ*, more *chump*. For someone who often felt like the ultimate "goofy" outsider, he had at long last begun featuring the imperfect people and performers who were a reflection of the less-than-perfect LeRoy Ripley.

As something of a misfit himself—obsessive, eccentric, monomaniacal—Norbert Pearlroth also left his mark on *Believe It or Not*, but it was Ripley's show, and always would be. Pearlroth's complicated and semivisible role, established from the start, would be that of Ripley's behind-the-bushes voice of authority—his Cyrano.

As he helped Ripley stoke and feed his newly invigorated cartoon, Pearlroth offered to expand his job duties and help prepare travel itineraries for his boss, knowing that Ripley considered travel "an unfailing source of oddities." In fact, Pearlroth seemed to want Ripley to more regularly flee his daily grind, but, for the benefit of the cartoon, in a way that involved more precision, preparation, and purpose. "You can't just take off for a country and ask the natives where their curiosities are," he once told Ripley. "You have to come primed, you have to already know about them."

So when Pearlroth learned that Ripley would soon travel to Amsterdam for the 1928 Olympic Games, he suggested a side trip—*to Hell.*

* * *

INSTEAD OF SAILING directly to Europe, Ripley first visited Iceland and then Scandinavia. In Norway, in the coastal city of Trondheim, he bought a train ticket for the town that was on Pearlroth's itinerary. Ripley's visit to the small village of Hell would ever after loom among his proudest little side trips. Though hardly an adventure, it was a perfect reflection of his offbeat explorer's sensibilities and his appreciation for tongue-in-cheek travel. He loved describing his "descent into Hell."

There wasn't much to see. Just a train station and a few vine-covered cottages. Ripley had befriended a woman (either on the train or on the ship from Greenland) and she snapped photos of him standing beneath the HELL sign, looking dapper in a three-piece wool suit and tie, a wool cap tilted just so.

Ripley wrote an article and drew a cartoon depicting himself and his lady friend having a cocktail—*"Skaal!"*—beside the train station. (Ripley would later tell a colleague that he'd spent the night with his new friend—a one-night tryst in Hell. Another new discovery: for some hard-to-believe reason, women *liked* him!)

The subsequent headlines in US papers would read: RIPLEY GOES TO HELL.

"It has frequently been suggested that I come here," Ripley wrote. "Hell is delightful! . . . Hell is restful, quiet and pleasant . . . Dante must be mistaken."

In a nod to the letter writers who were always asking for proof and information, he explained that Hell meant "gentle slope" in Norwegian.

"Go to Hell!" Ripley advised his readers. "I mean it."

The *Evening Post* admen had a field day. Not only had he visited fifty-three countries, Ripley had been to Hell and back.

CHAPTER 12

M. Lincoln "Max" Schuster was a savvy editor and marketer, with a nose for the public's tastes. With his equally acute partner, Richard L. "Dick" Simon, he'd published the first-ever book of crossword puzzles in 1924, inspired by Simon's aunt, a fanatic crossworder who wanted more than her newspaper's one-a-day puzzle.

⌁ BELIEVE IT! ⌁

Joseph Pulitzer's pioneering World *introduced the first crossword puzzle on December 21, 1913—a diamond-shaped puzzle created by an English journalist, who called it a "word-cross." Later renamed "crossword puzzle," it become a regular* World *feature, and other newspapers quickly copied the idea.*

With only a shared secretary between them, Simon & Schuster published *The Cross-Word Puzzle Book*, which came with a cute little pencil attached. It was an instant bestseller and within a year the duo published three more crossword-puzzle books, selling more than a million. After a few flops (including a failed Joseph Pulitzer biography), they signed popular gossip writer Walter Winchell to a book deal, and by 1928 Simon & Schuster had established itself as a serious publishing house.

Now Max Schuster wanted Ripley to put a collection of *Believe It or Not* cartoons and essays between hardcovers. Schuster had been wooing Ripley since his 1926 start at the *Evening Post*. He often wrote with praise or suggestions, sometimes promising to dig up curiosa for Ripley if he'd only stop by Schuster's office.

"Renewed congratulations on the way your work grips the popular imagination," Schuster wrote in late 1927. "I never miss an issue."

Schuster knew it might be tricky to sell Ripley in book form. "The big problem now will be to consider Ripley as a writer as well as an artist," he said in one of his letters, while insisting that a *Believe It or Not* collection could be a hit.

For many months, Ripley demurred, claiming that he was just a newspaperman, "just a two-cent man," not an author.

In time, Ripley realized that, with Pearlroth often providing more than he could use, a book might be the perfect place for his backlog of material. So, to Schuster's great relief, he finally signed a two-page contract.

In the book's introductory chapter, Ripley wrote that his humble sports-cartooning career now relied solely on the idea that "truth is stranger than fiction." He thanked a few of the groupies he'd attracted, folks who mailed in *Believe It or Not* suggestions, but he failed to mention Norbert Pearlroth. In fact, throughout Ripley's entire career it seems as if he never once credited Pearlroth in print, having decided that he would be the solo explorer, Pearlroth the invisible staffer geek.

Ripley submitted the final pages to Schuster in late 1928, including a quote from Thomas Moore at the end of his introductory chapter:

This world is all a fleeting show,
For man's illusion given.

RIPLEY'S 188-PAGE BOOK went on sale in January of 1929, for $2.50. The response was immediate, widespread, and uniformly laudatory.

Reviewers of all journalistic tiers declared it an instant classic and crowned Ripley "the Marco Polo of our time." The *Akron Beacon Journal* called it "an odyssey of oddities," and the *Sioux City Journal* declared it perfect "for anyone who likes the queer and the unusual."

Compared to Ripley's "repertory of freaks," said one writer, carnival barker P. T. Barnum looked like a schoolboy stamp collector. According to *Vanity Fair*, Ripley had resuscitated "the dying art of dinner conversation." The most glowing review came from William Bolitho, writing in Pulitzer's *World:*

> Such books are rare. It pricks the sluggish mind and coaxes the doubtful one to a true realization that the world, and life, is miraculous and interesting. Read Ripley and see with what wild eccentricity, what infinite good spirits, what fantastic jokes the world is administered. This is a pamphlet for truth, for the incontrovertible truth that life is miraculous, breathless and good to live.

Bolitho compared Ripley to such iconic explorers as Marco Polo, Sir John Mandeville, or Herodotus, calling him "the equal of them all."

"He is not merely retailing empty wonders to make yokels gape. His research is for the very highest type of curiosity, the unbelievably true," Bolitho continued, predicting a long shelf life: "It will drift about the world, second-hand, wherever curiosity and English occur together . . . It will automatically make the eye stop and the hand reach out."

On the advice of such raves, readers bought Ripley's book in vast quantities. It flew off bookstore shelves and via mail order. Kids and adults loved it; cartoon aficionados and history buffs loved it—all drawn to the promise of the enticing subtitle, "A Modern Book of Wonders, Miracles, Freaks, Monstrosities and Almost-Impossibilities." Ripley wisely mailed scores of autographed copies to former colleagues, reporters, and editors, which earned even more press.

Rube Goldberg praised Ripley's "striking innovation," telling him, "You have no peer." The wildly influential Walter Winchell devoted a full column in the *Evening Graphic* to "the sort of tome you cannot put down." Everywhere, reviewers hailed "a book that should be bound in leather and saved for future generations to read," as *The Chattanooga Times* put it. Philadelphia's *Public Ledger* compared Ripley's "eye of the child" to that of Voltaire, while the *Saturday Review of Literature* likened him to Poe. The esteemed *Daily News* critic Mark Hellinger said Ripley amused and startled readers in "one of the most interesting books I have ever read."

One reviewer, after reading a hundred pages, dropped the book into his lap and wondered aloud, "What sort of mind has the man who collects so much freak data?" The question was asked again and again—*Who is this guy?*—and the *Evening Post* went so far as to enlist a group of professors to attempt an answer in a series of promotional articles. Ripley's cartoons "are thrill pills," explained Professor Rudolph Pinter. "They give us a quick vicarious thrill." And Professor Clyde Miller said Ripley's *Believe It or Not* drawings "are a blessing to everyday people. In contrast to humdrum life, they are an emotional tonic."

Simon & Schuster kept printing copies and was soon into a fifth printing, then a ninth, eventually reaching forty.

✦ BELIEVE IT! ✦

Over the next twenty years, Ripley's books would sell more than two million copies.

* * *

SUCH SUCCESS INEVITABLY inspired copycat efforts, such as Ed Wolff's *Why We Do It,* which explained the stories behind why people throw rice at the bride, why men tip their hats, why women wear rouge, and how barber poles began. One critic complained that Wolff's book too closely resembled *Believe It or Not,* and that publishers were rushing to cash in on "the fascination of blobs of knowledge."

In truth, Ripley's imitators had been multiplying for years. Bernarr Macfadden's *True Story* magazine (tagline: "Truth Is Stranger Than Fiction") had been around for a decade, and in 1928 a talented young artist named John Hix launched his syndicated *Strange as It Seems* cartoon.

But the competition hardly compared with the original. As Ripley's book climbed the bestseller lists, fans clamored for more of the curious author and Ripley was showered with offers. *Collier's* invited him to contribute a regular cartoon feature to the magazine. A company called Famous Speakers Inc. offered a lecture series, and Ripley signed a contract that would give him half the proceeds from those lectures. He was even offered a nationwide vaudeville tour, and was soon being wooed by radio networks looking for ways to capture the *Believe It or Not* magic on the airwaves.

After twenty years in the newspaper business, he was finally in league with men such as Peter Kyne: an author, a lecturer, a world traveler, a *celebrity.*

While some fans wrote letters marveling at how he "keeps it going" for so many years, Ripley was finding it easier by the day, thanks to Pearlroth, his staff, and his fans. One *Evening Post* contest earned thousands of mailed-in reader submissions, including celebrity entries from Franklin D. Roosevelt, Jack Dempsey, and New York Giants manager John McGraw. With so much assistance, the supply of cartoon material seemed inexhaustible.

Believe It or Not was a self-perpetuating *machine,* and Ripley was suddenly being wooed by the biggest names in newspapers.

ROBERT L. RIPLEY and *Believe It or Not* were now entwined, indivisible. His cartoons weren't just some widgets he manufactured, they had become extensions of his personality. Yet, the real Ripley remained a mystery. In person and onstage, he seemed jovial and fun, though hardly at ease in public, often coming across as unrehearsed, a bit awkward and clumsy. He had a singsongy, faux-aristocratic voice (not unlike Hearst's), but his buckteeth hampered his articulation. He still stuttered—or, with too much nerve-calming booze, slurred—and his hands seemed to be constantly waving about. Such foibles only endeared him further to fans.

Ripley knew he needed to make himself available to readers and fans, or at least show a version of himself. He hired an assistant to manage his schedule and financial affairs. With a crew of employees toiling behind the scenes, he began spending more time as the public face of *Believe It or Not,* some days only working for an hour on the cartoon and the rest of his day managing offers from those wanting him to sign books or speak to their organization. Requests poured in for product endorsements or charitable donations, and Ripley had a hard time saying no. With an affinity for boys' and orphans' groups, he donated cartoons and cash to the Boys' Work Committee of the Rotary Club, the National Tuberculosis Association, and the Orphans Automobile Day Association.

When the publicity demands slowed, in the late spring of 1929, Ripley felt he could take time off to travel once again. He planned a two-month tour of Central America, but the trip was delayed when Bugs Baer's wife fell ill, and Ripley stayed with his longtime pal in New York. When Marjorie "Cass" Baer died of pneumonia, Ripley attended the funeral, serving as a pallbearer.

Finally, in late May, he sailed to Guatemala, El Salvador, and Honduras. Pearlroth had read about an ancient and primitive Central American civilization that an aviator had recently discovered in Guatemala and, though he hated the idea of flying, Ripley decided to search for the tribe himself. He hired a pilot who told Ripley that he always brought weapons when flying into the wilderness—a shotgun, a machete, and a blackjack—as precautions against the swarms of curious natives who always surrounded his plane. (It's unclear whether Ripley found the tribe he was seeking.)

In Mexico, he traveled deep into the Yucatán Peninsula to tour the Chichen Itza ruins, and would later claim to have "discovered" the origins of basketball there.

☜ BELIEVE IT! ☞

Pre-Columbian tlachtli *ball courts discovered at Chichen Itza and elsewhere in Central America featured stone hoops built into the walls. Using heavy rubber balls, players competed in a mash-up of soccer and basketball, a game later called* ulama.

In the blistering Yucatán heat, Ripley's exploration was cut short when he contracted an inner-ear ailment and was rushed to Cuba for treatment. By now he had visited dozens of countries, and friends found it remarkable that Ripley never got sick, an accomplishment he attributed to his miles-long New York walks, his rounds of handball, and his steady intake of germ-killing alcohol. Plus, he always traveled with a jar of disinfectant.

When he was released from the hospital and sailed from Havana toward home, Ripley was suddenly eager to get back to work. While traveling, word had leaked of the new job he'd been offered. Reporters and photographers would be waiting for him, having learned that their colleague was about to join the big leagues.

* * *

MONTHS EARLIER, Max Schuster had wisely sent one of the first copies of Ripley's book to William Randolph Hearst. When Hearst finally got around to reading it, he sent one of his men to tempt Ripley with a hard-to-ignore offer.

Hearst, like Ripley, had started his newspaper career in San Francisco, taking charge of his father's struggling four-page *San Francisco Examiner* in 1887. Over the next forty years, Hearst amassed thirty-four other newspapers and assorted magazines, and by 1929 employed twenty *thousand* people. At age sixty-four, he still put in twelve-hour days tending to his massive journalistic empire. His personal fortune, *The New Yorker* magazine had recently estimated, "mounts into nine figures."

Although Hearst's legacy would become that of a spoiled son who squandered his family's fortune in a maniacal quest for acquisition, he was actually a forward-thinking newsman obsessed with hiring the best of the best. "Your search for talent must be incessant and sleepless," Hearst told his editors. He pioneered global syndication and new methods of advertising, such as running ads for his publications in rival newspapers. An early supporter of moving pictures, he had partnered with the Vitagraph company as early as 1915 to distribute newsreels, and later turned a few of his newspapers' cartoons into animated short films. Ripley knew that Hearst had lifted many cartoonists' careers, not only paying them well but bringing their art to animated life on-screen.

To be sure, they had their differences. Hearst never drank, for example, and had stayed married and fathered five sons, despite an imperfect relationship with his wife and a longtime mistress (Marion Davies, Ripley's ex-wife's former Ziegfeld contemporary). But in many ways the two men shared a professional kinship. Hearst had an uncanny sense of public opinion, an ability to predict what the masses wanted to see in his pages. He must have sensed that Ripley knew something about mass appeal too, that he "understands the popular mind," as author Stephen Crane once said of Hearst.

In the spring of 1929, Hearst had sent a two-word telegram to one of his editors in New York: "HIRE Ripley."

* * *

THE RECIPIENT OF Hearst's directive was Joseph V. Connolly, head of King Features Syndicate, the world's largest purveyor of comic strips, columns, and assorted newspaper features. Connolly's first stop was the New York Athletic Club. Striding up to the front desk, he asked the receptionist, "Where can I find Bob Ripley?"

At that exact moment, Ripley was exiting the elevator, about to step into the lobby. One glimpse of the grim-looking

Connolly, who looked like a lawyer or a cop, told him he didn't want to meet the man. (He'd later say he was worried about an ex-girlfriend's threatened lawsuit.) Ripley slipped out a side exit and disappeared into Central Park. Connolly returned days later, cornered Ripley, and explained that "Mr. Hearst" wanted to hire him.

Due to the huge success of his book, Ripley had met with others like Connolly, men in suits bearing offers from newspapers and syndicates. This time, he sought advice from Bugs Baer, who wrote for Hearst's *New York American* and whose columns were syndicated by King Features. Baer told Ripley that Hearst's kingdom was the best place for him. He retold the story about his overnight stay at San Simeon, Hearst's castle on the California coast: "I left my shoes outside the door and they were gold-plated in the morning." Baer's advice: "Stick to Hearst, Bob."

At the time, nearly one in four Americans read a Hearst newspaper.

* * *

WHILE STANDING in the lobby of the NYAC, just before leaving for Central America, Ripley signed a three-page contract, good for three years. The terms required him to produce six daily *Believe It or Not* cartoons for King Features, starting July 9, plus a new full-page Sunday cartoon. At the time, Ripley was still earning about $10,000 a year. Hearst offered Ripley a base salary worth six times as much. But that was just part of it.

Ripley would also get 70 percent of the net proceeds of *Believe It or Not* sales to non-Hearst newspapers, plus a 50 percent cut of Sunday cartoon sales, with a written guarantee that his share of the profits would be no less than $400 a week. Ripley stood to make at least $100,000 a year.

Walter Winchell, who had recently signed his own contract with Hearst, announced the deal in his new "On Broadway" column in Hearst's *Daily Mirror*. Winchell said Ripley's new six-figure salary "must have made his competitors' heads swim." At the time, the influential gossip columnist was making $500 a week at Hearst's *Mirror*—an impressive salary, but still just over a quarter of what Ripley would be earning.

Ripley's new editor and boss would be one of Hearst's most trusted managers, and one of the more powerful men in news syndication.

Joseph V. Connolly had been a reporter before serving in World War I. He started at King Features as a promoter in 1920 and within three years was running the show. Sensing that postwar readers wanted to know more about the world, but also be entertained, Connolly encouraged Hearst to expand the number of syndicated news and feature stories—and comics. Connolly also played a hands-on role with his cartoonists, helping new artists develop their strips and counseling veterans on how to keep their cartoons fresh. Earlier in 1929, Connolly noticed a new character in Elzie Segar's ten-year-old strip, *Thimble Theatre*, an illiterate, tattooed, and muscle-bound sailor with a good heart whom Segar called Popeye. Connolly advised Segar: "Feature the sailor."

Connolly was also assistant manager of Hearst's other syndicates, International News Service, International Features Service, and Universal Service, whose deep roster of cartoonists included George Herriman (*Krazy Kat*), George McManus (*Bringing Up Father*), Billy DeBeck (*Barney Google*), and Ripley's pal Rube Goldberg, who must have told Ripley that working for Hearst and King Features was as good as it got for a cartoonist.

Ripley had once dreamed of becoming the next Goldberg or Tad, who'd died that May, and whom Ripley called "the greatest influence on my professional life." Though his ascent had been slow, and his path rocky, Ripley was now outearning them all.

✳ ✳ ✳

WHEN RIPLEY ARRIVED home from Cuba on July I, after his abbreviated trip to Central America, word had already spread that he'd be leaving the *Post* for King Features. He was greeted on a Manhattan pier by a crowd of reporters and photographers who clotted around him on the deck of the SS *Orizaba*.

Looking tanned and ebullient in a straw hat and bow tie, posing beside an *Orizaba* life preserver—"like the Ancient Mariner with his tale to tell," one reporter said—Ripley explained that he'd just added four more countries to his checklist and had now visited sixty-seven nations. He was already planning to visit Africa the following year.

On July 9, 1929, Ripley's first day with King Features, Connolly threw a lavish dinner party aboard the SS *Vulcania* ocean liner. He invited dozens of Ripley's friends—artists, journalists, athletes, and actors, including Al Jolson and Eddie Cantor. Cartoonist Harry Hershfield roasted Ripley and crooner Rudy Vallee devoted a new song, written by Irving Berlin, called "Believe It or Not."

It was Hearst's way of saying to Ripley, *Welcome to the family.*

Hearst then followed up his generous salary offer with a barrage of supportive publicity. Via internal memo distributed shortly after he hired Ripley, Hearst ordered his empire: "Please instruct all our papers using Ripley to promote him heavily in full page and half page advertisements in other papers and also on billboards."

In response to The Chief's instructions, Ripley's likeness began to appear in the *Seattle Post-Intelligencer,* the *San Antonio*

Light, the *Detroit Times,* the *Shreveport Times,* the *Asheville Citizen,* and scores of other King Features papers, announcing that Ripley had "joined the staff" or "Rip's coming" or "Ripley starts work tomorrow!" Profile writers dug up and repackaged the story of Ripley's tryout with the New York Giants, many of them claiming Ripley had been a starting pitcher. Hearst's *New York American* ran a half-page ad announcing "another brilliant star to shine on the sports pages."

Though Ripley had worked at three different New York newspapers since 1912, his true home had been Associated Newspapers, and his ultimate boss had been the syndicate's general manager, H. H. McClure, who had played the role of mentor, father figure, and friend. McClure and Ripley's day-to-day editors, like Walter St. Denis, had mostly given him a long leash, allowing him to do his own thing, to pursue new ideas or write about non-sports topics or sail to Europe on a whim. Connolly would be the first to actively manage Ripley, to mold and shape his magic. And Hearst would be the first to issue edicts and restrictions from on high.

In a mid-1929 telegraph message to "cartoonist Ripley," for example, Hearst insisted that Ripley stop drawing for magazine ads, which "injures the paper and also the artist." He reminded Ripley that his contract required him to "devote all time, attention, and energy" to the cartoon and "not work gratuitously or for hire . . ."

"The effect on your work is something for you to decide but the effect on the paper I can surely say would be unfortunate," Hearst said.

Hearst closed by adding, "We are happy in your association with our papers and hope everything will continue happily."

The message was clear: *Do as I say, and all will be well.*

*　*　*

THREE MONTHS into his new job, Ripley learned that his Hearst contract was the gift that kept giving.

Connolly informed him in late October that King Features had decided to start selling *Believe It or Not* cartoons overseas. Since this hadn't been addressed in the initial contract, Connolly suggested that they apply the same fifty-fifty split they'd set for profits from the full-page Sunday cartoons. "I believe that we can build up a worthwhile foreign business," Connolly said, adding that *Believe It or Not* could be as big in China and Australia as it was in the United States.

Ripley was given office space at the *New York American* in Lower Manhattan, but he often chose to work from home. The NYAC had opened a new clubhouse in 1927, a block east of its previous clubhouse on Central Park South. (Ripley helped design the new handball courts). As a longtime resident, he was given one of the two-room bachelor's suites, with a front-room parlor that he converted into an art studio and a bedroom in back. Room #1801 was the biggest place he'd lived in since leaving Santa Rosa twenty years earlier.

For someone who considered himself "indolent" and "the laziest man in the world," Ripley was soon working harder than ever. To produce the required quota of cartoons, he honed a new routine: starting work at dawn, drawing sketches in a robe and bare feet, eating a light breakfast, and skipping lunch. Though he always wore suits and ties in public, at home he could be downright slobbish. After a few hours of work, his hands would be caked with ink and charcoal, his fingernails black. When he ran out of socks, he'd rinse a pair in the sink.

He had been a NYAC resident for a decade but still treated

the club more like a hotel than a home, just a temporary stop-over between travels. The apartment had become cluttered with souvenirs and artwork accumulated from overseas trips, some of which he had begun putting into storage. On his Central America trip he had picked up a foulmouthed parrot that he taught to say "Hello, Rip" and "Good-bye, Rip." From its previous owners, the bird had learned more colorful words. As one writer put it, Ripley's pet was capable of as "sulfurous a flow of potent language as ever horrified delicate ears."

When the bird got too loud and raunchy, Ripley turned up his radio. When the apartment got stuffy, he stripped off his robe and worked in gym shorts, chatting with the parrot above the crackling squawk of the radio. Sometimes he invited one of his cute new secretaries up to dictate a letter, all the while listening to his music, sketching at his easel, and taunting his parrot, wearing nothing but skimpy shorts.

As the workload increased, Ripley tried to keep his drinking in check. He established a new rule for himself: no drinks before four or after seven. Under this odd but productive arrangement, Ripley quickly made good on Hearst's hefty investment.

WITH THE FINANCIAL CRISIS looming that fall of 1929, Hearst feared that readers would have less time to spend on their daily paper. In order to present news "briefly as well as brightly," he gave the *American* a tabloid-like makeover—expanding the Sunday comics page and putting cartoons on the front page—jazzy touches that prompted the *New Yorker* to praise Hearst's "journalistic sixth sense." Hearst seemed to feel that Ripley's jazzy everyman appeal could keep and attract readers, especially working-class and ethnic readers. Ripley's cartoon and sensibilities meshed nicely with Hearst's love of contests and stunts.

↩ BELIEVE IT! ↪

After Lindbergh's 1927 transatlantic feat, Hearst had sponsored a New York-to-Rome flying contest. One of his editors, Phil Payne, joined the crew of a Hearst-sponsored plane, Old Glory, *which crashed into the Atlantic, killing Payne and the others aboard.*

Ripley already knew how to goad readers with a tricky puzzler or far-fetched declaration. On November 3, a week after the stock market crash, as the markets continued their historic plunge, Ripley made this provocative statement in his first Sunday cartoon for Hearst: "America Has No National Anthem."

The sketch featured a chubby man raising a glass, singing to a packed barroom, with a caption that said Congress had repeatedly refused to endorse "The Star-Spangled Banner" as America's official anthem. Furthermore, "The Star-Spangled Banner" melody was based on "a vulgar old English drinking song." According to Ripley (with details provided by Pearlroth), while the lyrics to America's unofficial national anthem were written by Francis Scott Key, the music was based on the song "To Anacreon in Heaven," written around 1780 by members of the Anacreontic Society, a men's club in London. Intended as a homage to Greek poet Anacreon, known for his erotic poems, it became a popular drinking song whose lyrics celebrated wine and women—nine feisty maids, the myrtle of Venus, and Bacchus's vine made cameos.

With the nation's financial system in turmoil, some viewed this as indelicate timing, if not treasonous. One furious columnist called the cartoon "scurrilous" and derided Ripley as "one of the most offensive animals in the Hearst stable of odiferous zebras." Others were tickled, or inspired into patriotic action.

Letters poured in from all camps, demanding that Congress officially adopt the anthem. Within a year, Veterans of Foreign Wars activists and others would collect a petition with five million signatures. A one-sentence bill would make its way through Congress and on March 3, 1931, President Herbert Hoover would sign Public Law 823, making "The Star-Spangled Banner" America's national anthem. (The Hearst machine would credit Ripley in print for this achievement, and Ripley would become a devoted Hoover supporter and friend.)

* * *

IN AROUSING READERS, Ripley sometimes went too far for Hearst's tastes.

"St. Patrick was neither a Catholic, a saint, nor an Irishman! And his name was not Patrick!" Ripley declared in a late-1929 cartoon, which generated more animosity than any Ripley cartoon to date. Besieged by irate phone calls from offended Catholics, Hearst personally telegrammed all King Features papers, telling them to kill the cartoon. But it was too late and only a few afternoon papers were able to scrap it.

An Irish priest editorialized that Ripley should steer clear of religion and stick with "interesting little facts of nature or trick problems in arithmetic." A priest in Hawaii told the *Honolulu Star-Bulletin* the cartoon was "unpardonably inaccurate" and "stupid." When Ripley responded with a letter accurately explaining that Saint Patrick was not born in Ireland and not officially canonized, the priest shot back that "nobody pays attention to the silly cartoons of Ripley to question their exactitude."

It was just the kind of publicity Ripley thrived on, even if it angered Hearst, who was wary of offending immigrant Catholic readers. (In an effort to appeal to Italians, Hearst once hired Benito Mussolini to write a column.) Hearst's support for Ripley barely wavered, though. In fact, King Features launched a series of contests, offering autographed *Believe It or Not* books or cash to readers with the best strange-but-true items.

Submission letters poured in by the tens of thousands. One winner submitted the shortest sentence containing all the letters of the alphabet ("A quick brown fox jumps over the lazy dog"), only to be outdone a week later by a sentence one letter shorter ("Pack my box with five dozen liquor jugs").

Such contests were an ingenious scheme for the man contractually required to produce seven cartoons a week, each containing as many as six unbelievably true tidbits. Ripley's readers were now carrying some of the load and by the end of 1929, as he told one lecture crowd, he had *Believe It or Not* ideas "piled up three years ahead." With such a cache of believe-it-or-nots, he was hoping to get back on the road.

* * *

THOUGH THE GREAT DEPRESSION would soon consume the nation, forcing most Americans to hunker down and travel little or not at all, Ripley would see his fortunes and global travels soar in reverse correlation. His brand of printed entertainment—*See the world with Ripley for just a few cents! A thrill a day for less than a nickel!*—would grow to become just the kind of affordable diversion a troubled nation craved. Now that he was making more money every few weeks than he'd previously earned in a full year, he began planning an expanded list of alien lands to visit—*North Africa! The Holy Land! The Middle East! Russia!*

Back in Santa Rosa, Ripley's former hometown paper summed up his hard-earned success. ROY RIPLEY HAS WON FAME: SANTA ROSA BOY REACHES TOP OF LADDER, blared a *Press Democrat* headline, above a story calling him "one of the leading cartoonists of America, if not of the world . . . while a few years back he was a mere school boy with a hobby."

Ripley's *Believe It or Not* book finished the year ranked among 1929's top sellers, in the elite company of Ernest Hemingway's *A Farewell to Arms* as well as books by Edith Wharton, Bertrand Russell, Sinclair Lewis, Will Rogers, and Ripley's old San Francisco pal Peter B. Kyne, who had encouraged him to move to New York back in 1912.

His path had been rockier than that of his peers, and *Believe It or Not* had hardly been an overnight success. But now, at age thirty-nine, the obsessive pursuit of the aberrations of humanity had at long last become Roy Ripley's entire life. The kooky cartoonist and his kooky cartoon were inextricably entwined.

"Now it looks as though I will never do anything else," he had written in the introduction to his book. "And I don't care if I do."

CHAPTER

13

Within weeks of agreeing to join Ripley's staff, Dick Hyman found himself shivering and trapped in a snowstorm, stranded at a southern Indiana railroad depot, wondering what he'd gotten himself into by agreeing to become Ripley's new business manager and publicity director.

Since meeting Ripley years earlier in Rio, Hyman had been working as a reporter in Rhode Island. When Ripley lured him to New York, his first assignment was to visit the town of Santa Claus, Indiana, to mail thousands of pre-addressed letters just before Christmas, a scheme hatched at the last minute. He learned this was typical of Ripley.

A blizzard had shut the railroad, leaving Hyman stuck far short of Santa Claus. He was forced to travel the final miles by horse-drawn sleigh. When he finally reached the town—population thirty-two—he found the postmaster, who also ran the general store, lugging sacks of potatoes in from the snow. Hyman convinced the man to pose for pictures and to postmark Ripley's letters, then wrote a story about it all for King Features.

When the letters reached their recipients, hundreds of

newspapers around the world published photographs of the envelopes, each bearing a note preprinted on the front—*Believe It or Not, This Is a Letter from Santa Claus*—with an arrow pointing to the now-stamped "Santa Claus" postmark. Hyman learned that Ripley could be disorganized and unpredictable and difficult to work for, but his publicity instincts were impeccable.

"He never missed a beat," Hyman said years later, looking back on the start of his long partnership with Ripley.

Just as Ripley needed Pearlroth's research skills at a critical moment in his career, he now needed someone like Hyman to help him promote and manage himself. In Hyman, Ripley found the loyal aide he'd need to control the coming explosion of his career—the fame, the wealth, and the women.

⁎ ⁎ ⁎

BY MID-1930, nearing his first year of employment with Hearst and having just turned forty, Ripley looked back on the headiest months of his life.

The year began with a nonstop publicity blitz. In Akron, Ohio, he spoke to university students and then soared above the city in a blimp, terrified but waving gamely to the photographers. In Michigan, he spent an afternoon with Henry Ford at his Dearborn estate. In Washington, DC, he spoke to a standing-room-only crowd at Central High School, gave a midnight lecture at the Earle Theater, and the next day visited disabled veterans at Walter Reed Hospital. During a three-day visit to Boston, he met the mayor and governor, lectured and signed books, visited sick kids at Children's Hospital, and played pool at the Boston Boys Club, sinking fifteen in a row. Each night he appeared in a vaudeville-style show, outdrawing stage favorites Amos and Andy, who were performing at a rival theater.

Suddenly, everywhere he went, Ripley was trailed by photographers and autograph seekers. A *Boston Daily Record* editorial raved, "Believe It or Not is more than a feature, it's a *craze*."

Followers began calling themselves Bonfans (*Believe It or Not* fans) or "Rip-O-Maniacs." Even his former paper, the *Post*, acknowledged that Ripley had become "a nation-wide vogue . . . a one-man fad." According to one news report, he received more mail than Will Rogers, Rudy Vallee, and Herbert Hoover. He had received a *million* letters in 1929, nearly three thousand a day, and was considered to have broken all records for mail received by one person. In 1930, he became the target of some of the oddest envelopes ever to pass through the postal system.

One correspondent taped Ripley's photograph to an envelope, pasted on a two-cent stamp, and mailed it with no address. The letter would normally have been dumped into the dead-letter office, but postal workers by now knew where to send it. When King Features published a story about this feat—and awarded the letter writer a cash prize—it triggered waves of mischievous missives. One sent only a stamp, with the address and a forty-seven-word message inked on the back. Another sent an envelope with a drawing of a bird in place of an address. It took a magnifying glass to reveal the words "Robert Ripley" repeated thousands of times in the shape of the bird. Others sent letters addressed in Confederate Army code, in Boy Scout semaphore, or simply addressed to "the damndest liar in the world."

Ripley, meanwhile, was a terrible correspondent, and horribly disorganized when it came to paperwork. For a while, he simply threw it all away, until Hyman suggested it might be good publicity to respond now and then. Ripley then began saving *all* his mail, reluctant to toss it but unwilling to process it. When secretaries tried to categorize the letters, he'd say, "Just put it aside, put it aside. I'll decide later." Occasionally, before heading out of town, he'd grab a stack of letters and stuff it in his bag, with plans to write to a few correspondents. Friends loved to repeat the story about the stack of unopened mail Ripley flung from the window of an airplane above the African plains. Back in New York, the same letters were waiting for him.

Finally, the US postmaster general decided his employees had better things to do than manage Ripley's fan mail. On April 19, 1930, Walter Brown issued a directive to all postal workers, instructing that "such letters hereafter will either be returned to the sender or sent to the dead letter office."

Said Brown: "Postal clerks have had to devote too much time recently to deciphering freak letters intended for Ripley."

When King Features published Brown's directive, word for word, in hundreds of Hearst newspapers, it only inspired the letter writers to get freakier.

✳ ✳ ✳

KING FEATURES had exposed Ripley to a massive, global audience, and except for a minority of curmudgeons who considered Ripley's tastes too downscale and creepy—"devoid of conscience or brains or both," said one critic—the public mostly loved him. Hearst had given him a huge new stage, and Ripley found he was ready for the spotlight. No longer a mere reporter, he was now the man *other* reporters sought to interview.

He would invite interviewers up to his NYAC apartment and spend an hour casually answering their questions, whether it was a national magazine correspondent or a student reporter from Julia Richman High School's *Bluebird* newsletter. "Go right ahead, I'm not busy," he would insist, putting aside his nub of charcoal.

"Rip is quite unspoiled," said Hugh Leamy, who interviewed Ripley for the *American* magazine. "One of those soft-spoken, unobtrusive souls who can do a half dozen jobs at once without getting confused or excited."

Ripley worked hard to avoid the business side of his job. Contracts, letters, and phone calls were Dick Hyman's job. But he always made time for friends and fans, even if they put him behind schedule. He felt fortunate to have attracted so many followers, and was grateful for their loyalty. As he told Leamy, "If I hadn't hit on a lucky idea, I'd have been just another cartoonist."

Every day brought new offers. *Billboard* magazine described the "spirited salary-bidding contest" between RKO and Warner Bros., both hoping to sign Ripley to a vaudeville contract. Ripley signed with Warner Bros. for $4,000 per show. That was followed by a similar bidding war between radio networks, which led to Ripley signing with the National Broadcasting Company's Red Network and agreeing to a year of weekly programs, a contract worth $52,000—$1,000 for every fifteen minutes of airtime. *Billboard* said Ripley was the only performer besides Jack Dempsey who could earn so much without singing or dancing.

Becoming a stage and radio performer was a bold move for someone still uneasy with public speaking, and Ripley considered turning down the offers, knowing he was "not very good at it." At Hyman's urging, he began taking speech lessons to improve his elocution and diction. He also started attending theater performances and films, studying how professional actors spoke and carried themselves. "I'm getting better," he told one reporter. "And it's good discipline for the spirit."

It turned out that spirits were also good discipline. Ripley performed best with his paper cup of gin or whiskey nearby. But even with the emboldening assistance of alcohol, he remained a less-than-natural entertainer. His hands shook and his talks were speed-bumped with "ums" and "ahs." He hoped to prove to sponsors and fans, though, that he was a good sport, willing to try anything if it helped the cartoon. "Shyer than a white rabbit," a radio colleague said. "But he threw himself heart and soul into everything he did."

Fans and radio listeners would come to appreciate Ripley's awkward, earnest manner.

As would Hollywood.

* * *

WARNER BROS. had been founded by four Polish brothers from western Pennsylvania who, after World War I, began producing their own Hollywood films. After a successful run with the heroic soldier-dog Rin Tin Tin, the brothers bought the Vitagraph Company in 1925 and took over that company's Vitaphone studios in Brooklyn, where they produced "talkies." In 1927, Warner Bros. unveiled *The Jazz Singer*, starring Al Jolson, followed a year later by *The Lights of New York*, considered the first true talking picture. By 1930, Warner Bros. had produced hundreds of experimental short films called "Vitaphone Varieties" or "Broadway Brevities," starring vaudeville stars, comedians, singers, and even media celebrities like Walter Winchell.

✌ BELIEVE IT! ✍

In 1930 Vitaphone launched a series of animated cartoons called "Looney Tunes" that would create such characters as Porky Pig, Daffy Duck, Bugs Bunny, and Elmer Fudd. Introduced as Egghead in the late 1930s, the speech-impeded and stuttering character who became Fudd was believed to have been partly modeled on Ripley. One cartoon, "Believe It

*or Else," featured a bucktoothed Egghead wearing a loud suit
and spats. The narrator introduces the world's loudest hog
caller, the human basketball, and the world's fastest woodcutter.
"I don't believe it!" says Egghead. Egghead/Fudd also made a
cameo appearance in* The Isle of Pingo Pongo, *a faux South
Seas travelogue cartoon that was later banned for its racist
depiction of black islanders.*

Hearst had been working with Vitaphone for more than a decade, and it's likely that his influence led Warner Bros. to offer Ripley four ten-minute "Vitaphone Varieties" shows, at $3,500 per episode—the start of Ripley's long-term and lucrative relationship with both Warner Bros. and the big screen. Ripley's name began to appear on theater marquees in mid-1930 and the films became instant hits, sometimes prompting applause at their conclusion.

In Ripley's first-ever film, he introduced viewers to a six-year-old Chinese boy from Chicago named One Long Hop, said to have been born the day of Lindbergh's transatlantic flight, and a woman who could speak ten words per second. (The boy was actually the son of Ripley's cartoonist friend, Paul Fung—"One Long Hop" was a nickname; fast-talking Cygna Conly was a romantic interest who would soon come to work for Ripley.) In his next film, Ripley emerged from behind a six-foot mound of letters to thank a few letter carriers for handling so much of his mail. Then he displayed some creatively addressed envelopes, including one addressed in Braille, others in Greek, sign language, and one with a tear in the envelope next to a sketch of Robert E. Lee—*Rip + Lee.*

The films offered the first in-the-flesh look at the famed cartoonist. For many, it likely came as a shock to see how badly his teeth protruded and how significantly they affected his speech.

Like a craggy wall between upper and lower lips, Ripley's misshapen and misaligned teeth prevented him from fully closing his mouth, making it difficult to pronounce certain letters. With the help of his speech lessons (and liquor) he had grown accustomed to compensating, but certain letters and words still sounded awkward—*b*'s sounded like *v*'s, *p*'s sounded like *fee*, and *s*'s emerged in a slushy lisp.

On-screen, Ripley appeared swishy and loose-limbed, almost effeminate—possibly due to his self-prescribed doses of hooch. He walked with a sheepdog's waddle and constantly fiddled with the nubs of charcoal he kept in his pockets. After introducing guests, he'd shuffle to an easel and sketch a cartoon—an "Up-arm Man" from India or the boy who died of old age at six years old or the man-eating tree of Madagascar. He wore nice suits with bow ties and spats over his shoes. He appeared fit and confident, though he was starting to develop a paunch and lose hair, the remnants of which were slicked back and shiny.

The director, Murray Roth (who cowrote *Lights of New York*), grew frustrated as Ripley mangled the scripts. In his *On Broadway* column, Walter Winchell teased, "Ripley, who knows everything, can't remember his lines over at the Long Island studios. heheheh." Speaking before a small audience assembled on a stage designed to look like a ship's lounge or an airplane cabin, Ripley introduced guests and shared film footage of his travels to Morocco or Jerusalem or film clips of real people doing weird things. His human queeriosities included a sixteen-month-old roller skater, a six-year-old boy who smoked, and an armless trombone player. By featuring odd performers from Scranton, Flint, Tacoma, and Toledo, he showed an appreciation for small-town America as well as genuine awe for the fetishes and fixations of those willing to spend years of concentrated effort carving a chain of matchsticks or building a violin entirely of sugar or printing an eighth-of-an-inch copy of the *Rubáiyát of Omar Khayyám,* which Ripley stored inside a pinky ring.

In one episode, Ripley is arrested and tried in a mock court, forced to prove some of his controversial statements: *America had no official national anthem? The Statue of Liberty was built atop a prison?* He patiently defends himself on all charges and once again explains the details of his famous claim that Lindbergh had been the sixty-seventh man to fly across the Atlantic. Finally, the judge intervenes and declares, "Mr. Ripley, believe it or not, you are *acquitted.*"

* * *

HEARST'S SYNDICATES were reaching more Americans than any one news source had at any time in history, which meant Ripley was reaching them, too. But as the financial crisis worsened—Hearst ordered his papers to *never* use the term "depression"—circulation declined, prompting Hearst to aggressively expand his media empire into radio. He told employees that radio publicity was "the greatest promotion in the world today."

Ripley had done occasional radio shows since his 1922 debut, a thirty-nine-minute show on WDY in Roselle Park, New Jersey (the nation's first broadcast station). He had appeared on *The Collier Hour* show in 1929 and in early 1930, but those shows had all been one-time events. By mid-1930, he was ready for a show of his own, and signed with NBC.

Sponsored by Colonial Beacon Oil Company, Ripley's program would air Monday nights in New York and a dozen other cities. As with his Vitaphone films, Ripley would introduce listeners to some of the strange people he'd been featuring for years in print. His first guest was speed-talking Cygna Conly, who read Lincoln's Gettysburg Address in thirty-two seconds—eight and a half words per second. Eventually, by putting sextuplets on the air, a girl who roller-skated on her hands, a legless boy swimmer named Zimmy, a girl named June Bugg, a man who survived being buried alive, a seventy-year-old contortionist, and scores of other "living Believe-It-or-Nots," he would join Jack Benny, Al Jolson, and Kate Smith as a star of 1930s radio.

* * *

WITH *BELIEVE IT OR NOT* on the air and in the theaters, it was getting harder for Ripley's doubters to prove him wrong. Instead of existing as black-and-white newspaper drawings, Ripley's oddities and their feats could now be seen and heard. In time, some of his achievers would become minor celebrities themselves, bringing even more mail from people with odd abilities or physical deformities or unlikely tales, all wanting to become part of Ripley's famous world of the weird.

As a self-described odd duck, Ripley felt justified in encouraging other odd ducks to share with him their peculiarities and abnormalities, even if he knew it might not be in their best interest. Some had accidental talents, such as the Kansas man with the iron stomach who ate glass, newspapers, raw cow livers, and a sack of cement. Others were born with deformities or became disfigured by accident and developed unique new skills, such as the Missouri man who lost his arms and eyesight in an explosion but learned to read Braille with his tongue—an accomplishment worth $5,000 in one of Ripley's contests.

By now, Ripley realized that he owed his success to the "twisted folly" of such volunteers. And at a time of rising unemployment and a malaise spreading like a disease, the escapist distractions of his world travels and his expanding menagerie of misfit characters was the ideal tonic for an ailing nation.

His book was now in its fourteenth printing and still on the bestseller lists, having sold more than 70,000 copies. The *Believe It or Not* brand was succeeding overseas, too, with the book's foreign editions earning rave reviews in Dublin, Cape Town, Stockholm, Munich, Bratislava, Tokyo, and Peking. Simon & Schuster wanted him to write another book in 1931, so he began saving readers' letters to recycle their material. Fans wrote to him constantly, sharing their lives with him. They wanted Ripley to know about their empty rocking chair that rocked each night at the same time. About the man who bowled two games at once—lefty in one lane, righty in the other, scoring 270 in each. About the eight-year-old girl who'd been driving a truck since she was five. About the man who could lift a table and six chairs with his teeth, or the man who had smoked ten cigars a day for sixty-five years, or the sisters who made clothing from newspapers.

Such letters were proof, as the *New York American* put it in a promotional ad, that "there's a little bit of Riplianism in all of us," that everyone harbors a "fascination with the apparently untrue facts of life."

It seemed people needed Ripley's affordable brand of entertainment, treasured it during an otherwise troubled time. America was hunkering down, suffering a Roaring Twenties hangover. But with Ripley in their papers and on their radios, they could experience foreign lands, meet strange and interesting people. Ripley was becoming the country's know-it-all professor of history, geography, science, and anthropology. His offbeat lessons gave people hope.

Bucktoothed LeRoy Ripley, age eight. "Every-one at school picked on him because he was so different," a classmate would later say. "Not one of the guys," said another.

"THE VILLAGE BELL WAS SLOWLY RINGING"

Though he'd later claim to have sold his first drawing at age fourteen, Ripley was actually eighteen when this cartoon was published in *LIFE* magazine, in June of 1908. He was paid $8, which inspired him to pursue cartooning as a career.

ART STAFF
S.F. CHRONICLE — 1912

At far right with the *San Francisco Chronicle* art staff, 1912. After moving to San Francisco in 1909, Ripley was fired from his first newspaper job, at the *San Francisco Bulletin*—"My work was poor," he admitted—but was quickly hired at the *Chronicle*.

Having played in California's bush leagues after high school, Ripley dreamed of playing professional baseball. While covering the New York Giants' 1913 spring training in Texas, he was invited to suit up and try out for the team. An injury would put an end to his baseball career.

At the drawing board, 1915, working for the *New York Globe*, which would be his home for a decade.

A model and a Follies Girl, Beatrice Roberts sang and danced with the *Ziegfeld Follies*. A week after her eighteenth birthday, she married Ripley in Newark, New Jersey, and the couple honeymooned in Atlantic City. The smiles would not last.

Ripley the handball player, showing off his athlete's physique.

In late 1922, Ripley began his life-changing "Ramble 'Round the World" voyage, a four-month adventure that exposed Ripley to the country that would become his favorite: China—"the vast, old decaying land of the Celestial."

At the Taj Mahal, during his Ramble. Ripley found India to be fascinating and revolting. "Nowhere on earth can you see such a weird cross-cut of human life," he wrote, after a visit to the holy city of Benares. "All this pagan panorama."

SCAN THIS PAGE TO SEE VIDEOS, CARTOONS, AND PHOTOS

THE GLOBE AND COMMERCIAL ADVERTISER, NEW YORK, WEDNESDAY, APRIL 11, 1923

World's Champions Finally Gets Under Way

IT'S NOT SUCH A WICKED TOWN AFTER ALL

ABOVE: In April 1923, Ripley returned from his circumnavigation a changed man. Having witnessed the "demented, delusioned, diseased, and devout" of the world, his cartoons grew stranger, more gruesome and eccentric—and more popular.

With his best friend, the writer, humorist, and cartoonist Bugs Baer, mid-1920s. The two Mutt-and-Jeff pals would become rich and famous together.

At the railway station in Hell, Norway, 1928. "It has frequently been suggested that I come here," Ripley wrote in a column for the *Globe*, describing Hell as "delightful!" and advising his readers, "Go to Hell! I mean it."

Ripley forcing a smile—in truth, he hated to fly.

Ripley's one-eyed dog, Cyclops. A habitual collector, Ripley collected pets, too. Some visitors to his mansion felt he seemed more at ease with his dogs than with people.

Outside his mansion on BION Island.

BELOW: Ripley with some of his lady friends, paddling in one of his many boats on the pond behind his mansion. Associates would refer to his collection of girlfriends as his "harem."

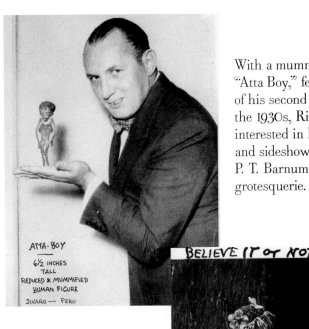

ATTA-BOY
6½ INCHES
TALL
REDUCED & MUMMIFIED
HUMAN FIGURE
JIVARO — PERU

With a mummified fetus known as "Atta Boy," featured on the jacket of his second book, 1931. Through the 1930s, Ripley became more interested in human deformities and sideshow freaks, displaying a P. T. Barnum–like obsession with grotesquerie.

BELIEVE IT or NOT —

"BULUM BALUBA" from Ripley
SUVA, FIJI ISLANDS

During an extensive 1932 journey through the South Seas and Asia, Ripley insisted on visiting with a tribe of alleged cannibals in Fiji. He proudly managed to bring home a "cannibal fork," which he would display in his museums and exhibitions.

In Port Moresby, New Guinea, with members of a tribal dance troupe, March 1932.

In a dug-out canoe at Waikiki Beach with the love of his life, Ruth Ross, whom he called "Oakie," February 1932. In his travel journal, he described how much they drank—and how little clothing they wore—during their South Seas cruise.

With Oakie and Olympic swimming star Duke Kahanamoku, considered the godfather of modern surfing. Ripley first met Kahanamoku at the 1920 Olympics.

At his peak, Ripley received more than a million letters a year. In 1930, the U.S. postmaster general issued a directive: "Postal clerks have had to devote too much time recently to deciphering freak letters intended for Ripley."

With Arjan Desur Dangar, one of the performers at Ripley's Odditorium exhibition at the 1933 Chicago World's Fair. Just before the fair started, Dangar fought with his manager, who ripped off half his mustache. Ripley sent them back to India.

With lion mask from Bali, 1932. Ripley amassed many crates of collectibles during his years of world travel, and in 1934 he finally bought a home to display his masks, weapons, beer steins, artwork, and other strange collections—including his erotica.

For $100, Ripley bought his first shrunken head from a tribe in Bolivia in 1925. Such heads would become *Believe It or Not* emblems. (The head in the photo was stolen from a Ripley's museum in the 1980s and has never been recovered.)

On a ship with his friend, the writer and radio personality Will Rogers. Ripley once ran into Rogers in the middle of the Syrian Desert at a fortress called Rutbah Wells, on his way to Baghdad, and later sailed home from Europe with Rogers and his wife.

His years as a sports cartoonist led to friendships with boxers (left to right) Jack Dempsey, Gene Tunney, and Floyd Gibbons. Ripley also befriended Babe Ruth and Lou Gehrig.

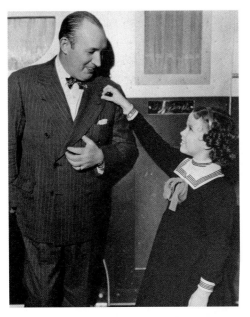

Ripley with child movie legend Shirley Temple, mid-1930s.

BELOW: After traveling from Jerusalem to Damascus to Baghdad to Tehran, Ripley entered Soviet territory for the first time. En route from Azerbaijan to Georgia, he insisted on a foolhardy crossing of the Caucasus Mountains—by car. Incredibly, two farmers with oxen were coming across from the other side and pulled Ripley's car free.

Another risky mountain crossing—this one traversing Khyber Pass, from Afghanistan into Pakistan (then northern India), 1936. Ripley eventually had to abandon the car and make the next portion of the trip by camel.

With a Hindu holy man in India, 1936. Ever since his 1922–23 trip around the world and his visit to the holy city of Benares, India, Ripley had been obsessed with the strange things mankind did in the name of their various gods.

Ripley's beloved statue of Hananuma Masakichi on display at the New York Odditorium in 1939. The sculptor, working in the nude and surrounded by mirrors, painstakingly re-created every muscle, wrinkle, and sinew of his body.

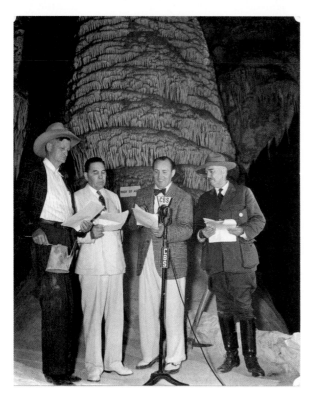

One of the *See America First with Bob Ripley* radio shows, this one airing from 850 feet underground in Carlsbad Caverns, New Mexico, June 1939. Left to right: James White, who discovered the caverns as a young boy; New Mexico governor John Miles; Ripley; Carlsbad National Park superintendent Colonel Thomas Boles.

Descending into the Grand Canyon—with a young Barry Goldwater—for another technically challenging *See America First* radio show.

During a 1936 live broadcast from Silver Springs, Florida, Ripley and his snake-handling, crocodile-wrestling host Ross Allen entered a pit full of poisonous snakes. When the lights suddenly went out, Allen yelled, "Let's get the hell outa here!"

First underwater radio broadcast—from the bottom of the shark tank at Marineland in St. Augustine, Florida. One shark got too close and knocked Ripley on his bottom.

Posing with the inaugural 1918 *Believe It or Not* cartoon (originally titled "Champs and Chumps"). He hung the cartoon behind a backlit mirror above the massive fireplace in his mansion and loved to flip the light switch that illuminated the hidden cartoon.

With a customs agent and a collection of masks after his 1940 travels through South and Central America. World War II would curtail Ripley's global travels.

ALL THE BEST! from Ripley.

Believe It — or Not 1948

A King Features Syndicate publicity photo shows Ripley at work on a cartoon. Owned by William Randolph Hearst, the syndicate exposed Ripley to a global audience.

Ripley and his staff, rehearsing a radio show in his Manhattan apartment over-looking Central Park. To the right of Ripley are the two long-time employees who were crucial to his career: Doug Storer and Norbert Pearlroth (on couch).

With close friend Li Ling-Ai (on Ripley's right) in Ripley's China-themed New York apartment, called Nirvana, which he had purchased from famed travel photographer Burton Holmes.

Visiting Hiroshima, during his somber postwar journey through Asia, which would be one of his last adventures.

The Ripley family tombstone in the Odd Fellows Cemetery in Santa Rosa, California. Like his parents, Ripley died before reaching sixty.

That's how Norbert Pearlroth saw it too. Ripley's cartoons "show that life is not all cut and dried, that nature is not always so workaday, that it has its own exceptions. Life *does* play strange tricks." While Ripley's lifestyle soared, Pearlroth's remained workaday. He still visited the library each day and came home late each night, despite complaints from his wife and son. He was making about $75 a week by 1930, but he continued to believe that his search for "the marvelous, the incredible" was a worthy mission. In fact, he seemed addicted to the thrill of finding what he called "a good one."

"A really good item," he once said, "is one where your heart has some part of it, where your heart begins to beat."

* * *

WHEN RIPLEY HEADLINED the National Automobile Show in January 1931, he was preceded onstage by President Herbert Hoover, who assured the crowd that "despite the depression" he was looking forward to "a prosperous New Year." While 1931 would hardly be a prosperous year for most Americans, Ripley's fortunes would mount.

For two years, his life had been a nonstop whirl. He'd tried to keep up his traveling pace, but every trip now carried obligations. If he visited Toronto or Havana, he was expected to do interviews with Hearst papers and radio stations. If he wanted to see Europe, King Features expected stories and cartoons, NBC expected him to make up for his absence from the airwaves, and Vitaphone wanted more film. Such duties rarely stopped him from leaving the country as often as possible, though—often on a moment's notice.

In March of 1931, he and Bugs Baer escaped New York on the SS *Roma*, bound for Northern Africa and the Middle East.

Shadowed by a Hearst cameraman, Ripley toured Morocco, Algiers, Tunis, Egypt, Palestine, Istanbul, and the Balkans. He returned home in May, and while the SS *Leviathan* was moored off Fire Island, still fifty miles from Manhattan, he broadcast a radio show from the ship back to NBC's New York studios, which his producers touted as the first ship-to-shore radio program.

The next day called for another stunt. In order to reach Newark for a radio show that night, Ripley climbed into a lifeboat that was lowered over the side of the *Leviathan*. The boat delivered him to an awaiting seaplane. Looking disheveled in a rumpled three-piece suit and crooked tie, his thinning hair askew, Ripley tipped his hat to passengers crowded along the *Leviathan*'s rails, then climbed inside. As the plane took off from choppy seas, a cameraman from Hearst's Metrotone Newsreel circled above in another plane, filming the whole scene.

What the cameras couldn't see was Ripley's fury. He hated to fly and hadn't been told about the stunt until the last minute. The scheme had been concocted by Dick Hyman, his new business manager and publicity assistant, who rode beside him. During the short flight, Ripley glowered, refusing to speak to Hyman. His anger melted the next morning, though, when he saw the front-page newspaper coverage, including maps, diagrams, and photos of Ripley waving from the seaplane.

The stunt allowed Hearst's papers to declare that Ripley had completed his most recent foreign journey "by liner, boat, plane, train, and motorcar." When Ripley summoned Hyman to the New York Athletic Club that afternoon, he was beaming.

* * *

FIRED FROM HIS first two newspaper jobs and on the brink of unemployment just five years earlier, Ripley was suddenly being described in print as "the highest paid artist in America today." At the time, Arthur Brisbane was making $250,000 as editor of Hearst's *New York American* and was considered to be the country's best-paid newsman. But Ripley's income from King Features, Warner Bros., Simon & Schuster, and NBC actually surpassed that of Hearst's most trusted employee. Ripley's income—an astounding $350,000 a year in 1931—accidentally found its way into print, thanks to a lawsuit.

Famous Speakers Inc. sued Ripley, claiming that the contract he signed in 1929 required him to give lectures exclusively for Famous Speakers. Company president Betty Smythe wanted *half* of the earnings from Ripley's films, radio shows, and vaudeville performances. In his testimony, Ripley revealed to a Supreme Court judge his six-figure income, which was hungrily picked up by the gossip columnists. The judge ruled in Ripley's favor, but the experience spooked him. He realized he needed to be more protective of his lucrative franchise.

After hiring Hyman in late 1929 he hired NYAC handball partner Robert Hyland to manage his finances and legal affairs. Next, he formed a company, Believe It or Not, Inc., and invited his brother, Doug, to help run it.

Now in his late twenties, Doug had lived a nomadic life. After leaving Santa Rosa, he'd briefly lived with sister Ethel and her husband in Sacramento but then quit school and moved to Ohio, staying with his father's relatives and working as a carpenter. That lasted a few years until Doug escaped altogether, moving into the hills to live in a cabin. Ripley had been trying to lure Doug to New York for years. He would visit or send money to the grocery store Doug frequented, but instead of buying a train ticket Doug would buy more supplies and head back to his cabin. By 1931, Ripley had finally convinced his brother that it was time to move to New York and become part of the *Believe It or Not* machine.

Even with Doug added (somewhat reluctantly) to the payroll, Ripley's pace never slowed. He typically arose at dawn to start his twelve-hour workdays. After twenty-five years of cartooning he remained a skilled artist with an almost obsessive focus on the smallest of details. Intense morning sketch sessions were typically followed by film work in the afternoon and radio at night, then a late dinner or drinks. The release of his second book in late 1931 required another round of nonstop publicity. The *New York Times* called it "better, more entertaining, more surprising than his first one." When the book tour ended, he was back in the Vitaphone studios, filming a musical called *Seasons Greetings.*

Ripley hired a clipping service to collect articles in which his name appeared, another effort to keep track of his empire. One clip summed up the dizzying expansion of the Believe It or Not brand, adding: "Fortunately for him he enjoys a strong physique or he would break down beneath the celebrity strain." But at forty-one, the strain was showing. With no time for exercise or handball, he was losing his athlete's physique, losing hair, gaining weight, and drinking too much. He told friends he had started having headaches.

He was an artist, not a businessman, but he now needed to be both. His popularity and fame had grown so quickly, he suddenly found himself with "no time for anything," as he put it in a woe-is-me story for *Reader's Digest.*

I am blessed with an indolent nature. I detest business. But since the publication of my Believe It or Not book, I have not had time, nor rest nor peace. . . . There are lectures, talking pictures, radio; syndicate features to prepare and illustrate, more books to write. . . . All this pressure has taught me the necessity of tightly packed entertainment, recreation, self-instruction, into the little, scattered, ten-minute fragments of time that are left to me.

What he needed most was a vacation. And a companion.

14

The boy who once ran from girls was now being chased by them. Even with his bad teeth (which he was thinking of getting fixed, now that he could afford to), he was among the most eligible men in New York, often seen with an attractive young actress, singer, or dancer on his arm. He had come close to proposing a time or two, but always reminded himself he was not spousal material. Monogamy, he had learned, was not his forte.

Three years after Hearst and King Features hoisted him onto a global stage, he had become rich, famous, and beloved. But he also wanted to love and to *be* loved. Or at least not be alone. He had discovered there were plenty of women who wanted to spend time with a needy cartoonist. Even married women.

Part of Dick Hyman's job was to manage the love interests that were playing a larger role in Ripley's daily life. If Ripley wanted to be alone with a lover, they had to meet in hotels, since women weren't allowed at the NYAC. Wary of seeing his name in the gossip pages, he would instruct Hyman to pack a heavy telephone book or two into an empty suitcase, take it to the hotel, then check in under an assumed name. Hyman would later hand a key to Ripley, who would slip into the hotel room later that night, where his girlfriend would be waiting.

Despite such attempts at discretion, one lover refused to stay in the shadows. Her name was Marion Ohnick, but she went by the stage name Haru Onuki. "That delectable morsel of Japanese femininity," the *Los Angeles Times* once called her. Onuki performed on Broadway and in traveling vaudeville shows from 1916 through the late 1920s, making her operatic debut in 1926 as the lead in *Madame Butterfly* with the touring San Carlo Opera Company. The *New York Times* described Onuki's "striking entrance" and "dramatic talent," but added that her voice "was not quite heavy enough for the tragic demands of the role."

Ripley had known Onuki since the mid-1920s and had featured her in a 1926 cartoon, calling her the "beautiful Japanese prima donna" who took a full day to fix her hair. Now thirty-seven, she was past her prima donna days but still regal and glamorous. Ripley had been seeing Onuki on and off for years, and proposed to her in 1931. At least, that's what Onuki would claim. He apparently kept delaying the event and soon started avoiding her. In September of that year, Onuki waited in the lobby of the NYAC, demanding to see "Bobbie." When Ripley repeatedly refused to come downstairs, she lay down on the lobby floor.

"I won't move until I get five hundred dollars from him!" she yelled.

Ripley eventually sent down the cash and Onuki left New York to be with her family in California. Shortly afterward, she sued, accusing Ripley of breaking his promise to marry her and seeking $500,000 in damages. The lawsuit initially went unnoticed by the press until Ripley's lawyer challenged Onuki's lawsuit due to her "diversity of citizenship." (Ohnick's father was Japanese.) A New York State Supreme Court judge agreed to transfer the case to the US District Court, and that's when word leaked to the newspapers—*Ripley sued by scorned lover.*

The breakup and lawsuit were reported in *Time* magazine, the *New York Times,* the *Los Angeles Times,* and others, putting Ripley's love life back in the headlines, ten years after the divorce from Beatrice earned similar notoriety. As before, Onuki wanted Ripley to pay for his alleged wrongs.

"I love Bobbie as much as I did when I first promised to be his little Japanese sister," she told *Time.*

One benefit of his wealth was the ability to quickly escape such troubles. So when Onuki moved back to New York, to the St. Moritz Hotel—right next to the NYAC—Ripley made sure he got as far away as possible. By March 1932, he was on the opposite side of the globe "seeking new incredible facts," as *Time* put it.

He was also seeking love—and Onuki's replacement.

THE SS *MARIPOSA* was a speedy, triple-smokestack liner that, if tipped on its nose, would reach almost halfway up the newly built Empire State Building. She began her maiden voyage on January 16, leaving New York with five hundred passengers. Ripley caught up with the ship in Los Angeles and began sailing toward the South Pacific, to explore "the wonderlands of the south seas," as the travel brochure promised.

With first-class dining halls, a hardwood dance pavilion, a library, two outdoor swimming pools, and the largest promenade deck of any American ship, the vessel would be Ripley's home for nearly three months and thirty thousand miles.

Capt. J. H. Trask, who had been sailing the Pacific for as long as Ripley had been alive, was entrusted with such notable passengers as former Hawaiian territorial governor George R. Carter and filmmaker Howard Hawks, who had just finished work on his latest film, *Scarface*. Ripley's entourage included a small radio crew to help conduct long-distance NBC broadcasts along the way, and a young man from Utah named Joe Simpson, who had been hired by King Features as Ripley's traveling secretary and cameraman. Simpson would film and photograph the journey for use in future Vitaphone films. (Based on the passenger logs of the *Mariposa* and many other ships Ripley had sailed, it seems Norbert Pearlroth never joined Ripley on any of his overseas travels.)

Ripley promised Joe Connolly he'd mail home a steady supply of cartoons. In the meantime, he intended to forget about the pending lawsuit and his near-miss second marriage to the litigious Onuki, and unwind with his feisty young female companion in their two-room suite with a private balcony.

Entrusted to Ripley's care was the woman he referred to in his journal only as "M." An employee would later describe her as "some pretty young thing he was hanging around with at the time" and a friend referred to her as "a beautiful, amusing woman whom he doted upon."

Based on photographs, passenger logs, and other documents, it seems Ripley's "pretty little shipmate" was actually Ruth Ross, a woman he'd met in the late 1920s in Europe who would become a constant traveling companion, employee, and, in time, his secret lover.

She was Eastern European (from either Russia or Hungary; Ripley's friends were never sure) and had left home to study in Paris. By the time Ripley met her she had become a successful antiques dealer. One colleague would describe her as "a flashing-eyed Jewess, handsome, intelligent, and vital." Ripley had initially hired Ross to accompany him during a tour of

France and Germany and to serve as his translator and cultural guide.

During their European travels they fell in love—or, at least, Ripley fell for her. By 1930 she had moved to New York, and friends came to believe Ripley had pulled strings to help her immigrate, though he was vague about her route to America, as well as her country of origin. Her English was good and Ripley adored her accent—"OK" sounded like "oakie," and she frequently used the term "okie-dokie," which he found cute. He nicknamed her Oakie.

Ripley kept a detailed journal, which provides a blow-by-blow account of the trip and, at times, the intimacy he and Oakie shared in their lovers' suite.

* * *

RIPLEY AROSE EACH MORNING around five o'clock to wander the decks barefoot, stopping to read *National Geographic* in the library. By late morning he'd find Oakie beside the pool, slowly turning brown. The two of them spent their days wearing only bathing suits—"or less," he wrote in his journal. By the time they reached Fiji, Oakie's skin had turned deep tan—"that golden brown is so attractive," said Ripley—while his own skin was the "ugly color of sickening pink and white." As on previous trips to Asia, Ripley sometimes felt self-conscious about the extreme whiteness of his skin, in contrast to the exotic darkness of the "natives."

Though Ripley enjoyed the multinational city of Suva, he wanted to see native Fijians, with their wild and reddish hair, whose ancestors were known cannibals. He was never much interested in postcards and typical tourist trinkets, but he did like the idea of bringing a "cannibal fork" home with him.

～ BELIEVE IT! ～

*A Fiji chieftain named Ratu Udre Udre was believed to have
eaten nine hundred people in his lifetime.*

In a rural village north of Suva, Ripley and Oakie toured among grass-roofed huts and watched native "spear dances" and a fire-walking demonstration, then reluctantly agreed to participate in a "kava ceremony." Villagers chewed the leaves of a kava plant, spit the juice into a bowl, and handed it to Ripley, who sipped the leaf-and-saliva concoction, winced, and told his hosts it tasted like soapy water with pepper sprinkled into it, but no worse than the liquor back home.

Before leaving Suva, Ripley befriended a bartender who sold him a few bottles, and over the next few days he and Oakie drank by the *Mariposa*'s pool while Ripley nursed his feet, which had become swollen and sore after his walking tour in Fiji. Ripley and Oakie sometimes spent whole days in their cabin, emerging only for dinner and some nights not dressing at all. Ripley hinted in his journal at Oakie's "free-air fiendishness" and how she'd get so "goofy about Bob" he'd wake up in the mornings with a sore back and neck. One morning he awoke with such a raging headache that he vowed not to allow himself to "be duped with drink and beautiful women."

Of course, Ripley's *Believe It or Not* duties were never far away. While crossing the Tasman Sea, Ripley and his NBC crew set up equipment for a planned radio broadcast to be sent back to New York—billed as the first South Seas–New York radio show. One of his guests was Czech pianist Rudolf Friml, formerly a *Ziegfeld Follies* composer. A known tippler, Friml forgot his lines and cues despite two days of practice. "Well, what do you want me to do," Friml said when Ripley introduced him on-air, but Ripley managed to keep him more or less on track and had him play a few songs.

When the ship stopped in Sydney, Ripley was confronted by a throng of newsmen and spent three days giving lectures and meeting with editors at Hearst's newspaper, *The Sun*. He and Oakie had an awkward dinner with his friend Whupsie Strelitz, the woman he'd dated in Buenos Aires in 1925 and had stayed in touch with. (Oakie was not happy; Ripley told his journal he was tempted to throw her overboard.) His last night in Sydney called for another complicated transoceanic radio broadcast, linking the show to New York via a network of Australian stations. Captain Trask agreed to delay the *Mariposa*'s departure to allow Ripley to finish his broadcast, but the show ran late and Ripley sprinted to the ship to meet the angry stares of passengers and crew.

Over the next month, the *Mariposa* sailed among tropical islands, hopping from port to port as Ripley and Oakie drank gin and dined with Rudolf Friml. In New Guinea, Ripley posed for photos with beautiful narrow-waisted and topless Papuan women, who warned him not to venture into the nearby jungle. A local tribe had recently invited another tribe to a peace conference, but the visitors slaughtered their hosts—"quartered them and ate their flesh," Ripley reported. As guests at the home of the Port Moresby police chief, Ripley and Oakie drank cocktails while watching performances by native dancers, including a prohibited "sex dance." He and Oakie were again the last passengers back aboard the *Mariposa* that night, just barely reaching the gangplank before it was pulled up.

* * *

WHAT RIPLEY LOVED most about traveling were the slow-paced moments of "delightful fatigue," far from New York's madness—walking barefoot on the empty decks at sunrise, hitting golf balls out over schools of flying fish, watching Oakie spread tanning oil on her glistening body.

He also loved visiting exotic locales that felt original and untouched by modernity. He found Bali to be one of the most peaceful, beautiful places he had ever seen, inhabited by "lovable, brown-skinned people" who were "the most artistic on earth." Ripley preferred his "natives" to be authentically *native*—barefoot and bare breasted, living simply in their huts of grass. In Bali and throughout Java, he eagerly captured more film footage of native dances and ceremonial rituals.

In Singapore, Ripley introduced Oakie to John Little's bar, where he had first tasted Singapore Slings in 1923. The bar seemed more run-down than he remembered, though after a few midday Slings he decided it looked pretty good after all. He had to practically carry Oakie back to the ship, where she collapsed unconscious into her bunk, but rebounded for a late night on the town. They got back to the ship at four a.m., and found a monkey and a parrot in their cabin.

Sailing into Bangkok, Ripley watched children diving off the horns of a partially submerged water buffalo. That night, he experienced the "wonderful quality" of Thai opium before watching a performance by Siamese dancers, whose kaleidoscopic costumes were "the most magnificent I have ever seen."

Days later, the *Mariposa* entered Hong Kong Harbor, its pale-green waters jammed with thousands of sampans, fishing boats, and ferries. Thrilled to be back in the Orient, Ripley quickly immersed himself, riding rickshaws down ancient narrow alleys and exploring streets alive with clicking mahjong games and clubs overflowing with the gaudy music of singsong girls—*his* China. After two heady days in Hong Kong he decided he wasn't ready to leave and made a last-minute decision to visit Shanghai. Twenty minutes before the scheduled departure from Hong Kong, he, Oakie, and Joe Simpson packed a bag, disembarked, and watched the *Mariposa* sail away.

The *New York Times* advertisement for the *Mariposa* tour had promised "a dramatic journey with a scintillating prologue." Now, the South Seas prologue of semi-clad native dancers and Singapore Slings was about to be replaced by the drama of war.

* * *

RIPLEY AND HIS COMPANIONS reached Shanghai at a volatile and dangerous time. Seven months earlier, Japanese troops had invaded the Manchuria region of northeast China and just two months before Ripley's arrival Japan had attacked Shanghai. The Chinese Army had pulled back, but sporadic fighting continued and Ripley witnessed evidence of the conflict: corpses and unexploded shells, charred buildings and fifty-foot bomb craters. He was stopped and questioned often by Japanese soldiers, who confiscated his movie camera and film. (Simpson managed to retrieve the camera and Ripley would return to the States with grisly footage of an execution: A group of prisoners is led through the streets, lined up on their knees, then shot in the head by a firing squad. It's unknown whether he purchased the film or if he and Simpson shot it. Years later, Ripley would admit during a lecture, "I have seen numbers of people executed because they disagreed politically.")

In some sections of town, Japanese soldiers dined easily in Chinese restaurants. Elsewhere, machine-gun fire popped and dark smoke curled into the sky. Ripley tried to cheer himself by visiting clubs he'd sampled years earlier. At the St. Georges, he was recognized by American sailors, who bought him a beer. To his surprise, he didn't feel like drinking. At the Del Monte, a group of Japanese naval officers invited Ripley to drink with them. As the Japanese officers drank beer, Ripley sipped coffee, then walked sullenly and alone back to his hotel.

"Felt low all day due to the influence of the war," he wrote in his journal.

The next morning, despite Ripley's fear of flying, he and his companions boarded an American seaplane and flew above a crazy quilt of rice paddies to Nanking. There, they toured past the conference hall where peace talks were being held and past the home of Chiang Kai-shek, who was quietly preparing for all-out war with Japan. Ripley also had dinner with Pearl S. Buck, who had just won the Pulitzer Prize for her novel *The Good Earth*. "It is very tense here," Buck had recently told a friend, and Ripley was about to discover just how tense his favorite country had become.

Unlike his previous visit, touring China was now risky and disturbing. On a crowded train to Peiping (as Westerners called Beijing at the time), Ripley was refused service in the dining car and forced to sit in a passenger car crammed with Chinese men drinking brandy and smoking cigars, many of the men staring intensely at the only white people aboard. He had always considered China peaceful and loving, but now he felt threatened and unsafe—which helped explain the scarcity of other American or Western travelers.

Still, he tried to pretend it was just a vacation and not an error in judgment. He and Oakie toured the Great Wall in sedan chairs and walked through the Forbidden City and the Temple of Heaven, where he was startled to meet two former Santa Rosa classmates. In a market Ripley found a comfortable pair of Chinese slippers for his aching feet, the sight of which earned some laughs from passengers on that afternoon's steamer journey to Dairen.

From Dairen (as Dalian was called at the time), they traveled north to war-shredded Mukden. The city, now under martial law, felt spooky and on edge. On the pier, Ripley was met by a man who called himself Chris Shibuya, who worked for the "News Bureau" and offered to give Ripley a tour. When Ripley explained who he was, the man abruptly turned and walked off. Ripley assumed Shibuya was a spy, and over the next two days felt as if he was being followed.

Mukden proved to be a stressful stop for the American tourists. Just days before Ripley's arrival, twelve suspected bandits had been executed and decapitated, their heads hung from the arch of the city gate. By day, shops remained closed and citizens walked nervously through town, eyeing Ripley with suspicion. Each night, machine guns sputtered. Ripley was forbidden from taking photographs or even scribbling notes. He had to secretly send cables to New York addressed "Dear Elsie . . ." to prevent his messages from being intercepted by the Japanese military.

Despite the dangers and images of war, he left China as enchanted and beguiled as ever. Though besieged by Japanese invaders, the country struck him as resilient and magical, a place "of superstition and religion, of mercy and goodness," as Pearl Buck once put it, "of dreams and miracles, of dragons and gods and goddesses and priests . . ."

Ripley's group left China by boat, traveling to the Korean city of Pusan and then across to Japan, where Ripley spent a few days visiting temples, sitting for interviews with Japanese newsmen, and catching up on his cartoons before reuniting with the *Mariposa* once again for the journey home—to California.

His latest big adventure put him in a philosophical mood, and his journal captured his sometimes pessimistic view of mankind, and possibly himself:

Nature is strong and man is weak
The earth turns green and man turns dark
Nature is virulent and man is impotent

ON FRIDAY MORNING, April 29, thousands of Santa Rosa citizens gathered outside the courthouse to celebrate "Ripley Day," an event timed for Ripley's return from the Orient. Ripley's sister met the *Mariposa* at the pier in San Francisco and drove him straight to Santa Rosa, which he hadn't visited since his mother died.

Bands marched, flags waved, and residents cheered the return of their now-famous former citizen as Mayor George Cadan presented him the keys to the city and Ripley thanked the crowd. At a luncheon, ex-classmates sang high school fight songs and bombarded Ripley with backslaps and bet-you-don't-remember-me's. Ripley told the group that in the seventeen years since his last trip home he had visited Santa Rosa, Mexico; Santa Rosa, Chile; and Santa Rosa, Philippines.

Ripley was escorted by civic leaders to his old grammar school and then to Santa Rosa High, where he told 1,500 students the story of leaving town in 1909 to work at the *San Francisco Bulletin* for $8 a week. He was joined onstage by his former English teacher, Frances O'Meara, whom he embraced in an enormous bear hug. Ripley thanked O'Meara for encouraging his drawing, then gave her a gold-and-jade necklace he'd purchased in China. After the event, O'Meara grew weepy recalling the 1921 fire that destroyed the old high school, torching all of

Ripley's drawings: "Part of me was destroyed in that fire . . . Their loss can never be replaced."

At one last reception that evening, the mayor gave Ripley an unexpected gift—a section of the roof beam from his old Orchard Street house. As a lonely little boy, LeRoy Ripley had sometimes crawled into the attic. He once etched his name into the beam with a pocketknife. The beam had been salvaged from the house and still bore Ripley's hand-carved name. Visibly moved by the gesture, he seemed on the verge of tears. Fortunately, he had the excuse of a plane to catch. He quickly thanked everyone, then drove off in Ethel's car.

✸ ✳ ✳

IN 1932 ALONE, Ripley estimated that he covered sixty thousand miles—equal to two and a half times around the Earth.

In recognition of his relentless global explorations, he was elected to the prestigious, century-old Royal Geographic Society of London. (Ripley thought it was a prank and initially ignored the society's congratulatory letter.) Joining the society put Ripley in the company of one of his heroes, Burton Holmes, the famed creator of the "travelogue," who for forty years had been telling stories about his globetrotting experiences in popular lectures and films.

Ripley had much in common with Holmes, who harbored a deep admiration for Marco Polo, loved the Orient, slept on a futon at night, and often wore a kimono by day. Ripley likely heard Holmes speak at the San Francisco World's Fair in 1915, or read about Holmes witnessing the eruption of Mt. Vesuvius in 1906. He surely knew of Holmes's much-publicized wanderings, which far outpaced his own. Along the way Holmes had collected massive amounts of art and curios, stored in his numerous residences. He now lived in a sprawling apartment, called Nirvana, overlooking Central Park.

Holmes's motto—"To Travel Is to Possess the World"—seemed to have become Ripley's as well. And while Ripley enjoyed sharing his experiences with the public, he preferred the road to the radio booth or the lecture stage. At the start of 1933 he cut back on his radio and lecture schedule to prepare for even more far-flung travels.

* * *

BY NOW, Ripley had become something of a wayfaring snob. For foreign lands to be interesting, they needed to challenge him, enlighten him, surprise him, or at least disgust him. South America and Europe had been too ordinary compared to the countries that most fascinated him, mainly India and China.

He was hoping for some surprises from Africa when he booked a last-minute sea-and-air tour from Cairo to Cape Town in early 1933.

As on previous travels through Muslim lands, he found himself troubled by the "fanatical" teachings of Islam and the Koran. He was also annoyed that the "natives" suddenly seemed so *Western*—drinking whiskey, wearing English suits, mixing socially with white Brits and Yanks.

His curiosity was finally aroused when he and Joe Simpson and a camera crew (no girlfriend this time) reached Sudan, where he fell into a typical rhythm. One day he'd be amazed by the sword-wielding Bishari tribe. The next day he'd be repulsed by the "unwashed horde" traveling in the third-class barge towed behind his ship down the Nile. As on other travels, he was shocked at how hard the women worked. "In this country, there are three beasts of burden," he wrote in a dispatch, en route to Khartoum. "The camel, the donkey, and the woman." The men, meanwhile, spent much of their time horizontal. Although he'd sometimes be accused of mistreating the women in his life, there was a complicated duality to Ripley's contradictory attitudes on gender and racial equality. He had fallen in love with Africa, for example, but disparaged African males' work ethic, sometimes referring to Africans as "darkies" and at times claiming admiration for the British "white standard" in its colonies.

"The English know how to run colonies," he wrote, while the Americans "have a knack for spoiling natives."

Friends could never quite resolve the seemingly bipolar attitudes of Ripley the traveler. On the one hand, he was the worldly anthropologist, concerned about women being treated as beasts of burden in male-dominated cultures, and seemingly envious of the simple lives of the poor. (In New Zealand, he had admired the Maori, who seemed peaceful and lived "in the moment.") On the other hand, he was the narrow-minded hayseed, relieved to get off the Nile and into the Grand Hotel in Khartoum, which he called "a first-class white man's oasis in the desert, where they have pink gins, and Scotch and sodas." He was sometimes being ironic in such statements, or self-mocking. Still, it was often hard for Ripley to disguise his unease amid the dark-skinned poor or conceal his fluctuating compassions. In Khartoum, when his car was surrounded by swarms of beggars, he found them menacing but also "curious [and] good natured."

Ripley flew south to the city of Juba and, in his adopted traveling uniform—pith helmet, khaki shorts, and two-toned shoes—he walked through a village of thatched-roof huts shaped like beehives, gathering footage for an upcoming Vitaphone film (in which he would describe the "African Beehive Village"). He filmed some of the topless women, but many rushed to cover themselves when the strange-looking white man approached.

In Nairobi, Ripley toured a Kikuyu village with an Englishman named John Boyes, who had lived in Africa for years and once fought beside the Kikuyus against a rival tribe, afterward declaring himself their king. Boyes was also a known elephant poacher who exploited what he called the "Dark Continent." Discussing colonialism with Boyes gave Ripley the chance to explore topics that had nagged him since his arrival in Africa. He disagreed with Boyes on a few points—for example, that the "savage" native was inferior to the educated Westerner or that the Kikuyu practice of female genital mutilation was acceptable— but felt there was something valid about Boyes's argument that white men had upset the natural order of Africa. Just as he hated to see signs of Westernization in Cairo, Ripley disapproved of what he saw in Nairobi: "stupid white people trying to change the age-old habits of the Africans."

"Missionaries are the curse of Africa, the same as they are the curse of the Islands of the South Seas. The black man of Africa in his savage state is a gentleman," he wrote in his journal. "Only when he starts to become civilized does he lose his character and become diseased, immoral, unhealthy, and criminal."

* * *

ONE APRIL MORNING, Ripley worked in his hotel room in his undershorts, catching up on overdue cartoons while nursing a hangover. He'd been celebrating the previous day, after hearing the news from back home: Congress had voted to repeal the Eighteenth Amendment, and Prohibition would come to an end later in 1933. Nairobi was an expensive city—a pair of socks cost $2.50—but for the price of two socks Ripley managed to buy a celebratory quart of scotch.

Ripley loved to drink when he traveled (and when he didn't), but usually found time to work off the liquor through exercise. Lately, it had been getting harder to squeeze in a swim, a long walk, or a game of tennis or handball, and he worried often about his weight. That didn't stop him from drinking and eating more and more freely. His weakness for alcohol was something else he shared with Burton Holmes, who never smoked but would boast in his autobiography that he "violated the Volstead Act at every convenient or inconvenient opportunity."

Even with the extra pounds and rounded face, Ripley was recognized everywhere in South Africa. He traveled from Mombasa to Zanzibar to Maputo (known then as Lourenzo Marques), then to Swaziland and onward to Durban, where he judged a *Believe It or Not* contest and gave a radio address. During the show, he made frequent trips to the adjacent Durban Club, but later felt "utterly disgusted" with himself. After a visit to Victoria Falls, he again drank too much during a "disgraceful" appearance at the Plaza in Johannesburg and awoke feeling embarrassed about his public drunkenness "and more or less sore at the world in general."

He forced himself out of bed for a scheduled trip to the Robinson gold mine, which turned out to be the perfect hangover cure. He descended by elevator nearly two miles underground into a buried city of railroads, electric lights, blacksmith shops, and hospitals, all squeezed beneath a low ceiling propped up by crooked timbers. He was amazed that man's "lust for gold" had inspired him to dig so deep into the earth's crust. Though overwhelmed by the thick heat, he was grateful for the perspiration, the previous night's scotch seeping from his pores. When he emerged from the elevator and back into sunlight, he felt euphoric.

During a radio interview in Cape Town, he described his experience in the gold mine as "the most thrilling of my life."

＊　＊　＊

BY NOW RIPLEY had visited 147 countries, traveling "farther than the distance from the earth to the moon," by his estimation. When asked about his favorite country, he usually listed China first, but told a South African interviewer, "at the present time, after my trip from Cairo to Cape Town, I am a little bit in doubt." He flew to Argentina by seaplane— among the earliest transatlantic passenger flights—then flew to New York, lugging many crates of artifacts he'd purchased in Africa.

He also returned home armed with more strange scenes with which to entertain a depressed nation.

In Mombasa, he had watched a two-hour tribal dance that climaxed when one frenzied dancer "stuck the blade of a dagger into his mouth and twisted it around and then spouted blood all over." Just like the holy men of India who tortured themselves, he continued to be fascinated by religious fanaticism. He had come to believe that "the strangest places on earth are the holiest." He was also developing a guilty fascination with disfiguration. In Zanzibar he searched for victims of elephantiasis, offering two rupees to anyone who would expose their large and gruesome limbs to his camera.

While flying (nervously) home from Africa, he had tried describing in his journal what he loved about travel, how the rewards were always worth the hardships:

I don't know what my position in life really is—I don't like to fly, I don't like to walk, I don't like to swim, and I don't like to be underground . . . Yet each time I do either one of these things I am thrilled, but more thrilled after they are finished. Every time I go up in an airplane, I am exhilarated after I am on the ground again.

CHAPTER 15

Ripley's fame would soon expand significantly thanks to the promotional instincts of a fellow Santa Rosan named Charles C. Pyle.

Known as "Cash and Carry" or just "C. C.," Pyle was a born promoter. As a boy, he had created a goodwill tour to lure businesses back to Santa Rosa after the 1906 earthquake. In 1925, he became publicity agent for Chicago Bears star Red Grange, considered a first in pro football. Pyle next formed his own football team, the New York Yankees, and founded his own nine-team American Football League to compete with the NFL.

When the AFL flopped and was absorbed into the NFL, Pyle switched sports to promote a 1928 L.A.-to-New York marathon called the Bunion Derby. Most of the runners dropped out along the way, struck by cars or felled by illness, and only a handful made it to New York. Pyle lost at least $150,000.

Another money-losing venture was a sideshow tour with the mummified corpse of a train robber named Elmer McCurdy, which Pyle bought for $50, dubbing him the "Oklahoma Outlaw." Critics—and the police—eventually forced Pyle to bury poor McCurdy.

Ripley had attended grammar school with Pyle's sister and was willing to listen to an intriguing business proposal from a childhood acquaintance.

Pyle's idea was to bring the Believe It or Not franchise to the upcoming World's Fair in Chicago in the form of an exhibit that would display some of the curios and artifacts Ripley had been collecting. The highlight of Pyle's proposed exhibition would be live performances by some of the bizarrely talented people Ripley had featured in his cartoons, films, and radio shows. Pyle would run everything and pay Ripley a licensing fee plus a share of the profits. With Ripley traveling and still overcommitted to his lecture, film, and radio obligations, the arrangement could spread the Believe It or Not brand name without much heavy lifting by Ripley.

Ripley's initial contribution to the partnership was to give the exhibition its name: the Ripley "Believe It or Not" *Odditorium*.

RIPLEY TAPPED his Hearst-appointed secretary and frequent traveling partner, Joe Simpson, to help Pyle track down performers and negotiate contracts. Simpson and Pyle sent out scores of letters and telegrams seeking the world's oldest man, the shortest man, contortionists, Hindu ascetics, and other *Believe It or Not* subjects. "We have done our best to trace the Horned Man of South Africa but have been unable to do so," read one reply from an overseas acquaintance.

Performers were offered travel expenses, a $40 weekly salary, and free room and board. Half their pay would be withheld until the end of the fair, to prevent premature quitters. (Delayed payments were implemented after the early loss of a performer from India. When Arjan Desur Dangar learned that his manager/translator was keeping two-thirds of his income, he cracked open the man's head with a brick. The manager fought back and accidentally ripped off half his client's seventy-eight-inch mustache. Pyle sent them both back to India.)

The Century of Progress Exposition opened on May 27, 1933, commemorating Chicago's hundredth birthday and its recovery from the 1871 fire that had leveled much of the city. Spread across 424 acres south of downtown, the fair was scheduled to last five months.

Ripley visited in July for a dizzying three-day Odditorium kickoff. He hosted a huge contest in Hearst's *Herald and Examiner*, gave radio interviews and lectures, and autographed books at Marshall Field's. At a luncheon of the Chicago Association of Commerce, he was introduced as "one of the world's greatest explorers," and he was a special guest at the first-ever Major League Baseball All-Star Game, held at Comiskey Park.

⌒ BELIEVE IT! ⌒

The All-Star Game was intended as a one-time matchup between the two Major League divisions but would become an annual event.

At Pyle's air-conditioned exhibition hall, visitors walked past display cases with shrunken heads, medieval torture devices, and hundreds of other treasures and trinkets that Ripley finally released from his boxed-up personal collection, including Jesse James's first gun and a "cannibal fork" from Fiji.

Farther inside were sixteen small stages, where entertainers performed vaudeville-style acts. On one stage, an attractive sword swallower plunged a two-foot neon light down her throat, where it glowed. Another performer lifted weights with hooks attached to his eyelids, then used the same hooks to tow a wagon carrying his wife. Other stages featured a man who could smoke a cigarette and inflate balloons through his eye socket, a man who could dislocate his jaw and "swallow" his nose, and a one-man orchestra who could play twenty-one instruments simultaneously.

Some of the two dozen performers had been featured in *Believe It or Not* cartoons over the years, including E. L. Blystone, who wrote more than two thousand letters on a grain of rice, and a man who crammed his huge mouth with four golf balls and a full-sized baseball. As one newspaper writer pointed out, "You'll not have to wonder about these men and women from a pen and ink illustration. They'll be right there in person."

In the first weeks, however, business lagged, and Pyle worried that the Odditorium might be a bust. He considered dropping the forty-cent admission price to lure visitors and shared his nagging concerns with another sideshow operator named Lou Dufour. "I don't understand it," Pyle lamented.

Somewhat audaciously, Dufour had come to the fair with a display of human embryos in jars of formaldehyde, including a two-headed fetus. His other exhibit, "Darkest Africa," was a village of thatched-roof huts inhabited by Zulu and Senegalese immigrants from Harlem dressed in loincloths and carrying spears. "Darkest Africa" also included the hut of a man named Captain Callahan, who had been mutilated during an expedition to the Congo. A show barker told patrons that savages "had decapitated his penis and testicles," and that Callahan would remove his robe to reveal the scars—for an extra fifty cents.

Dufour told Pyle to find better acts, like Callahan. His advice: *less vaudeville, more torture.* "The public loves to suffer," he liked to say. Dufour offered to help Pyle find more interesting performers—a man who could drive long nails into his nose and stick hatpins through his cheeks, one who licked red-hot bars with his tongue—in exchange for 3 percent of the ticket receipts. But Pyle was hesitant to create a blatant freak show.

"People will faint," he protested.

Dufour assured him, *"That's* when the business will start."

Ripley had by this point stepped back to let Pyle take charge, having learned in recent years that he could hardly manage his empire alone, that he was still a better traveling artist than a businessman. Though he had grown wary in recent years of tainting the Believe It or Not brand and was quick to sue anyone who misused his trademark, with a fellow Santa Rosan in charge he freely turned over the "Ripley" name and hoped for the best.

Meanwhile, as Pyle worked to save the struggling Odditorium that summer of 1933, Ripley was in a Jerusalem hotel, wondering how to find the Garden of Eden.

* * *

RIPLEY COULD BE CYNICAL when he spoke or wrote about religion, but he was still a Christian and believed in the stories of the Bible, which he read frequently. (If caught, he'd claim he was just searching for *Believe It or Not* material, but close friends could tell the book was more than a research tool.) Whenever he found himself at some holy site, he always thought to himself, *Christ was here.* While sitting alone at the King David Hotel leafing through the Bible, he read from the Book of Genesis: "And the LORD God planted a garden eastward in Eden." Suddenly, he decided to see Eden for himself.

Though his initial destination had been the Middle East, he now wanted to push ahead to Iraq and Iran (then called Persia), since Iraq was home to the alleged site of the real Garden of

Eden. He contacted the Persian minister in Washington, whose office arranged for a letter of introduction. Persian consul general Phiroz D. Saklatvala assured Ripley that by presenting the letter to the first official he encountered in Persia, he would "receive courteous treatment."

Ripley first traveled north along the coast to Haifa, then stopped in Nazareth and Cana, where he visited a display of the two clay jars in which Jesus was said to have converted water into wine. In Damascus, Syria, he dined on pigeons and watched a cabaret show but found the beggars "more annoying than ever." Joining up with a caravan of buses and cars headed east, Ripley and his one-man camera crew, Simpson, bounced and bucked five hundred miles through the rock-strewn desert. Their chariot was a modified bus whose twelve balloon tires helped it surf over inches-deep sand. With no sign of anything that could be called a *road*, the whole stifling hot expanse of flat desert was a gritty-dusty highway. Ripley sent home a *Believe It or Not* featuring "The Widest Road in the World! It is wider than it is long!"

The caravan drove all day, stopping occasionally for sandwiches (Ripley preferred scotch and sodas), and finally parking for the night at a sprawling compound in the middle of the desert, the fortress of Rutbah Wells, where Ripley was confronted by the drawling voice of his friend, Will Rogers, who was on his way to Damascus.

The two men ate fish for dinner and spent a few evening hours touring the fortress, walking atop the walls and looking out at the fires of the thousands camped outside.

* * *

AFTER A MUCH-NEEDED BATH at Baghdad's Tigris Palace Hotel, Ripley found a tour guide to help him explore his 152nd country. The guide arrived in a brand-new Studebaker. Folded in Ripley's pocket was the letter from the Persian minister's office, which he hoped would ease his travels through this unfamiliar terrain.

At the police station in Karbala, Ripley pulled out the minister's letter and was provided a police escort through the city, "to protect us from any fanatical outbreak on the part of the devout Mohammedans," he wrote in his journal. He witnessed plenty of devotion on the road to Najaf, clogged with Iraqis delivering their dead—in cars and on donkeys—to the massive cemetery in one of the holiest Islamic cities. But the "magic letter," as he called it, failed to protect him and Simpson in Najaf. A group of men started shouting when they saw Simpson's camera aimed at their Koran studies. Simpson was scratched and punched while shoving his way to the Studebaker.

After the roughing-up in Najaf they toured the crumbling remains of the alleged site of the Tower of Babel, which Ripley found to be "a glorified pigeon house." He was even more disappointed upon reaching the alleged site of the Garden of Eden, which was just a barren patch on the banks of the Euphrates. In a forthcoming *Believe It or Not* panel he would dispute the biblical tale of Adam and Eve and speculate that mankind's original transgression was probably eating a fig, not an apple.

Ripley called rural Iraq a land "where ancient history is written in sweat and blood, where life is mixed with horror." Baghdad, on the other hand, was "a man's town, the most masculine place I have ever seen." He spent two more days in Baghdad, filming circular "guffa" boats bobbing along the Tigris River and learning a few of the thousand words for "sword." After a few German beers at a café, Ripley donned the white robe and headdress he'd purchased at a bazaar.

Later, when photos of Ripley in Bedouin garb were transmitted to Hearst's papers, eager copy editors added a bogus description of how Ripley traveled "in disguise during a trip through forbidden country of Near East." An overnight train ride took him to Persia, where he ate herring and drank beer for breakfast. His magic letter barely prevented his film from being confiscated, and he became mesmerized by Persia's women, swathed in black veils and head-to-toe blouses and pantaloons.

* * *

RIPLEY'S LETTER from Persia's minister eventually turned out to be an invaluable traveling aid. During the seventeen-hour drive from the Iraq border to Tehran, he was stopped nearly every hour by police. He noted in his journal that even with the letter his passage across Persia became entangled in red tape, and "we almost wished we had never heard of this police controlled country." It took a full day to get permission to visit Isfahan, but he soon appreciated the access to "the most beautiful city in Persia."

As usual, Ripley managed to find a drink in the most unlikely of places. In Isfahan he bought strange-tasting beer for $1.25 a bottle and sampled two local drinks, which he soon regretted. He spent his last day and a half in Persia complaining about "too much *pelo* and *mastique*."

On his final night in Tehran—a "much overrated" city—he attacked his nagging hangover with a bottle of warm wine and cheap caviar. As on many previous travels, Ripley was hardly squeamish about sampling local foods, the more exotic the better. He had particularly enjoyed cold tongue salad and oxtail ragout in Baghdad.

Driving north to the Soviet border for a planned crossing into Azerbaijan, Ripley was again stopped often by police, and at every stop a swarm of beggars surrounded his car. He considered Persian beggars "the raggedest and dirtiest of any place in the world." Of course, they may have been just curious locals— Ripley often viewed rural villagers as "beggars." He was an intrepid traveler but not always a compassionate one.

After exiting the many gates of Tehran, Ripley's car, his bags tied atop, slogged for hours through dozens of small towns and walled cities, bypassing nomadic families and their sheep and camels. As the starry night descended Ripley felt the first reluctant stirrings for the age-old beauty of Persia. Stopping for the night in Zingan (later called Zanjan), Ripley followed a tall blond tourist around town but soon learned she was married. He spent his final hours in Persia sulking on his balcony.

At the Aras River Bridge crossing, Ripley and Simpson were forced to wait for hours—at first held up by sluggish Persian border guards savoring their afternoon tea, then by stone-faced Russian solders on the Soviet side, toting rifles and aiming their bayonets at the unarmed cartoonist and his Mormon sidekick.

Ripley jumped when he heard a loud *pop*. It was only the huge bottle of disinfectant he'd been carrying for the past five thousand miles, expecting to need it in Russia. One of the guards had dropped it on the bridge.

* * *

BACK IN CHICAGO, C. C. Pyle had enlivened his exhibit with a cast of performers that gave the Odditorium a kinky new reputation. Pyle had dropped all pretense, replacing gee-whiz novelty acts with freak-show entertainers. By late summer, as Lou Dufour put it, the Odditorium was "packing them in like sardines in a tin."

Among the new acts: "Crocodile Man" and "Leopard-Skinned

Man" (both victims of skin disease); "Rubber-Skinned Girl" (Agnes C. Schmidt, whose skin ailment caused thick skin on her hips to droop to her knees); "Mule-Faced Lady" (Grace McDaniels, who had enormous, disfiguring facial tumors); and "The Armless Wonder" (who shaved himself, brushed his hair, lit a cigar, and threw knives at a female model—with his *toes*).

A crowd favorite was Betty Lou Williams, "The Girl with Four Legs and Three Arms." Betty Lou was born two years earlier to a poor family in rural Georgia with the remains of her twin sister's undeveloped body emerging grotesquely from her torso—two lifeless legs, pelvis, and one arm. Odditorium visitors were told that X-rays showed the "perfectly developed" head of Betty Lou's parasitic twin inside her abdomen. Doctors had been unable to remove the extremities of Betty Lou's sister, so her parents agreed to let a sideshow man take her to New York. Pyle paid Betty Lou's parents $250 a week to appear in Ripley's show—more than five times what other performers received. The toddler stood in diapers and white booties, or sat in the arms of a nurse, her deformed body exposed to bug-eyed crowds for twelve hours a day.

Another popular new performer was Martin Laurello, the "Human Owl." Laurello had spent three years in training, twisting his head and neck farther and farther until he could turn his head 180 degrees and look backward. Equally unsettling were the feats of Singlee, the "Hindu Fire Worshipper," who aimed a flaming blowtorch at his face, and Leo Kongee, "The Human Pin Cushion," who nailed pins into his head, sewed buttons into his flesh, and fastened socks to his legs with safety pins.

Then there was adorable Frieda Pushnik, the "Armless, Legless Girl Wonder." A healthy baby, except for her missing arms and legs (the result of a botched appendectomy performed during pregnancy), Frieda grew to be impressively independent, learning to dress and feed herself, to sew, write, and draw using her teeth, chin, and the small nubs where her arms should have been. Frieda traveled the sideshow circuit with her mother and sister but always introduced her own performances, sitting atop a pillow and telling audiences, "I'm Frieda Kathryn Pushnik. I'm nine years old and I attend public school." She would thread a needle and sew a few stitches, piece together a jigsaw puzzle, then write a few words on a notepad by wedging a pencil beneath her chin. Her show lasted just a few minutes, but she repeated it over and over, sometimes sixteen hours a day. Frieda earned extra money signing souvenir photographs in her near-perfect, swooping script, "Best Wishes, Frieda." (Her handwriting had received a national penmanship award from the creators of the Palmer Method.)

Said one newspaper reporter, "At the Ripley 'Believe-It-or-Not' Odditorium her cheery smile has won her a host of friends."

RIPLEY OFTEN CLAIMED to detest the word "freak," preferring to think of his religious fanatics and disfigured performers as "oddities" or "queeriosities." But as more spectators sought out Cash & Carry Pyle's revamped exhibit that summer and fall in Chicago, it quickly became obvious that Ripley's Odditorium had become nothing less than a spiffed-up adaptation of a Barnum-esque *freak show*.

P. T. Barnum had launched his own showbiz career by tight-roping between entertainment and exploitation, starting in 1835 when he toured with a blind, emaciated slave billed as George Washington's 161-year-old former nurse. Barnum gave his acts catchy names, nearly identical to the ones Ripley now used—"Human Pincushion" and "Armless Wonder"—while avoiding the term "freak." Barnum preferred to call his performers "living wonders" or "human curiosities."

After Barnum's death in 1891 (and the death of his partner, James Bailey), his shows were bought by five Wisconsin brothers named Ringling, who turned the Ringling Bros. and Barnum & Bailey Circus into the largest purveyor of human oddities during the first decades of the 1900s. Many Ringling Bros. sideshow performers were featured in a controversial 1932 film called *Freaks,* whose graphic portrayal of Siamese twins and fat ladies, half boys and armless girls disgusted critics and viewers alike. Some theaters posted warnings: "Children positively not admitted. Adults not in normal health are not advised to see this picture." The film was banned in many cities, which may have heightened the public's curiosity and lured them to Ripley's 1933 show.

Burton Holmes roamed the fairgrounds, too, filming and photographing the sites—"Midget Village," nudie shows, the smallest couple in the world, and "the world's tallest man"— having "the time of my life," as he put it, collecting footage for a travelogue about the fair that he'd present in 1934.

With the Odditorium costing forty cents and most exhibits and rides costing a quarter, *Variety* magazine called it all "a poor man's carnival." There was plenty of traditional wholesomeness— carousels, Ferris wheels, and the midway; roving clowns and jugglers; nightly fireworks. But the dominant theme was guilty pleasure, with the most popular concessions and nightclubs peddling sexuality or freakishness. Even Texas Guinan, Ripley's friend and speakeasy matron from New York, brought a troupe of beautiful, barely clad women to her "Dance Ship" exhibit.

* * *

BUGS BAER, in his Hearst-syndicated column, called the Odditorium the fair's highlight. "Rip has collected every amazing freak in the world," Baer wrote.

Ripley later claimed he had to keep six beds on hand for the hundred people a day who fainted. Despite the exaggeration, people *did* faint after seeing some performances, and Pyle stowed cots in an alley, a makeshift hospital where a nurse cracked smelling salts beneath the noses of queasy or unconscious patrons.

Though Ripley wouldn't learn the details until returning from his travels later that fall, the Odditorium was an unexpectedly huge success, earning $400,000—proof that makeshift sideshows were another lucrative outlet for his Believe It or Not franchise, even if it also earned some harsh accusations of exploitation. Syndicated *Chicago Tribune* columnist Westbrook Pegler had mercilessly mocked Pyle that summer for his "exotic educational innovations." Pegler reminded readers of Pyle's failed Bunion Derby and his ownership of the Oklahoma Outlaw corpse, calling Pyle "an insidious teacher who stoops to conquer ignorance." The implication was that, by association, Ripley was insidious as well.

Until now, Ripley had mostly avoided any close affiliation with the sideshow world of the deformed and the abnormal. If his cartoons featured people with birth defects or disfiguring injuries, they were often long dead or distant foreigners—the Chinese man with two sets of pupils, for example, or the horned African. But by leasing his name to Pyle's show, he had crossed a boundary, moving further away from athletes or prodigies or even religious fanatics as his hard-to-believe subjects.

In truth, the terrain had beckoned for years. Ripley's contorted teeth had fostered a kinship with those afflicted by bodies or faces that had failed them, sometimes horribly, but who still managed to live useful or at least hopeful lives. It's that attitude that allowed Harry Overdurff, whose bones had fused and turned his body stiff and boardlike, to earn money at Ripley's Odditorium as the "Ossified Man." To Ripley, such people were the ultimate underdogs, wonders of nature and worthy of attention.

Now that he was famous enough to pursue personal obsessions, he had grown comfortable filling his cartoons, radio shows, and now his Odditorium with such people. He had also grown more comfortable exploiting the legions of devotees who did bizarre things to their bodies in order to gain Ripley's attention. If these people were willing to invest the time necessary to learn how to swallow three gallons of water and regurgitate it into a jar, Ripley had no problem giving "The Human Fountain" a moment in the spotlight.

"A man may be too foolish for his own good, but not for mine," he once said. "Their folly is my fortune. I'll get rich off the ridiculous yet."

* * *

ALTHOUGH IT OCCURRED during one of the lowest points in the Depression, the Century of Progress Exhibition succeeded far beyond its organizers' hopes. Even recently inaugurated president Franklin Roosevelt went so far as to encourage Chicago officials to resurrect the fair for a second year. Ripley's Odditorium was among the concessions that would be invited back for an encore run in the summer of 1934.

Instead of sending his performers home until mid-1934, Pyle quickly put together a traveling show, loading entertainers onto buses and driving to Cleveland, where a temporary downtown Odditorium was created, and from there onward to Pittsburgh and Washington. A Pittsburgh sports editor who had previously worked with Ripley wrote, "Who would have thought that the young Bob Ripley we knew as a sports cartoonist some years ago would put together a show such as this one? Bob was such a quiet, bashful guy, and now he's knocking the world's eye out with his amazing exhibit."

At that moment, Ripley had finally embarked on the last legs of his most exhaustive—and controversial—journey in years, performing his part in the broader *Believe It or Not* show. Because, while freaks onstage were clearly profitable, for the formula to succeed Ripley needed to maintain his reputation as an outlandish traveler.

AFTER BEING FORCED to wait for hours in no-man's-land, halfway between Persia and Azerbaijan, Ripley was finally allowed to cross into Soviet territory. His bags were delivered late that night by ox-pulled dray to an inn, where he and Simpson dined hungrily on canned salmon and slept a few hours in a dirty room, then awoke before dawn to board a train. They immediately fell asleep, but woke at sunrise to catch Mount Ararat out their window as they passed through Armenia.

The slow-moving train was filthy, the toilets backed up and black, and there was no food or water available during the day-long trip into Georgia. Ripley and Simpson were joined by two official escorts from InTourist, the Soviet travel agency created four years earlier by Joseph Stalin. The view outside their windows was a sprawling blur of concrete buildings that Ripley joked was the Soviets' "last word in modern housing." During layovers in small towns, the best Ripley could find to eat was cabbage soup and black bread. At each town he saw gaunt-looking families hovering around the station collecting scraps of food. With the help of some vodka, he managed to sleep and to avoid the rainy, homely landscape outside. He would soon publish his initial assessment of the Soviet Union, describing "the filthiest train I have ever seen in 158 countries" and impoverished citizens who never smiled.

During an overnight stop in the Georgian capital of Tiflis (soon to be renamed Tbilisi), he had to maneuver his way across a treacherous train platform maligned by missing planks and rotted holes toward a smelly hotel room. In Tiflis, Ripley decided to abandon the train and drive into Russia, against the advice of his InTourist guides, who warned that the Caucasus Mountains had received eighteen inches of snow the previous night and the pass might be closed.

When Ripley insisted, his escorts reluctantly found a car and a chauffeur, but the car broke down a few hours into the next morning's drive. While waiting for a replacement, Ripley and Simpson ate lunch with a family of "peasants" (Ripley's word) as dogs and pigs scurried beneath their legs. The driver returned with another car and they continued into the mountains, but at a crowded mountainside inn they were warned not to proceed, that they'd all freeze and die. Ripley agreed to wait until morning and drank vodka with his hosts until he grew sleepy, then curled up on a cot still wearing his clothes and overcoat.

The next morning, his driver inched through deep snow toward the pass, the car sliding on and off the serpentine road. The driver had forgotten to bring tire chains, but it looked like they might have enough momentum to climb the final mile—until they were stopped short by a farmer's horse-pulled wagon, stuck in the snow and blocking the pass. Ripley and Simpson helped the farmer push his horse cart aside, but then the car refused to budge and it looked as if the previous night's warnings had been correct, that they'd perish up there at 7,800 feet. Incredibly, four hours later, two poor farmers came plodding through thigh-high snowdrifts with a team of oxen. The men hooked their oxen to the car and slowly pulled it over the top, with Ripley and the others pushing and shoveling. In film footage of the dangerous crossing (recorded by Simpson), Ripley appears giddy, almost euphoric, having the time of his life.

Later that afternoon, they snaked down the north slope of the Caucasus range into a mining village and ate their first meal of the day—cabbage soup. Ripley wisely decided to ditch the car and catch a train. A mile from the station, though, the driver pulled over with a flat. Hearing a train whistle, Ripley and Simpson grabbed their bags and ran to the station, only to learn their train would be five hours late.

It would take another month to reach New York, an extended anticlimax after the experiences of Iraq, Persia, and Georgia. Ripley briefly visited Moscow ("a hard, severe, unromantic, and inartistic city") and Leningrad ("clean and dignified"), where he was given a tour of a hospital and watched Russian surgeons perform an abortion. He was surprised by Soviet health care, especially the free contraceptives. Two things he admired: Russia's vodka and its liberal sexual mores. "Sexual intercourse in Russia is not looked down upon at all, as it is in our conventional country, but is regarded purely as a human necessity and treated as such," he wrote, revealing his own view.

Still, he was hugely relieved to reach Finland, which felt instantly cleaner, more civilized, and friendlier. It seemed as if everyone on the train sighed and smiled with relief "to be out of Sovietland." During two weeks in Russia, he had seen few smiles.

* * *

RIPLEY OFTEN JOKED that he traveled so much—two-thirds of the past five years spent on the road, by his estimate—to stay ahead of Prohibition agents and find a good drink. While roving the world he had swilled gin slings in Singapore, chota pegs in Bombay, cold Champagne in Panama, and even cold beer in Iraq. Days after his return from Russia, however, the Twenty-first Amendment was ratified, repealing the Eighteenth Amendment and finally putting an end to Prohibition.

Burton Holmes was among those who cheered the end of "the dark fourteen years." With Prohibition good and dead, Ripley no longer needed Manhattan's speakeasy scene to accommodate his drinking bouts. That scene had been diminished anyway by the passing of Texas Guinan, who died in November at age forty-nine, a month shy of seeing the conclusion of America's experiment in abstinence.

During the same fourteen years of Prohibition, Ripley had been living at the NYAC, in what one interviewer described as a newspaper's city room—"if a city room had hats and shirts and things strewn around it as well as crumpled newspapers and such." Until recently, it had been all the home Ripley needed, since his real home had been foreign hotel rooms or ocean-liner cabins. But the NYAC—and even the city itself—had begun to feel a bit tight.

By early 1934, Ripley had come to the conclusion that, at age forty-four, it was time to move out of the NYAC, and even out of Manhattan, leaving the handballer/bachelor/Prohibition-violator lifestyle behind to find a residence suitable for a middle-aged millionaire.

CHAPTER

16

Five years after the Wall Street crash, President Roosevelt ramped up his New Deal efforts to get hungry and unemployed Americans back to work. Violent dust storms scoured the Great Plains. Farmers lost their homesteads to foreclosure. Factory workers were striking.

And Robert Ripley flourished, making money seemingly without trying. Unscathed by the lumbering events of the Depression, cash and new contracts and profitable new offers found him, practically *chased* him, and his income kept dancing skyward. Even Uncle Sam threw money at him, issuing a much-publicized $20,000 Treasury Department refund after Ripley complained he'd been overtaxed in 1931.

Though exact numbers are elusive, his income from newspaper, radio, books, endorsements, film, and his Odditorium was believed to be at least half a million dollars a year (the equivalent of nearly $9 million in 2012 dollars). He was far outearning any cartoonist in the business. One columnist referred to him as "the six-figure gent."

"Last year was the worst year of the depression but it affected cartooning very little compared to other industries," said a 1933 article in *Modern Mechanix* magazine titled "How Comic Cartoons Make Fortunes," which featured Ripley atop the list of "big money makers in the funnies," ahead of Rube Goldberg, George McManus, Bud Fisher, and even Walt Disney. "Why? Because editors wanted more and more 'funnies' to cheer people and help them forget their troubles."

For two decades he had lived and worked in the heart of a metropolis that featured more floodlit glitz than any similar patch of land. But with the means to live wherever and however he chose, he decided to leave the island of Manhattan and buy an island of his own, trading his cramped apartment for an over-the-top residence twenty-five times larger.

Using his acronym for "Believe It or Not," he called his grandiose new home BION Island.

THE DECISION TO LEAVE New York surprised many friends, who assumed he would be content to live at the NYAC forever. Said one columnist, shortly before Ripley moved north, "Those close to him perceive no indication that he'll ever move into more commodious quarters. Probably he feels that to keep two rooms littered is work enough."

Yet, as he would explain in a magazine article, Ripley had been feeling rootless—"like the proverbial sailor who is always a-sea but looks forward to the time when he may have a home of his own, to be embellished with mementoes of his sea travels." Traveling so far and so often, he had accumulated too many artifacts and collectibles, stashing them in warehouses but frustrated by the inability to *do something* with them. He was finally ready to free that booty from its storage crates, to put it on display, and enjoy it.

Ripley had been visiting Mamaroneck and surrounding Westchester County for years. The NYAC had built its Winged Foot Golf Club there in 1922. Joseph Connolly, Ripley's boss at King Features, and Max Schuster lived in Westchester County, as did other newspaper and radio friends.

An old town, full of odd historical facts and characters, Mamaroneck was an ideal fit. An ethnically diverse home to shipbuilders, textile workers, and fishermen, it began attracting theatre people after D. W. Griffith, director of the 1915 film *Birth of a Nation*, bought an estate there and built a studio, turning Mamaroneck into a miniature Hollywood. Mary Pickford and Lillian and Dorothy Gish moved there, as did Ethel Barrymore, who wrote in a memoir that Mamaroneck was just twenty miles from New York but "might just as well be a million miles."

Trolleys ran up and down the main street, an old Indian trail now called the Boston Post Road, and Manhattan was less than an hour away by train. In a sense, it was like an East Coast version of the Santa Rosa–San Francisco link of his youth, with Ripley living in the country village an hour north of the big city.

Ripley's island was at the end of Taylors Lane, which branched off Boston Post Road. He bought it for $85,000 from John Eberson, an architect who had designed movie theaters but lost his fortune as the Depression took its toll on the film business. A stone causeway led out to three acres of lawns, gardens, tall pine trees, rocky outcroppings, and swampy marshes. The centerpiece was a twenty-eight-room English-style manor of stucco and stone, built in 1910 atop a rock mound at the center of the island. The homestead also contained a smaller house, a garage, and a boathouse, all of it surrounded by a tidal pool that had been severed from Long Island Sound by a dam.

With oak floors and dark-wood paneling, the mansion's shadowy interior resembled an elegant lodge or the NYAC's dining hall and saloon. Scattered across three stories were bedrooms, sitting rooms, a solarium, a dark room, a steam room, and a gymnasium. Windows were scarce, but drafty. Ripley soon learned the old house was difficult to heat in the winter, musty in summer.

A Gothic living room looked out onto the Sound, always busy with boats and gulls. Above the huge fireplace, Ripley hung the 1918 "Champs and Chumps" cartoon in a frame, with the original title crossed out and "Believe It or Not" written beside it. Later, he would encase the cartoon behind a mirror and surprise guests by flipping a hidden switch that turned on a light, revealing the cartoon that had started it all. He now had a place to display the beam he'd received from his childhood house. He hung it in his favorite room: the basement bar.

He began unpacking crates that had been in storage, some of them for years. In time, the mansion would become his personal Odditorium, more a museum than a house and surely one of the more bizarre dwellings in all of New York. At first, it was an absolute mess, the rooms cluttered with javelins, mastodon and elephant tusks, boomerangs, skeletons, and war drums. Hand-carved cabinets of teak and mahogany set askew. Turkish and Oriental rugs piled up on the floors. In the garage were scores of crates, boxes, and trunks stuffed with wooden statues and carvings, musky-smelling python skins and stuffed animals, a huge bell from Japan that could ring for twenty minutes, all waiting to be unpacked.

There wasn't much time to get settled, though. He first had to loan some of his souvenirs to the Odditorium in Chicago, where C. C. Pyle's exhibition was reopening for its encore season at the Chicago World's Fair.

✳ ✳ ✳

RIPLEY PLAYED a more aggressive role in the 1934 Odditorium, promising in a King Features press release that the new Odditorium would be "bigger and in every way better . . . the greatest congress of oddities and curios in the world today."

After the surprising success of the 1933 Odditorium, Ripley followed Pyle's lead and willingly crossed more fully into Barnum territory, advising Simpson by handwritten letter: "No sword swallowers. Too Coney Island." Instead, he wanted an "Up-Arm man" from India, a "Sun-gazer," and a "Hindu sitting on nails." He wanted the seven-foot-nine-inch Buddhist monk from Korea and Kikuyu women wearing plate-sized earrings from Africa. He wanted men who ate glass, drank boiling water, stuck knives through their cheeks or spikes in their noses. He wanted a horned girl.

Ripley considered himself and his sideshow more reputable than P. T. Barnum, who was known for fakery and deceit. Instead of Exit signs, Barnum sometimes posted signs that said Egress, luring rubes and illiterates outside and forcing them to pay to reenter. Barnum sometimes claimed that the public *liked* to be tricked, that it was all a game. Ripley disagreed, once telling an interviewer, "Barnum was wrong. The public doesn't like to be fooled. And I'm happy to say I've never fooled my public. Not that the public always thinks so."

Among those returning for the 1934 Chicago show were Frieda Pushnik ("The Little Half Girl"), Leo Kongee ("The Human Pincushion"), Singlee ("The Fireproof Man"), and Betty Williams, who had learned to walk and could display the gruesome remains of her twin sister while standing on two of her four feet. New acts included a man who puffed cigarettes through a hole in his back and one who could break six-inch nails in half with his teeth. Ripley hired Swami See Ram Lai, a Hindu ascetic he'd met in Benares, who skewered his tongue with a long needle, then meditated. Ripley called him "The Great Tongue-Tied."

His proudest oddity was a recently purchased statue, a freakishly lifelike and anatomically correct self-portrait of a Japanese artist.

Diagnosed with tuberculosis in the mid-1800s, Hananuma Masakichi had intended for the sculpture to be a dying gift to his lover. Working in the nude and surrounded by mirrors, he painstakingly re-created every muscle, wrinkle, and sinew of his body. Starting with his feet and moving upward, he glued together thousands of wood strips, then etched and sanded his likeness into the wood. He crafted startlingly realistic glass eyes and then—Ripley loved this part—drilled tiny holes to match each pore on his body and filled them with strands of his own hair. Upon completion, with hair on its arms, legs, head, face, and genitals, the statue looked like its creator in every way. Some newspaper stories later falsely claimed that the artist even pulled out his own fingernails, toenails, and teeth and inserted them in his statue.

After finishing his masterpiece in 1885, Masakichi held exhibits, standing perfectly still next to his creation as viewers tried to figure out which wiry figure was statue and which was man. Masakichi died ten years later at age sixty-three.

Ripley had known of the statue for years, having seen it at a curio shop when he'd first moved to San Francisco. When he learned it was still there, he arranged to have it shipped to Chicago—one worker shrieked when they unpacked the crate. (In one retelling, Ripley claimed to have bought the entire store from the reluctant proprietor in order to get the statue.) Ripley called it "the greatest piece of art in the world."

Missing from the May-through-October fair would be Lou Dufour's "Darkest Africa," the victim of an NAACP antidiscrimination campaign, and the girly joint run by Texas Guinan, now dead. But the fair's second season would be as popular as the first, with more than forty million visitors during the two seasons combined. Ripley's Odditorium would draw more than two million and Pyle's final balance sheet showed a profit of $500,000.

What Pyle didn't reveal was the $10,000 he'd paid Lou Dufour for helping to restyle the show. Dufour felt he deserved more, complaining that Pyle had agreed in 1933 to pay him 3 percent of the *gross* ticket sales. Pyle refused. Since they only had a handshake deal, Dufour accepted the $10,000 but promised to get revenge someday.

The half-million-dollar success of the partnership inspired Ripley and Pyle to create an ongoing series of Odditoriums, a self-perpetuating side business. Pyle started making plans for the next World's Fair events: San Diego in 1935, Dallas in 1936, and Cleveland in 1937.

※　※　※

AFTER CUTTING BACK on his radio schedule to travel during the previous two years, Ripley returned to the airwaves in 1934 with a global gimmick that made headlines and earned him another new partner.

He assembled a team of sixteen linguists and squeezed them onto a stage. Surrounded by rows of microphones, they translated Ripley's show into their respective languages. The show was broadcast using a transmitter linked to radio networks and shortwave transmitters in other countries, allowing Ripley to claim he had performed the first radio show to be broadcast simultaneously around the world.

RIPLEY TALKS TO WHOLE WORLD, said the next day's headlines, noting that the show had been picked up in China, Japan, Italy, Germany, Sweden, Holland, Argentina, Persia, and beyond. The man behind the curtain on that record-setting broadcast was Doug Storer, a self-taught master of such gimmicks.

Born near Harlem in 1899, Storer had graduated from Dartmouth with a medical degree but ditched his doctoring plans to run the radio department at a Chicago ad agency. He left advertising to manage a cousin's radio stations in Toledo and Detroit, then became director of radio for the Blackman Company, producing shows for the United States Rubber Company, Procter & Gamble, and Hudson Motor Car.

Ripley had first met Storer a couple years earlier during an appearance on NBC's *Saturday Night Dancing Party* radio show, which Storer helped produce. An hour before airtime, Storer was running around the studio, handing out scripts and barking orders. He saw Ripley sneak quietly through a side door and would never forget Ripley's outfit: a pale-blue shirt, an orange batwing tie, a plaid jacket, tan slacks, and black-and-white shoes.

"*You're* Bob Ripley?" Storer asked.

Ripley bowed slightly, "grinning like an embarrassed schoolboy," as Storer later put it. He suspected Ripley had been drinking.

All Ripley had to do that night was read a brief introduction to a dramatic reenactment of one of his *Believe It or Not* cartoons, which would be performed by actors. At the microphone, he stammered through the introduction, his voice shaky, his hands shakier. He dropped the script and, when he bent to retrieve it, almost knocked over the microphone. After the show, he went straight to the control room.

"H-how'd I do?" Ripley asked Storer, who couldn't believe the celebrity cartoonist cared what *he* thought.

Feeling obliged to be honest, Storer said, "You need a little practice."

Storer was shocked to find Ripley so shy and self-conscious, yearning for approval. But he was impressed that Ripley seemed game for anything, especially broadcasts that accomplished something new and unique. Storer knew of Ripley's previous exploits over the airwaves: transmitting a cartoon from London to New York (1926), broadcasting from ship to shore (1931), and broadcasting from Australia to New York (1932).

It had been Storer's idea to hire translators and attempt the simultaneous worldwide broadcast, which served its intended purpose and earned Ripley a new radio show.

On Hudson Motor Car Company's *Terraplane Program*, with bandleader B. A. Rolfe conducting the "Terraplane Orchestra," Ripley played a smallish role introducing live reenactments of scenes depicted in his cartoons. Sometimes Bugs Baer served as emcee—he was a natural—and Ripley had a scant few lines. Storer felt that with more speech lessons and practice, Ripley could land an even bigger sponsor. Ripley agreed and invited Storer to work for him full-time, offering Storer 10 percent of all his radio income. Storer soon proved worth his commission. When the *Terraplane Program* ended in 1935, he convinced NBC that Ripley was ready for a show of his own. He landed a deal with the *Baker's Broadcast*, sponsored by food conglomerate Standard Brands. The show would air in prime time on Sunday nights, with Ripley as the host, assisted by a sidekick/ bandleader named Ozzie Nelson and Nelson's soon-to-be wife, the singer Harriet Hilliard.

Storer made sure the new Ripley-and-Ozzie-and-Harriet

partnership received plenty of newspaper ink, and telegrammed congratulations poured in. "You're the nuts," the actress Beatrice Lillie wired, and Jimmy Durante wished him "good luck." Jack Dempsey wrote, "You're a knockout to me." Storer became a true believer in the Believe It or Not brand and, like Norbert Pearlroth and others, another moonstruck apostle eager to lash his career to Ripley's.

Storer loved Ripley's lack of pretense or polish, his unrehearsed authenticity. The public seemed smitten too. "In fact, the pubic *liked* Ripley's awkward manner," Storer said later, describing him as "boyish and appealing, so earnest and honest."

It was that same boyish, earnest appeal that had drawn Pearlroth to Ripley a decade earlier. Back in 1923, as Frank Munsey tore apart the newspaper network that had been Ripley's support base, Pearlroth was Ripley's most loyal accomplice. Lately, though, as Joseph Connolly and Ripley's brother and now Doug Storer came aboard, Pearlroth felt a distance growing between him and his boss. Yet, even as he felt shoved aside a little, he was unwilling to walk away from his "dream job."

Storer, meanwhile, seemed to have found his own dream job. He felt that his previous careers, as adman, radio producer, and talent agent, had all been leading him to Ripley.

Like Ripley's other benefactors—Max Schuster, William Randolph Hearst, and C. C. Pyle—Storer possessed a keen sense of what the audience wanted, even if he sometimes tested sponsors' patience. He and Ripley pitched one show in which circus performer James Mandy—alleged owner of the hardest head in the world—would head-butt a goat. When a humane society accused Ripley of cruelty to animals, NBC officials nixed the idea. Ripley and Storer also once considered the proposal of a terminally ill man who wanted to kill himself on the air—for $5,000.

Though they declined the offer, Ripley told Storer, "It would have been a helluva show."

* * *

HEARST CONTINUED to be a tolerant patron, letting Ripley push the boundaries of radio and indulging his cartoonist's perpetual traveling and forays into freak shows. Hearst also protected Ripley from the economics of the troubled news business. When King Features proposed cutting costs by reducing the size of Ripley's Sunday cartoons, Ripley complained to Hearst that it would be "harmful" to the Believe It or Not name.

"This is quite true," Hearst wrote back. "We will resume the larger sizes later."

Hearst was less accommodating when Ripley defied him, as he did when he continued to accept offers to endorse products in magazine ads, or when Ripley willfully crossed into territory that might cost Hearst subscribers.

Ripley had grown more politically conservative by the mid-1930s, distrustful of Roosevelt's New Deal and suspicious of Communist-friendly politicians and policies. He and Storer tussled frequently over Ripley's spontaneous pontificating on the air. When Upton Sinclair lost his 1934 campaign for governor of California, Ripley congratulated his birth state for its "good sense in rejecting a man who would turn [California] into another Soviet state."

As fear of communism and socialism slowly infected America, Ripley became more vocal in airing his views on the dangerous shortcomings of the Soviet way of life. His tiff with the Soviet empire had begun in late 1933, following his trek through Azerbaijan, Georgia, and Russia. Months later, he'd written an article for Hearst's *International Cosmopolitan* magazine, describing his Soviet travels as the most miserable of his life.

"It is always misty in Russia . . . the sun never shines," he wrote, claiming that citizens had grown dour and fearful after more than a decade of Soviet rule. "There is no God in Russia. Lenin has taken the place of Christ," said Ripley, who called Lenin "the Deity of the Downtrodden."

True, Ripley had been reluctantly impressed by Russia's social liberalism, free health care, and liberal sexuality, and he even worried that "Sovietism" might catch on, that the USSR could become "one of the strongest nations in the world." In early 1935, however, he shared a more critical account of his Russian visit in a speech to the Crusaders, an organization initially created to fight Prohibition that had grown into an aggressive anti-Communist consortium. Ripley claimed that Russians never smiled or laughed because they were *starving to death.* The Soviet government stole farmers' grain, he said, forcing people to "subsist on dogs, cats, weeds and grass." Ripley's address was broadcast on radio and reprinted on the front page of Hearst's *New York American.* The headline: "I SAW STARVATION IN RUSSIA," SAYS BOB RIPLEY.

His accusations were extreme. And, as they appeared to give voice to Hearst's own outsized fears of communism, they raised some eyebrows:

"Everybody in Russia is a prisoner of the government."

"Russia is a gigantic poorhouse where millions of people are on the verge of starvation."

"Outside of Moscow and Leningrad—the Soviet show-places—starvation stalks through squalor and filth."

The *Daily Worker* newspaper, published by the Communist Party of America, ridiculed Ripley's claims, pointing out that he was only in-country for two weeks and spent most of his time on trains. The writer called Ripley a "well-known Hearst stooge" and a "phony."

It's unknown whether Hearst, no fan of communism himself, played any role in Ripley's tirades. Hearst complained often of Roosevelt's "socialistic" tendencies and felt the New Deal nurtured a socialist movement in America, and he'd recently argued that his media empire needed to "make a powerful crusade against Communism . . . if we want to retain our liberties." So it's plausible that Hearst and/or Connolly lurked behind Ripley's vocal accusations.

Still, Ripley's scuffle with Russia might have petered out if he hadn't mischievously attempted another visit to "Sovietland."

✳ ✳ ✳

IN EARLY 1936, Ripley began planning yet another around-the-world trip and applied for permission to enter Siberia, in far eastern Russia. When his visa application was denied, he complained to the US secretary of state, whose office responded: "It is not the practice of this Government to intervene in such matters." Ripley then sent copies of his letter, as well as the secretary of state's response, to the media and members of Congress, igniting a political firestorm.

Legislators tripped over themselves to denounce Ripley's "ban" from Russia. Congressman John McCormack of Massachusetts, who chaired a committee investigating un-American activities, called it "a suppression of the truth" that would "crystallize American opinion" of the failures of communism. One New York representative defended Ripley as an "outstanding American cartoonist whose honesty has never been questioned."

Such foot stomping made Ripley an instant hero among

nationalists and right-wing organizations. Harry Jung, head of the American Vigilant Intelligence Federation, thanked Ripley on behalf of his "group of patriots" and encouraged him to "Go after the Bolsheviks!" Ripley suddenly had to consider how far to exploit this new renown. He asked Joe Simpson to look into a possible series of anti-Communist radio broadcasts, but Simpson warned that it might alienate advertisers and listeners. "Not on a commercial radio program," Simpson advised. "Also doubtful of NBC letting it on the air."

Ripley kept stoking the anti-Communist theme. In one Sunday-night broadcast he complained about his inability to visit Russia and promised to discuss the reason for the ban the following week. He immediately received a letter of admonishment from the advertising firm J. Walter Thompson Company, warning that the show's sponsor, Standard Brands, wanted no mention of "Russia, Soviet or Communism." Ripley then petulantly fired off letters directly to Standard Brand executives and board members, scolding them while also imploring them to reconsider.

"I am astounded that Standard Brands takes this attitude, because I feel everyone should do all possible to combat the un-American institutions," he wrote.

When a Standard Brands executive replied that his company had to remain "non-partisan and non-political," Ripley appealed to a higher authority. In a telegram to Hearst, he wrote:

I cannot understand such attitude of men who would be first to lose their shirts and heads should Communism succeed in America STOP I would like to write a speech like one I did April fourth last year and broadcast special half hour program over National Broadcasting nationwide STOP Would appreciate your suggestions and assistance.

Hearst's response, if any, is lost to history, but Doug Storer soon received an urgent letter from NBC vice president John Royal. "Be sure Ripley doesn't say anything about Russia in any way, shape or form on Sunday night," said Royal, advising Storer that "everyone will be saved embarrassment."

Ripley complied, but found other ways to snipe. At St. Thomas Episcopal Church in Mamaroneck, he delivered an address titled "How God Is Worshipped All Over the World." With religion banned in Russia, he said it was vital for other lands to explore "the mystery of whence we came and whither we are going." The many religious customs he'd witnessed over the years "are all pointing in the same direction," he said. "They are trying to make the pathway of life more pleasant."

He continued: "The greatest thing in life is faith. . . . Whatever your religious belief is, believe in it very much."

A nonpracticing Christian, Ripley never made it clear exactly where his own faith lay, except maybe a deep belief in the strange truths of life. And in himself.

*　*　*

IN JANUARY OF 1936, Congress released a report on the previous year's highest-paid Americans. While not a definitive list, the report found that sixteen people had earned more than $300,000; nine were General Motors employees, with GM president Alfred P. Sloan Jr. topping the list at $561,311. Ten movie and radio stars reported income in excess of $200,000, with Gary Cooper making $370,214.

Ripley was not mentioned, possibly because his income came from various sources and no single corporation. Nonetheless, the curious cartoonist from Santa Rosa was now earning as much as GM's president and ranked among the highest-paid men in America.

He was also, by at least one measure, one of the most popular.

The Boys Club of New York conducted a nationwide survey that spring of 1936, asking thousands of boys between the ages of eight and eighteen one question: "If you had your choice of all the jobs in the world, whose job would you want?" Walter Winchell ranked tenth—"because he knows everything before it happens," one boy wrote. President Roosevelt was seventh, boxer Jack Dempsey sixth. Such notables as Henry Ford, golfer Bobby Jones, and aviator Charles Lindbergh didn't even crack the top dozen. Movie star James Cagney ranked third, preceded by FBI director J. Edgar Hoover.

Overwhelmingly, the boys preferred the job of that buck-toothed cartoonist, world traveler, and radio and film star Robert L. Ripley—who must've felt an extra thrill to have beaten Roosevelt. Among the boys' reasons:

"He gets 'round a lot."

"He is so busy with his radio speeches, drawings, and trips that he doesn't have time to get into mischief."

"He meets interesting people and freaks." (Rube Goldberg noted in his column that President Roosevelt also met many freaks, "only he keeps quiet about it.")

The widely publicized survey set off a flurry of editorials seeking to make sense of the values of America's youth. "He is engrossed in life, as shown by a desire to go places and see things," said the *Nashville Tennessean*. A *Columbus Dispatch* editor said, "Ripley makes a great deal of money just doing the things which the youth would like to do."

Boys recognized in Ripley a kindred spirit, a whimsical child in a man's body who displayed "that priceless quality of naive and youthful wonder," said a columnist friend of Ripley's.

"The wide-eyed, innocent curiosity that started Bob Ripley along the trail of fame more than 15 years ago burns as brightly today as ever," O. B. Keeler wrote. "He is still a youngster . . . and he can never grow old, for the freshness of life is an eternal dew in his heart."

LeRoy Robert Ripley was becoming a real-life Peter Pan.

Later that year, the New York Boy Scout Foundation honored Ripley at a star-studded benefit dinner chaired by Hearst and held at the Waldorf-Astoria in New York. Among the attendees were Lou Gehrig, Walter Winchell, and many of New York's top cartoonists. More than two thousand people paid $10 apiece to attend, raising scads of money for Ripley's favorite charity, the Boy Scouts of Greater New York.

Ripley had been traveling and arrived, theatrically, just in time for dinner. Wearing white socks with his dark suit, Ripley was surrounded by autograph seekers, patiently signing copies of his book, the backs of envelopes, scraps of paper. As if striving to live up to recent accolades, he told the attendees about his latest exploration throughout Greece, Africa, India, and Afghanistan.

But the world as Ripley knew it had begun changing. Due to political upheaval and the storm clouds of war, lands he had recently visited were shifting allegiances and changing names. Latvia had become a dictatorship. Persia had become Iran. Adolf Hitler, Germany's hawkish president, was expanding his army, building an air force, conspiring with Italy. In China, Mao Tse-tung's Communist Army had been forced into retreat by Japan's Imperial Army, even as many rural Chinese, left hungry and homeless by famine and civil war, wondered if communism might save them. Across Europe and Asia, nations were realigning—Communist or Socialist or Fascist—teaming up and choosing sides.

None of which was good news for a man who, as fourteen-year-old Leroy Smith had put it to pollsters, "goes all around the world, has brains, and is always having adventures."

The future for adventure was looking bleak as Ripley's foreign playgrounds tilted toward war, one after the other. For Ripley, it was like watching a curtain slowly close. And he worried: If he couldn't travel at will, what would fuel his cartoons? If he couldn't experience the wonders of the world and translate and reinterpret them in print and on air, what would stoke his followers' dreams?

CHAPTER

17

As one of the most popular men in America, Ripley reigned among the most eligible, with an international playboy's reputation nurtured in the gossip pages.

"Almost always in public he is squiring with much gallantry something especially slick and saucy," columnist O. O. McIntyre wrote in the *New York American.*

"Who are the most beautiful women in the world?" a teenager shouted one night after a lecture at a Connecticut boys' school, and Ripley professed an appreciation for Icelandic women: "Blond and blue eyed, with beautiful skin and marvelous figures." The boys wanted to hear about French and Spanish women, but Ripley said Europeans were "overrated" and that Oriental and Arab women were the most lovely and mysterious.

Then again, he added, "You can see more beautiful women any day in the week in one New York block than you can find anywhere in the world."

With newspaper and magazine photography now commonplace, Ripley was often caught in the act of sharing drinks or dinner with actresses and dancers. Long gone were the requisite ball games and boxing matches, replaced by Broadway parties, charity balls, or cocktails at midtown nightclubs, often in the company of his raspy-voiced sidekick, Bugs Baer. Pictures of Ripley and Baer appeared regularly, posing with some attractive unnamed woman at a table with Gene Tunney or Babe Ruth. Ripley always looked dapper, in tailor-made suits, bright-colored shirts, bow ties, and his trademark black-and-white wing tips. He wore a pinky ring and twirled a walking stick. Columnists stoked his reputation as a fop. "All shyness disappears as Ripley goes to town sartorially," said one writer. "High colors are his choice—green that is green, red that is red."

Yet, Ripley suspiciously remained a bachelor, and the question lingered—*Why aren't you married?* "Women have a way of falling in love with Ripley," wrote a female reporter who spent a weekend at BION Island while researching a story for *Radio Stars* magazine. "Popular, wealthy, fabulously famous, extremely attractive to women—and still not married!" Ripley usually explained that his hectic travel schedule limited his marital prospects to women who were extremely tolerant, adventurous, or both. "If she didn't like to travel," he said, "she'd be a widow most of the time." He told another reporter that he sometimes dreamed of having children and "growing old at BION." But it seemed that anytime he fell in love he would leave for a trip and return to find his lover betrothed to another.

In truth, he had already found the ideal partner, beautiful and loving, adventurous and tolerant . . . yet married.

RUTH "OAKIE" ROSS had for years been the mystery woman of Ripley's life, the one who appeared and disappeared and reappeared again without anyone ever catching her full story, even as she became his constant traveling companion and a paid employee of Believe It or Not, Inc.

Through the mid-1930s she had frequently joined in his travels, including the 1932 South Seas and China adventure. In 1934 they had toured throughout Northern Africa—Morocco, Tripoli, Libya (then known as Cyrenaica), Algeria—and on to Northern Europe. Though she was listed on his payroll as "secretary," Ripley once introduced her to reporters as "Mrs. Ripley" during a visit to the Shetland Islands. At the end of that trip, he and Oakie sailed home with Will Rogers and his wife.

When Ripley bought BION Island in 1934, Oakie helped organize the messy contents of his new mansion. She lived in Manhattan but spent many days and nights at the Mamaroneck house. Their lives were woven tightly together and at times they lived practically as man and wife. One contemporary called her "a combination social secretary and companion [who] earned the right to move in and out of Ripley's life as she pleased."

But sealing the deal by proposing was apparently never a consideration, largely due to dark memories of his failed marriage to Beatrice. In one of the why-aren't-you-married stories, a reporter asked if he ever *had* been married. "Oh, nooooooo," he said, then quickly admitted, "I guess I was once. But she's married and got children."

Ripley had occasionally run into Beatrice over the years, once while searching for Mayan ruins in Mexico. The captain of Ripley's ship had introduced him to the owner of a hemp plantation, who invited Ripley to stay the night. At dinner he introduced his wife—it was Beatrice. Ripley later told Bugs it felt "a little creepy." In another version of that story, Beatrice sent him a note later that night: "Roy, you'll always be the only one I love." An employee would later claim that the run-in was no accident, that Ripley knew Beatrice was living there and staged the encounter with her husband in order to see her.

Ripley so rarely talked about Beatrice that her true identity would become mixed and muddled. For decades, *Believe It or Not* fans thought she was the same Beatrice Roberts who became a Miss America contestant, a small-time actress, and Louis B. Mayer's lover. Based on census records, Ripley's marriage license, Miss America documents, and newspaper articles, it turned out they all had the wrong Beatrice. After divorcing Ripley, Beatrice returned to Massachusetts to live with her family. She eventually married a Cuban man and lived with him in Cuba, but her husband died of tuberculosis, leaving her with two children. She moved back to Massachusetts, and Ripley helped by continuing to send occasional checks to his widowed ex.

Beatrice wasn't the only ex-lover who'd remained part of his life. After Haru Onuki (aka Marion Ohnick) sued him in 1932, Ripley settled out of court, paying an undisclosed sum. She eventually moved back to California, and Ripley would visit during trips to Los Angeles. He once received a cable from Onuki, who had lost her purse while traveling and wondered if her "Bobbie" could wire some money. Though his attorney smelled "a frame," Ripley complied.

A collector and sentimentalist, Ripley seemed unable to sever ties to the women he once loved, and had even continued to contact his high school love, Nell. But he had at least learned not to remarry, that he could "never make a wife happy," as he once put it. Besides, there were too many beautiful women in the world. Ripley was no braggart, but he once told Doug Storer that he intended to have sex in every country he visited and wasn't far off that goal. One of his proudest conquests was still his tryst in Hell, Norway—"Just for the hell of it," he told Storer with a wink. A self-professed connoisseur of the female form, he wrote in his third *Believe It or Not* book that he adored Nordic women ("pure unadulterated beauty"), Eurasian women ("always beautiful"), and Turkish women ("lovely"), adding, "I doubt if anyone ever saw anything cuter than a Javanese."

In Oakie, he found someone possessing the best features of all the world's women. Though he appreciated slim, dark-skinned women—especially Asian women—Ripley also liked intelligent, independent, and worldly women. Oakie was all of that.

At thirty-eight she was older than most girlfriends, but carried herself with poise and assurance, always well-dressed, a confident strut, often grinning. While in the tropics, she wasn't shy about removing her top and sunning herself. In one of Ripley's home movies, he and Oakie are lounging on a boat someplace steamy, Ripley sweating in just white skivvies and Oakie with her bathing suit pulled down to her waist, her head thrown back to soak up the sun.

Elsewhere in Ripley's home movies the two seem perfectly at ease walking along cobblestone streets or beaches, sharing a pedicab or a meal or a dance. With her, Ripley seemed carefree and happy, and friends could tell there was something special about their relationship. Other serious partnerships had ended in divorce, lawsuits, headlines, allegations of abuse—indications that Ripley preferred drama and conflict in his liaisons. With Oakie, he sought simplicity and domesticity. Though he would remain secretive about the details of their affair, it became obvious to those close to him that he truly loved her.

But there was that one complication in their otherwise romantic love story, which compelled Ripley to be furtive. His lover was a married woman.

FRIENDS WOULD LATER say that Ripley declined to marry Oakie, so she eventually wed someone else, sometime in the mid-1930s. Others assumed she had been married all along, and that Oakie gave Ripley the ideal duty-free relationship. The particulars would remain murky, as would the identity of Oakie's husband. However it came to be, the strange arrangement might have been for the best.

Until meeting Oakie, Ripley had seemed incapable of fully sharing his life with just one woman. He admired the male-dominated cultures of certain countries, even those practicing polygamy, and he complained often about American-style marriages. In one interview he declared his admiration for Muslim-style marriages. "Men are left to enjoy themselves," he said. "Women aren't making noise all the time with court litigation like they do here." Oakie apparently decided there was no sense in forcing Ripley to commit. She simply married another and became Ripley's favored mistress. They seemed to have made a pact, each agreeing to the ruse in which their separate lives sometimes overlapped.

At BION Island, Oakie left her imprint everywhere. She had initially helped him find and hire domestic help—cooks, chauffeurs, gardeners, and maids—and then began arranging his antique furniture and artwork. By 1936, Ripley was living and working there nearly full-time, roughly two years after buying the place.

* * *

WITH HIS VARIOUS collections now on display across BION Island, he loved to show off his extraordinary and eccentric estate to guests. With Hitler stirring up conflict in Europe, it wasn't an ideal time for overseas passenger travel anyway, which meant Ripley couldn't venture too far abroad. He tried to take at least one long vacation each summer (usually with Oakie), but scaled back from his two or three global trips a year, and was forced to stay away from Europe and parts of Asia. He compensated by displaying some of the world's weird artifacts on his private island, reminders of previous adventures that helped him relive life on the road.

In 1937, he visited Alaska, then stopped at Ye Olde Curiosity Shop in Seattle, where he spent $1,000 on more BION decorations, including totem poles and a "man-eating" clamshell. He decorated his island with Buddha sculptures, Japanese bells, African idols, and covered nearly every inch of floor space in thick rugs from India, China, Turkey, and Persia. (Ripley's feet frequently ached and swelled, and he preferred to walk barefoot across rug-draped floors). Oakie helped fill rooms with velvet-covered chairs and a hodgepodge of dark-wood, hand-carved furniture. Walls bristled with weapons—spears, masks, torture devices, and pieces of armor—giving the house a medieval warlord motif. Here and there, Ripley added sentimental touches. In addition to the ridgepole hanging above the bar, he had purchased the front door from his childhood home, handmade by his father and with the metal numbers of his old street address still attached. He installed it as the entrance to his bedroom.

On weekends, he'd invite friends, employees, newsmen, sports stars, and celebrities to his island. He hosted swimming, boating, and seafood feasts in summer, ice-skating and bonfires in winter. His brother and a carpenter built a new bar in the boathouse, and Ripley purchased (or relieved from storage) boats to use on his pond, including a sealskin kayak from his Alaska trip, a boat of woven reeds from India, a dugout canoe from Peru, and a circular guffa boat from Iraq. Columnist O. O. McIntyre, after a weekend ride in a guffa, raved about Ripley's "moated castle."

Guests lingered in the low-ceilinged basement bar, cool and dark as an Irish pub, where Ripley happily played barkeep. He stocked the bar with fine wines from California, many of them sent by the mayor of Santa Rosa. He'd serve drinks beneath the flags of countries he'd visited, scores of them dangling from the walls. Shelves were cluttered with unusual souvenirs, sheep's bells and bullwhips, a collection of rare goblets, steins and tankards, a narwhal tusk, and the dried penis of a whale. When guests asked what *that* was, Ripley would explain, "Let's just say it was very dear to the whale." When the mayor of Hell, Norway, passed through New York, Ripley threw him a party and hired waiters dressed as monks to serve hell-themed dishes like deviled eggs and sizzling meats.

In one rock-walled, grotto-like basement room, which was off-limits to most visitors, he displayed his erotica: pictures, statues, books, and carvings from around the world. One visitor described the collection as "ranging from the revolting to the exquisitely executed." In this dimly lit room he also stowed a few of the gruesome photographs he'd acquired over the years—men being tortured in China, elephantiasis victims in Africa.

He began collecting pets, too. His first dog, a cocker spaniel named Dokie (as in *okie-dokie*), had been joined by Suzy the Dalmatian; Flash the collie; Sin and Virtue, both spaniels; and others. Some visitors observed that Ripley seemed more at ease with his animals than his guests.

HIS KOOKY HOME became his primary workplace, where six to ten employees tended to the Believe It or Not realm. For nearly thirty years he had worked in either a newspaper office, his NYAC apartment, or hotel rooms and cruise-ship cabins. By 1937, he had developed a new set of work routines.

Before eating or even dressing, he'd begin drawing cartoons at dawn in the spacious studio he created on the top floor. Barefoot and clad in a kimono, he worked feverishly to catch up on his quota of cartoons. By late morning, with a few sketches completed, he'd eat a light breakfast in the massive kitchen, where he employed two full-time chefs from China. (He favored oxtail soup.) Then he'd return to the studio with snacks and work until dusk, while staffers scurried around on the floors below. In warm weather, he kept the studio windows open and scattered nuts and cracked corn on the sill to attract squirrels, chipmunks, and birds. On midday walks around the island, he always kept a stash of nuts in his pockets, to feed the rodents.

Norbert Pearlroth still worked at the New York Public Library and would send *Believe It or Not* ideas to the island. Robert Hyland continued to work as Ripley's financial manager, Dick Hyman as publicist, and Joe Simpson as traveling secretary, while C. C. Pyle oversaw the Odditoriums, and Doug Storer managed his radio shows. Ripley's domestic staff included a personal assistant named Mac, Joe the chauffeur, Barry the gardener, Elinor the housekeeper, and his chief secretary, Cygna Conly, the speed-talker featured in cartoons and on the air. Another ten employees worked at the King Features offices in New York, managing the daily deluge of mail.

Ripley's brother, Doug, was now a full-time fixture in Believe It or Not, Inc. He'd spent a few years living in New York after Ripley first lured him away from his cabin in the Appalachian hills of Ohio. Now living at BION Island, he preferred working with his hands, fixing things or assisting the carpenter or gardener, but Ripley kept giving him business duties, such as delivering cartoons into New York. Doug was a quiet, moody presence among the others, seemingly immune to his hardworking brother's work habits and more at ease with the household staff than the newsmen. He drank a lot—sometimes even more than Ripley—and occasionally scuffled with King Features staffers. He developed an especially scrappy relationship with Ripley's boss, Joe Connolly, a regular visitor to BION Island. Doug once called Connolly a "freeloader" and kicked him off the island. Connolly retaliated by barring him from Hearst's offices in New York.

Ripley usually defended Doug, trying to make good on his long-ago promise to their mother. He must have sensed Doug's unease amid the hubbub of his celebrity lifestyle. When Ripley got permission to build a pier off the island, he bought Doug a yacht, and Doug would disappear for days at a time, motoring all over Long Island Sound. In time Doug learned to navigate the tricky waters around Manhattan and would shuttle his brother into New York. Some nights Doug would wait at an East Side pier to take Ripley back home, but he'd end up waiting past midnight before realizing his brother wasn't coming. Doug would head back to Mamaroneck alone. He eventually sold the yacht and bought a speedboat.

* * *

AS A DISORGANIZED MANAGER of his own affairs, notorious for running late, losing keys, and forgetting important phone numbers, including his own, Ripley relied on his brother and his staff more than ever. He communicated by intercom, sometimes testily calling downstairs for more paper or ink, food or drink. Employees became the buffer between Ripley and King Features. They stayed in touch with the downtown office by phone or mail, sending requests for more art supplies and arranging for the delivery of Ripley's sketches, which were often behind schedule. Editors wrote back regularly asking Ripley to *please* send more cartoons.

Unlike other big-name cartoonists, Ripley continued to draw

his own sketches. "That's fundamental," he once said. But he had begun to allow other King Features artists to ink the captions. He would send drawings to New York with instructions on how the captions should be arranged. In the coming years, Ripley would turn more artistic duties over to subordinates, even though he would publicly insist that he drew every last cartoon with his own hand.

Despite some tensions caused by Ripley's move to Mamaroneck, Believe It or Not remained a profitable enterprise for King Features, which now sold Ripley's cartoons to hundreds of papers. In late 1937, when Ripley agreed to extend his partnership with Hearst for three more years, Joe Connolly sent a personal note expressing his pride in a partnership that "has been so satisfactory and so personally pleasant to me." As Ripley's most vocal advocate, Connolly used all his resources to promote *Believe It or Not*, instructing reporters and photographers to give coverage to all of Ripley's travels and radio shows.

At a time when he had begun to feel threatened by rivals and competitors, Ripley needed to stay in the public eye.

JOHN HIX, whose cartoons featured unusual historical facts and scientific phenomena, had been nipping at Ripley's heels for a decade. Ripley initially viewed Hix's *Strange As It Seems* as both a blatant knockoff and a sign of flattery.

By the mid-1930s, however, Hix had become a true threat, his cartoon getting picked up by more and more papers. Hix had expanded into comic books and radio, his show closely resembling Ripley's, with curious tales dramatized in reenactments. But Hix wasn't the only competitor. A cartoon called *Screen Oddities* featured odd facts about actors, actresses, and other celebrities. Bernarr Macfadden's *True Story* magazine now reached a circulation of two million, prompting Macfadden to create more stranger-than-fiction offspring: *True Romances, True Ghost Stories, True Detective.* Other knockoff magazines included *Amazing Stories, Weird Tales,* and *Science Wonder Stories.*

Rivalry was advancing on all fronts. The Depression had become a heyday for cartoons, launching such soon-to-be favorites as *Dick Tracy, Flash Gordon, L'il Abner, Prince Valiant,* and *The Gumps.* Many of those cartoons had also earned their own radio shows.

With Hix and other competitors on the radio, in comic books, and in newspapers, Ripley realized he needed to protect his brand at all levels. When he heard about a Massachusetts theater show featuring performers who had appeared in his cartoons, he ·sued, accusing the show of copyright infringement. He also sued the "House of Mirth" carnival and its sideshow, titled "Robert (Believe It or Not) Ripley's Freaks." One act featured men and women of "abnormal sex nature," which Ripley's lawyers called "indecent, lewd, immoral, disgusting." A judge agreed and sent sheriff's deputies to halt the show's railroad cars in Connecticut.

Ripley complained to a *Popular Mechanics* writer that he felt "besieged by lawsuits, taxes, and imitators." One columnist, in a mid-1930s Ripley profile, said, "He has more imitators—some of them extremely good—than any other artist of his type the world ever saw. But there is only one 'Rip.' He combines with the gift of his art that glowing spark of curiosity and the beautiful quality of wonder as no one else ever has."

Despite the competition, *Believe It or Not* continued to inspire boys and artists. When a young Minnesota cartoonist noticed his dog's propensity to eat broken glass and sewing needles, his first thought was Ripley. The boy drew a picture of his dog Spike and mailed it to New York. In early 1937, Ripley published the sketch inside a *Believe It or Not* panel with a caption explaining that C. F. Schulz's dog "eats pins, tacks, screws and razor blades."

Charles F. Schulz, whose ill-mannered dog became the cartoon legend Snoopy, was just fourteen.

AFTER NEARLY THIRTY YEARS of cartooning, Ripley's newspaper panel could feel as constrictive as a cell. He sometimes preferred the excitement of NBC's radio studios at Rockefeller Center over the solo grind of the drawing table. This was partly thanks to Doug Storer, who by 1937 had begun managing Ripley's radio career with brio.

When a successful two-year run with Ozzie and Harriet ended in July of 1937, Storer sought a new sponsor with deeper pockets. He signed with General Foods, which was promoting a new breakfast cereal called Huskies. "Believe It or Not Featuring Robert Ripley" would air over NBC's Red Network.

In addition to Ripley's $3,500 weekly salary, General Foods agreed to fund an annual vacation of eight to thirteen weeks, at $1,500 a week. The thirty-minute show was set to air Friday nights but soon switched to the prime eight p.m. Saturday slot, temporarily easing Ripley's concerns about upstarts and imitators.

Ripley felt restricted by his previous show and had urged Storer to find a more progressive sponsor. He'd developed a sense of the growing power of radio and hoped to take his show in a new direction, attempting more groundbreaking broadcasts from remote locations, such as airing from the Cave of the Winds beneath Niagara Falls, where he would interview the man who in 1928 had soared over the falls inside a huge rubber ball.

Storer encouraged the concept, impressed by Ripley's enthusiasm for radio adventure. In Ripley's view, he *needed* to take risks to keep a step ahead of his rivals. Just before launching his new show, Ripley told a reporter that as a former baseball and handball player, he'd retained a competitive streak. "I take a great delight in competing on the air as a radio artist, not as a cartoonist," he said. "It makes me very happy to be a success in radio, for it's the last thing I'd ever imagine I could do."

His new shows, beginning in mid-1937, featured two types of segments. The first were interviews with Ripley's "living Believe-It-or-Nots"—the blind woman whose sight was restored, the woman who had lived for years inside an iron lung, and the story of a man who survived getting blown by pressurized air through a hole in the roof of an underwater tunnel. The other segments were dramatic reenactments of Ripley's cartoons, including the story of a Mexican man who survived a firing-squad execution and whose scarred flesh still carried the bullets. But Ripley and Storer constantly reached for fresher, weirder ideas, offering to pay the expenses of anyone with a good story who was willing to come to New York and bare their soul on NBC.

Occasionally, Ripley welcomed celebrity guests—Shirley Temple or Somerset Maugham or Lou Gehrig, whom he interviewed within hours of Gehrig's record-breaking two thousandth game. Gehrig accidentally veered off script and said his favorite breakfast cereal was "a big bowl of Wheaties"—a competitor of the show's sponsor. When Ripley invited the mayor of Hell, Norway, onto his show, he proudly persuaded Lorentz Stenvig to state on the air, "It's hotter than Hell in New York!"

Toward the end of the first twenty-six-week season, with a hiatus upcoming in early 1938, Storer convinced Ripley to finally allow a dentist to attempt to fix the offensive teeth that had been a lifelong handicap. Public-speaking lessons had greatly improved Ripley's stuttering, and he rarely went on air anymore without a nerve-calming cup of liquor. But the teeth had continued to mangle certain letters and words.

His dentist felt it wasn't possible to corral them with braces, that Ripley's situation required more drastic measures. He yanked out the front teeth and replanted them at a less disfiguring angle. (Ripley asked not to make them *too* straight, since the imperfection was part of his brand.) After the procedure, his teeth were held in place for weeks by thin wires, and they slowly settled back into the gums. Ripley was soon back on the air, though not without months of pain and discomfort.

One columnist wrote that "the sudden oratorical ease of Robert L. Ripley over the radio is the celebrity accomplishment of the hour . . . He devoted a year to it and now has everything under control."

* * *

RIPLEY'S MOST POPULAR SHOWS were those in which unknown people shared their most personal stories. He reunited a sister and brother born seventy years earlier, allegedly in a set of sextuplets, who hadn't seen each other for twenty-five years. Another show reunited twin sisters who had been separated at birth and adopted by different families. "Marjorie, meet your twin sister Shirley," Ripley said, as the estranged sisters tearfully embraced.

One show featured a couple who got married forty-four years after their original wedding date. They had fought that day, canceled the wedding, and later married others. When their respective spouses died, they found each other again and wed. Ripley also introduced listeners to "The Modern Adam and Eve," who married after the woman was injured in a car accident and the man donated a rib to help surgeons repair her injuries.

It turned out that Ripley was well suited to moderate family reunions and on-air retellings of odd marriages and divorces, of reunited twins and orphans. He was a patient and empathetic interviewer, whether his guests were disfigured or handicapped or from some distant land. As one who had suffered humiliation and loss in his own life, he seemed to understand the discomfort of others. As one who had mingled with all classes, he seemed to possess some reserve of compassion, coming across as gentle and nonjudgmental. Guests responded by speaking honestly and emotionally, as they would decades later with Phil Donahue or Oprah Winfrey.

* * *

IN JULY OF 1938, a pilot named Douglas Corrigan touched down in Ireland after allegedly flying across the Atlantic by accident. Within hours, "Wrong-Way Corrigan," as the press would soon call him, received a call from Doug Storer, and the next night he was live on NBC discussing the Brooklyn-to-Dublin flight with Ripley.

"A fellow can't help it if he gets mixed up, can he?" Corrigan asked Ripley.

A month later, Ripley hosted an even more memorable show starring an Indian "mystic" named Kuda Bux, known for performing such stunts as firing a gun at targets with his eyes taped shut. Storer invited Bux to attempt a far more impressive stunt: to walk barefoot across a bed of flaming coals.

Workers dug two ten-foot ditches in a parking lot beside Radio City Music Hall, filling them with bags of charcoal topped by stacks of oak wood. By the next night, the fiery coals had reached 1,400 degrees. Thousands of onlookers crowded around the site as ambulances and fire trucks stood by. From his studio high above the fire pits, Ripley explained to listeners: "In my travels to the Orient, I have always been fascinated by the unexplainable miracles that the holy men of India perform."

As Bux removed his shoes and rolled up his pant legs, some in the crowd covered their ears or pinched their noses, afraid to hear or smell burning flesh. Ripley signed off briefly and descended from Rockefeller Center to street level. Announcer Graham McNamee took over the play-by-play, describing "red-hot coals that shine brightly in the night," and then excitedly announcing Ripley's approach. "The crowd is milling about now . . . the cameras are grinding," he enthused. "And, O-*ho*! Here comes Bob Ripley. He has a police escort and he's getting nearer; he's fighting through the crowd and here he comes!"

When Ripley took the microphone, he described Bux as "completely cool and unruffled." A team of doctors—New York's health commissioner; a skin specialist; and Doug Storer's father, a doctor—examined Bux's feet to make sure there were no abnormal calluses or chemical coatings, and pronounced his feet to be normal. Then, before anyone could stop him, the diminutive man in the turban scampered through the smoking-red pits, hiking his pant legs and sinking ankle-deep in glowing coals. When the sluggish cameramen realized they'd missed the money shot, they encouraged Bux to "do it again, do it again." So he did.

Afterward, doctors found a small burn where a coal had become embedded in his heel, but otherwise no scars. Bux's body temperature was normal and he seemed pain-free. Ripley called it "the most amazing thing I have ever seen."

When the crowd and the cameramen settled down, Ripley sat beside Bux and asked the obvious question—*How?*

"It is faith, Mr. Ripley," replied Kuda Bux. "It is faith I have that allows me to do it."

"Well, Kuda Bux, it must be faith," said Ripley. "Because

that fire was so hot that none of us here could get within three feet of it."

MONTHS LATER, radio listeners tuned in for a Halloween-night drama by Orson Welles on WABC. In a reenactment of H. G. Wells's *The War of the Worlds,* fake newscasters read mock news flashes about aliens landing in metal cylinders in New Jersey and tentacled Martians killing residents with death rays. Across the New York metropolis, people ran from their homes, fleeing to parks and police stations, believing America was under attack, despite the three (albeit brief) announcements that the performance was fictional.

Already edgy from a recent hurricane that had ravaged New York and New England, radio listeners were furious, accusing Welles of intentionally causing a panic. Welles weathered the outrage, which helped launch his career. But he'd upped the ante in the game of bold radio achievement.

Radio had become America's favorite pastime, the nightly schedule packed with plays and music, comedy and baseball. At the time of Welles's headline-grabbing feat, however, Ripley was no longer in the game. He had lost his radio show weeks before.

Two years earlier, Ripley's *Baker's Broadcast* with Ozzie and Harriet had been one of America's favorite shows, in league with the top-ranked shows of Jack Benny and Bing Crosby. But his Huskies-sponsored program had struggled to find an audience. Its initial Saturday-night success in 1937 slumped when General Foods moved the show to Tuesdays. When the show switched to Mondays, ratings dipped further and his sponsor pulled the plug.

He was still earning a mid-six-figures income, but he hated to be off the air when John Hix and other cartoonists *were* on the air. Cartoons and comic strips had continued to infiltrate American culture, becoming what *Fortune* magazine described as America's "adult dream life." *Action Comics* had debuted in mid-1938, its cover dominated by a flying strongman called "Superman." *Believe It or Not* had changed little over the years, and Ripley worried constantly that the whole concept might grow stale. He was desperate to find more stunts like the Kuda Bux show to keep things fresh.

In December of that year, Ripley celebrated his cartoon's twentieth anniversary. Though the original hadn't been called *Believe It or Not* and was a sporadic feature until the mid-1920s, King Features had established 1918 as its birthday. The syndicate ran commemorative ads, prompting an outpouring of celebrity telegrams. Babe Ruth wrote that he "learned a lot of things from following [Ripley's] work" and Kate Smith sent congratulations to "my favorite cartoonist." Rube Goldberg, noting that they had both been Hy Baggerly's trainees in San Francisco, wrote: "I believe Ripley has done more for the profession of cartooning than any one man in our time. May his great influence for good both in the entertainment and educational worlds continue for many years to come."

But his entertaining influence seemed to be waning, and Ripley the pioneer ended the year searching for a new radio sponsor, only to find potential advertisers skittish as Europe edged closer to war. Normally, during times of stress and anxiety, he'd hit the road and attempt to outrun his troubles. But it was not a promising time for world travel. Indeed, America was about to clamp shut, caging Ripley like an animal and separating him from his playground.

CHAPTER

18

In early 1939, the planet seemed to be at war with itself. Civil war raged in Spain. Thirty thousand were killed in a Chilean earthquake. Ripley's favorite country, China, was now eighteen months into full-on bloody warfare with Japan. Germany had taken over parts of Czechoslovakia and was planning to invade Poland, while Italy was planning an attack on Albania. These were dark days for world travelers.

Unable to cross the Atlantic or Pacific, Ripley and Oakie started the New Year in the Caribbean, having sailed there just before the holidays for a month-long escape. Ripley wanted to see the tribe on the San Blas Islands off Panama that celebrated Christmas with cockfights, adding San Blas to the list of countries he'd visited, even though it wasn't really a country. (San Blas, later renamed Kana Yula, was an autonomous territory and part of Panama.)

Still, *Time* magazine dutifully reported that "buck-toothed Ripley" had visited two hundred nations and was now "more widely traveled than Marco Polo, Magellan, and any other human being that ever lived." By Ripley's count, he needed to visit thirty more countries to have visited them all.

After Panama, Ripley and Oakie visited Haiti and Jamaica, where he received an urgent telegram from Doug Storer. By phone, Storer told Ripley that he had finally found a sponsor for a new weekly *Believe It or Not* program, starting in March 1939. Due to a muffled connection, Ripley thought his sponsor was Coca-Cola, and he and Oakie spent the next few days celebrating with rum and Cokes. Ripley wouldn't learn until arriving back in New York that his sponsor was actually Nehi Corporation's *Royal Crown* Cola. He was hardly disappointed, however, when he learned that he'd be paid $7,500 per show.

By now, Ripley had entrusted Storer with more duties. In his role as agent, adviser, and personal manager, Storer had negotiated other deals to keep Ripley busy—endorsements and magazine ads in which Ripley (despite Hearst's earlier warning) would lease his name and drawings to Macmillan Oil Company, Flexo Tray ice-cube trays, Parker Pen Company, Gillette razors, and Realsilk socks. Even better, Storer was in discussions with Twentieth Century Fox, which wanted to produce half a dozen short Movietone films about Ripley's travels, netting Ripley $3,000 per film.

Storer even managed to score Ripley a college diploma, convincing his alma mater, Dartmouth College, to give Ripley an honorary degree recognizing his "artistic contributions." Weeks later, Ripley the high school dropout received an honorary *doctorate* from Missouri Valley College, and president Thomas Bibb's proclamation read like a eulogy, touting "Ripley's contributions to human knowledge; his stimulation of widespread interest in science, history, literature, and the arts . . . and his own achievements in overcoming personal handicaps to become one of America's and the world's best-known and best-liked personalities."

After the ceremony, Ripley somberly shared with a reporter his concerns that the world had become "topsy turvy . . . a very difficult world of depression, millions of unemployed, the outlook is not very encouraging I will admit."

When the reporter asked Ripley to describe the most unusual thing he'd ever seen, Ripley said he hadn't seen it yet: "If I had, I would lose my ambitions and I would not travel any more."

* * *

WITH THE DOOR closing on overseas travel, Ripley decided a key feature of his new radio show would be "on-the-spot" broadcasts from remote locations, allowing him to explore more of his own country. He was ready, for a change, to see America.

One of his first *See America First with Bob Ripley* shows took place deep inside New Mexico's Carlsbad Caverns in the summer of 1939. Engineers unspooled a thousand feet of electrical and audio cable to allow Ripley to conduct a live interview with Jim White, the man who discovered the caverns in 1901.

"I am now speaking to you from 750 feet below the surface of the earth, from the most inspiring place of beauty in the world," Ripley reported. A Fox film crew recorded the event for one of Ripley's Movietone films, and a *Look* magazine photographer snapped pictures. Back in New York, B. A. Rolfe called it "one of the most thrilling broadcasts ever heard" and NBC estimated that twenty million listeners tuned in.

Seeing more of America awakened Ripley's patriotism and public spirit, and he began donating time and money to an increasing number of charity events and humanitarian organizations, such as the Finnish Relief Fund, established by Herbert Hoover to assist Finland after an attack by Stalin's Red Army.

But his favorite charities remained orphan groups, youth organizations, and scout troops.

In mid-1939, to raise money for the Boys Club of New York, he co-hosted a charity softball game at Madison Square Garden, serving as captain of the celebrity-packed "Believe It or Nots" team, which included Babe Ruth, Jack Dempsey, Rube Goldberg, and Jimmy Durante. The opposing "Nine Old Men" team, captained by writer/broadcaster Lowell Thomas, included Walter Winchell and boxer Gene Tunney. A crowd of fourteen thousand watched Ripley's team emerge from the dugout wearing comically baggy uniforms of pantaloons and turbans. The *New York Times* said Ripley and Bugs Baer "looked entirely out of place and most uncomfortable."

Ripley, in a reprise of his bush league days, pitched the first two innings. He gave up two runs, but Babe Ruth swatted their team to a 7–2 lead. Frequent interruptions for "refreshments" in the dugout caused the crowd to grow restless, and the umpire, New York mayor Fiorello La Guardia, called the game after four innings. The *Times* said the event raised $12,000 for the Boys Club and "a grand time was had by all."

✸ ✳ ✾

WHEN IT CAME TO GIRLS, meanwhile, he associated with a very different kind of club—the deformed, the disfigured, the armless and/or legless.

Ripley's traveling Odditorium show had visited half a dozen cities in recent years, and in 1939 his cast of entertainers was called upon to appear in *two* Odditoriums at once. C. C. Pyle put together an exhibition for the upcoming Golden Gate International Exposition in San Francisco, at the same time organizing an even bigger show for New York's 1939 World's Fair. Ripley was looking forward to having Odditoriums on both coasts.

Two weeks before the San Francisco fair opened, Pyle suffered a stroke at his Los Angeles home. The fifty-six-year-old showman hadn't finished setting up the two Odditoriums and his partner struggled to launch both shows simultaneously.

Ripley then learned that New York officials decided they didn't need his Odditorium after all. Lurking behind this last-minute decision was Lou Dufour, who after the 1933–34 Chicago fair had vowed to exact revenge on C. C. Pyle. Dufour felt he deserved more than the $10,000 he received for helping Pyle fix his ailing show in Chicago, and had promised to "get my compensation in some other manner."

That day had come. Dufour partnered with John Hix to produce a "Strange As It Seems Show" and museum, a near replica of Ripley's Odditorium, replete with razor-blade eaters and contortionists. Hix soon launched a new CBS radio show too. A *New Yorker* magazine profile of Dufour that summer referred to Hix as "Ripley's bustling young rival," and said Ripley was "peeved by the affront to his prestige."

With performers and exhibits already lined up for the New York fair, Ripley decided to create his first *permanent* Odditorium in a vacant restaurant building at Forty-eighth Street and Broadway. There, he would present exhibits from his personal collection on the ground floor, and live performers on a second-floor rotating stage.

Ripley and an investor sank $2 million into renovating the building and creating display cases for his collection of curiosities, including shrunken heads, a box made of human skin, the lifelike Masakichi sculpture, and the shoes of the world's tallest man, Robert Wadlow.

Huge neon signs hung off both sides of the corner building, welcoming visitors to Ripley's "exhibit of curioddities from 200 countries" and "40 living Ripley radio oddities." For the grand opening, a piano player named Bill Hajak sat out front, insisting he'd play nonstop for a month. He lasted two weeks, setting a world's record for marathon piano playing, but quit after missing his daughter's birth. Inside, sword swallowers, glass eaters, superhuman contortionists, and unfortunates with physical deformities performed their acts of self-mutilation or pseudo-torture from noon until one a.m.

Shortly after the grand opening, though, the crowds thinned and the museum began to falter. Busy with cartoon and radio duties, Ripley had turned the museum over to his financial manager, Robert Hyland, and his brother, Doug, whose blue-collar skills didn't translate to running a business.

Shy and solitary, Doug drank to find courage in social settings. Too often he crossed the line. He frequently scuffled with Robert Hyland over management of the Odditorium, and Hyland accused Doug of always being late and/or drunk. Hyland hired his teenage son to pick up the slack, but his son and Doug regularly argued and often came close to blows. Patrons sometimes overheard the shouting, and Ripley's financial partner started asking why he hadn't seen any returns. By the fall, other creditors came knocking, and the Odditorium, $100,000 in debt, seemed headed toward insolvency.

The only good news in the whole mess was that Hix's World's Fair exhibition also flopped. Fair organizers invited Ripley to replace Hix and bring a *Believe It or Not* show to the fair's second season, in 1940. The San Francisco fair also planned an encore season in 1940 and invited Ripley back as well. This time, Ripley would put Pyle's partner, Frank Zambreno, in charge of both Odditoriums. Even in death, Pyle found a way to make money for Ripley.

* * *

AS HIS BROADWAY MUSEUM floundered, Ripley fled, making a trip in early 1940 to the only countries still safe enough to visit. He and Oakie covered ten thousand miles during three weeks in South and Central America, then joined Herbert Hoover on a tour through the southern United States to raise money for the Finnish Relief Fund. At each stop Ripley showed movies of his recent travels and tribal masks he'd purchased in Brazil and Mexico.

His restlessness inflamed, Ripley asked Storer to expand the *See America First with Bob Ripley* radio series and strive for even more technically complex broadcasts from remote corners of the nation. Ripley even announced plans to take his on-the-spot broadcasts to Europe and South America, that he would start sending shortwave radio reports from war zones and even the North and South Poles. More realistically, Storer reached an agreement with the Department of the Interior to begin touring America's national parks, starting in the summer of 1940 with trips to the Grand Canyon and Yellowstone.

But first, Ripley and Storer took their *See America* show to Florida.

Marineland, the world's first "oceanarium," had opened two years earlier in St. Augustine and quickly became one of Florida's most popular tourist destinations. Ripley's crew arrived with plans to broadcast part of the show underwater. Ripley fed a couple porpoises, which leapt out of the water to snatch fish from his hand, then milked a female porpoise that was lifted from the water in a webbed harness. A Marineland attendant had to cut a harness strap so Ripley could reach his hand around the porpoise's teat, but in doing so accidentally cut the porpoise. A spurt of blood splattered onto Ripley's diving suit.

Next, Ripley put on a huge diving helmet, which fit over the headphones and microphone that would allow him to broadcast from a huge pool containing sharks and porpoises. Burdened by the cumbersome suit and helmet, Ripley and a Marineland expert slowly descended to the bottom of the pool. Ripley had grumbled about this stunt all day. He was not a good swimmer and was anxious about speaking on the air without a script. One of his writers quickly prepared a few remarks, but Ripley snapped, "How do you expect me to read underwater!"

On the floor of the pool, Ripley and his attendant, a professional diver, tried to feed a pair of sharks, using a long stick to shove dead mullets into their mouths. For some reason, the sharks weren't interested. They began circling Ripley and one shark bumped him backward onto his butt. The diver grabbed Ripley's arm and dragged him to the stairs, where he was pulled from the water. The diver figured the sharks must have picked up the scent of porpoise blood on Ripley's suit. The experience frightened and infuriated Ripley, but the show was a thrilling hit.

His encounter with a hungry shark did little to dampen Ripley's intrepidness. When he heard about a snake and alligator farm at Silver Springs, Florida, he wired his New York office: "Change next week's schedule." He wanted to milk a rattlesnake on the air. He moved the radio team inland, where he began his broadcast on a boat with Ross Allen, founder of the Silver Springs Reptile Institute. "Don't be frightened by that noise you hear in the background," Ripley told listeners. "It is just the bellowing of the alligators, who are all excited by this broadcast from their homeland!" He then described how, moments earlier, Allen had dived into the Silver River to wrestle a ten-foot alligator.

"Ross, how did you conquer that alligator?" he asked Allen, who stood beside him still dripping in his swim trunks.

"I tired him out," Allen said. "You've just got to understand them."

Allen and Ripley next climbed down a ladder into a pit slithering with five hundred poisonous snakes. The plan was for Allen to grab a rattlesnake and show Ripley how to "milk" it and collect its venom. Ripley wore thick rubber boots, while Allen remained barefoot.

"Nervous, Bob?" Allen asked.

According to the script, Ripley was supposed to say that after man-eating sharks and deadly snakes, "these *Believe It or Not* programs will be the end of me yet." He didn't get the chance. Just as he and Ross lowered themselves into the pit, the lights went out.

"Let's get the hell outa here!" Allen yelled, his words barely audible over the air. (Allen later found that muskrats had chewed into the wiring.)

He and Ripley fumbled their way out of the pit, and Ripley managed to turn the show over to his New York studio.

"Take it away, B. A. Rolfe!" he ad-libbed.

After the sunny Florida broadcasts, Ripley returned to BION Island, which was immediately slammed by an ice storm that turned every surface into an icicle. For days Ripley and his staff lived without heat or electricity, warming the mansion by keeping the fireplaces stoked. As was usually the case when confronted with adversity, Ripley was dazzled by the freak storm, walking childlike and wide-eyed around the island with his dogs, filming the surreal, glimmering beauty.

People frequently disappointed him—women, employees, even his brother—but nature, and his dogs, rarely let him down.

* * *

IN MAY OF 1940, a special railroad car was attached to the back of the *20th Century Limited* and the *Believe It or Not* radio crew rolled west for a month-long tour. (Instead of Oakie, Ripley brought along a new Japanese girlfriend.) The highlight would be a broadcast from the bottom of the Grand Canyon. To achieve this, engineers would have to transmit the audio signal up to the canyon rim, send it along the nearest town's lone telephone line, then relay the show to ninety-two CBS stations.

Crew members grumbled that the whole idea was nuts, even as they marveled at Ripley's willingness to attempt the impossible. It took thirty mules to carry actors, writers, guides, and two thousand pounds of equipment down the seven-mile trail to the canyon floor. Ripley, in cowboy garb atop a white mule, kept waving his hat and yelling *yee-haw*. The crew was divided into thirds. One group would set up a dramatization around a fire pit, using local cowboys as actors. Another crew would record the sounds of the Colorado River, using a boom microphone stretched over the water.

The third and most complicated piece of the broadcast was a live report from a river guide as he shot through a section of rapids. Emery Kolb had been navigating the river for decades, but rarely at night, and never with expensive radio gear. Kolb suggested to Doug Storer that they hire an announcer to accompany him and operate the shortwave radio. Ripley grew concerned when he saw the announcer Storer had chosen: six-foot-two and over two hundred pounds.

"Why didn't they send a little guy?" Ripley grumbled. "This fellow will sink the boat."

Thus was Ripley introduced to a young department store manager and aspiring Phoenix politician named Barry Goldwater.

The first half of the show went according to plan. But during the shoot-the-rapids sequence, Goldwater and Kolb missed the flash of a lantern that was to be their signal to start downstream. As per the backup plan, they started rowing at what they believed to be the correct time. Ripley and his engineers waited to hear Goldwater describing the rapids, but at first all they heard was a police dispatcher asking fellow officers to be on the lookout for a stolen green Chevrolet—the radio signals had gotten crossed. Fifteen long seconds later, Goldwater's voice came through, but his report was brief. Water had begun slopping over the gunwales, threatening to short-circuit the equipment and sink the boat. Goldwater reacted quickly. "Take it away, Bob," he said. "I can't talk. I have to bail."

Ripley picked up the description of the moonlit action, but in doing so missed his own cue to throw a rope out to the boat, which swept past the sandbar where it was supposed to pull out. Ripley watched helplessly as Goldwater and Kolb rolled farther downstream.

ℰ BELIEVE IT! ℰ

Five months later, Goldwater joined pioneering river-runner Norman Nevills on the first-ever commercial paddling trip through the Grand Canyon. Goldwater wrote to tell Ripley about it, and Ripley invited him to New York. The two men hit it off (like Ripley, Goldwater was a foe of Roosevelt's New Deal), and Ripley encouraged Goldwater to use his photographs to create a slide show and lecture. While delivering his travelogue presentation to packed audiences, Goldwater discovered a knack for public speaking and, after serving as a pilot in World War II, entered politics, eventually making his run for the presidency of the United States.

✴ ✳ ✴

AFTER A MONTH on the road, the *See America* train returned east, stopping in Birmingham, Alabama, for another unique broadcast, from the National Air Races.

"Ladies and gentlemen. Now I shall present a *Believe It or Not* which has never been done on the air before," Ripley announced at the start of the show. "Jack Huber is a young man who will make a parachute jump of twelve thousand feet—almost two and one half miles—and actually describe his sensations to you as he falls."

Storer had convinced Huber, a Hollywood stuntman, to jump from a plane with a clunky twenty-pound radio transmitter strapped to his chest. Later, no one could ever say for sure whether Huber actually "spoke" during his 160-mile-an-hour plummet to earth. All that listeners across America heard was the muffled shush-and-whistle of air whipping across the microphone attached to his harness. One reason for Huber's lack of commentary was that his main parachute failed to open and ripped away from the harness. Unknown to those in Radioland, Huber spent a few terrifying moments plummeting toward his death until his backup chute finally bloomed open.

Even with his backup chute, Huber had lost altitude and slammed into the ground. His wife, watching nearby, burst into tears as an ambulance sped toward the drop zone. Doug Storer got there first and found Huber slumped at the edge of the field, certain that the daredevil was dead.

Ripley, back at the makeshift studio, improvised: "You have just heard, in his own words, Jack Huber's sensations as he made a twelve-thousand-foot parachute drop . . . And I must say that I, for one, never heard a more thrilling description in my life." Ripley announced that at any moment Huber would be on the air "to prove that he landed safely, and that all is well." Storer was relieved to find that all actually *was* well—Huber was alive, having only had the wind knocked out of him.

* * *

BY NOW, Ripley's Odditorium on Broadway was in its death throes. Doug Ripley and Robert Hyland had tried to revitalize the show with a two-headed baby from Sumatra, but the deal fell through and attendance slumped further. Ripley's main investor sued, forcing the money-losing venture toward closure. The museum's parent company, International Oddities, of which Doug Ripley was president, would soon file for bankruptcy.

When Hyland learned that a sheriff's deputy was planning to confiscate Ripley's collectibles, he asked Doug to intercept the officer and stall while he secreted Ripley's valuables out the back and into a moving van. Doug helped by getting the officer drunk, giving Hyland enough time to deliver Ripley's stuff back to BION Island.

Ripley had been anxious during his museum's final weeks, terrified that the papers would write about the biggest financial flop of his career. He blamed Hyland for mismanaging the enterprise but defended his brother, bringing an end to his longtime friendship with Hyland, who quit.

The Odditoriums at the San Francisco and New York World's Fairs, meanwhile, had performed surprisingly well. Yet, by the time those shows closed in the fall of 1940, fewer Americans were in the mood for that type of entertainment. Freaky sideshows had been a welcome diversion during the Depression but now seemed out of place at the troubled start of a new decade.

* * *

ON OCTOBER 30, 1940, a farmer living on an island in the Bahamas watched a small wooden boat wash ashore. Inside, he found two emaciated and disoriented men, sailors from a British cargo ship that had been sunk by German torpedoes off the coast of Africa.

Germans had strafed the ship's life rafts but seven crewmen, including Roy Widdicombe and Robert Tapscott, escaped in an eighteen-foot "jolly boat." Their craft contained just a few portions of food and water. Within a week, four men died. A week later Widdicombe wrote in a journal, "2nd cook goes mad dies. Two of us left." Rainstorms provided some drinking water, but the food ran out and Widdicombe broke his teeth trying to eat a shoe. In one log entry he wrote: "Getting very weak but trusting in God to pull us through." Days later: "All water and biscuits gone but still hoping to make land."

That was the final journal entry. Five weeks later, the farmer found Widdicombe and Tapscott on his beach, nearly three thousand miles from where their ship sank. When they recovered enough to speak, the men explained that flying fish had landed in the boat one day to provide nourishment. Small bits of seaweed helped too, but they often went days without water, sliding in and out of consciousness. Widdicombe lost eighty pounds, Tapscott lost sixty. Both were severely sunburned. Doctors called it a miracle that they'd survived.

When Doug Storer heard the story, he immediately made plans for a live broadcast from the Bahamas. He, Ripley, Oakie, and a technical crew flew to Nassau to set up the show. While getting his script approved by Bahamian officials, Storer was introduced to the former king of England. Now known as the duke of Windsor, Prince Edward had been sent to the Bahamas to serve as governor after abdicating his throne to marry an American divorcée.

The day before the broadcast, the duke unexpectedly offered to join the show—a potential coup for Ripley and Storer, since

the ex-king had never spoken on commercial radio. His partici-
pation remained uncertain until just hours before airtime due to
CBS concerns about Rolfe's orchestra, stationed in New York,
playing both "The Star-Spangled Banner" and "God Save the
Queen." CBS didn't want to give the appearance that the United
States was allied with England, now at war with Germany. The
duke learned about CBS's concerns (Storer suspected his phone
had been tapped) and offered to withdraw, but Storer begged
him not to cancel. Hours before the show, Ripley paced his hotel
room in a loose robe that kept flapping open, unconcerned that
he was flashing Storer's former secretary, Hazel, who had become Storer's wife.

"You're crazy," he kept telling Storer. "He'll never do it."

The broadcast began that night at ten o'clock in the ball-
room of the Royal Victoria Hotel. After Ripley interviewed Widdicombe and Tapscott about their ordeal at sea, and the two men
gamely answered questions about the slow deaths of their crew-
mates, the duke approached the microphone. He read a brief
prepared speech, calling the sailors' journey "an extraordinary
adventure up to the standard of Mr. Ripley's famous feature."
The show was rebroadcast to ninety stations across North America, and the next day's papers were filled with reports about the
biggest scoop of Ripley's radio career.

☜ BELIEVE IT! ☞

*Widdicombe would not enjoy his miraculously spared life for
long. After recovering, he traveled to New York, then sailed
toward England to reunite with his wife and child. With
Liverpool in sight, Widdicombe's ship was torpedoed and sunk.
All were killed. Tapscott recovered and enlisted in the Canadian
Air Force, then rejoined the Merchant Marine. He served at sea*

for twenty years, until his premature death at age forty-two. Hellmuth von Ruckteschell, the captain of the German ship that had attacked Widdicombe and Tapscott's ship, was convicted of war crimes and died in prison.

Satisfied with the publicity, Ripley and Oakie left the Bahamas the next morning for a seaplane ride to the island of San Salvador, to tour the site where Columbus allegedly landed in the New World, believing he'd circled the earth and reached Asia.

But for Ripley and Oakie, it would be their last adventure together. As they would learn within a few months, Oakie was sick. Incurably so.

✳ ✳ ✳

AS 1940 WOUND DOWN, Ripley must have exhaled, having survived a year of tumult. Threatened by rivals such as Hix and enduring the financial distress of his Odditorium failure, he never slowed down, and in fact kept pushing himself further, always striving to reinvigorate his oft-mimicked brand.

That fall he earned a glowing two-part profile in the prestigious fifteen-year-old *New Yorker* magazine, whose writer, Geoffrey Hellman, summarized the Ripley legend and touted the cartoonist's astronomical wealth, his $500,000-plus annual income, the thirty annual lectures at $1,000 a *pop*. Hellman rehashed vignettes of Ripley's charmed career, like the time he fell into an orchestra pit during a lecture, couldn't find the stairs, and had to exit the theater and pay admission to reenter . . . or the time a group of Nicaraguan kids chased him down Managua's streets shouting, *"Reep-lee! Reep-lee!"*

A late-1940 Advertising Research Foundation survey found

that *Believe It or Not* had become the second most popular newspaper feature. Only the front page was of more interest to readers. Ripley had survived imitators' threats, lovers' lawsuits, and risky radio shows.

Now he had to find a way to keep his career alive through another world war.

CHAPTER

19

Though frustrated by the global wartime travel limitations, Ripley managed to transfer some of his excess energy into further sprucing up BION Island and hosting his increasingly audacious parties. Among the many impressive skills the once-shy cartoonist had developed was the ability to throw a bash. In New York he emceed star-studded galas for politicians, sports stars, military leaders, and visiting royalty, from Malaysian princesses to Spanish and Portuguese counts. On BION Island, he entertained as if ringmaster of his own circus.

At scores of dinners, luncheons, barbecues, wedding showers, and even christenings, he spent freely on the best food, drink, and entertainment. For summer cookouts he'd have six chefs grilling meats and seafood while magicians or musicians entertained the crowd, including his lovely new accordion-playing friend, Gypsy Markoff. Sometimes Bugs Baer would entertain guests with ad-lib comedy routines, and Ripley was always ready to initiate a game of softball or badminton or a dance on the outdoor dance floor. Any holiday was reason enough for a party—St. Patrick's Day, the Fourth of July, Chinese New

Year. Ripley loved to hustle around, bossing his staff, introducing guests to one another, giving speeches and toasts.

Not every party went according to plan. Ripley once invited newsmen to honor a seventy-year-old bride and her twenty-four-year-old husband, whom he'd featured in a radio show. He forgot it was his kitchen staff's day off, so his housekeeper and gardener had to prepare and serve lunch for thirty. Another time, Ripley invited a Boy Scout troop for a luncheon but neglected to tell the staff, who scrambled to prepare a suitable feast. Then there was the Sunday morning when his brother announced he was marrying his German girlfriend, Crystl, that afternoon at four. Doug preferred a simple affair, but by five his brother had invited guests and launched a fully catered party.

Ripley often strained his staff's tolerance by calling a dozen friends over for impromptu get-togethers or making impulsive plans to roast whole pigs or sides of beef all day on a spit. "Rip never cared for being alone," Doug Storer's wife, Hazel, once said. One housekeeper later said, "I cannot remember a dinner without at least one or two guests . . . one or two *lady* guests."

Ripley had installed a wiring system for lights and an outdoor sound system. During daylong affairs he would make announcements over the loudspeakers before the start of a swimming or boating contest, a softball game, or a toast. Some parties brought a hundred guests or more and Ripley stocked the guest bathrooms with extra bathing suits, slippers, robes, towels, and sun lotion. At larger parties, if anyone drank too much—or, in one case, started a fight—Ripley was quick to enforce order. "Throw that bum out!" he bellowed late one night after a scuffle between guests. "Throw *all* those bums out!"

By 1940, magazine writers and photographers had learned that Ripley's strange abode and massive parties made for good copy. Visitors included *LIFE* magazine (headline: BELIEVE IT OR

NOT: THIS IS WHERE ROBERT L. RIPLEY LIVES), *Radio Guide* (AT HOME WITH RIPLEY), *Liberty* magazine (WHERE A GLOBETROTTER HANGS HIS HAT), and even *Good Housekeeping,* which interviewed his housekeeper (IF YOU WERE HOUSEKEEPER TO MR. RIPLEY).

In the summer of 1940, *LIFE* co-hosted a party at BION featuring a dozen Odditorium performers. Guests arrived in limousines and the day's events were captured in a four-page spread. One photo shows Linda Lee, a singer on Ripley's radio show, pouring a beer beside a sword-swallower in mid-swallow. In another photo, a woman lights a cigarette while sitting on the chest of a man lying on a bed of nails. One particularly creepy picture shows Martin Laurello (The Human Owl) getting a drink at the bar, his head turned gruesomely backward. By afternoon, "the novelty of examining one another's peculiarities had worn off," as *LIFE* put it, and guests went swimming, spun around the pond in Ripley's boats, and played musical chairs. A fire breather tried to cook hot dogs on a skewer.

Also at that party was one of Ripley's heroes, Burton Holmes, who sat in a wheelchair nursing an injured foot. Ripley wheeled Holmes around the island, showing off his totem poles, bronze statues, and his boat collection. During the tour, Holmes mentioned that his injury had lately kept him from enjoying Nirvana, his bi-level apartment beside Manhattan's Central Park. He was thinking of selling the Asian-themed place, which would come fully furnished with artifacts Holmes had collected from the Orient. Holmes wondered: *Was Ripley interested?*

Weeks later, Ripley called from New York to tell his housekeeper, Almuth Seabeck, "I have found the apartment I have been looking for." Ripley's chauffeur delivered Seabeck to Sixty-seventh Street and Central Park West and they spent the afternoon inspecting Holmes's ten-room apartment, the dark hallways, ornate teak molding, two-story living room, and the balcony overlooking Central Park. A week later, Ripley was moving in. Employees dubbed it his "new baby."

Ripley rationalized that he could now work in the city during busy weeks of radio shows and lectures, then spend weekends at BION Island. His staff knew the arrangement would be more complicated than that, and would surely involve extra work for all. Seabeck, a middle-aged woman who had traveled the world before settling in America, had been Ripley's housekeeper since 1938 and had come to predict and even appreciate Ripley's frenetic pace and his antics.

She immediately ordered duplicates of Ripley's favorite clothes—one set for the city, one for the country.

* * *

BUGS BAER and other longtime friends found it astonishing that a man who'd spent so many years living out of a suitcase had become consumed by his domestic surroundings, to the point of obsession. Baer had even begun worrying about Ripley's health now that he'd stopped exercising. "Bob walks twice around that island of his and collapses," Baer told the *New Yorker*, which remarked on Ripley's "increasing tendency toward plumpness."

A doctor tried to impose a diet, but regular parties thwarted doctor's orders. At age fifty—the same age his father died—Ripley had become downright beefy. Though he tried to eat right, preferring vegetables and rice over steak and potatoes, his decade with King Features had enriched him at the expense of his athlete's physique. The youthful obsession with fitness had been fully sacrificed on the altar of fame. The former champion, once touted as someone who "plays handball as well as he draws," hadn't danced across a handball court for a decade, and the effects were mounting—high blood pressure, stress, sleeplessness, and fatigue. He'd previously held a new religious belief in the curative effects of exercise. Now he clung to the hope that if he just kept busy, kept traveling and having fun, he'd outrun his father's fate.

It wasn't just work that prevented Ripley from exercising so much as a transference of obsessions. Instead of good health he'd become fixated on good housekeeping.

Incapable of turning all household duties over to his staff, Ripley could be finicky about the smallest of domestic details. He once grew furious when an actress visited for a weekend at BION Island and clogged the plumbing with her blond hair, calling her "the dirtiest female I have ever known." He constantly relocated furniture and artwork, often redecorating entire rooms on a whim. He would tell a staffer to start working on a remodeling project that seemed important one day, but the next day he'd change his mind, telling the same housekeeper, gardener, or carpenter, "Drop it, it's not important!"

AS A BOY, Ripley once paid a hard-earned nickel for a postcard-sized duplicate of a painting by a Russian artist named Konstantin Makovsky, titled *The Boyar Wedding Feast.* When he couldn't convince his mother or sister to pose, he would sketch the postcard for practice, over and over.

One day, Seabeck found two rolled-up canvases in an attic, one of which appeared to be the original *Wedding Feast.* She framed and hung it in Ripley's New York apartment. The other painting was a portrayal of a Russian nobleman selecting a frightened girl to become his wife. Unaware of Ripley's complex views of wedlock, Seabeck encouraged him to hang *The Choosing of the Bride* in his mansion, and for some reason he decided to devote an entire room to the painting. He had the domed ceiling painted blue, to match the painting, and had the floor tiled in black and white, to match the tiled floor in the painting. When guests entered the room, the effect made it seem as if they were entering the choosing-the-bride scene itself—an oddly sentimental gesture for someone who claimed never to have been in love.

Among his more ambitious projects was digging a tunnel beneath his house, to connect the basement bar to an outdoor rotunda. Workers soon discovered they'd have to blast through bedrock to get the job done, but Ripley gave the go-ahead and put his brother in charge. Crews spent weeks boring into rock with pneumatic drills, setting off small explosives that shook the house and caused spiderweb plaster cracks in the ceilings. The tunnel eventually reached its destination, but was quickly neglected, a rarely used passageway that became a dimly lit space for Ripley to display his collection of tribal masks, which the staff called the Mask Room.

Some visitors didn't understand this need to convert a home into a museum. One writer, after a tour, said that walking through Ripley's house felt "like getting lost in the mummy section of a museum after its been closed for the night. It's just plain creepy."

Creepy or not, people loved to visit BION *and* to be around Ripley, whose quirks of dress and personality could be endlessly entertaining. Ripley had always been an oddball, but his eccentricities seemed to amplify with age. He walked quickly and pigeon-toed, with a slight butt-waggle. He sucked his teeth and twiddled his now-necessary eyeglasses. He wore a small sketch pad on a cord around his neck and was always scribbling ideas or doodling. When someone told him an interesting story, he would pop open his mouth and bug out his eyes in exaggerated astonishment.

After so many years on radio and in film, onstage and before audiences, he had become an unexpectedly adept performer, though he now sometimes performed more than necessary. In social settings, he could be pedantic and a bit of a bore. Some visitors were put off by his know-it-all history lessons, his stories about some artifact he had discovered in Bolivia or Afghanistan or Egypt. "Listening to Bob was sometimes like attending a lecture," Seabeck once said. But longtime friends and employees tolerated Ripley's monologues as fair trade for his vast generosity, for his willingness to turn his home into a carnival for *their* entertainment.

THOUGH GENEROUS and compassionate, Ripley could be atrociously forgetful. B. A. Rolfe once bumped into him on a date with a beautiful blonde, and Ripley pulled Rolfe aside to ask, "Do you know the name of the girl I'm with?" Still, he seemed able to remember anyone who had assisted him along the path to success.

Over the years he had stayed in contact with Carol Ennis, who helped him get his first newspaper job in San Francisco. If he visited San Francisco, he would always treat her to lunch or dinner, and if Ennis visited New York he would make sure she had a chauffeur-driven limousine to squire her around town.

Norbert Pearlroth, though sometimes feeling underappreciated by King Features, remained as devoted as ever to Ripley after twenty years. Pearlroth once mentioned to Ripley his frustration over the cost of his daughter's private-school tuition. The next day, Ripley handed him a $500 check, then another check each of the following six days. When Pearlroth thanked his boss for the $3,500, Ripley said, "Next time ask me something really tough."

Ripley seemed aware of his good fortune, the beam and

front door from his Santa Rosa house reminding him how far he'd come. He always showed guests the original "Champs and Chumps" cartoon hidden behind a backlit mirror above his fireplace, telling them with a gesture toward his paintings, rugs, and furniture, "If it weren't for that [cartoon], these wouldn't be here." He also seemed to feel grateful for the years of support and loyalty of longtime friends, especially Bugs Baer.

While traveling, he would often send postcards to friends, and though he might forget the day of the week he rarely forgot birthdays. He'd send hand-drawn cards, like the one drawn for Baer's fiftieth that showed Baer's head growing out of a long stem, above a caption that read "Long Life to the Half Century Plant."

Ripley frequently invited friends to stay at BION for a night or two, including his King Features boss Joe Connolly, or Doug Storer and his wife, or Vyvyan Donner, who had made him feel so welcome during his first years in New York. (It helped that Donner, as fashion editor for *Movietone News*, often brought along pretty young models.) Donner would laugh at Ripley and Baer, both now past the half-century mark, calling them "overgrown boys." Seabeck the housekeeper noticed that, whether it was softball or drinking, a political argument or girl talk, Ripley and Baer went at it "with the eagerness of two youngsters playing hooky from school."

Maybe to compensate for his abbreviated boyhood—the premature departure from high school and his teenaged entry into the workforce—Ripley performed well in the role of heedless adolescent. He loved to play pranks, such as hiding the nude Masakichi statue in guests' closets and then waiting outside for their shouts of terror.

Friends assumed there was something *chemical* at work, that

Ripley was neurotic and compulsive, perpetually sophomoric and impetuous, that he simply couldn't help himself or control his urges. Empty floor or wall space? It seemed to make him uncomfortable and needed to be filled with a statue or a weapon or a chair or a painting. Uncluttered ledges? The shelves surrounding his bar were now jam-packed with figurines, carved tusks, pistols, tureens, and old currency.

This pathology extended to his collection of pets. He now owned collies, Dalmatians, spaniels, and cats, including a six-toed Manx named Peter who loved to hide under the fridge, waiting for a dog to walk past to attack. Ripley still owned his foulmouthed parrot and had recently obtained a twenty-eight-foot boa constrictor as thick as a Dalmatian.

One weekend, on an early-morning stroll around the island, Joe Connolly practically tripped over the fat snake, named Gertie, who had gotten loose from the pen.

"Don't worry, Joe," Ripley said. "He's a friend of mine."

Though Ripley fed Gertie a steady diet of rabbits, the snake escaped regularly. Baer especially hated Gertie, and Ripley once created a barrier of broken glass around the snake's pen, assuring Baer, "A snake won't cross broken glass."

"Neither will I," Baer replied, vowing not to come back to BION while Gertie was still on the loose. (The snake was later shipped off to a zoo.)

* * *

WHEN HE WASN'T OCCUPIED with his curiosities and his pets, he used BION Island to nurture his nostalgia for the boozy Prohibition-era NYAC/bachelor's lifestyle. He installed beer kegs in the bar so that even during the workweek he and his staff could slip downstairs to draw a cold pint. Whenever

B. A. Rolfe visited, the tubby bandleader would immediately grab a quart-sized tankard from Ripley's collection and insist that it never be allowed to dip toward empty.

Everyday life at BION was like a fraternity party, with a Keystone Kops aspect to the workaday. Ripley's desk was surrounded by file drawers, stacks of papers, reference books, sticks of charcoal, leftover food and drink, and two phones. While drawing he'd reach for a phone to ask a secretary to find some tidbit at the library or call some scholar—or Pearlroth—to verify an elusive fact. He was always falling behind schedule, always late for meetings. Trips to New York escalated into madcap flurries. Thursdays were the worst, since Ripley was due for rehearsals for his Friday-night radio show. Everyone scurried about collecting script pages, cartoons to deliver to King Features, Ripley's glasses, extra clothes for the New York apartment, drawing materials, and maybe a bottle of sherry for the drive south.

Still, Ripley seemed immune to the persistent backlogs, almost amused by the never-ending demands and the sometimes-angry insistence from King Features to "send more cartoons!" At the worst possible moment he would call for a spontaneous softball game or tell staffers to meet on the front lawn to help assemble some new boat he'd ordered from India. He managed to find time for fishing, boating, sunbathing, and afternoon naps. He believed in the healthy effects of a good sweat, and liked to lie in the hot sun, then cool off with a glass of beer. He took steam baths before dinner, and after dessert would lead guests downstairs to the bar for cordials, radio, and conversation. He rarely went to bed before midnight, often ending his night with a drawn-out card game, a glass of milk, or a late-night snack in the kitchen.

Seabeck the housekeeper often complained to Ripley about

his collections of curios "with no place to put them" and about the odors his crates and boxes emitted, especially anything from Tibet, which smelled like "rancid butter." One night Seabeck retired to her bedroom, exhausted as usual. She was about to climb into bed when, with a shriek, she discovered the Masakichi statue tucked beneath her bedcovers.

Over time, Ripley's staff became its own semi-functional family. Years later, friends and staffers would wonder whether the parties and gags, the dog and snakes, were Ripley's way of staving off a festering sadness.

ONE NIGHT IN 1941, the staff sat in the kitchen, drinking and reading aloud from some of the bizarre letters submitted to Ripley's latest contest. They were laughing their heads off when Ripley, who was supposed to be in Central America, walked through the kitchen door with terrible news.

After nearly fifteen years as his most consistent female companion, his traveling partner and not-so-secret lover, Oakie, was dead.

When Oakie had gotten married—sometime in the mid-1930s, though no one seemed sure when or where—Ripley became even more vague with friends about the details of their relationship, though it was hard to ignore that they continued to spend enormous amounts of time in each other's company, on BION Island or touring the world: Morocco, Tripoli, and Libya; Germany, France, and Italy; Mexico, Brazil, and Bermuda. They once visited the Mediterranean island of Djerba, which in Greek mythology had been home to the lethargic Lotus Eaters, whose diet of lotus leaves brought them peace. He and Oakie had plucked a few leaves and fed them to each other, and Ripley declared, "One taste of this plant and man forgets all his troubles."

Over time Oakie had apparently come to accept his particular views of love and fidelity, and she seemed to agree with Ripley that America's moral standards were out of whack. Ripley felt the American preoccupation with monogamy was to blame—the same moralistic fixation that led to Prohibition. "You can't force people *not* to drink," he told one reporter—just as you can't force people to love only one person.

And yet, though he had chosen not to marry her, and allowed her to wed another, he would later confess that Oakie was "the only woman I ever loved." He had assumed she would be his covert love forever. When she succumbed to breast cancer, it clearly rattled him.

In his mourning, Ripley launched himself into a project that he hoped would honor her memory. He began designing a room that he planned to endow to a New York hospital, a place where women suffering from cancer might live during their treatment—or during their final days. He wanted the room to have soothing colors, inspiring paintings, and comfortable furniture, "to delight the eye of the sufferer." (He would work on this project off and on over the next few years, but it seems as if he never saw it through to fruition.)

After Oakie's death, Ripley seemed to resort, almost desperately, to his collector's habits. Having amassed a small zoo of pets, *four* homes (he still had his NYAC apartment and had purchased a beach house in New Jersey), plus enough employees to field two baseball teams, he began to add more and more beautiful women to his cluttered and manic life.

* * *

NO ONE COULD SAY for sure when and where he found some of his companions. A random woman would show up one day, introduced as a new "secretary" or "housekeeper" or "publicist." She'd stay for dinner, then be at the breakfast table, then still around the next night, until she was part of the BION Island family. Later, there would be another new arrival, and another. Almost all were young immigrants, predominantly Asian, some in seemingly murky roles—they worked for him, lived with him, and sometimes shared his bed.

Among the first to commit herself unreservedly was a quiet and fragile Japanese woman named Ming Jung, referred to by one colleague as "an exquisite creature." As was often the case, no one at BION seemed to know the woman's full story, but Hazel Storer would sometimes chat with Ming and in time learned that she had been married to a man who had worked as a cameraman in Los Angeles. The couple split after their only child died, and Ming kept the baby's ashes in a lacquered box.

Ming accompanied Ripley on a few trips, and at parties she was often dressed in a snug-fitting Chinese gown. She became part of a rotating cast of Ripley companions who, by the early 1940s, began regularly occupying BION's guest bedrooms.

Toshia Mori, an actress whom *Time* once called "a sloe-eyed Japanese girl," was hired as a "research assistant" for Ripley's Movietone films and soon moved in. She once fainted after wandering into the secret basement room where Ripley kept his erotica and torture photos. Ripley had added to this collection over the years, including a shrunken head from Ecuador that had arrived by mail with a note: "Please take care of this, I think it is one of my relatives." One ghastly photo showed an African family, all ten of their legs terminating at the knee, and another featuring a man whose testicles were so swollen by elephantiasis he had to carry them in a wheelbarrow.

"Oh those terrible things," Toshia whispered as one of Ripley's staffers carried her to a couch and gave her some brandy.

Ming and Toshia were joined by a pert young assistant

housekeeper from Spain who napped constantly, and a histrionic Japanese singer who sought Ripley's attentions with halfhearted suicide attempts. She once swallowed half a bottle of aspirin and another time threatened to stab herself in the heart—with a bread knife. One night, she leapt dramatically off a balcony, but the four-foot drop was only enough to inflict a bruise.

Women came and went, some semi-famous, though it was never entirely clear who was friend, girlfriend, or just a curious visitor. Gossip columnists found euphemistic ways of referring to Ripley's female coterie without naming names: "a very charming friend of Ripley's" or "tall, quite dark, and full of sparkling vitality." One frequent guest was Ann Sheridan, a redheaded actress and pinup girl who was between marriages when she befriended Ripley and became a fixture at his dinner parties, occasionally photographed by his side in magazine profiles. Another regular was singer and actress Anna May Wong, a Chinese American beauty who had pulled away from Hollywood to raise money for Chinese war refugees and, in Ripley, found a sympathetic supporter of her causes.

ᚖ BELIEVE IT! ᚖ

Known for her dragon lady and diva roles of the 1920s and '30s, Wong had appeared with Toshia Mori in Streets of Shanghai *and* Mr. Wu *in 1927. Laws against interracial marriage prevented both actresses from becoming leading ladies, since they weren't allowed to kiss white men on-screen.*

There were others: Daniel Boone's great-granddaughter; a leggy blond Hungarian actress, Ilona Massey; singer/actress Marion Hutton, whose mother was a bootlegger and speakeasy proprietress; Marquita Nicholi, a model who lived at the famed Barbizon Hotel for Women. Ripley had little tolerance, though, for women who didn't make themselves useful in some fashion. A publicist named Kay Lawrence was another regular at BION, always drinking white wine and giggling. Ripley called her the "goofy blonde" until she mishandled a magazine story that Ripley felt was less than flattering, after which he called Lawrence "half-assed."

Sometimes these girlfriend-secretary-housekeepers would leave, to be replaced by another. Sometimes they overlapped and two or three would be living on BION Island at once. "The ones with gumption and pride left him," Hazel Storer would write years later. "Those that stayed found plenty of compensations—easy living, easy money, not too much work, and plenty of liquor."

Ripley kept bedrooms and bathrooms stocked with necessities, as well as fragrant soaps, talcums, oils, and lotions. One writer speculated that Ripley stocked his life with women so he wouldn't have to choose just one. The women had their reasons to appreciate his attentions. Though he dressed sloppily during the day—no shoes, bathrobes, charcoal-covered fingers—he cleaned up well and dressed elegantly at night. He could be funny, charming, and wildly generous. And he doted on them, sometimes taking three or four women shopping at once.

One night Doug and Hazel Storer visited to find Ripley reclined on a chaise in his living room, wearing only a robe and framed by four gorgeous women—Hungarian, English, German, and Russian. Two sat on silk pillows, massaging his feet, while two rubbed his neck and shoulders. "It looked just like a harem," Hazel recalled, and would later claim that Ripley (who had now become her boss) "lived in open concubinage."

One of Ripley's radio writers referred to them as his "Broads Brigade." If Ripley announced he was headed to New York for the day, the women would declare they'd been planning to go there too. If he was headed out of town they'd try to position themselves to be chosen to join him. Once, Ripley was headed to the Caribbean and told a girlfriend (probably Ming) that she couldn't come along because he was visiting a British colony and, since she was Japanese, she wouldn't be permitted. She saw Ripley off at Penn Station and by Philadelphia he had hooked up with the woman who *would* accompany him.

Ripley knew plenty of women were desperate to become Mrs. Robert L. Ripley. They competed with and undermined one another and sometimes went too far. A married woman from Buffalo sent a torrent of love letters and warned that if Ripley didn't write back she'd show up at BION Island. When her furniture and suitcases arrived, Ripley had to pay to send everything back. (The husband apologized for his wife's behavior.) Another fan sent a barrage of valentines, telling Ripley she was unhappy with her husband and her life. When she died, the woman's teenaged daughter took up the letter writing. One girlfriend cornered him at a train station in Vienna, a minister in tow, and Ripley hid in an empty rail car until the hopeful bride gave up.

By now, he had learned from past mistakes. Lovers who had sued or threatened to sue upon realizing a proposal wasn't forthcoming had taught him to be careful with his affections. As Hazel Storer would tell a writer years later, "He liked, needed, and distrusted women." He would admit as much, telling one interviewer, "Women are wonderful, simply wonderful—in their place." At BION, he actually took the extreme precaution of having some female guests sign a one-page waiver, in which they acknowledged that they were living on the island "voluntarily."

Slow nights featured just the "intimate circle," as Seabeck the housekeeper put it in an unpublished memoir: Ripley's brother and his wife, Crystl, plus two of Ripley's handpicked women, one on his left, one on his right. Some nights the women jostled for the more respectable position to Ripley's right.

Sometimes the arrangement flat-out collapsed. Ripley once invited Bugs Baer and others for Christmas dinner, but Baer had plans and Ripley found himself alone with just four guests: a widowed ex-girlfriend and her teenage son, a French actress, and an Asian girlfriend. As Ripley later described it to Baer, the ex-girlfriend propped a framed photograph of her late husband next to her plate while her skinny son sulked. The two other women glared at each other silently through the meal until one of them reached into the Christmas turkey, grabbed a fistful of chestnut stuffing, and threw it in her rival's face.

Ripley called Baer the next day. "It's just as well you and Louise didn't come," he said. "You probably wouldn't have had a very good time."

* * *

IN 1941, Ripley installed two massive bronze Chinese warrior statues at the end of the causeway crossing to his island. Mounted on stone pedestals, each menacing figure weighed a ton, and he would tell guests they were to ward off evil spirits. With America edging closer to war, he wasn't taking any chances.

Ripley had desperately wanted his country to remain neutral, for political and personal reasons. Earlier in 1941 he had given a radio address encouraging President Roosevelt and Congress to do everything possible to avoid the war. Former president Herbert Hoover, with whom Ripley had become friends, thanked Ripley for his efforts. "Believe it or Not, that speech has surprised me in the effect which it has had," Hoover wrote. "Your opportunities to help are very great." Hoover's encouragement prompted Ripley to write to congressmen, some of whom wrote back with promises of neutrality. Ohio senator Robert Taft replied, "It is always encouraging to hear from those who feel as I do on this issue."

Of course, the events of December 7, 1941, changed everything. By early 1942 Ripley had immersed himself emotionally and professionally in the war and in relief efforts. He began spending more time at his New York apartment, to be closer to the radio studios, and even bought the top two floors of the building to gain extra space for guests, staffers, and offices. He continued decorating Holmes's former Nirvana with Asian artifacts, including a Chinese bridal bed and a sedan chair. At one of his Chinese-themed parties, he parked the chair in the living room with Ming Jung sitting inside most of the night. Guests wondered if she willingly stuffed herself in the passenger compartment or if Ripley had encouraged it for theatrical effect.

Oddly, it seemed as if Ripley's female companions were all from lands at war—Japan, Russia, China, and Germany. Shortly before the bombing of Pearl Harbor, Ripley had hired a tall and striking new secretary, a German immigrant named Lieselotta Wisse. She was nineteen when she joined Ripley's stable of female "employees," although, unlike some others, she was a hard worker and a well-organized secretary who was soon managing Ripley's social and business schedules. *Liberty* magazine called Liese, as she was known, "a disarming-looking brunette." When Liese received her citizenship papers, Ripley threw her a party at his New York apartment. She and twenty friends arrived to find a huge Nazi flag laid out on the living room floor. Ripley toasted Liese's citizenship and, gesturing to the flag, told her to "stomp on it." He meant for it to be a cathartic event, but guests felt embarrassed for Liese as she jumped on the flag.

Ripley's hatred for Hitler was soon far outweighed, however, by mounting worries over the land that had established itself through the years as his favorite: China.

CHAPTER
20

It had been a decade since Ripley and Oakie witnessed firsthand the evidence of Japan's brutal invasion of China—the craters and rubble, the corpses and executions.

By 1942, word had reached the United States of China's many years of suffering. Eleanor Roosevelt had begun encouraging Americans to host "Bowl of Rice" parties to raise money for humanitarian aid to Chinese refugees. Ripley hosted one such charity luncheon at his apartment and invited an elegant and witty Chinese American divorcée named Li Ling-Ai to speak to guests about the United China Relief program.

Li had been raised in Honolulu and studied theater and dance in China. The war with Japan and a failed marriage inspired a move to New York in the late 1930s. She lived in near poverty in a closet-sized apartment until she was hired to run the Chinese Pavilion at the 1940 World's Fair (along with Anna May Wong). Li then helped produce and finance a 1941 documentary that exposed China's struggles against its Japanese invaders. *Kukan: The Battle Cry of China* won an honorary Academy Award and Li was invited to the White House for a special viewing with President and Eleanor Roosevelt. Soon Li was being invited to give lectures and performances, and she used her newfound fame to raise money for aid to China. She even took flying lessons, in hopes of delivering food to war-torn Chinese villages.

After seeing *Kukan* and reading about Li, Ripley invited her to his luncheon that day, one of many such fund-raisers he hosted during the early 1940s. Ripley was instantly impressed by her eloquence, humor, and charm. And it was hard to ignore that she was stunningly beautiful. Li designed her own clothes and jewelry and was always dressed as if she were a costumed stage actress, wearing shapely, intricately embroidered gowns, bejeweled headdresses, and flowers in her hair.

Li found herself drawn to Ripley, too. Though he was surrounded by other women "all the time," she found him to be "a rough diamond, but a gentleman." In an interview decades later, she recalled their first meeting: "This man, I looked at him and I thought, a real gentleman in the Chinese sense."

Ripley introduced his new friend in a cartoon as a "celebrated Chinese actress, author & lecturer." The cartoon contained a close-up sketch of Li's pretty face and the statement "Chinese eyes do not slant!! It's an illusion." (She was mad at first, since he hadn't asked for her permission.) Elsewhere in print she was described as a noted Chinese feminist, dancer, dramatist, designer, and aviatrix. She was soon being featured in *Harper's Bazaar* and *Vogue*. When Li sang at one of Ripley's dinner parties, gossip columnist Louella Parsons wrote about Li's "sweet, low, throaty voice . . . I never saw such a personality."

In no time Li became one of Ripley's "favored lady friends," as Seabeck put it, and he asked her to join his staff, giving her an impressive title: Director of Far Eastern Research. She became a regular on BION Island and at the New York apartment, and the others could tell from the start that there was something different about their relationship. They would co-host parties together, cooking up Chinese meals dressed in matching costumes. Sometimes she would pick him up in her beat-up Chevrolet and squire him to some small family restaurant in Chinatown, or she'd arrive unannounced at the mansion and he'd demand, "Hurry up and make something good to eat." A self-described "sassy girl," Li was the only one who could get away with teasing Ripley, arguing with him or making fun of him. It helped that she could match him drink for drink.

Ripley loved to spar with Li. War had caused his political views to skew further to the right, which was at odds with the left-leaning bent of some of his guests, particularly Li. At a party for Li's film he embarrassed guests by raising a toast to "that son of a bitch" Roosevelt. Often he'd instigate a political argument, taking a contrary position, egging on both sides, and it was sometimes unclear whether he felt strongly or just wanted to rile things up. At dinner tables Li would mischievously take the position of the stubborn liberal and never backed down. Ripley would get up from the table and, with a smirk, turn his radio up to full volume.

Friends couldn't quite tell if Ripley and Li were lovers or just pals, but it was hard to ignore the similarities between her and Oakie. Just as Oakie had left a war-ravaged homeland after World War I, Li was a refugee of sorts—her hometown of Honolulu had been attacked, as had her adopted homeland of China. Like Oakie, Li was sophisticated, independent, and educated, worldly and multilingual. And most important to Ripley, she was strong-willed and passionate.

Commenting years later on their friendship, Li said, "He likes to argue, likes when you argue back. He's annoyed by stooges and yes men."

Ripley and Li began traveling together—to an air show in Cleveland, lectures in Boston, and "Chinese Night" in Mamaroneck, among other destinations—to promote Li's film and to raise money for British and Chinese relief agencies. With help from Ripley and the Hearst publicity machine, Li was soon becoming famous herself. She and Ripley were frequently photographed together—a Boston newspaper photographer captured them eating cheek to cheek from a shared bowl of rice—and writers began referring to Li as "China's leading dancer."

A beautiful partnership had blossomed. Li would later describe how Ripley had given her a break when nobody else would. He encouraged and supported her, provided a leg up. She believed that, through her, he was repaying a favor to those who had helped him. She called such gestures the "reflection of the heart."

Ripley preferred people who served a purpose—those who were either funny or smart or talented or beautiful. If someone didn't enrich his life somehow, they weren't useful. He cherished those who enhanced *Believe It or Not* in some way too. And while there was a price for admission to Ripley's inner circle—he was obsessed with work and impatient with distractions—there were also rich rewards. "He pretends to be tough but he's always doing little things for people," Li told a reporter at the time, describing her new friend's loyalty and generosity.

In that manner, Li viewed Ripley as an American with a Chinese soul. She liked to think he viewed her as a Chinese with an American soul.

Though Ripley was pleased with this new relationship—especially so soon after losing Oakie—by 1942 the war had completely closed off most of the planet, sealing him inside US borders. It was a harsh blow to his wanderlust. Ever resilient,

however, he managed to find a new and reliable source of unbelievably true stories for his cartoons: *war.*

AFTER PEARL HARBOR, the Nehi Corporation exercised a
clause that allowed it to kill Ripley's RC Cola radio show in the
event of "dire international calamity." With the country about
to devote all its resources to a two-front war, it seemed Ripley's
decade-long run on the air might come to an end. But then his
years of vocal pro-Americanism paid off in a surprising way,
as did his trust in Doug Storer, who negotiated a new program
with the biggest sponsor of all: Uncle Sam.

By now, Storer's own career had progressed, thanks to the
exposure he'd earned as Ripley's manager and radio producer.
He'd taken on other clients—self-help guru Dale Carnegie,
King Features writer Bob Considine, and bandleader Cab Cal-
loway, for example—and by late 1941 had been named head of
programming at NBC's new Blue Network. Wielding his new
title, within days of the Pearl Harbor attack Storer had reached
an agreement with the coordinator of inter-American affairs for
Ripley to broadcast twenty-six half-hour episodes featuring pro-
American, war-related believe-it-or-nots. Just as he had drawn
patriotic cartoons for the US government during World War I,
Ripley would lend his artistic talent to the current war effort.

There was one catch: the deal had to remain a secret. The
coordinator of inter-American affairs, millionaire Nelson Rockefeller, wrote to demand that Storer and Ripley never publicly
mention Rockefeller, nor his department, nor the US government
"as sponsoring or in any way being connected with or responsible for carrying out the project." NBC would air the shows
with no reference to the real sponsor.

The Coordinator of Inter-American Affairs Office (CIAA) had been created within the State Department to disseminate news reports, films, advertising, and radio to Latin America, an effort to counteract pro-Italian and pro-German propaganda there. By 1942, CIAA had a $38 million budget and a staff of a thousand, all devoted to shaping South America's public opinion in favor of its neighbor to the north. Walt Disney performed duties similar to Ripley's on CIAA's behalf, notably a 1941 South American goodwill tour that produced the film *Saludos Amigos* ("Hello, friends"). Rockefeller's reaction to the film—"exceeds our highest expectations"—prompted Disney to produce more thinly veiled propaganda films for the CIAA.

❖ BELIEVE IT! ❖

US intelligence later discovered that the CIAA Office had been infiltrated by Soviet intelligence. Federal employees at the CIAA were sharing information with Soviet spies, whose code name for the CIAA was "Cabaret."

Ripley's directive was to broadcast positive stories about Americans at war and promote the United States' commitment to "Western Hemisphere defense." The primary goal was to comfort South America, as Ripley's $1,500-per-show contract put it, with stories of "every-day life, history, famous institutions, science, heroes, soldiers, statesmen, artists." Rockefeller's office, the War Department, and the State Department would be allowed to review Storer's scripts and veto guests.

See All the Americas with Bob Ripley launched in January of 1942 on Saturday nights. An announcer told listeners that "our modern Marco Polo, the most traveled man in history" would "make you better acquainted with the twenty neighboring republics to the south of us." Each show highlighted a different country, and Ripley told stories of visits to Quito, Rio, and Buenos Aires. "The principal delight in my Believe It or Not work is the pleasure of traveling," he said in one show. "But if someone should ask me where I have derived the greatest content, I would have to say, truthfully, South America." (*Truthfully,* Ripley preferred Asia to South America, having once scorned Bolivians as "stupid" and "weak.")

Ripley was proud to be playing a role in the war effort and intoxicated by the covertness of the project. Plus, he would now be able to verbally attack communism and fascism on the air without fear of being muzzled. The new show was important to Ripley, who felt he was doing something more valuable with his passionate patriotism than just entertaining. Ever the competitor, he was doing something heroic for his home team.

RIPLEY'S FIRST THIRTEEN-WEEK season was extended for thirteen more weeks, and Nelson Rockefeller wrote to thank him for doing such a "marvelous job."

Then Ripley received a letter of censure from the Office of Censorship, slapping his wrist for identifying the location of a US fighter squadron in the South Pacific. Soon after that, he received a letter from President Roosevelt's radio department thanking him for "the valuable service you have rendered to the government" but informing him his contract would not be renewed. Ripley wondered if his opposition to Roosevelt was partly to blame.

Thus began a yearlong period in which Ripley would not be on the air, the longest such gap in a decade. He tried to stay busy, lending time to war efforts and charities. He cooperated with the Office of War Information by donating *Believe It or*

Not sketches—of Medal of Honor winners or star athletes in the military—which were reprinted as posters or in military newspapers. He performed onstage for servicemen headed overseas and even agreed to draw sketches for a military booklet warning soldiers about venereal disease. Still, he felt a growing need to devote more of himself, somehow, to the war.

"I wanted to get into this war," he would soon tell a reporter, concluding that radio might be "my greatest opportunity for serving my country." Storer assured Ripley that he was searching for new shows and sponsors, but there were limited opportunities "with the war picture as it is."

In late August 1942, he received more bad news. Linda Lee, the sultry-voiced singer who had performed for years on his show with B. A. Rolfe's orchestra, was dead at age twenty-seven. Lee had been under a doctor's care for "a nervous condition" and had been fretting over her husband's enlistment in the Army. She fell to her death—or possibly jumped—from the low-silled window of her seventh-floor apartment on Central Park South. Wearing a nightgown, she landed on the sidewalk across from horrified diners at the Hotel St. Moritz café.

Lee's death was the latest in a series of personal losses for Ripley, starting with the 1940 death of his high school teacher Miss O'Meara. (Ripley wrote a letter that was read at the funeral, avowing that O'Meara's teachings "will be cherished throughout my life.") That was followed by the devastating death of his lover, Oakie, and then the unexpected death of his travel secretary, George Wieda.

Even his dogs had begun dying. Barking and roughhousing had become part of everyday life at BION Island. Ripley raised Dalmatians and donated his pups to Mamaroneck's fire department. He adopted a shaggy-haired English sheepdog named Rhumba, and for promotional photos and holiday cards he would comb Rhumba's hair over one eye and pose beside his one-eyed dog, Cyclops. With so many dogs and their offspring on the island, he often gave puppies to friends as gifts.

Inevitably, not all the pets survived. Ripley's first dog, Dokie the cocker spaniel, had been killed by a delivery truck. A spaniel named Virtue crashed through the ice and drowned in the pond. His collie Flash was killed by the gardener's Saint Bernard. Ripley buried his dogs in a pet cemetery on a knoll atop BION Island. One pet's headstone read, HE LIVED A DOG'S LIFE.

As he was absorbing the deaths of colleagues and pets, he received the heartbreaking news that his companion Ming Jung had been sent to an internment camp, one of the detention centers into which Japanese Americans were forcibly relocated, beginning in 1942. It's unclear how she ended up there, since Executive Order 9066 applied primarily to Japanese Americans living on the West Coast. Ripley acted quickly and used his influence to secure Ming's release, but she'd gotten sick at the camp and had to be hospitalized. The details of her illness remained unknown to friends, but Ripley once told Storer that she'd developed problems with her circulation, that her blood pressure dropped to dangerously low levels and at one point doctors thought she'd die. Ripley fretted during her months in the hospital and visited her often. Ming eventually recovered and moved back to BION Island, but the internment and illness had taken a toll. She would spend hours paddling alone on the pond and rarely spoke about her imprisonment or illness.

By 1943, it seemed as if everything in Ripley's life had been upended by war. Newspaper friends were headed off to war assignments, trusted chauffeurs and butlers were being drafted or enlisting, and other employees found stateside jobs related to the war effort. When Almuth Seabeck's husband enlisted, the housekeeper resigned and Ripley decided to shutter BION Island for a while. It was too difficult to keep the place running without a full staff, so he hosted one last party—a farewell for Seabeck and her husband—then mothballed his mansion and moved into the New York apartment.

* * *

MONTHS EARLIER, Storer convinced NBC to allow him to create another new Ripley show to promote stories about aviation and encourage youngsters to become pilots. Sponsored by the Junior Air Reserve, with the support of the air forces of the US Army and Navy, *Scramble* would broadcast coast to coast each Friday.

Ripley aggressively took up this new cause, advocating the future of flight to America's youth. Lending his voice to the aviation community was a natural fit. He'd always had an interest in flying, and he realized that he owed a portion of his success to the airplane—his Lindbergh cartoon remained one of his best known, and the Wrong-Way Corrigan interview had been among his earlier radio coups. Over the years, he'd befriended famous flyers, including Eddie Rickenbacker, a frequent BION visitor whom he'd known since Rickenbacker's pre–World War I days as a race car driver.

Scramble gave Ripley an opportunity to tap into his memories of a world before war, to describe to radio listeners his actual visits to the places that were now gory battlefields—in China, North Africa, the South Pacific, and Europe. "When I was in Tripoli . . ." began one such episode.

Ripley's success with *Scramble* prompted the National Aeronautic Association in 1943 to name him "special assistant" to its Air Youth Division, and he embarked on a nationwide tour. He spoke to junior aviation groups, high schools, Boy Scout troops, and orphanages, encouraging young men and women to pursue a career in aviation. "The air age is on us," he told a group in St. Louis. "The airplane has made the world so small and drawn the peoples of the world so close together that in a not very long time they all may speak the same language and wear the same clothes." Fifteen years earlier, Ripley had been terrified of flying. Now he was declaring throughout the Midwest that aviation would "bring about lasting peace."

Finally, with Ripley so much in the public eye, Nelson Rockefeller contacted Doug Storer to say his office had decided to renew Ripley's CIAA show. Rockefeller said Ripley's return, with more episodes on Latin American countries, "would be in the best interest of the United States." Through the fall of 1943, Ripley was back on the air, and Rockefeller wrote in a letter, "You are certainly making a real contribution toward better understanding between the Americas."

Just as Ripley had thrived during World War I and during the Depression, he was flourishing through the second world war, at least career-wise. The year ended on a professional high note, with a twenty-fifth *Believe It or Not* anniversary party at the Waldorf-Astoria. Max Schuster couldn't attend but sent a gushing telegram: "After twenty-five years of awed and breathless admiration I am more convinced than ever that the greatest Believe It or Not of them all is the story of Bob Ripley."

✳ ✳ ✳

BACK IN LATE 1942, a German U-boat had torpedoed a British merchant ship off the South American coast and only one of the fifty-four crewmen survived.

Poon Lim, a Chinese steward, had grabbed a life vest and dived overboard, then climbed into a life raft stocked with enough food for sixty days. Lim drifted for twice that long before being rescued by fishermen off the coast of Brazil. His 133 days alone at sea—nearly twice as long as the castaways Ripley had interviewed in the Bahamas—was an all-time record.

In January of 1944, Ripley interviewed Poon, a slight and quiet man who described singing folk songs to pass the time and, when his food ran low, making a fishhook from the spring of a flashlight. On the air, while actors dramatized his plight, Poon could be heard in the background, sobbing. In his column the next day, Walter Winchell listed the emotional broadcast among his weekly "headliners."

Ripley's new show, *Rhythm, Romance, and Ripley*, sponsored by Pall Mall cigarettes and airing over the Mutual Network, became an instant hit. It was also Ripley's most lucrative radio partnership, with Pall Mall coughing up $4,000 a week for Ripley's salary. Airing five nights a week at 9:15 p.m., the fifteen-minute broadcasts focused exclusively on hard-to-believe war stories. "Amazing wonders culled from a world at war" was how publicists described it.

One night Ripley profiled a soldier whose pet monkey saved his life on a North African battlefield, and he later featured a man who was honorably discharged for snoring too loud. One show introduced listeners to Ray and Curtis Ewing, a father and son from Bellingham, Washington, with an inconceivable story. Curtis Ewing's army base in northern Australia was bombed in 1942, and while picking through rubble he found a chunk of shrapnel with his father's name etched into it. Ray Ewing, a Boeing airplane mechanic, had years earlier chiseled his name into the engine block of the family car. The scrap metal from the old car had somehow ended up in a Japanese bomb factory.

With his new show up and running, Ripley hired a press agent, and the gossip columns were suddenly packed with

Ripley stories and snippets. He earned ink in the columns of Hedda Hopper, Louella Parsons, Louis Sobol, Dorothy Kilgallen, E. V. Durling, and, on a regular basis, Walter Winchell. Some writers said Ripley was thinking of taking his strange life story to Broadway, working with a writer on a *Believe It or Not* play. Others rehashed certain facts (some questionable) about Ripley's life so frequently, so consistently word for word, that it was obvious they were writing from press releases: *born on Christmas Day . . . visited 201 countries . . . designed tombstones as his first job . . . likes the company of chipmunks . . . first man to broadcast around the world . . . still uses the front door of his boyhood home . . . only wears bowties.*

Columnists raved about evenings spent at "one of Ripley's fabulous parties," with guest lists ranging from Jimmy Durante, Jack Dempsey, and Carmen Miranda to Chiang Kai-shek's personal physician. Louella Parsons described the "heartwarming" birthday party Ripley threw for his longtime boss and friend, Joe Connolly, who had been ill. When Bugs Baer, Eddie Rickenbacker, Vyvyan Donner and others sang happy birthday to the famed King Features president, Parsons pronounced the evening "one we'll all remember."

THOUGH PARSONS PRAISED RIPLEY as "a grand host" for celebrating Connolly's fiftieth, the relationship between Ripley and his superiors had in fact become quite strained.

Ripley's radio show often stretched him to the breaking point, and his obligations to King Features got pushed down the priority list. In addition to prepping for five weekly shows, he was still drawing seven cartoons a week. And while columnists sometimes gushed that Ripley remained "one of the few famous cartoonists who still does his own drawings," the truth was that a growing stable of young King Features artists was drawing more of Ripley's cartoons.

Ripley had become overwhelmed by obligations many times before, and always emerged intact. A sheepish shrug seemed to repair all ills. Lately, however, with trusted staffers off to war and Ripley neck deep in one of the busier periods of his career, something had to give. Too often it was the cartoon. King Features executives regularly wrote or wired, from 1942 through 1945, about "your late schedule" or "further complications" or being "weeks behind our war-time schedule."

At one point, with Ripley a month behind schedule, one of Connolly's associates, Brad Kelly, pleaded: "Something has got to be done quickly . . . Won't you remedy this situation immediately and supply two weeks [of cartoons] every five days until you are on the war-time schedule?" The situation grew worse when mail restrictions forced Ripley to send cartoons an extra week ahead of schedule. "The situation is serious," another King Features executive wrote.

Ripley's secretary, Cygna Conly, tried to help him avoid the $5,000 fines King Features began threatening for missed deadlines, but her boss seemed almost intent on sabotage. In late 1944, desperately itchy to travel, deadlines or no deadlines, Ripley escaped to Cuba for the Christmas holidays. When he returned to New York, King Features colleagues must have all slapped their foreheads as they read headlines about Ripley's latest effort—trying to buy a Mexican volcano.

At a New Year's Eve party in Cuba he'd learned about a volcano that had mushroomed up from a cornfield in Mexico. A fissure in the cornfield began vomiting up lava and ash in 1943 and within weeks it had bulged to a five-story mound. By 1944 it was a 1,100-foot cone of steaming cinders called Paricutin, which continued to belch smoke and lava. Ever since the 1906 California earthquake, Ripley had been fascinated by natural disasters and the violent tics of the earth. Earlier in 1944, Italy's Mount Vesuvius had also erupted, the first such eruption since 1906, inciting Ripley's obsession with owning his own volcano.

When he learned about Paricutin, he began telling dumbfounded friends that owning it might fill a spiritual void, or that the volcano might contain minerals that would be a good financial investment. After returning from Havana, Ripley began negotiating by phone and mail with the farmer, whose claim to the land turned out to be somewhat vague. Mexican authorities finally told Ripley they weren't keen on having an American own Mexican land, and the legislature hastily passed a bill making the volcano state property.

"I could have charged admissions and made money off it," Ripley complained, vowing to search for another volcano elsewhere and proposing a *Believe It or Not* volcano contest.

Soon after the failed volcano purchase, Ripley learned that Joe Connolly, his mentor for more than fifteen years, had died. Connolly and his wife were coming home from a movie when Connolly suffered a heart attack. He died later at the hospital, in April of 1945, a week after President Roosevelt's death.

Connolly had been in poor health for years, but never slowed down. Six hundred people attended the funeral, at which Ripley served as pallbearer. Connolly's replacement at King Features, Brad Kelly, told Ripley, "You were his pride and joy."

Ripley's own health had been in continual decline. The man once called America's most eligible bachelor, who in 1942 had ranked sixth in a columnist's "Catch of the Season" list, was now described in print as "stocky" and "a heavyset middle aged man with dark laughing eyes."

He had recently learned that one culprit behind the years of suffering from sore and swollen feet was a heart condition that caused poor circulation and dropsy. When he told Li Ling-Ai about the diagnosis, she could tell he was shaken, knowing that his father had died young of a heart attack. And while there is no record of it, Hazel Storer would say years later that Ripley also suffered a small stroke in the mid-1940s—"in a hotel out in the Midwest on a lecture date."

After attending so many funerals in recent years, Ripley had to be contemplating mortality during this period, especially as America tallied its dead at the conclusion of four years at war. As World War II finally ended, Ripley tallied his own losses— friends, bosses, dogs, and even the luxury ships he had once sailed upon. War's end seemed to bring Ripley little peace, and friends worried that the years of global conflict had strained his ties to the exotic lands he'd so obsessively pursued.

"We want to be a part of somebody and something," Li Ling-Ai later observed. "We might fall in love to say we're a part of somebody's life. But to be a part of humanity, the world . . ."

Li knew Ripley well enough to sense that a man so attuned to the weird, wide world around him needed, now more than ever, to be part of *something*.

CHAPTER

21

Until 1941, Ripley had stubbornly pretended that World War II wasn't spreading like a cancer, that Earth wasn't becoming a battlefield. He kept lobbying for neutrality while poring over maps and atlases, making lists and notes and lofty travel plans. Even as it became obvious that America would join the fight, he had obsessively compiled possible itineraries, optimistic but unlikely tours of Greece, Romania, Turkey, Egypt, Italy, France, West Africa, and the South Pacific.

In fact, just a year before the attack on Hawaii, he had communicated by mail with the Japanese Tourist Industry, which offered to cover the expenses for a railway tour of Japan. His travel secretary at the time, George Wieda, advised Ripley that some of his ideas were "impractical."

Now that the war was over, he couldn't wait to get back overseas after five years of wartime restrictions. Unfortunately, the travel industry was hardly ready to accommodate him. Indeed, many of the beautiful vessels that had once delivered him to exotic ports had been lost during the war and now lay in pieces on the ocean floor.

The SS *Santa Luisa,* aboard which Ripley had sailed to South America in 1925, had been sunk in the Aleutian Islands. The *Conte di Savoia,* which carried him home from Europe in 1932, had been set afire and bombed by the Germans, sinking in the English Channel. The *Savoia's* sister ship, the SS *Rex,* which ferried Ripley back and forth across the Atlantic a few times, had also been sunk, by the British.

He had tried to explore close-to-home waterways during his decade at BION Island, paddling his pond in his international collection of boats from Iraq, Alaska, and Peru, or occasionally commuting into Manhattan on his brother's yacht. Though Ripley had championed the power of aviation, he preferred being on the water. And when he learned that no luxury liners would be available for passenger travel anytime soon, in early 1946 he decided that he was ready for a boat of his own.

As usual, no ordinary purchase would suffice. For $7,500, he bought the strangest and least practical vessel on the eastern seaboard.

✳ ✱ ✲

THE *MON LEI* had been built in 1939 for a wealthy Hong Kong businessman. (Ripley always referred to him as a "war lord.") According to one version of the story, when the Japanese invaded China, they captured the boat and sold it on the black market to British employees of Dollar Steamship, who were stranded in Hong Kong. The new owners sailed with a Chinese crew across the Pacific, through the Panama Canal, and up to Baltimore, where Ripley found the boat. In another version, the boat was sailed across to California, to keep it out of Japanese hands, and was later found sunk in the mud in Florida.

Ripley invested $40,000 to restore and repaint the worn-out

vessel. He installed a powerful new diesel engine and, in recognition of a Chinese belief that boats are propelled by the spirits of dragons, had eyes, teeth, and whiskers painted on the engine. In the wheelhouse he painted a Chinese saying that translated as "May she sail like a flying dragon and move like a leaping elephant." For the boat's flag, he chose the entwined yin and yang symbols. He installed a gong to ward off evil spirits and, because Chinese sailors believed that only a golden anchor could hold fast, he gold-plated his anchor accordingly. Belowdecks, there were sleeping cabins with six bunks and a tiled bathroom with a shower stall. He refinished the elaborately hand-carved teak wood, and the paint scheme throughout was heavy on gold and red lacquer.

Ripley loved to explain how the name *Mon Lei* (in a Cantonese dialect) meant "ten thousand miles" or "infinity," that it was sometimes used to imply "bon voyage." She was a fishing boat known as a "junk," fifty feet long, seventeen feet wide, and her draft—the depth of the hull below the waterline—was just shy of five feet. The flat-bottomed boat was designed for the shallow waters of the lower Yangtze in Shanghai. Rather than carve through water, "she slides over it," Ripley liked to explain. Of course, that made the *Mon Lei* ill suited for the chop around New York and along the East Coast. But it wasn't so much navigational proficiency he valued as the exotic worldliness his boat represented, and the freedom from US shores she offered.

Though it had been built for sailing, the three scalloped sails were now decorative, made obsolete by the new engine. But Ripley insisted on keeping the sails up, and local boaters snickered at the diesel smoke coughing from the alleged sailboat's rear. On weekends, Ripley would invite friends aboard for floating parties around Long Island Sound, serving cocktails and

Chinese food in his captain's outfit—a double-breasted jacket, white pants, and sailor's cap. Ripley hired a real captain and crew to navigate, but he loved to dress the part. He'd invite guests belowdecks to rub the belly of Ho-Tei, his statue of a Chinese good-luck god. He kept a prayer wheel aboard with 1,000 prayers inside a cylinder that, when spun, was said to release the prayers toward heaven. One writer said that descending belowdecks "is like entering a different world, one in which grinning Buddhas, flaming-mouthed dragons, and prayer wheels are necessary accoutrements."

Ripley soon grew bored with the waters of greater New York and began planning more distant *Mon Lei* adventures. Though global hostilities had mostly ended, it was still risky for civilian vessels to sail beyond American waters, so Ripley came up with routes that would allow him to safely play captain for weeks at a time. He rationalized that these trips would perform double duty as colorful *Believe It or Not* publicity campaigns. In April of 1946, he and his crew sailed to Florida, stopping in a dozen ports along the way. Liese Wisse and Ming Jung joined him on the sluggish journey south—the boat was only capable of 11 knots. When the *Mon Lei* finally arrived in Miami, a newsman said she "looks like something between an Orange Bowl float and an opium dream."

On one trip to Connecticut, Ripley was scheduled to be feted by the *Hartford Times*. The publisher and editor waited dockside with a King Features publicist named Joe Willicombe, all of them looking down the Connecticut River for the *Mon Lei*. Willicombe finally excused himself and drove south until he found the *Mon Lei* docked in Middletown, fifteen miles away. When Willicombe asked why they weren't in Hartford, the captain insisted, "This *is* Hartford!" Willicombe found Ripley relaxing below and convinced him that they were still an hour's sail from Hartford, then drove him north to the day's festivities.

The next day, the rival *Hartford Courant* teased, RIPLEY ERRS, MISTAKES MIDDLETOWN FOR HARTFORD.

In a similar display of Ripley's nautical naiveté, he agreed to sail up the Hudson River for a day of festivities in Albany. The *Mon Lei* was expected by ten a.m., to join a flotilla of yachts and Navy ships. Hundreds lined the shore, awaiting the flamboyant boat and her owner, but by noon there was no sign of them. Joe Willicombe again found himself nervously driving downriver, where he found the *Mon Lei* bobbing lifelessly. Her engines had died and the captain had no luck attempting to sail the final miles. Willicombe wired a message to Albany and a Navy boat sped to the rescue, hooked a rope to the *Mon Lei*'s bow, and towed her into port.

For a day trip into Manhattan to view a flotilla of Navy ships, Ripley, Baer, Li Ling-Ai, and others dressed in Chinese costumes and swilled cocktails as the *Mon Lei* chugged south, passing beneath drawbridges. When a bridge tender asked Ripley's captain to identify himself, Baer taunted, "We can't tell you. We're smuggling in dope from the Orient." At another bridge, Ripley pointed to Li Ling-Ai and yelled, "You better let us pass, we have Madame Chiang Kai-shek aboard."

When the *Mon Lei* sailed too close to the USS *Missouri*, which President Truman was scheduled to visit by helicopter, a Coast Guard patrol boat motored up and began nudging the *Mon Lei* away. An officer ordered Ripley's crew by megaphone to "pull to the Jersey shore," and the party came to an end with Ripley, unable to talk himself out of trouble, being interrogated and paying a fine.

✳ ✳ ✳

THE *MON LEI* quickly became Ripley's refuge, and his favorite toy. After hiring a full-time captain, a first mate, and a cook, he spent as much free time as possible exploring East Coast ports. Ripley found the deadlines, the phone calls, and the demands of his fame all melted away while sailing.

Over the years he had often told reporters that he sometimes imagined himself as the reincarnation of a Chinese warlord, or that he wished he could come back in his next life as "a Chinaman." On the *Mon Lei,* he could live out such fantasies. When he brought girlfriends along, he expected them to dress their part. In newspaper and magazine photographs, Ming Jung, Liese Wisse, and other female friends and secretaries are usually wearing embroidered Chinese dresses. He'd invite well-known Chinese entertainers aboard, including actresses Anna May Wong and Jessie Tai Sing. For one magazine photo shoot he hosted beautiful dancers from the China Doll nightclub, and his itinerary for press tours always included a request for "Chinese girls for pictures." (Joe Willicombe actually received a letter from King Features with the exact instructions: make sure good-looking Chinese women are always aboard, and reserve hotel suites for Ripley and his "secretaries.")

Li was a frequent passenger, always dressed in elegant Chinese garb. She even put together a stump lecture about the *Mon Lei*'s features and oddities, which she would deliver to visiting journalists. During a trip to Greenwich, Connecticut, Ripley left the *Mon Lei* at the pier to play golf with Samuel F. Pryor, a vice president with Pan American Airways. Pryor delivered his mother and her friend to the pier and Li gave the older women a tour. One of them asked about the large symbol over Ripley's bed and Li explained, "It means 'I wish you one thousand lays.'" The older women nodded their heads, thinking of leis, the flowery Hawaiian wreaths.

That fall, he docked the boat in Long Island and put Ming Jung in charge of an overhaul, which included adding a barroom and converting one of the cabins into a bedroom/art studio. Ripley then spent most of the winter of 1946–47 living and working aboard the *Mon Lei* (with Liese Wisse along as his companion) traveling south to Charleston, Savannah, Miami, and Key West, where newsmen gawked at Ripley's "pretty secretary," who felt woozy after weeks at sea. Ripley never got seasick, Wisse said with a pout to the reporters: "It makes me *mad.*"

The *Mon Lei* sailed up Florida's west coast to St. Petersburg, where he signed autographs at the pier for hours.

His staff would later learn that he had signed something else on aboard the *Mon Lei* that spring in St. Petersburg. The "Last Will and Testament of Robert L. Ripley" was witnessed and signed by Liese Wisse and the *Mon Lei*'s skipper, William L. Platt, on April 4, 1947.

After Ripley signed the document, he hid it aboard the *Mon Lei,* hoping its services wouldn't be required for years to come.

✶ ✳ ✳

LATE THAT YEAR, he concluded another season of radio and sailed once more to Florida for the winter. When the *Mon Lei* arrived in Miami in the final days of 1947, she was surrounded by so many curious onlookers that Ripley (and Liese) had to check into a hotel to get some rest. A reporter cornered Ripley and asked him to describe "the greatest oddity," but Ripley said he was still looking.

"When I find it, I'll retire," he said.

Having been diagnosed with high blood pressure and warned by doctors to take better care of himself, he must have sensed that retirement was near. During the Christmas holidays, he decided he liked the idea of sunshine in winter, and bought himself yet another house—a Spanish-style mansion called Hi-Mount—in Palm Beach. He immediately had a special dock and boathouse built for the *Mon Lei*, right on the shore of Lake Worth, a lagoon that connected to the Intracoastal Waterway.

His first night at Hi-Mount, in early February 1948, was spent eating take-out food on the floor with a girlfriend and Doug and Hazel Storer. Two employees were still driving south from New York with furniture. The only items in the house were a couple of chairs and cabinets, a Chinese rug, and a beat-up wooden drawing table from the *Mon Lei*, which Ripley had been using for thirty years. He set up a small buffet on the table and they all sat on the rug eating cold cuts and drinking Michelob beer.

The Storers thought Ripley seemed more at ease than he'd been in years. Far from the demanding New York lifestyle, Florida seemed to relax him.

He certainly wasn't thinking about his recently signed will that first night at Hi-Mount. The will that named those who'd befriended him or hired him or worked for him or slept with him over the years. The will that listed in detail the amount of money each of the most important people in his life should receive when he was gone. The will that named his brother and sister, as well as an inventory of current and former secretaries, housekeepers, and lovers.

"He was utterly happy that night," Hazel Storer later said. "He was happy and relaxed and felt free to be completely natural."

When the Storers left for their hotel, Ripley and his companion curled up in a pile of jackets on the Chinese rug and fell asleep.

CHAPTER

22

Within weeks of that happy first night in his new Florida home, Ripley was back in New York, back to the lifestyle he'd been denied during the war. He reopened BION Island, started hosting parties again at his New York apartment, and was back on the air. Ripley's *Believe It or Not Radio Odditorium* had broadcast three times a week in 1947, but NBC decided to bump the show to five days a week for the 1948 season.

Just as quickly, he was back to planning his long-delayed escape from American soil. By now—two and a half years after the war—the full onset of peace meant Ripley could travel once more. The *Mon Lei* and the new Florida house had been exciting distractions, but apparently not enough.

He suddenly, *urgently,* wanted to return to Asia, especially China. Ripley had first mentioned this surging desire to Doug Storer at a Christmas party. "How about you and Hazel going to China with me?" he had asked. Weeks later, he invited Storer to his apartment, ostensibly to discuss details of the radio show. Instead, Ripley again raised the topic of China. He'd been reading news reports about his favorite country's tilt toward communism after World War II and felt the need to act fast if he wanted to see China again.

"It won't be long before the Reds gobble up the rest of the country—gobble it up and close it up," he said. "This will probably be our last chance to go back."

Storer reminded Ripley of his contractual obligations—the NBC program and the cartoon, to name two—and that he couldn't just sail off to the Orient. But Ripley seemed insistent, almost desperate, and suggested that they broadcast radio shows by remote along the way, as they had during the *See America* series. Storer said he'd look into it, doubtful that he could pull it off but worried that Ripley wouldn't let it go.

A solution practically fell into Storer's lap. He spotted a *New York Times* ad for the upcoming maiden voyage of the SS *President Cleveland*, which would be making a speedy tour through the South Seas, China, and Japan. Storer immediately called the head of American President Lines and pitched an idea: Robert Ripley would air his weekday radio show from aboard the *President Cleveland*. Fully warming to Ripley's harebrained adventure, Storer suggested bringing a technician along so they could create audio travelogues from each country. The fifteen-minute shows could be performed in foreign ports or at sea from the ship's deck, recorded, and transmitted back to New York.

Storer convinced the president of the cruise line that the gimmick, and Ripley's presence aboard ship, might be good publicity. The president finally agreed to host Ripley and his party free of charge. The ship would leave San Francisco in April, giving Storer less than a month to prepare the Believe It or Not machine for the road.

RIPLEY KNEW THE drill. As with his regular trips before the war, he promised King Features he'd mail cartoons and promised NBC he'd send radio shows, even if such commitments would make for an exhausting vacation with little time for unplanned diversions. As usual, there were girlfriend issues to manage. Liese Wisse, Ripley's longtime secretary (and part-time lover), insisted on coming along. Ripley initially didn't want her aboard, having already invited Li Ling-Ai, who was out west and would meet him in San Francisco. Ripley recklessly instructed Storer to tell Wisse the trip had been canceled, but of course she discovered the truth, and Ripley relented. She packed a huge trunk full of dresses and joined him on a westbound train.

Storer, meanwhile, arranged to have his wife, Hazel, come along to help with radio scripts, and an NBC production manager named Ed Dunham to set up the radio equipment. Liese would help photograph everything—Storer wanted to make sure he captured it all on film, knowing that Ripley's return to Asia might be his last.

But first, the entourage had to stop in Los Angeles, to offset the cost of Ripley's troupe's ride to China. As part of a complex scheme Storer had worked out with NBC, Ripley had to appear on the *Truth or Consequences* radio show before earning his free passage on the *President Cleveland*.

* * *

GEORGE MCMILLIN was a young stockbroker from Chicago whose father had recently died. When George's girlfriend dumped him, George moved to Los Angeles to live with his widowed mother and twin brother, and to pursue his dream of breaking into radio. When a friend gave him a ticket to the *Truth or Consequences* radio show, George was plucked from the audience as one of the show's contestants.

The host, Ralph Edwards, instructed McMillin that his challenge was to exit the studio and convince the first person he met that he was the cartoonist Robert Ripley. In the studio hallway he met a man named Roberts, from Des Moines (actually Ripley in disguise), and tried selling himself as Ripley, but quickly gave up and confessed that he was "just George McMillin." Edwards then asked McMillin if he'd like to meet the *real* Ripley, and McMillin said, "Sure!"

"Well, shake hands with him," said Edwards. "He's right in front of you!"

When McMillin recovered from the shock, he was told that he'd been chosen to spend an expenses-paid trip with Ripley, leaving from San Francisco in less than a week. McMillin would receive a spending allowance of $600 a week, and in a note to his mother he gushed that he'd won a trip to the Orient "with the most traveled man in the United States—and they are going to *pay* me to go."

The ship left port on April 9, and as McMillin settled into his bunk he couldn't sleep a wink, thinking how lucky he was. "How can this all happen to me?" he wrote in his diary. "I'm not that good a boy. I will be from now on, tho." McMillin learned the next day that his trunk had been left on the San Francisco pier, and that he was headed to China with just the clothes on his back. He had to borrow $50 from Ripley to buy clothes from the ship's store.

Also aboard the ship was Ripley's composer/conductor friend Rudolf Friml. The two men reminisced about their travels to the South Seas together in 1932. Friml was accompanied by two beautiful Chinese "secretaries," and McMillin told his diary that Friml's companions were the prettiest women aboard.

McMillin's first days on the *Cleveland* were spent half-drunk beside the pool, ogling Friml's friends; earning a blistery sunburn; dancing (badly) on the wooden dance floor; sharing late-night cocktails with Li Ling-Ai, who could hold her liquor better than most men; and sweating off hangovers in the ship's gymnasium with Doug Storer.

Ripley, meanwhile, made himself scarce, holing up in his stateroom, scratching out cartoons while sipping gin and grapefruit juice. Sometimes he emerged full of mirth at cocktail hour and joined the others for dinner, after which they'd roll games of dice. One night they all crowded around a radio to listen to a rebroadcast of the *Truth or Consequences* show.

McMillin found Ripley to be generous and entertaining, always willing to offer a bottle of beer or a sandwich. He also glimpsed the melodrama of Ripley's VIP lifestyle. Ripley once blew up when he learned that his favorite masseur had missed the ship at San Francisco. Storer had to hunt down someone to attend to Ripley's sore back, and to the rescue came a bass player in Friml's orchestra who was studying to become a chiropractor.

Still, Ripley spent most of his days inside his darkened cabin, possibly to avoid Liese Wisse, who hadn't learned until San Francisco that she'd have to share a cabin with her perceived rival, Li Ling-Ai. During the first days of the journey, Liese made frequent visits to Ripley's cabin, where she and Ripley launched into terrible arguments like an embittered married couple. No one was quite sure what they were fighting about, but their shouts spilled into the hallways.

IN HAWAII, the "land of romance and happiness" where Ripley once imagined himself retiring, he finally emerged from his stateroom for an eighteen-hour layover packed with the duties and obligations of fame.

He reunited with former Olympic swimming champ and

famed surfer Duke Kahanamoku, who was now fifteen years into his term as Honolulu's sheriff. Duke escorted Ripley's group to the Outrigger Canoe Club at Waikiki Beach, where Ripley recorded one of three radio shows scheduled for his short Hawaiian visit. He then climbed into an outrigger canoe with McMillin, Wisse, and two beefy guides. The fivesome paddled offshore, surrounded by Duke and other local surfers. When a big swell approached, the guides yelled, "Paddle! Paddle! Paddle!" Ripley's boat caught the wave, as did the nearby surfers, and they all surfed the curl toward shore.

Ripley had surfed in an outrigger canoe during his memorable South Seas trip with Oakie sixteen years earlier. Now he threw his head back, lifted his oar in the air with both hands, and laughed giddily as water sprayed over the sides. It would be one of the purest, happiest moments of the trip.

During that night's radio show, Ripley interviewed a local boy with the shortest Hawaiian name (Mi) and a girl with the longest (eighty-one letters). In another show, Ripley gave an impassioned plug for Hawaiian statehood and interviewed Li Ling-Ai's parents, both doctors for fifty years. Li's parents threw a dinner party, after which Ripley made an emotional toast to his Hawaiian hosts, who escorted Ripley's entourage back to the *Cleveland* for its midnight departure.

For the next twelve days, Ripley mostly retreated to the sullen cave of his stateroom while the rest of his entourage fell into a lazy schedule, the leisurely life-at-sea pace Ripley once loved. McMillin, the Storers, Wisse, Li, and the others sunned themselves by the pool, played tennis and shuffleboard, ate buffet lunches, and on the rare cool days sipped hot bouillon. Tea was served at four each afternoon, followed by highballs at five, then dinner and a carefree night of card games, slot machines, or bingo. One night the ship's staff threw a costume ball and the men in Ripley's group borrowed clothes from Wisse and showed up in drag. (Liese brought along so much clothing her trunk blocked the bathroom entrance. During a cabin inspection, the ship's captain asked Li how she got in and out past Wisse's trunk. She winked at him and said, "Easy. I go Chinese fashion—sideways." Li's quip later got back to Ripley, who bugged out his eyes and roared with laughter.)

As the days wore on, Ripley's absence from most activities began to feel awkward. McMillin noted Ripley's truancy in his journal: "Very seldom see Mr. Ripley during the day. He is usually working in his stateroom . . . Once in a while he gets up on deck for a couple of hours of sun." Ripley seemed to spring to life just before his broadcasts, and performed dutifully. Then he'd disappear back to his room. With windows shut and shades drawn, it became rank with leftover food, fruit peelings, unwashed clothes, and empty cocktail glasses. In a rare display of hospitality, Ripley hosted a cocktail party one night for thirty guests, all of them getting bombed and silly. Li sang "When Irish Eyes Are Smiling" and Storer and McMillin performed a mock *Believe It or Not* radio show that had Ripley howling.

"Gosh, life is wonderful," McMillin declared in that night's journal entry. But as the *Cleveland* steamed toward the Philippines, Ripley's laughter was again replaced by quiet solemnity.

Ripley one day asked the ship's florist to prepare a wreath of flowers. He'd arranged with the captain to visit the spot where a Japanese ship carrying American POWs had been accidentally bombed by US planes. One of those killed was the son of Ripley's friend in New York, and Ripley had offered to toss a wreath atop the spot where the so-called hell ship went down. Coincidentally, another passenger aboard the *Cleveland* had prepared a similar ceremony for his twin brother, who was lost on the same ship. Ripley and the other man stood beside the railing as the *Cleveland* slowed to a crawl. A small crowd gathered as a priest said a quiet prayer and they each tossed their wreaths overboard.

Ahead in Manila waited more celebrity duties and more reminders of war: a city in ruins, buildings and churches gutted and crumbling, pocked with battle scars. In port, children swarmed around Ripley's group, begging for coins and Cokes and shrieking, "Hello, Joe!" Ripley, drenched in sweat, swatted them away, looking stricken as he scanned the gaping wounds and lopsided buildings of the downtown skyline.

With special permission, Ripley's crew received a tour of Corregidor Island, at the entrance to Manila Bay. Douglas MacArthur had used the island's tunnel network, Malinta Tunnel, as his headquarters at the start of America's entry into World War II, but the island fell to Japanese invaders in 1942. When it was retaken by US forces in 1945, many Japanese soldiers committed suicide to avoid capture, detonating explosives that brought sections of the tunnel down on top of them. Across nearly five years of battle, Corregidor had been shelled to rubble. Only Filipino demolition squads and some American soldiers lived there now, and the island remained a dangerous place, rigged with land mines and booby traps. Just weeks earlier, twenty men were killed by an explosion in Malinta Tunnel, their bodies still trapped inside. Some of the soldiers stationed on the island believed Japanese fighters were still hiding deep inside the tunnels, unaware the war had ended.

Ripley's tour guide was a young Filipino lieutenant who oversaw the demolition crews. As he drove Ripley inland, the lieutenant said a land mine was found on the road that very morning—Ripley could have been killed. Ripley had brought along a case of cold Dutch beer, but he and his companions hardly felt festive, and the beer quickly turned warm. At the top of the island, they all began climbing a tower, its metal staircase rickety and damaged. Ripley, now a much portlier specimen than the athlete he'd once been, was exhausted and refused to climb the last steps to the top. The others continued up, then looked out over the complete devastation of a once flowery and magical island, silent except for a few birds.

"Once, many people lived over there," the lieutenant said, pointing. "They laughed and danced and the island was very alive. Now, there is nothing here but death."

On the boat ride back to Manila, one of the engines died and the two-hour trip stretched to four. Ripley arrived shamefully late for a banquet with Army officers and orphans who had been held during the war at nearby Santo Tomas Internment Camp.

In the next day's radio show, Ripley solemnly described the "extent of the damage done by the Japs."

* * *

AFTER A ONE-DAY VISIT to Hong Kong, during which Ripley visited the Wo Hop shipyard where the *Mon Lei* had been built a decade earlier, the SS *President Cleveland* steamed into Shanghai, finally delivering Ripley back to Chinese soil. The arrival wasn't nearly as cathartic as he'd hoped.

Ripley had first visited Shanghai twenty-five years earlier and it had always ranked atop his list of most fascinating cities—"the Paris of the Orient," he'd called it. Now he found chaos, poverty, and anti-American angst. The city had taken a steady beating since the Japanese bombing in 1932, shortly before Ripley's visit that same year. After so many years of battle, the recent postwar economic collapse, and the rising influence of the Communist Party, Ripley hardly recognized Shanghai. As one employee later put it, for Ripley it was like meeting "an old flame who had become soiled and shabby with age, illness, and misfortune."

"Shabby" didn't come close to describing what had occurred in Shanghai after Japan's more aggressive second invasion in 1937. More than 200,000 Chinese soldiers were killed and thousands of civilians raped or beheaded. Eleven years later, Ripley found himself dumbstruck by Shanghai in her wrecked and soiled postwar state.

In a radio broadcast he announced that every time he turned a corner his eyes popped from his head, that he was in a "continual mental tailspin." He was sorry that the man-powered rickshaws had been replaced by pedicabs, and it almost hurt to see the ruined swimming pool at the French Club, which had been used to store Japanese bombs. The city's economy was in turmoil, the exchange rates fluctuating hourly. At one point an American dollar was worth a million Chinese dollars. Ripley described for Radioland how near-worthless $1,000 Chinese bills blew down the streets, how a newspaper cost $50,000 and a single cigarette cost $6,000. In order to buy a new suit from his favorite tailor, Ripley had to hire two men to lug wheelbarrows of Chinese currency from Chase Bank.

Despite the eye-popping distractions, Ripley stuck to the work schedule, drew his cartoons, and spoke into his microphone to NBC listeners. But he seemed disturbed by China's sad state of affairs. During a dinner party at the ambassador's residence he learned that the Communist Army was literally at Shanghai's city gates. He gruffly excused himself and went back to his hotel. Hazel Storer, who had once lived in Shanghai, could tell that Ripley was a wreck. "Shanghai was all but unrecognizable . . . a ravaged caricature," she would write years later. "The whole city seemed to be covered in a thin, gray scum.

The people were silent, indifferent . . . He knew that he would never see China again." Ripley would later describe how it was "beyond all belief" for him to watch the citizens of Shanghai "sit idly in the streets waiting for the Communist armies to roll in and take over."

The next day, Ripley told Doug Storer he wanted to leave Shanghai immediately and fly ahead to Tokyo, to prepare for their planned broadcast from Hiroshima. He argued that he and Storer could use the extra days ahead of the *Cleveland*'s arrival to ensure that their stay in Japan was fruitful. Storer agreed, and he and Ripley caught a hastily arranged flight.

In Tokyo, Douglas MacArthur's staff arranged for Ripley to broadcast from Radio Tokyo, the infamous station where Tokyo Rose had aired her taunting wartime propaganda. MacArthur's PR officer then helped Ripley visit Hiroshima. Security was tight, so Ripley traveled alone, carrying his own camera to film the spot above which the atomic bomb "Little Boy" had detonated nearly three years earlier. He taped his radio show from that site, interviewing survivors of the US attack. Surrounded by mounds of rubble and a crowd filled with injured and sick victims, Ripley told radio listeners that vegetation had begun to grow again and that residents "look very well and they're beginning to wear their bright clothes again." But his voice seemed shaky and unsure.

Meanwhile, back on the *Cleveland*, the others were having "a gay old time," as McMillin put it. He and Li one night competed in a "chug a lug" contest of martinis. When the ship reached the port at Yokohama and they all reunited, Hazel Storer became worried at how "sobered and saddened" Ripley seemed after Hiroshima.

He was becoming more somber as the trip progressed.

ONE NIGHT, the ship's captain hosted a dinner and invited Ripley to sit beside him at the head of the table. Ripley began drinking heavily, and was soon grousing about Franklin Roosevelt, a tirade that escalated into shouts about "that son of a bitch."

The others at the table—including congressman Emmet O'Neal, a Democrat from Kentucky, who'd been appointed ambassador to the Philippines—later said Ripley acted like "a wild man," cursing and waving his arms, his face turning purple. Friends were never entirely sure of the source of such venom. Ripley had for decades lived among wealthy men who had resisted Roosevelt's New Deal. He then became one of those millionaires who hated the idea of sharing his income with the government. He could be generous with charities, he was patriotic to a fault, but he didn't trust the US government with his tax dollars.

Ripley had once met Roosevelt, in the 1930s, and initially claimed to like the man. He served on a March of Dimes committee at one point and sketched a few *Believe It or Not* cartoons that were sympathetic to Roosevelt. Over the years, however, his animosity grew, and even three years after Roosevelt's death his hatred was on full, fuming display that night at the captain's table. Years later, friends would speculate that maybe the poverty of Ripley's youth fueled his belief that the New Deal helped people who should be helping themselves. Li wondered if it had something to do with China—Roosevelt's hesitance to help China during its war with Japan, or maybe Ripley's pride in the fortitude of the Chinese. "He liked China because he saw people working despite poverty, working in spite of war," she said. Ripley seemed to believe the New Deal prevented people from finding their inner strengths (as he had) and made them "beggars forever."

Whatever the complicated reasons, Ripley seemed to know he'd gone too far that night. The captain, Hobart Ehman, finally rose and put a hand on Ripley's shoulder, then whispered in his ear. Ripley hung his head and excused himself from the table.

✳   ✳   ✳

HOMEBOUND TOWARD SAN FRANCISCO, the *Cleveland* stopped once more in Honolulu, where Ripley received special permission and a military escort to tour the devastated naval yard at Pearl Harbor. Here again he came face-to-face with lingering scenes of the war's most terrible moments.

Many of the ships that had been wounded or destroyed on December 7, 1941, had been scrapped or sunk, leaving only the towers, turrets, and antennae of the USS *Arizona* visible above the waterline. Ripley told radio listeners the *Arizona*'s remains looked "like bony skeleton hands." More than 1,100 men had died on the *Arizona*. Ripley was shocked to learn that most of the bodies were still entombed inside.

Standing above the rusting battleship, trying to describe on-air what he was experiencing, Ripley's voice quavered and he struggled to proceed. The others stood back nervously and watched him peer down into the water, the *Arizona*'s deck visible just feet below the surface. He seemed so sad.

"You have no idea how shocking was the sight of that twisted, tortured steel," Ripley said at the close of his broadcast. "I'm sure that all my listeners will join me in tribute to the heroes of Pearl Harbor."

Li Ling-Ai had decided to stay in Honolulu with her parents, and as the *Cleveland* left she stood on the pier waving up at Ripley and the others, wiping tears from her eyes.

While sailing toward home—just ahead of warnings that a tidal wave was roaring toward Hawaii—Ripley told Storer that he wanted to design a memorial for the *Arizona*, some monument that could become a national shrine and forever honor the men who had died there. Ripley even hoped to convince the Navy to raise the *Arizona* and give the dead sailors a proper burial. Storer promised he would get the idea and a few drawings into the right hands, and Ripley began sketching various designs during the final days of the three-week, 26,000-mile journey.

ON THE LAST LEG to San Francisco, the Storers, McMillin, and Ed Dunham (NBC's radio manager) held a small party for Ripley in his stateroom. Dunham performed a mock radio skit, pretending to be Ripley celebrating his ninety-second birthday. But the party was cut short by stormy seas; not quite the predicted tidal wave but a violent thrashing that tossed the ship and caused Ripley to miss his final radio broadcast, scheduled for that night in San Francisco. It was the only show he missed during the journey.

In San Francisco, as he often did during visits there, he stopped briefly at McAllister Street to look into the basement windows of his first apartment. He and the others then traveled by train to Los Angeles for one more *Truth or Consequences* show. That night, Ripley invited McMillin to dinner at the Brown Derby, along with two beautiful blond Hungarian actresses, Mitzi Bruce and Ilona Massey. Massey gave McMillin her phone number and told him, "Call me sometime."

McMillin had fallen in love a dozen times during his weeks abroad, and noticed that Ripley—who "dresses colorfully and in good taste for a big man"—seemed to attract beautiful women, seemingly without trying. The trip had been a young man's fantasy and McMillin filled his diary with giddy descriptions of all the stunning women he'd met. Though he had seen little of

Ripley during the cruise, he was suddenly sitting at Ripley's side in the company of two Hollywood starlets.

Ripley left the next morning for a train ride to San Simeon, to meet with William Randolph Hearst. McMillin, meanwhile, was soon back with his widowed mother, unemployed and planning to look for a job. Yet, as he put it in the final line of his diary, he'd always be able to say, "I went to the Orient with Bob Ripley.

"I could learn more facts in 10 minutes of conversation with Mr. Ripley than I could in reading a whole volume of Book of Knowledge. What a guy."

CHAPTER

23

Those who'd watched Ripley grow moodier and more unpredictable in recent years had hoped that the trip to Hawaii, the Philippines, China, and Japan would refresh him. Instead, he returned home crankier and more volatile than ever.

He snapped at employees and friends. He fired and rehired one of his personal secretaries, Bill McDonald, almost weekly. Once during a dinner party he barked at Ming Jung, telling her not to speak to the other guests, saying, "Get off to your room." He even took his frustrations out on Doug Storer. When one show ran behind schedule, Storer interrupted Ripley during the final moments in order to reach the commercial break in time. Ripley seethed for days and then sent Storer a furious letter. "I don't recall being so disturbed or humiliated as I was on the last program when you cut me off on the air," he wrote, complaining that the dramatic sketches were too long. "This definitely I will never permit again under any circumstances whatever."

Storer dutifully wrote a lengthy letter of apology, blaming the director and promising, "It won't happen again."

King Features was also a target of Ripley's wrath. In a 1948 memo to his editor, Brad Kelly, he complained about changes to a cartoon in which an artist who drew the caption had covered up a small portion of the drawing and, in Ripley's view, ruined the whole thing. "I seriously object to any change being made in the Sunday cartoon," he wrote. "Certainly the greatest newspaper feature in the history of the newspaper business should not be cut down at any time."

Doctors had continued warning Ripley to work less and lose weight, to relax and slow down. Instead, he kept plunging into new projects, including one that he hoped might outlive him. It seemed Ripley had begun giving serious thought to his legacy, to what he would leave behind, and for the past few years he'd been looking for a location for a permanent Believe It or Not museum, ideally one in his former hometown.

In 1945, he had come close to buying a building on the former Santa Rosa estate of Luther Burbank (who'd died in 1926), but the deal fell through. Then, just before the ship left San Francisco for his 1948 Far East trip, Ripley made a quick drive north to Santa Rosa with his sister, Ethel. They visited their parents' graves at the Odd Fellows Cemetery and their mother's church, which was in bad shape. Ripley told Ethel he was thinking of buying the run-down Church Built of One Tree and turning it into his personal museum. It could be a memorial to Lillie Belle, he said, and a place to display his thousands of collected curios.

Back in New York in mid-1948, he contacted Santa Rosa's city manager and offered to pay half the cost of restoring the church, if the city would pay the other half. He suggested moving the building to a new location and adding a special museum wing while keeping the original church intact. The city council initially agreed to the idea, but then a new city manager was hired and argued that the church was too old and would cost too much to move. "Besides," said the new city manager, Ed

Blom, "the building is not fireproof and not a good place for housing valuable curios."

While waiting for his hometown to make a final decision, Ripley continued to work on his Pearl Harbor memorial.

He'd initially proposed raising the *Arizona* and removing the bodies, but the secretary of the Navy's office informed him by letter that it had already decided that recovering the bodies would inflict "needless cruelty" on the victims' families. Ripley agreed to modify his proposal, the design for which included a marble causeway that would give visitors access to the *Arizona* from land. He even wrote to William Randolph Hearst, seeking help with the costs.

"I feel so very deeply about this," he told Hearst, adding that he was ready to appeal to readers and listeners for support.

Storer felt that, with Hearst behind the memorial and Ripley promoting it on radio, it could be "a monument of great importance." He encouraged Ripley in letters through the summer of 1948, reminding him that the Navy was receptive to his idea and that top Navy officials were awaiting Ripley's sketches. Storer nudged him to "send them along shortly." When Ripley finally finished his designs, Storer sent them to Rear Admiral John J. Manning, head of the Navy's yards and docks bureau, who called Ripley's idea "most commendable" and "one that would give me great pride."

Manning offered to provide $8.7 million in military funding, but suggested that the memorial become one that honored not just those killed aboard the *Arizona* but "all of the heroic Pearl Harbor dead." He further suggested building the memorial in a different location, so it could be viewed by ships entering Pearl Harbor, the Hawaiian equivalent of the Statue of Liberty.

Storer then watched in frustration as Ripley slowly, inexplicably backed away from the project through the latter half of 1948, distracted by other tasks and apparently unwilling to modify his designs to meet the Navy's suggestions. Ripley also pulled away from his plans for a Santa Rosa museum after the city hesitated to cooperate.

In no time, both opportunities were lost.

⚡ BELIEVE IT! ⚡

It would take another fourteen years for the USS Arizona *to be declared a national shrine. A memorial would be built above the ship's sunken remains; instead of Ripley's causeway, the memorial is now reached by boat.*

⁎ ⁎ ⁎

TOWARD LATE 1948, at the end of his current radio program's cycle, Ripley made plans to travel once again, arranging to join a four-day trip around the world by airplane. By now, however, it had become clear that his hair-trigger temper and angry outbursts weren't solely emotional but were physical manifestations of his increasingly bad health. His doctors refused to allow him to make the trip. Doug Storer wondered if the small stroke Ripley had apparently suffered a few years earlier was partly to blame for his erratic behavior.

Then again, in his recent travels Ripley had discovered the world to be a much different place. His cruise on the *Cleveland* had taken him to or past the battlefields and morgues of the Pacific war, all of which had ruffled and saddened him, as had China's unstoppable slump toward communism. He'd returned home in an exhausted state but continued to work at a frenzied pace, and now the doctors were telling him: *No more traveling.*

What he needed most was to take a *real* vacation and recuperate. To escape to Florida and lounge beside his pool. To dawdle aboard the *Mon Lei,* which now sat docked behind his house like a neglected toy. Instead, he added yet another massive commitment to his perpetually overbooked life: a television show.

✳ ✳ ✳

THOUGH TWENTY YEARS of live radio had prepared Ripley reasonably well for a transition to television, it turned out the mediums were hardly interchangeable.

As Ripley sat on a soundstage behind a hand-carved desk and cameras began to roll during the filming of his pilot episode, he seemed startled when co-host Norman Brokenshire (a popular radio announcer) appeared beside him, accompanied by a spectacularly beautiful young woman. *"We-elll,* who's this pretty lady," Ripley asked, and Brokenshire introduced Nellie Jane Cannon, a cover model whom *LIFE* magazine referred to as one of "New York's loveliest girls." Ripley seemed flustered and promptly mangled her name, welcoming "Miss Jennie Ling" to his show. It's possible he'd leaned too heavily on his radio-show crutch and tossed back too much drink.

When Brokenshire asked Ripley if he still actually drew all of his own cartoons, Ripley insisted that he got up at six o'clock every morning to draw. Brokenshire dared him to prove it, and Ripley turned to Nellie/Jennie and asked what she'd like him to draw.

"How about the strangest man you've ever seen?"

Ripley walked over to an easel, picked up a piece of charcoal and quickly slashed a few thick lines, then scratched some waves and squiggles that seemed to be hair. As he stroked and swished, the vague shape of a man's face appeared. Ripley smeared parts of his drawing with his fingers and palm and, as if by magic, the disjointed black scribbles came into focus. The man was clearly African, practically a caricature, with a wide nose and high forehead.

It was an impressive impromptu drawing, but as Broken-shire quickly pointed out, there didn't seem to be anything strange or unique about the face. Ripley then explained: "The reason he really is so strange is because on his head he has *horns* . . ."—and here he drew on his man's forehead a long, black horn—"*twenty . . . eight . . . inches . . . long!*" Ripley said that years earlier in Africa he had met the humble man, who shed his horns the way deer shed antlers.

"Each year they grew again," Ripley told Nellie Jane. "He is without a doubt the strangest man I've ever seen."

Despite Ripley's awkward hesitations and occasional stumbles, NBC executives decided they liked what they saw in the pilot, which also featured Nellie Jane gamely choking down a bite of a hundred-year-old Chinese egg that Ripley fed her with a spoon. The network decided the Believe It or Not brand was ready for prime time and offered Ripley a weekly show that would launch on March I, 1949.

While Storer was thrilled to introduce his best client to the untested waters of broadcast television, he was worried about Ripley, who was clearly unwell. Ripley promised Storer he'd take it easy during an upcoming Florida vacation. But first he closed out 1948 in style, dressed in a checked suit and sporting a fake mustache.

In mid-December, King Features hosted a massive celebration for the thirtieth anniversary of Ripley's *Believe It or Not*. The Gay Nineties–themed costume party was held at Toots Shor's on West Fifty-first Street. Ripley and Baer had become fans of the restaurant/bar and its wisecracking owner, Bernard

"Toots" Shor, a rough-edged storyteller beloved by such celebrity eater-drinkers as Jackie Gleason, Frank Sinatra, Orson Welles, and Ernest Hemingway.

All the top King Features executives attended, as did many syndicated Hearst columnists and cartoonists. Dressed in a baggy houndstooth suit and wearing a derby and his fake mustache, Ripley posed for silly pictures and signed autographs for King Features employees who'd worked for him for years but who rarely got the chance to see the man in person. Liese Wisse looked stunning in an extremely low-cut burlesque outfit and Li Ling-Ai came dressed as a sexy Chinese peasant. Surrounded by so many friends and colleagues—Vyvyan Donner, Cygna Conly, Bugs Baer, and many others—Ripley drank and sang and danced all night, having the time of his life.

*　*　*

EVER SINCE HIS STEEP RISE to fame in the 1930s, Ripley had been nursing a plan. He'd explained it in a 1935 interview with one of his first editors, Harry B. Smith, who was still working as a columnist at the *San Francisco Chronicle*. During the interview, Smith asked about the sudden wealth and renown, remembering Ripley as so shy and seemingly vulnerable to exploitation. But Ripley assured Smith that stardom didn't trouble him because once he'd earned enough money he would buy a dream house on the Atlantic coast and, as he put it, "spend his last years in leisure and ease."

Fourteen years later, he'd found the house but not the leisure and ease.

Into 1949, he spent busy weeks obsessively sprucing up Hi-Mount. He'd already moved some of his household staff down from New York and now had ten people working at the house or on the *Mon Lei*. His longtime carpenter came south to install new cabinets and fixtures throughout the house, to build a special ramp beside the saltwater swimming pool, to help Ripley's dogs get in and out of the water. It was all in preparation for what Ripley intended would soon become his permanent relocation to Florida, the dream he'd described to Smith.

Doug and Hazel visited for a few weeks so that Ripley and Storer could discuss the upcoming TV show. At first, Ripley seemed like his old entertaining self. He invited another couple to visit and they all rang in 1949 together, swimming in the pool and strolling on the vast lawn that sloped down to Lake Worth.

Ripley one day invited a dozen friends over for a floating cocktail party on the *Mon Lei*, handing everyone colorful straw hats as they boarded. Despite heavy winds and protests from his captain, Ripley insisted on sailing beyond Lake Worth, through an inlet into the Atlantic. Waves battered the flat-bottomed boat and Ripley's guests were nearly tossed overboard. The captain quickly returned to the calmer waters of Lake Worth and the party continued on Ripley's dock. That night, the Storers watched Ripley slip into a sodden funk. He complained that his guests had taken the valuable Chinese hats he'd handed out, thinking they were souvenirs.

Soon, there were more signs of instability. One day, Hazel walked into the living room to find Ripley's secretary, Cygna Conly, holding a hand to her face and seething with anger. Conly and Ripley had argued about some business matter and he'd slapped her. He later apologized and bought Conly a mink coat—not the first time a mink served as an apology. (Ripley once enlisted Li Ling-Ai's help in buying *twelve* mink coats for "the ladies that he went out with once in a while," as Li put it years later. When Ripley gave Li the money to make the purchase, he told her, "Choose one for yourself.")

Among his many messy, overlapping relationships, the one with beautiful Ming Jung remained especially mysterious to those who witnessed Ripley's occasionally harsh treatment. Hearst sportswriter and columnist Bob Considine and his wife once spent a summer living across the pond from BION Island. They visited frequently for cocktails, despite some competitive tension between Ripley and Considine (who would write a less-than-flattering and wildly inaccurate mini-biography of Ripley in 1961). The Considines were visiting the night Ripley ordered Ming, "Off to your room," and Millie Considine went to comfort Ming, who talked about keeping her child's ashes in a lacquered wooden box. "They are not there now," Ming allegedly told Considine. "When Bob gets mad at me he hides them."

Millie Considine would see Ming paddling alone on the pond and wondered what made Ripley's women stay. Millie came to believe that "once Ripley took an interest in a girl there was a bond between them forever after—no matter what." Hazel Storer would similarly wonder about the women who stayed, later writing, "How some of those gals took what he handed out in the way of abusive and contemptuous language I'll never know."

Just a year earlier, in an interview with *American Weekly* magazine, Ripley had shared his ongoing belief that "the only time women are happy is when they are completely under the domination of men." Now, though, even Ming had had enough of Ripley's domination. She'd finally given up on him, moved out of BION, and married a man who ran the Mamaroneck auto and marine service station that refueled and repaired the *Mon Lei.*

Ripley was rarely without companionship, however. At Hi-Mount he presented a sexy new Cuban girlfriend to the Storers and other visiting friends, and for a few days they all had a grand time, taking turns riding Ripley's new motor scooter or his tandem bicycle around the lakeside path. They went to the movies one night and Ripley snored through *A Tree Grows in Brooklyn.* (Notorious for sleeping in theaters, and for snoring like a diesel engine, Ripley once annoyed a crowd by loudly sleeping through a performance of Rodgers and Hammerstein's *Allegro,* despite much hushing from an usher and the audience.) Ripley's girlfriend was soon joined by an attractive blonde who flew up from Havana bearing bottles of rum and an adorable springer spaniel puppy. Rum punches lasted until dawn, but the fun ended the next day.

Worried that the puppy seemed sick, Ripley suggested to his owner that she take the dog to a vet. She promised she would, but instead corralled the dog inside the kitchen. A household staffer found the dog there, sicker than before, and took him to the vet, where he died. Ripley was furious. To make amends, his Cuban girlfriend and her guest offered to make dinner. They clattered around in the kitchen while the Storers and another couple got dressed in upstairs guest rooms.

Ripley sat drinking rum, getting madder the more he drank. Hazel was the first to come downstairs and found Ripley alone at the dining room table, his head in his hands. She touched his shoulder and Ripley jumped up and exploded with a tirade about the death of the puppy and his visitor's carelessness. Hazel went to the kitchen and found the two women locked in an embrace, clearly terrified. Moments earlier, Ripley had apparently gotten fed up with the giggling and burst into the kitchen, yelling at his girlfriend's friend, accusing her of treating the puppy like "a toy." He'd terrified both women, and possibly himself.

And yet, Hazel doubted that Ripley's love of animals was the true source of his anger that night. She suspected some undiagnosed illness was to blame.

* * *

THE STORERS STAYED with Ripley a few more weeks. Doug Storer wanted to make sure his client and friend was emotionally and physically ready for the upcoming television season. Though Ripley was often surrounded by eager employees and devoted girlfriends, he had few truly close friends with whom to share his deepest troubles. This became apparent during the last days of the Storers' final visit at Hi-Mount.

One night they went to a quiet French restaurant in Palm Beach and Ripley relaxed and spoke freely, telling them the full story of Oakie, about his sorrow in losing her to cancer before the war. He broke into tears at the memory of the one true love of his life. Another night, Ripley sat alone with Hazel on the back deck and talked for two hours about his tenuous relationship with his brother, and their most recent schism.

He'd tried over the years to find the right fit for Doug in his world. Doug had done some work at King Features, until his conflicts with Joe Connolly got him fired. Doug's role as captain of Ripley's yacht hadn't lasted long either, and Doug mostly ended up doing manual labor around BION Island, more comfortable with chauffeurs and carpenters than his brother's newspaper friends. Doug was extremely introverted and often felt overwhelmed by the social scene that swirled around Ripley. In trying to relax and fit in, he usually drank too much. Tensions led to occasional fights between the brothers, with Doug once telling Ripley, "To hell with you!"

One frequent houseguest said Doug "changed from mouse to lion as the level on the bottle went down" and Li Ling-Ai thought Doug seemed "always high." ("He was a blue-collar guy who was caught up in a white-collar world," one of Doug's two sons, Robert, said decades later. "There were a lot of temptations there, be it alcohol or women.") Ripley eventually bought Doug and his wife a house in Mamaroneck and Doug ventured out on his own, working blue-collar jobs, including a stint at a naval shipyard. Even so, Ripley always tried to lure his brother back, calling and asking, "What are you doing? C'mon over."

Ripley explained to Hazel Storer that night in Florida how one particular fight with his brother had not yet healed. They'd been at Ripley's New York apartment and Ripley was on a ladder arranging some of his shelved curios. Doug had been drinking and the brothers began to argue about something. Voices were raised, arms flailed, and Doug knocked over the ladder, which nearly hit Ripley in the head as it crashed to the floor. Stunned, Ripley shouted, "Out!" He pointed to the door and told Doug he wanted him out of his life. He told Hazel he was thinking of cutting off any future financial support.

Ripley could be quite generous with friends, and in fact had recently loaned Doug Storer $1,000 to carry him through a financial rough patch until the new TV show began. He once bought Li a new car, as thanks for the many rides she'd given him in her beat-up Chevy. (She asked him to return the car.) Li wondered if Ripley, in the role of surrogate parent, had high expectations for his brother and didn't believe in "handouts." Ripley sometimes felt that Doug wasn't willing to care for himself, at least not in the manner that Ripley, as father figure, expected. Ripley set high standards for everyone who worked with him, and Doug had clearly fallen short. In his rant that night with Hazel, Ripley said he considered Doug "no brother of mine." Hazel tried to be sympathetic, but she was shaken by Ripley's bitterness.

* * *

AFTER THE STORERS left Hi-Mount, Ripley traveled to Cuba, possibly to reconnect with the girlfriend he'd scared off.

While in Havana, he concocted a new plan: to buy the property next to Hi-Mount and turn it into a studio from which he could broadcast television shows.

He mailed Doug Storer drawings of what the studio might look like, along with an enthusiastic letter: "I have many more and different ideas . . . What do you think?" Storer replied, in the kind of patient tone one might use with a child, "We don't know whether it would be mechanically possible to broadcast from that spot," adding that there might be restrictions that would prevent such a business from operating in a residential neighborhood.

After Havana, Ripley returned to New York, and a few weeks before the first TV show he invited a group of friends to his apartment for a party.

When the Storers arrived at Ripley's place, he was waiting anxiously at the elevator that opened directly into his tenth-floor apartment. He immediately grabbed Hazel by the hand and led her into his bedroom. He'd developed a kinship with Hazel, who assumed that Ripley took a special interest in her because she'd lived in Shanghai in the 1930s. Hazel could tell he was unusually distraught and had been drinking heavily. He sat at the edge of his huge bed and began to cry, tears dribbling onto his white dinner jacket. He'd read earlier in the day that the Communist Army had finally overtaken Shanghai.

Over and over, he told her, "We'll never see China again. *Never!*"

Hazel knew, as did Li Ling-Ai, just how passionately Ripley felt about China. "Rip really loved and admired this remarkable country and its people," Hazel once said. He had surrounded himself with women, employees, art, food, and furniture from his adopted land. Impressed by the Chinese ability to find happiness in poverty and war, he admired their resilience, believing that the survival of life's hardships made people stronger and more creative.

Li once said the Chinese "made him remember his own youth and feel good that he survived too."

It made sense, then, for Ripley to become so emotional the night he learned of China's latest setback. The Communist Army had taken control of all but southeast China, and it was just a matter of time before Chiang Kai-shek's US-supported Kuomintang forces fell to Mao Zedong's Soviet-backed People's Liberation Army.

For a man so inspired by all things Chinese, it also made sense that the decor and tone of his TV show would be distinctly Asian, a televised culmination of his lifelong obsession.

ON MARCH 1, 1949, at 9:30 p.m., anyone on the East Coast with a television set tuned to the NBC network would have seen their black-and-white screens fill with the image of a young Chinese man banging a gong, who then welcomed viewers to one of the more surreal programs in the short history of broadcast television.

After achieving such massive success in newspapers, publishing, radio, and film, Ripley the media pioneer was hoping the Believe It or Not magic would translate to this latest medium. His first show launched with a comedy duo, Ming and Ling, veterans of New York's cabaret scene who worked at the China Doll club and were known for their Chinese hillbilly routine and their Frank Sinatra impressions. (They'd soon score a radio hit with their song "Eggroll Eatin' Mama.")

Ripley then introduced his lovely sidekick, twenty-four-year-old Peggy Corday, a World War II pinup girl. Ripley bragged that Corday had recently been named "Miss Television of 1949." Her first moment as Ripley's on-air assistant was a shrill scream of pretend shock as she opened a closet door to find Ripley's lifelike Masakichi statue staring back at her. Corday was bright-eyed and quick on her feet; her role would in part require her to keep the unpredictable host on track.

Until now, Ripley had achieved celebrity as a mostly in-visible cartoonist and radio personality. Across the first half of 1949, he became an in-the-flesh television star.

While the show sometimes featured actors performing the same type of dramatic sketches he'd aired on radio, those acts now took a secondary role to Ripley's on-screen persona. He'd been in the public eye for three decades, but hadn't appeared in a film—or on a screen of any kind—since before the war. On the grainy screen of a Motorola set, he seemed older and paunch-ier than the global adventurer viewers may have expected. (His teeth looked better than ever, though. He'd had another ag-gressive surgical procedure to further straighten them, so much so that his upper lip, after a lifetime of protrusion, now dipped *inward*.)

Viewers liked what they saw. At the end of the first six epi-sodes, NBC had a chance to back out but instead affirmed its commitment to a full thirteen-episode season. Most shows fea-tured Ripley interviewing special guests, war heroes, and inter-esting people he'd profiled over the years, including a paralyzed Canadian artist who painted with a brush in his teeth. Ripley usually sketched a favorite cartoon, such as the self-mutilating holy men he'd seen in India or African Kikuyu women.

"I always like to draw pictures of the young ladies," he said flirtatiously to Corday.

He seemed most at ease during those pure moments of draw-ing at his easel while talking breezily about his travels. Ripley was still a supremely talented artist and NBC weaved plenty of on-air sketches into each script, with Ripley drawing scenes that he'd "bring to life for you" in segments called "Ripley's Sketchbook."

Ripley's favorite dramatic reenactment involved the story of a melancholy Italian man who could never laugh "because the whole world is ugly and unhappy." His doctor's prescription was to find laughter at the circus, where the famous Grimaldi the Clown performed. It turned out that the doctor's patient was Grimaldi himself, who eventually died of "melancholia." Said Ripley, "The funniest man in the world was also the unhappiest."

Turning to Peggy Corday, he added, "The difference between joy and sadness isn't so very much after all." Friends would note the irony of Ripley's affinity for Grimaldi's story.

As he'd done since breaking into radio in the early 1930s, Ripley drank whiskey or gin before each episode. Sometimes it helped, and he appeared smooth and calm. Other nights he seemed awkward and clumsy, forgetting guest names and mangling lines and, if one listened closely, slurring and swishing his words. While introducing a lord and lady from Scotland who were to perform a traditional Scottish dance—a surreal jig alleged to be the only time British nobility performed such a thing in public—Ripley told the couple, "Well, you'll have the joint a-jiving—or something like that."

Though he seemed to be finding some momentum, the shows were taking an emotional toll, and colleagues worried about Ripley's increasing agitation, how he often looked so drawn and tired. On May 4, he fired off one of his scathing telegrams, this one aimed at NBC executives. "This is a formal protest against the dreadful way in which the 'Believe It or Not' TV show has been mismanaged," he wrote, signing it "Believe It or Not Ripley."

Two days later, NBC received another telegram, this one from Liese Wisse, telling NBC that Ripley refused to come to the studio the next day. "Mr. Ripley is entertaining guests in New York apartment. Will not be available for rehearsal," Liese wrote.

NBC had to wonder what it had gotten itself into with the temperamental cartoonist.

PEGGY CORDAY WAS PAID $100 per episode and turned out to be worth every penny. Smooth and professional, even a bit sassy and flirty, she often ad-libbed when Ripley flubbed one of his lines or maimed some guest's name, deftly covering up the host's gaffes. She was the perfect and perky offset to the some-times confused and distracted Ripley, who seemed to enjoy hav-ing her by his side during his tenuous venture into television.

Even with Ripley's lack of polish, the show became instantly popular, at least among the limited number of households with televisions. Ripley could be clunky while interviewing others, but his unease somehow helped guests relax, as it had on radio. Like the daytime TV hosts who would later become megastars using a similar formula, he gently coaxed guests to open up, to share their emotions and vulnerabilities, often with surprisingly moving results.

He again interviewed Poon Lim, the sailor who'd drifted for 133 days in a life raft. He told Ripley, "I was never afraid." Ripley introduced viewers to a Philadelphia man who was in-jured in a car accident and, told that he'd be wheelchair-bound for life, trained himself to walk again—on his *hands*. Another guest was born blind and had taught himself to play piano—at age *two*. One show celebrated National Hospital Week and Rip-ley interviewed Army nurse Katherine Dollison, who'd been on

Corregidor when it fell to the Japanese. She broke down while describing her three years in a Japanese prison: "Well, Bob. It was pretty awful."

Off-screen, however, the troubles continued. He became disproportionately angry when NBC approved, then overruled, a guest list he and Storer had put together—*after* the guests had already been paid. Ripley also complained about the injustice of one writer (George Lefferts) getting full credit for writing the show when others (including Pearlroth and Storer) had been doing much of the work. In general, Ripley seemed burdened by this foray into TV land. A week shy of the final episode of his first thirteen-week season, Ripley bade his audience farewell with an impromptu and heartfelt prayer, concluding: "The blessing of the Lord be upon you."

Though frustrated with aspects of NBC's handling of the show, he appreciated those who worked on it, and in late May threw a party at a German restaurant for the cast and crew, just before the May 24 program, which would unexpectedly turn out to be his last.

CHAPTER 24

Thirteen weeks into the season, Ripley fans knew when and where to tune in. At nine thirty on Tuesday night, May 24, viewers saw the familiar introductory shot of a Buddha, followed by the sound of a gong. Announcer Fritz DeWilde explained that tonight Ripley would bring to life a dramatization of "the true story behind the world's most famous bugle call." With Memorial Day a week away, Ripley had decided to feature a patriotic tribute to taps.

First, Peggy Corday joined Ripley at his desk to introduce a reenactment of a Hungarian man and wife being separated during World War II and sent to concentration camps. Each thought the other had died and after the war they both moved to New York. While riding the subway one day, the man met another Holocaust survivor, Marcel Sternberger. As the two men talked, Sternberger realized that he knew the man's wife and he helped reunite the couple.

Calling it "one of the most touching love stories ever recorded," Ripley interviewed Sternberger, whom he called the couple's "guardian angel."

In the next segment, Ripley and Corday looked through his collection of crown jewels, gem-crusted replicas of crowns, and scepters from England, France, India, and Africa. Ripley explained how the duke of Windsor chose not to wear a crown during his brief reign as king of England (before abdicating to marry his American girlfriend). He added that he'd recently seen the duke in Palm Beach, and instead of a crown and scepter he wore a golf cap and wielded a golf club.

Suddenly, Ripley's eyes glazed over and he grew quiet, still holding one of the crowns in his hand. Corday realized something was wrong and quickly stepped in.

"Bob, they're beautiful," she gushed, and held a jeweled crown up to the camera. "Henry the Sixth!"

Standing offstage, Doug Storer knew something was wrong too, even though the rest of the crew didn't immediately react to the sudden stillness of the host. Storer had seen it before, these brief Ripley blackouts. But the show was live, with a studio audience, and couldn't be interrupted.

"Bob, they're absolutely astonishing," Corday continued, trying to keep the show rolling.

As Ripley slumped slightly, his eyes still open, Corday stepped closer and put her arm on his shoulder, to prevent him from falling over. Storer was amazed at Corday's poise but knew he needed to intervene. Just as he was about to walk onto the stage, Ripley emerged from his stupor and, with Corday's help, haltingly carried on.

After mumbling an introduction to a dramatization on the life of King Henry the Fourth, Ripley groggily introduced the planned reenactment of the story behind the funereal bugle call taps. He repeated the oft-told but apocryphal version of the song's origins in which a Union captain found the music in the pocket of his dead son, a Confederate soldier. (Taps was actually composed by Union general Daniel Butterfield in 1862 and later played by buglers at both Union and Confederate funerals.)

Instead of closing the show with his usual good-night prayer, Ripley looked into the camera and explained in a somewhat shaky voice that the program would end with the playing of taps, in honor of all the veterans whose ultimate sacrifice to their country was being commemorated that Memorial Day.

"May this call be a requiem not only for our dead but for the very act of war which took their lives," he said. "And to that all mankind must say *Amen.*"

As the program began fading to black, a lone bugler played the familiar notes of taps, his figure silhouetted against a backdrop of clouds.

When the final note expired, the show closed with the sound of a gong.

* * *

IT'S UNCLEAR what exactly happened to Ripley onstage that night—there is no known film footage of the episode, and eyewitnesses later shared differing accounts of what occurred next. Some witnesses said Ripley grew weary again after the show, passed out, and fell to the floor. Others said he collapsed on the air and was rushed to the hospital. One employee speculated that Ripley had suffered a small stroke, while others assumed that his heart problems had caused a temporarily sluggish flow of blood to his brain. (As a producer for the show, Doug Storer witnessed the entire scene, making his version the most reliable.)

In a detailed account written years later, Storer said he cornered Ripley in the studio while crews disassembled the set and the audience filed out.

"Stop," Storer said. "I want to talk to you about something."

Storer knew Ripley was physically in bad shape and that his doctor had been warning him to get a more complete checkup.

"You've got to go into the hospital and get those checkups," Storer said. "You're going to do it this week."

"No, no. I'm not going to do it this week," Ripley said. "Maybe next week."

"Bob, I don't care if we cancel the show. I'm not going to have you do what you did tonight and make it permanent," Storer insisted.

Storer was a few inches shorter than Ripley, who patted him on the shoulder as if he were a child and said, "Oh, Doug, Doug, stop worrying."

But Storer was familiar with Ripley's often-irrational optimism and well-honed delay tactics. He made Ripley promise to visit the hospital as soon as possible.

"You win, Doug," Ripley finally agreed. "I'm going to the hospital for a checkup at once."

But Ripley didn't check in the next day. Instead, he threw a party.

When Ripley called Li Ling-Ai the next morning and told her he wanted to host her birthday party, she told him he'd mixed up the dates and it wasn't her birthday yet. But he seemed desperate for an excuse to defer his promise to Storer, so Li relented. She could tell Ripley was nervous about the hospital visit and assumed he wanted to enjoy one more get-together with friends before letting doctors poke and prod him.

The day after that—Thursday, May 26—Ripley checked into Harkness Pavilion at Columbia-Presbyterian Medical Center, where technicians administered tests that confirmed what he already knew: like his dad, he had a bad heart.

His condition was hardly critical, though, and Ripley remained in fairly good spirits, even when doctors decided to keep him overnight for more tests. That night, Bugs Baer paid a quick visit, sneaking in a bottle of booze to ease his friend's discomfort.

The next morning, Ripley used his bedside phone to call other friends and start making plans for the weekend. One doctor, Ralph Boots, then arrived with two well-known heart specialists, who agreed that even more tests were needed. The specialists administered an injection of some kind, but Ripley insisted he still felt good and expected to be released soon. Li had promised to stop by for lunch and Ripley told his nurses that Madame Chiang Kai-shek was going to pay him a visit. When Li arrived, the nurses assumed she really was Madame Chiang until Ripley confessed to the gag.

But Li grew worried when she saw Ripley. Liese Wisse was already there, having volunteered to spend the day by Ripley's side, and she seemed troubled too.

"His face was a little lonely," Li said years later. She tried to cheer him up by ordering lunch from a nurse, asking if they had pheasant lips on the menu. Ripley laughed but then got back to business. He had previously asked Li to enlist a group of scientists and doctors for an upcoming episode about believe-it-or-nots in medicine and, specifically, Chinese herbs. Li said she was meeting with two scientists and a doctor that very night. When she left him, she could tell Ripley seemed anxious.

"I sensed an unease," she later said, recalling that he was "a trifle scared."

Still, Ripley tried to convince himself it wasn't serious and continued making future plans. At around five o'clock, at the end of his second day in the hospital, he called Baer, who now lived in Connecticut, not far from Ripley's home in Mamaroneck.

Ripley told Baer he was still suffering through his doctor's "checkup," but that he expected to be home for the weekend and wanted to see him.

"I'm going to get home this week," he said. "I don't care what happens. I'm going to go home and *be* home."

"Come on," Baer offered. "Join me. We'll do something."

Ripley seemed thrilled with the idea. "I'll be out to your farm tomorrow afternoon," he said.

When Ripley hung up the phone, he asked Liese to take some dictation, then suddenly clutched his chest and began to convulse.

Liese jumped from her seat and rushed to his side, calling out wildly for help. When no one responded, she raced down the hall to beckon a nurse, who quickly found the doctor on call. They all sprinted back to Ripley's room, but it was too late.

LeRoy Robert Ripley was dead, the victim of a massive heart attack. He was fifty-nine.

✷ ✳ ✻

WITHIN THE HOUR, Liese found herself all alone and tasked with making a series of painful, tearful phone calls—to Ripley's brother, to Norbert Pearlroth, to Robert Hyland, Doug Storer, and many others.

"Mr. Ripley is dead," she told each one, over and over. "He's *dead.*"

Liese next reached Cygna Conly, who in turn broke the news to Li Ling-Ai. Li couldn't believe that the man who'd just hosted her premature birthday party, who seemed so full of jokes and optimism just hours earlier, was dead. She gripped the phone in shock. *How could Ripley be gone?* "It is no good to be that famous and work that hard," she told Conly. "Because you die young."

A group of friends gathered that night at the hospital. Amid the gloom, Pearlroth quietly commented on how strange it was that Ripley's final broadcast had been his thirteenth, that the show had featured the story of a funeral song. He further told the others that ten years earlier Ripley had actually predicted his life might end in 1949.

They'd been having dinner together when Ripley observed that his life had thus far gone in ten-year cycles. Ever attuned to a hard-to-believe story, he explained how he'd started his cartooning career in 1909, had launched his *Believe It or Not* series ten years after that, and in 1929 had joined King Features. Ripley told Pearlroth that night in 1939 that he hoped Providence would allow him "another ten years of the same life."

Li told the others how Ripley once spoke to her about his hope to be reincarnated—in China. She said she believed Ripley had "the Chinese attitude."

"We are all born lonely," Li said. "We are all what we create."

Bizarrely, the day Ripley died was also a day of death for China. The last of the Nationalist Army troops retreated from Shanghai while others surrendered to Mao's soldiers, who then marched them off to POW camps. The world's fourth-largest city was now fully in the hands of the Communists.

✴ ✳ ✴

NEWS OF RIPLEY'S DEATH spread quickly. Hazel Storer was listening to music on the radio when an announcer broke in with a news flash. When Bugs Baer learned that his friend was dead, he immediately started writing a column, which would appear the next morning in Hearst's *New York Journal-American* and across America, via the International News Service.

"This one is tough to believe," it began. "The Believe-It-Or-Not man will not answer the gong [on his TV show] Tuesday night. It rang for the last time Friday afternoon when Ripley dissolved into the mysterious past whence came his amazing truths."

Baer had known Ripley for more than thirty years. They had grown up together, become famous and rich together. They'd shared innumerable drinks, laughs, and women. Baer had been with Ripley the night he created his first "Believe It or Not" (that is, "Champs and Chumps") cartoon, and the night he'd met Beatrice. Ripley had been with Baer when his first wife died, and earlier in 1949 had hosted a New York Heart Association fund-raiser for his second wife, Louise, who was ill. Now Ripley was gone and Baer was in mourning. But print was his life, his outlet, as it had been for Ripley, so he forced himself to mourn publicly. His column continued:

> He had the pride of craftsmanship in his drawings and the authority of knowledge in his statements. Nobody ever proved him wrong. If Ripley told me I had two heads, I would go out and buy two hats. And tip them both to the greatest cartoonist in the history of American journalism.

* * *

FOUR DAYS LATER, a funeral service was held at St. James Episcopal Church, a half-dozen blocks from Ripley's apartment. Though he'd nurtured a lifelong fascination with religion, he was never a churchgoer. The Episcopal church had been Storer's idea, and he asked the Rev. Dr. James W. Hyde to officiate.

More than four hundred attended, with hundreds more waiting outside. William Randolph Hearst's son, William Jr., served as an honorary pallbearer, alongside publisher Max Schuster. Former heavyweight champs Gene Tunney and Jack Dempsey attended, as did famed aviators Eddie Rickenbacker and James

Doolittle; numerous celebrities, journalists, and athletes; and a large contingent of artists and cartoonists, including such long-ago colleagues as Paul Terry and Herb Roth.

One by one, Ripley's lovers arrived, including Ming Jung, now married. She and a few other former BION Island inhabitants (the voluntary signers of Ripley's waiver) sat together in a pew, weeping behind black veils, an awkward reunion. Eight men carried the coffin, staggering at one point and almost losing their grip. Thousands lined the streets to watch the bronze, rose-covered casket roll toward Grand Central Station, where it would begin traveling by rail back to Ripley's native California. A group of his companions, including Liese and Ling-Ai, entered a black limousine behind the hearse as onlookers rubbernecked to see who was behind the veils.

One man on his lunch break turned to a man beside him and said, "They must be his models." A woman nearby made a crude joke ("You mean his whores?") and they all shared a laugh. Hazel Storer overheard and scowled at them.

Ripley then began his final transcontinental journey, loaded onto *The Chicagoan*, accompanied by his brother and sister. In Chicago, his body was transferred to a *City of San Francisco* train for the two-day trip west, back to the town where his cartooning career had begun. Nell Griffith, Ripley's first friend and first love, met the casket at the San Francisco depot and traveled in the hearse, led by police escort, for the last fifty-mile leg back to Santa Rosa. It was a suitable final journey.

SANTA ROSANS TURNED OUT by the thousands to say farewell, lining the streets and spilling out of Lillie Belle's Church Built of One Tree.

Classmates and neighbors told stories to the papers about

young Ripley the obsessed doodler, the aspiring ballplayer; how he never forgot his hometown, especially Miss O'Meara; how proud they were of the rangy and curious barefoot boy who left town and followed his whimsical dreams.

Nell Griffith wrote a story for the *Santa Rosa Press-Democrat,* describing the LeRoy Ripley she once knew: "a shy and rather awkward boy . . . a boy dressed in a brown suit with knee pants . . . a boy with a great gift and a driving ambition." Nell's husband had died two years earlier. Now widowed and raising her children alone, Nell said of Ripley's death, "It shouldn't have happened so soon."

Compared to the average Joe, Ripley seemed to have lived the life of twenty men. He had also poured everything he had into *Believe It or Not,* which became his life, his identity, his true religion. That commitment had fully consumed him, professionally and personally, leaving little room for anything or anyone else.

Some, like Hazel Storer, believed that losing China to a Communist regime had contributed to Ripley's ill health. (Mao Zedong would officially establish the People's Republic of China five months after Ripley's death.) His sister, Ethel, on the other hand, wondered if his inability to create a museum and a legacy in the Church Built of One Tree had been a factor. "He felt pretty bad about not being able to make it a memorial for his curios," she told a reporter after the funeral.

The likeliest reason for Ripley's health problems and turbulent behavior was one he'd been hinting at in print for decades.

An insatiable, incurable romantic, he loved women so much (and, apparently, so often) but had never managed to find his one true love—except Oakie. In fact, his physical and emotional decline seemed to have begun in full after Oakie died. In a revealing 1947 interview with *True Confession* magazine, entitled "Ripley Wants a Wife!" he admitted that for all the material success he had gained, what he still lacked was "the one thing that really matters to a man."

"I've discovered that fame and good fortune don't mean a thing unless you can share them with the right woman," he said.

After a prayer service at Lillie Belle's church, the church Isaac had helped build, LeRoy Ripley was buried beside his father and mother at Odd Fellows Cemetery, less than twenty blocks from his childhood home. Li stood beside his grave, tearfully praying that he'd get his wish to be reincarnated.

"He was such a mystery, like the Chinese. He loved the mystery of an idea," she said. "He loved life so much."

On one of his final *Mon Lei* trips, while moored in Savannah, Ripley told a reporter that his staff was so well organized he expected *Believe It or Not* to continue "many, many years after I die." In the weeks following his death, however, there were no guarantees Ripley's legacy would survive, let alone thrive. In fact, it seemed as if everything he'd built up might collapse into rubble without his stewardship.

At first, the television show limped ahead, airing Tuesday nights through the summer of 1949. A bearded announcer named Robert St. John introduced himself as the new host and "guest custodian" of Ripley's sketch books. Joined by Li Ling-Ai for a few shows, they'd flip through pages of Ripley cartoons, then introduce a dramatic reenactment, with no on-air mention of Ripley's demise. (The show would last another year. It would be revived in the 1980s, hosted by Jack Palance, and again in 2000.)

The daily cartoon also lurched onward. King Features editor Ward Greene announced that the cartoon would continue because Ripley's research files contained so much "interesting material." Norbert Pearlroth kept mining the library for hard-to-believe facts, as he had for twenty-six years, and Paul Frehm became the lead artist.

～ BELIEVE IT! ～

Ripley's Believe It or Not *remains one of the longest-running cartoons in history. In 2012 it was being drawn by John Graziano.*

Even with the television show and cartoon on seemingly stable ground, the rest of Ripley's empire—all the strange objects, peculiar people, and amazing performers he'd collected—began splitting apart and dispersing, and it seemed as if the magical Believe It or Not world might disappear altogether.

Earlier in 1949, when a secretary overheard a loud argument with Doug Storer, Ripley had ominously warned, "You think that was bad? It's nothing compared to the arguments and fights and lawsuits that will take place after I've gone." Indeed, a power struggle erupted within days of Ripley's demise as various factions, including Doug Ripley and Doug Storer, competed for control of the orphaned remains of Ripley's kingdom.

* * *

PARTLY THIS WAS Ripley's fault for never officially designating a successor. Months before his "many, many years" prediction to a Savannah reporter, he had signed his will and stashed it aboard the *Mon Lei*, where it was found in the days after his death. In it, Ripley was very specific about cash awards—bequests ranging from $500 to $5,000 to longtime employees and friends—but excruciatingly vague about what should be done with the lucrative brand he'd created.

The names in the will read like a guest list to Ripley's biggest party, among them patrons who'd helped early in Ripley's career—Carol Ennis, Vyvyan Donner, and his old editor Walter St. Denis; secretaries, housekeepers, and female companions; such longtime employees as Norbert Pearlroth, Doug Storer, and two captains of the *Mon Lei;* as well as close friends such as Bugs Baer and Li Ling-Ai.

Ripley instructed that the rest of his estate be formed into a trust, whose income and profits would be shared by his sister and brother.

Though Ripley did not specify who should actually run things, Doug had hoped to take charge of the company and keep his brother's menagerie of peculiarities intact. But he soon allowed the lawyers to auction off the estate, then watched in horror as moving vans pulled away from BION Island, loaded with Ripley's curios and collectibles. Unable to keep the employees on board, Doug watched them disappear too.

Three months after Ripley's death, nearly a thousand artworks and curios—collected from BION, the New York apartment, the Florida house, and the *Mon Lei*—were sold during a four-day session at the Plaza Art Gallery in New York. Scores of bidders competed for Ripley's totem poles, beer steins, Buddhas, Ugandan masks, opium pipes, and shrunken heads, along with the Makovsky paintings and the lifelike Masakichi statue. Among the bidders was Francis Cardinal Spellman, who was outbid for a statue of Saint Patrick, and a young couple from Queens vying for statuettes and brass dragons. "Oh what an apartment we're going to have," the woman whispered to her fiancé. "I can hardly wait till we're married."

The auction, featured in the pages of *LIFE* and *The New Yorker*, netted $90,000—no small sum, but a fraction of the booty's true value. The main bidder was John Arthur, who *LIFE* said was "trying to step into Ripley's shoes." Arthur spent

$50,000 for "several vanloads of stuff," as *LIFE* put it, and paid another $5,500 for the *Mon Lei*.

BION Island sold for $50,000 to Ferruccio Tagliavini, a Metropolitan Opera star, who never moved in. The mansion was sold a few years later and razed to make room for two new houses; the site remained vacant for years.

Proceeds from the auction and the sale of Ripley's homes netted $500,000 for Doug Ripley, who was forced to buy back from the estate any items of sentimental value. In 1951, he and Storer together purchased all shares of Believe It or Not, Inc., with Storer taking over as company president and Doug chairing the board of directors. It was an uneasy partnership from the start, and through the mid-1950s both men scuffled in court, as did Robert Hyland and John Arthur. When Doug Ripley was diagnosed with cancer, Storer saw a chance to take over, and Doug Ripley seemed to realize he'd been outplayed.

"He didn't know what to do without Roy," Doug's granddaughter, Rebecca Ripley, said decades later, using the family name for Robert/LeRoy. Doug's son, Robert, said his father was never entirely comfortable in his big brother's world. "I don't think it was my father's cup of tea," he said. "I think he was out of his element there."

Doug Ripley died in 1956. His sons, Robert and Douglas Ripley, were still living in Mamaroneck in 2012.

Storer took sole possession of the company, calling it "a frightening responsibility." He managed the cartoon and sold comic books and published new editions of *Believe It or Not* books, which sold hundreds of thousands of copies through the 1950s.

But the legal battles continued, as Ripley had predicted they would. In 1959, Storer sold out to John Arthur, the man who'd purchased so much of the estate at auction. Arthur had put his purchases on permanent display in an Odditorium-style museum housed in a former castle in St. Augustine, Florida, which opened in 1950 and was followed by Ripley museums in Las Vegas, Atlantic City, and Times Square. Arthur had also hoped to create a floating museum aboard the *Mon Lei*. But storage and repair costs, plus a threatened lawsuit, prompted Arthur to sell the boat, which fell into private hands.

In 1969, a Canadian named Alec Rigby bought out Arthur, moved the headquarters from New York to Toronto, and began expanding the company, opening museums in Niagara Falls; San Francisco; Chicago; Gatlinburg, Tennessee; and Myrtle Beach, South Carolina.

In 1971, Lillie Belle's church was finally restored and turned into the museum Ripley had once hoped for. Among the displays: a two-headed calf with six legs. The church/museum closed in 1998 and fell into disrepair; it was restored in 2010 by the city of Santa Rosa, which turned it into a community meeting hall.

In 1985, Rigby sold the company to Jim Pattison, one of Canada's wealthiest men, whom Toronto's *Saturday Post* credited with resurrecting Ripley's "multimedia entertainment conglomerate." The newly named Ripley Entertainment, Inc., relocated to Orlando and opened more museums and other attractions.

There are now dozens of Ripley-themed attractions worldwide—haunted houses, aquariums, mini golf courses—in Australia, England, South Korea, Thailand, and even India.

THROUGHOUT THE VARIOUS POST-1949 corporate iterations, Ripley's core staff scattered, and no one seemed to keep track of the whereabouts of his many secretaries, housekeepers, chefs, butlers, and lovers such as Liese Wisse, Cygna Conly, and Ming Jung. Though the brand had survived, quite impressively, the strange and international and eccentric family Ripley had gathered together on BION Island and beneath his Believe It or Not umbrella did not.

In 1959, after selling his interest in Believe It or Not, Inc., Doug Storer founded his own brand, Amazing But True, an attempt to reinvent himself as the new Ripley, with a similar multimedia array of books, radio shows, and newspaper columns. Using Ripley as his model, Storer traveled extensively through the 1960s and '70s, collecting stories and photographs. He eventually retired to Florida, where he died in 1985, at age eighty-six. His wife, Hazel, died in 2005 and bequeathed to the University of North Carolina Doug's trove of Believe It or Not materials (now known as the Doug and Hazel Storer Collection).

Norbert Pearlroth's association with *Believe It or Not* lasted longer than even Ripley's. He continued to work for King Features, visiting the New York Public Library daily to dig up new material for the cartoon. In 1972, he told the *Wall Street Journal* he never got bored. "It's just like being an explorer," said the man Ripley referred to as "the human encyclopedia." Pearlroth retired in 1975, at the age of eighty-one.

But after a fifty-two-year commitment to *Believe It or Not*, Pearlroth missed his days at the New York Library. ("He *lived* there," said grandson Jonathan.) Pearlroth died in 1983, a month before the ninetieth-birthday party scheduled for him at the library.

Li Ling-Ai, after co-hosting the *Believe It or Not* TV show, worked briefly with Doug Storer as his *Amazing But True* "Far East consultant." In 1973, she published a book about her parents, *Life Is for a Long Time*, whose mottoes and maxims seemed to be part commentary on Ripley's life. (Example: "Learn what it is to be a whole person in this new world.") Li also wrote children's books and over the years gave lectures and spoke regularly on radio and onstage about Chinese history, cooking, and culture. She died in 2003 at age ninety-five.

Before her death, in an interview for a documentary about Ripley's life, Li described him as "a special institution" who found his life and the world around him endlessly interesting and exciting, who felt compelled to share that shameless enthusiasm with his fans—and with anyone else who'd listen.

"He understood the psychology of the American public," she said. "He didn't really have hobbies. He liked to draw. He didn't talk about the stock market or good scotch or wine . . . because it doesn't matter whether you have caviar and Champagne or mink coats. It is life that is exciting and interesting, no matter what.

"That's all," said Li. "That's Ripley."

* * *

WHILE BELIEVE IT OR NOT has endured, as Ripley predicted it would, the brand is safeguarded by the spirit of its long-dead creator. This haunting has actually been more of a boon than anyone might have anticipated, an added mystique to Ripley's lasting appeal. At tourist-packed Believe It or Not museums on Fisherman's Wharf in San Francisco or Times Square in New York, Ripley is a spooky presence, a beneficent ghost, his face grinning from deep within faded black-and-white photographs.

Then again, he is something of a cardboard mascot. In today's world, it's hard to imagine an incarnation of such a man, a shy, goofy, portly, bucktoothed stutterer who becomes a world traveler, a multimedia pioneer, a rich and famous ladies' man, and one of the most popular men in America. Consumers of the twenty-first century are a jaded lot. In the belief that there's nothing new to discover, purveyors of popular culture created reality TV instead. The revelations that made Ripley gasp— burning ghats in India, shrunken heads in Ecuador, armless/ legless girl wonders—seem archaic compared to the intentional extremes of shows like *Jackass* and *Survivor,* the exploits of the masses on *Fear Factor* and *American Idol,* or the televised Burton Holmes–esque travels of Andrew Zimmern in *Bizarre World* and *Bizarre Foods.*

And yet, the phrase Ripley coined remains part of the English lexicon nearly a century later.

In 2011, "believe it or not" appeared more than twelve thousand times in the *New York Times* and on its website, and a mid-2012 Google search landed more than seventy *million* "believe it or not" hits. The spirit of Ripley lives on in shows like *Myth-Busters* and *River Monsters,* on *America's Funniest Home Videos* and all across YouTube. Also thriving, on the Internet, on TV, and on radio, are the aspirations that Ripley embodied—to show people something they didn't know, to entertain and educate and titillate, to question and challenge the truth—as are the driving passions of voyeurism, exhibitionism, and the base appreciation of freakishness, oddities, and pranks of nature.

The man who considered himself a rube and a farm boy, who indulged in a lifestyle as risky as that of any character in his cartoons, who taught readers to gape with respect at the weirdness of man and nature, who contributed to the adoption of America's national anthem and the creation of the Pearl Harbor memorial and so much more . . .

LeRoy Ripley, it turns out, may have been the most unbelievable oddity of all.

Ripley's ——∞ Believe It or Not!

FATHER AGAINST SON
JOE RUDDY DEFEATS HIS OWN SON
AT WATER-POLO.
N.Y.A.C VS NAVY, Annapolis, Feb. 1928

OUTFIELDER
HEWITT, of Moran, Kan... CAUGHT A FLYBALL ON HIS BACK

LINDBERGH
WAS THE 67ᵗʰ MAN TO
MAKE A NON-STOP FLIGHT
OVER THE ATLANTIC OCEAN !

"STRETCHED"
IS THE LONGEST
ONE-SYLLABLE WORD
IN THE ENGLISH
LANGUAGE

THE KIWI KIWI
— A BIRD
WITHOUT WINGS !

AUTHOR'S NOTE ON SOURCES

On Friday, August 24, 2007, while skimming the *New York Times*, I came across a story that diverted me from the book project I'd been working on and set me on the five-year path that led to this book. Headlined O, BELIEVERS, PREPARE TO BE AMAZED!, the story profiled a new museum that had opened in Times Square: the Ripley's Believe It or Not Odditorium. Reporter Edward Rothstein seemed genuinely shocked at the "entertaining and provocative" displays inside, and described the "voyeuristic sense of gaining entry to a forbidden, exotic and at times unsettling realm."

Channeling Ripley, Rothstein mused a bit about the people and places that celebrate the freakish: "The freakish is the ultimate avant-garde, a finger in the eye of the buttoned-up bourgeois vision of ordered life, like a tattoo parlor in the midst of a holistic spa."

Midway into the story, Rothstein introduced the proprietor of the metaphorical tattoo parlor—"a cross between the Coney Island barker and the cultural anthropologist"—and cited the 1936 newspaper poll that had ranked Robert Ripley as the most popular man in America.

As a former newspaper reporter and a lifelong newspaper

reader, I had read and known about Ripley's cartoons since childhood. But I'd never stopped to consider the man behind it all. I grabbed a pen and started underlining the *Times* reporter's words—"something refreshing about Ripley's enthusiastic refusal to homogenize humanity's extremes . . . his gaze roamed across his own culture's peculiarities too, treating them with the same amazement."

My curiosity aroused, I visited Amazon.com and quickly learned that there existed no definitive biography of Ripley. In fact, it seemed as if the only biographical retelling of any kind had been a slim 1961 volume, *Ripley, the Modern Marco Polo,* by Bob Considine, a used copy of which I ordered from Amazon. Unable to wait a few days, I scoured the Internet and in minutes found and began printing a PDF of that same book. By that afternoon, I was in awe of the life Ripley had lived, and soon decided to attempt to write the first full story about the freakish man who celebrated the freakishness of the world.

My early research led me to the Orlando-based Ripley Entertainment Inc., which manages the Ripley empire and publishes those fat and weird annual *Believe It or Not!* books. Through the generous cooperation of VP Norm Deska and archivist Edward Meyer, I was granted unfettered access to the climate-controlled room containing the company's archives, a one-stop-shopping trove of Ripley's personal and business papers, journals, photographs, home movies, letters, and more. It's no exaggeration to say this was a reporter's jackpot—this project could never have happened without the help of Ripley Entertainment, especially Meyer.

Six months after immersing myself in Ripley's life, almost by accident I learned about the Doug and Hazel Storer Collection at the University of North Carolina at Chapel Hill. Doug Storer, Ripley's business manager, had died in 1985, and his wife Hazel died in 2005, after which the family's papers were donated to UNC. After two years of being organized and catalogued, the collection was opened to the public in 2008. I spent many long hours in the manuscripts department at Wilson Library, taking digital photographs of thousands of documents that proved invaluable to this project.

In addition to gaining access to such long-buried treasures at Ripley Entertainment and UNC, I was grateful for the cooperation I received from Sidney Kirkpatrick, who had previously begun exploring Ripley's life and who agreed to share with me his many boxes of research. I'm humbled by his generosity.

Last but not least, I'm very thankful that Ripley's nephew Robert and grandniece, Rebecca, graciously accommodated my many phone calls and finally agreed to speak with me about Ripley and his brother, Doug. Their cooperation helped shed some light on one of the mysteries of this story, and I hope my portrayal of the brothers and their complicated but loving relationship is accurate. Any errors are my own.

NOTES

For more information on sources—including samples of Ripley's personal journals, business letters, travel photos, home movies, and more—visit www.nealthompson.com/books/curiousman.

KEY

Ripley Entertainment archives = RE

Ripley personal scrapbooks (Note: exact titles, dates, and even publication names are occasionally missing) = SCRAP

Doug and Hazel Storer Collection = DHS (http://www.lib.unc.edu/mss/inv/s/Storer,Doug_and _Hazel_Anderson.html)

Believe It or Not cartoon (and/or essay) = BION

Sidney Kirkpatrick papers = SID

Gaye LeBaron Collection = GLB (http://library.sonoma.edu/regional/lebaron/)

Sonoma Historian, journal of the Sonoma County Historical Society = SH

Santa Rosa Press Democrat = SRD

San Francisco Chronicle = SFC

San Francisco Bulletin = SFB

New York Globe = NYG

Associated Newspapers = AN

New York Post = NYP

New York Times = NYT

King Features Syndicate = KFS

The Incredible Life and Times of Robert Ripley: Believe It or Not, TBS Productions, Turner Home Entertainment, 1994 = TBS

CHAPTER I

On Ripley's childhood and family, see the following: RE "Ripley's Ramble 'Round the World," *Associated Newspapers,* December 4, 1922; "Strange Things Under the Sun," by Hugh Leamy, *The American,* October 1929; "Famous Cartoonist Tells Story of His Life," by Robert Boyd, *The Success Magazine,* January 1926; SH ("Robert Ripley, His Own Greatest Oddity," by H. Lightfoot, Fall 1967); SCRAP (untitled profile by Edgar T. "Scoop" Gleeson, *San Francisco Bulletin,* 1915; "Where a Globetrotter Hangs His Hat," *Liberty Magazine,* May 11, 1946); GLB (Ethel letter to Roy); SID (interview with Bruce Bailey, January 14, 2002); SID (interview with George Proctor, May 12, 2002); SID (interview with Nancy Jo Black Cafo, February 15, 2002); "I Remember When," unpublished essay by Clara VanWormer Black, 1958; SRD (Ripley obituary, May 28, 1949); SRD ("As Nell Wilson Knew Him," May 28, 1949); SRD (August 24, 2005); Li Ling-Ai interview with TBS, 1993; RE

("How to Draw," unpublished Robert Ripley manuscript, n.d.); "Recollections of Ripley," unpublished essay by Frances O'Meara; GLB (assorted SRD columns); "Believe It or Not, Ripley Was Almost as Odd as His Items," by Donald Dale Jackson, *Smithsonian*, January 1995; *Ripley, the Modern Marco Polo*, by Bob Considine, Garden City, NY: Doubleday & Co., 1961 (hereafter referred to as MMP); DHS (interviews, letters, and handwritten notes by Hazel Storer).

Note on Ripley's birth date: Census records from 1900 and 1910 show Ripley's birth year as 1890; so does his headstone. Family photos further confirm Ripley's birth in early 1890. A photo taken in July 1890 says "at six months."

Santa Rosa history: *Santa Rosa: A Twentieth Century Town*, by Gaye LeBaron and Joanne Mitchell; *How Plants Are Trained to Work for Man*, by Luther Burbank, PF Collier & Son, 1914, NY; *Images of America, Santa Rosa*, by Simone Wilson, Arcadia Publishing, 2004; *Santa Rosa California in Vintage Postcards*, by Bob and Kay Voliva, Arcadia Publishing, 1999; SH (Volume I, 2006); *The Garden of Invention*, by Jane S. Smith, Penguin Press, 2009.

CHAPTER 2

Santa Rosa history and earthquake: SRD (assorted clips); GLB (SRD columns and *Santa Rosa: A Twentieth Century Town*); author interview with Jeremy Nichols; SRD (anniversary story, April 19, 2006); assorted unpublished memoirs; "The Story of an Eyewitness," by Jack London, *Collier's*, May 5, 1906; RE "Ripley's Ramble 'Round the World," December 10, 1922; SRD (June 13, 1908); SH ("1906 Earthquake Issue," 2006).

Note on the higher death per capita compared to San Francisco: Santa Rosa had 64 to 100 deaths and 6,700 to 8,700 residents—1 in 80 died; San Francisco had 500 deaths and 400,000 residents—1 in 800.

Ripley at school, and home life: SH ("Robert Ripley, His Own Greatest Oddity," by H. Lightfoot, Fall 1967); SID (interview with George Proctor, May 12, 2002); SRD (Ripley obituary, May 28, 1949, including recollections by Helen Proctor and others); DHS (interviews, letters, and handwritten notes by Hazel

Storer); "Recollections of Ripley," unpublished essay by Frances O'Meara; "Panther Profile," Santa Rosa High School newsletter story, 1989; "Famous Cartoonist Tells Story of His Life," by Robert Boyd, *The Success Magazine*, January 1926; SCRAP (untitled profile by Edgar T. "Scoop" Gleeson, *San Francisco Bulletin*, 1915; SCRAP (untitled *Pittsburgh Chronicle Telegraph* story, date unknown, circa spring of 1916); "Odd Man," by Geoffrey T. Hellman, two-part profile in *The New Yorker*, August 31, 1940 and September 7, 1940.

Comics: *The Ten-Cent Plague: The Great Comic-Book Scare and How It Changed America*, by David Hajdu, Picador, 2009; *The Comics: Before 1945*, by Brian Walker, Harry N. Abrams, 2004.

CHAPTER 3

Moving to and living/working in San Francisco: "The Village Bell was Slowly Ringing," *LIFE*, May 18, 1908; DHS (Carol Ennis letter to Bob Considine); MMP (pp. 20–21); "Famous Cartoonist Tells Story of His Life," by Robert Boyd, *The Success Magazine*, January 1926; "Pictures from the Past," by John Baggerly, *Los Gatos Weekly*, September 19, 2001; SRD (March 2, 2009); SCRAP (*Saturday Evening Post* profile, 1932); GLB; RE (Ripley's Ramble 'Round the World, December 11, 1922); "Timeline of San Francisco History," www.sfhistoryencyclopedia.com/articles/timeline/index.html [accessed September 30, 2012]; US Census, 1910; SFC (June 10, 2009); *The Comics: Before 1945*, by Brian Walker, Harry N. Abrams, 2004; *Rube Goldberg: His Life and Work*, by Peter C. Marzio, Harper, 1973; SCRAP (untitled profile by Edgar T. "Scoop" Gleeson, *San Francisco Bulletin*, 1915; SID (Ripley letters to Nell, August 15, 1909 and October 6, 1909); DHS (notes by Hazel Storer).

Believe It! sidebar (TAD): *New York Times* obituary, May 23, 1929.

Note: Different versions of the end to Ripley's *San Francisco Bulletin* career would endure. He'd sometimes claim he was fired after a week. Other times he lasted a year, until an office boy tipped him off that Baggerly was thinking of bagging him and he quit. Occasionally he'd claim he was shown the door after demanding a two-dollar-a-week raise.

CHAPTER 4

Ripley at the *Chronicle:* 1909 San Francisco city directory; author interview with Bill Beutner, research assistant, San Francisco Architectural Heritage, July 29, 2009; "Famous Cartoonist Tells Story of His Life," by Robert Boyd, *The Success Magazine*, January 1926; SCRAP ("Ripley's Life a Believe It or Not," by Gladys Baker, *Birmingham News-Age-Herald*, May 12, 1936); RE and DHS (untitled, unpublished article by Herbert Corey, based on his interview with Ripley); RE (*How to Draw*, unpublished Ripley manuscript); "Believe It or Not," by Jack Banner, *Radio Guide*, November 9, 1935.

Note on baseball: Although Ripley would later claim to have been Ping Bodie's teammate and to have played in California's minor leagues, I was unable to find records in any Pacific Coast League archives to support this, and neither is he mentioned in any minor-league baseball stories in the *Bulletin* or *Chronicle* between 1908 and 1912. He may have continued to play at the semi-professional level, as he had in Santa Rosa—there were scores of "bush league" teams in the Bay Area. He once claimed to have played a season for "the Oakland team of the California State League." The Oakland Coasters were part of the State League, considered an "outlaw" minor league. Sources include books on the Pacific Coast League; e-mail interview with Dick Beverage; NYG ("Bodie Fans with Ripley," August 21, 1912); SCRAP ("Getting Acquainted with Rip," by Robert L. Ripley, *Strength* magazine, December 1929).

Ripley and Nell: SID (Ripley letters to Nell, August 15, 1909; October 6, 1909; December 9, 1909; and April 24, 1910); SRD ("As Nell Wilson Knew Him," May 28, 1949).

Reno and fight: "Struggle for His Soul," by David Remnick, *The Observer*, November 2, 2003; SFC (assorted 1910 clips); NYT (assorted 1910 clips); "Famous

Cartoonist Tells Story of His Life," by Robert Boyd, *The Success Magazine,* January 1926; International Boxing Hall of Fame, www.sweetscience.com; *Unforgivable Blackness: The Rise and Fall of Jack Johnson,* by Geoffrey C. Ward, Vintage, 2006 (also the PBS film with Ken Burns); MMP, p. 23.

Leaving San Francisco: "Believe It or Not Here's Ripley," by Lee Bevins, *Pageant,* October 1948; "Believe It or Not," by Jack Banner, *Radio Guide,* November 9, 1935; DHS (Hazel Storer notes); "Famous Cartoonist Tells Story of His Life," by Robert Boyd, *The Success Magazine,* January 1926; "Strange Things Under the Sun," by Hugh Leamy, *The American,* October 1929; SCRAP ("Ripley's Life a Believe It or Not," by Gladys Baker, *Birmingham News-Age-Herald,* May 12, 1936); RE ("Ripley's Ramble 'Round the World," December 11, 1922); SCRAP (*Pittsburgh Chronicle Telegraph* story, date unknown, circa spring of 1916).

Route to New York: Ripley likely left San Francisco on either the Western Pacific's Feather River Route or the Union Pacific and Southern Pacific's Overland Route, both of which offered daily departures (www.sfmuseum .org/hist1/skeds.html); route details and $85 trip cost estimate from Clifford Vander Yacht—best name ever!—editor of the Railway and Locomotive Historical Society newsletter, whom I interviewed on July 28, 2009.

CHAPTER 5

Story about arriving in New York: SCRAP (untitled profile by Edgar T. "Scoop" Gleeson, *San Francisco Bulletin,* 1915).

Believe It! sidebar (yellow kid): *The Chief: The Life of William Randolph Hearst,* by David Nasaw, Mariner Books, 2001; *The Ten-Cent Plague: The Great Comic-Book Scare and How It Changed America,* by David Hajdu, Picador, 2009; *The Comics: Before 1945,* by Brian Walker, Harry N. Abrams, 2004.

Looking for work in New York and starting at *New York Globe*: DHS (Hazel Storer notes); "Famous Cartoonist Tells Story of His Life," by Robert Boyd, *The Success Magazine,* January 1926; "Strange Things Under the Sun," by

Hugh Leamy, *The American*, October 1929; SCRAP ("How to Be a Cartoonist," *Saturday Evening Post*, October 19, 1940); SCRAP (Herb Corey, article manuscript, date unknown); "Odd Man," Geoffrey T. Hellman, *New Yorker*, 1940; *America's Oldest Daily Newspaper, The New York Globe*, by James Melvin Lee, *The Globe*, 1918; *The Encyclopedia of New York City*, edited by Kenneth T. Jackson, Yale University Press, 1995; NYG (assorted clips, February and March, 1912–1913); "Ripley, Believe It or Not—A Real Success Story," by Harry B. Smith, *San Francisco Chronicle*, February 13, 1935; "Friends Honor Bob Ripley," *Rochester Times-Union*, January 5, 1944; NYT (1949 obit.).

Believe It! sidebar (Yankees): "Red Sox vs. Yankees," Harvey Frommer, 2005, p. 266.

Assorted details about cartoons and comics: *The Ten-Cent Plague: The Great Comic-Book Scare and How It Changed America*, by David Hajdu, Picador, 2009; *The Comics: Before 1945*, by Brian Walker, Harry N. Abrams, 2004; *Over 50 Years of American Comic Books;* by Ron Gaulart, 1991; *Stripper's Guide*, http://strippersguide.blogspot.com/2008_04_01_archive.html [accessed October 1, 2012]; Billy Ireland Cartoon Library & Museum, cartoons. osu.edu [accessed October 1, 2012]; *Men of Tomorrow: Geeks, Gangsters, and the Birth of the Comic Book*, by Gerard Jones, Basic Books, 1995; author interview with Allan Holtz, March 25, 2009.

Ripley playing for the New York Giants: NYT (assorted clips, including "M'Graw Goes South," February 17, 1912); "Odd Man," Geoffrey T. Hellman, *New Yorker*, 1940; "Famous Cartoonist Tells Story of His Life," by Robert Boyd, *The Success Magazine*, January 1926; SCRAP ("Getting Acquainted with Rip," by Robert L. Ripley, *Strength* magazine, December 1929); SCRAP ("Ripley's Life a Believe It or Not," by Gladys Baker, *Birmingham News-Age-Herald*, May 12, 1936); MMP, pp. 33–34; "The Brighter Side," *Charleston Gazette*, January 15, 1939; "Believe It or Not," by Jack Banner, *Radio Guide*, November 9, 1935.

Believe It! sidebar (jazz): "I Remember the Birth of Jazz," Edgar Gleeson, *San Francisco Call-Bulletin*, September 3, 1938; Gleeson article, *San Francisco*

Call, March 6, 1913; "Art Hickman and His Orchestra," by Bruce Vermazen, www.gracyk.com/hickman.shtml [accessed October 1, 2012]; "How Baseball Gave Us 'Jazz,'" by Ben Zimmer, Boston.com, 3/25/12.

Ripley and Santa Rosa and family: SFB ("Ripley Returns to Scenes of His Early Triumph," Edgar Gleeson, circa 1915); RE (Ripley telegrams); DHS (Hazel Storer notes); "Odd Man," Geoffrey T. Hellman, *New Yorker,* 1940; interview with Bob, Doug, and Rebecca Ripley (nephews and grandniece of Ripley); NYG ("Ripley Interviews Ritchie," August 9, 1915).

CHAPTER 6

Settling in New York, and meeting Bugs Baer: *Green Book Magazine,* July 1916, http://historicalziegfeld.multiply.com/photos/album/252 [accessed October 1, 2012]; NYT (1949 obituary); NYT ("Bugs Baer Dead," May 18, 1969); NYG (April 7, 1915, and January 8, 1916); *Unforgivable Blackness: The Rise and Fall of Jack Johnson,* by Geoffrey C. Ward, Vintage, 2006; "Odd Man," by Geoffrey T. Hellman, *New Yorker,* 1940; MMP, pp. 27, 31–32.

Details on cartoonists and Disney: SCRAP (*American Magazine* story, 1916); *The Comics: Before 1945,* by Brian Walker, Harry N. Abrams, 2004; *Walt Disney: The Triumph of the American Imagination,* by Neal Gabler, Vintage, 2007; RE (*How to Draw,* unpublished Ripley manuscript).

World War I cartoons: NYG (December 6, 1915; August 16, 1916; July 28, 1914; September 8, 1914; June 2, 1914; July 18, 1918; and April 2, 1918); RE (*How to Draw,* unpublished Ripley manuscript).

World War I details: *How We Advertised America: The First Telling of the Amazing Story of the Committee on Public Information That Carried the Gospel of Americanism to Every Corner of the Globe,* by George Creel, Kessinger Pub. Co., 2008; National Archives, www.archives.gov/research/guide-fed-records/groups/063.html [accessed October 1, 2012]; assorted links from the Wikipedia page for the Committee on Public Information (http://en.wikipedia.org/wiki/Committee_on_Public_Information); NYG (letter to editor, August 20, 1917).

Champs and Chumps: "The Incredible 'Believe It or Not,'" by Robert Ripley, *Popular Mechanics*, February 1936; DHS (Hazel Storer notes, and letters to Hazel); "Strange Things Under the Sun," by Hugh Leamy, *The American*, October 1929; "Odd Man," Geoffrey T. Hellman, *New Yorker*, 1940; RE (*How to Draw*, unpublished Ripley manuscript); "The Story of Believe It or Not," by Mel Heimer, King Features Syndicate Biographical Series, No. 29.

CHAPTER 7

Bernarr Macfadden and Freddie Welsh: bernarrmacfadden.com [accessed October 1, 2012]; *Occupation: Prizefighter: Freddie Welsh's Quest for the World Championship*, by Andrew Gallimore, Seren, 2006; author interview with Allan Holtz, November 2, 2009.

On women: RE (typed manuscript of "The New Beauty for Women," by Robert Ripley—unpublished?); SCRAP ("Getting Acquainted with Rip," by Robert L. Ripley, *Strength* magazine, December 1929); SCRAP ("Why I Am Not Married," by Betty Brainerd, for her "We Women" column, date unknown).

Life at the NYAC and playing handball: *The First Hundred Years: A Portrait of the NYAC*, by Bob Considine and Fred G. Jarvis, 1974; New York Athletic Club, nyac.org [accessed October 1, 2012]; author interview with NYAC historian Tom Quinn, August 20, 2009; "Famous Cartoonist Tells Story of His Life," by Robert Boyd, *The Success Magazine*, January 1926; *Spalding's Official Handball Guide*, by Robert L. Ripley, American Sports Pub., 1923; "The New Beauty for Women," by Robert Ripley; SCRAP ("Getting Acquainted with Rip," by Robert L. Ripley, *Strength* magazine, December 1929); NYT (obituary, 1949); MMP, p. 38; SCRAP ("Ripley Owns an Egg Pen Now," undated article); "Believe It or Not, Ripley Was Almost as Odd as His Items," by Donald Dale Jackson, *Smithsonian*, January 1995.

Marriage to Beatrice: in addition to obtaining Beatrice's birth certificate and Ripley and Beatrice's marriage license, the details of their marriage are based on assorted articles found in Ripley's scrapbook (many from 1922 and 1923, and others undated), as well as letters from Ripley to his sister; "No One Would Believe It," by Ruth Biery, *Radio Stars* magazine, May 1936; and "Why I Am Not Married," by Betty Brainerd. At the time of their marriage, a few newspapers referred to Beatrice as Beatrice Carlisle. As I explain in chapter 17, for many years there was confusion over the true identity of Ripley's wife.

Ziegfeld and the *Ziegfeld Follies*: *Ziegfeld: The Man Who Invented Show Business,* by Ethan Mordden (2008).

Olympics: *The First Hundred Years: A Portrait of the NYAC,* by Bob Considine and Fred G. Jarvis, 1974; NYT (July 19, 1920); NYG (August 25, 1920); Official Website of the Olympic Movement, www.olympic.org [accessed October 1, 2012]; *Flanders Today,* flanderstoday.eu [accessed October 1, 2012].

Troubles with Beatrice: "No One Would Believe It," by Ruth Biery, *Radio Stars,* 1936; MMP, pp. 39–41; SCRAP (assorted stories about the court proceedings and divorce, 1921 and 1923); NYT (April 13, 1923); "The New Beauty for Women," by Robert Ripley.

CHAPTER 8

All details of the Ramble are based on Ripley's personal travel journals and his cartoons and essays that appeared in the *New York Globe* and other newspapers. [Note: Though the actual journey began in early December of 1922, some papers wouldn't start running the illustrated articles until January of 1923.]

Believe It! sidebar (Titanic): author interview with Tom Quinn.

CHAPTER 9

Frank Munsey: "Mr. Munsey Buys," *Time,* June 4, 1923; "Another Buy," *Time,* February 4, 1924; author interview with Allan Holtz; *Forty Years, Forty Millions:*

The Career of Frank A. Munsey, by George Britt, Farrar & Rinehart, 1935; NYT (Munsey obituary, December 29, 1925); "The Classic Era of American Pulp Magazines," by Peter Haining, www.crimetime.co.uk/features/peterhaining .php [accessed October 1, 2012].

More troubles with Beatrice: NYG (April 14, 1923); NYT (April 13, 1923); "No One Would Believe It," by Ruth Biery, *Radio Stars* magazine, May 1936; SCRAP ("Why I Am Not Married," by Betty Brainerd, for her "We Women" column, date unknown); SCRAP (assorted stories about the court proceedings and divorce, 1921 and 1923); NYP (Ramble 'Round South America, January 27, 1925).

Details about Doug and Ethel: interviews with Rebecca and Robert Ripley; RE (letter to Ethel, April 15, 1923).

Death of the *Globe*: NYT (Munsey obituary, December 29, 1925); *America's Oldest Daily Newspaper, The New York Globe,* by James Melvin Lee, *The Globe,* 1918.

Norbert Pearlroth: "In Search of the (Nearly) Miraculous," by Susan Lydon, *Village Voice,* October 22, 1979; "You Better Believe This," by Dan Carlinsky, *Modern Maturity,* 1974; Pearlroth obituary, *Time,* April 25, 1983; "Believe It or Not," by Kenneth Turan, *The Washington Post,* April 1, 1973).

Miscellaneous: NYP (Ramble 'Round South America, March 23, 1925 and January 27, 1925); The Circumnavigators Club, www.circumnavigatorsclub .org [accessed October 1, 2012]; SCRAP ("Why I Am Not Married," by Betty Brainerd, for her "We Women" column, date unknown).

CHAPTER 10

All details of the Ramble are based on Ripley's personal travel journals and the cartoons and essays that appeared in the Associated Newspapers and various other newspapers throughout early 1925. Additional details: MMP; DHS; RE.

CHAPTER 11

Munsey's death: *Forty Years, Forty Millions: The Career of Frank A. Munsey,* by George Britt, Farrar & Rinehart, 1935; NYT (Munsey obituary, December 29, 1925); "Uncensored Commentaries," by Theo Lippman Jr., *Baltimore Sun,* March 31, 2003.

Handball note: Ripley played at the 1927 National Championships in St. Paul but lost by a few points, in a best-of-three series against the eventual champ.

Believe It! sidebar (Curtis's income): *Time* (June 19, 1933); NYT (Curtis obituary, September 6, 1925); *Outliers: The Story of Success,* by Malcolm Gladwell, Little, Brown and Company, 2008.

Starting at *New York Post:* "Circulation Figures," *Time,* October 22, 1923; NYP ("Ripley's Returned," August 16, 1926); author interview with Jeff Pearlroth.

Macfadden: *Winchell: Gossip, Power, and the Culture of Celebrity,* by Neal Gabler, Vintage, 1995, pp. 72, 74, 77.

Lindbergh cartoon, lying accusations, and Marching Chinese cartoon: "You Better Believe This," by Dan Carlinsky, *Modern Maturity,* 1974; *Ripley's Believe It or Not!: In Celebration . . . A Special Reissue of the Original!,* by Robert Ripley, Ripley Publishing, 2004, p. 39; MMP, pp. 52–53; SCRAP ("Celebrated Caricaturist Entertains with Sketches and Interesting Facts," exact date and publication unknown; "Ripley to Talk . . . ," unknown publication, April 9, 1928; and "Ripley Loves to Have Fans Call Him Liar," *New York Herald,* day unknown, 1929).

Lectures and letters, and verifying facts: SCRAP (untitled clip, March 22, 1927; untitled article, by Joseph M. Ripley, *American Press,* 1929; miscellaneous clips); NYP (letter from Mabel Henry, October 1, 1928; letter to editor, April 12, 1928; assorted Ripley cartoons and essays); SCRAP ("Getting Acquainted with Rip," by Robert L. Ripley, *Strength* magazine, December 1929); *Ripley's Believe It or Not!,* by Robert Ripley, Ripley Publishing, 2004; MMP, pp. 45, 49, 50, 59.

Ripley lifestyle versus Pearlroth lifestyle: SID (Rube Goldberg letter to Bob Considine); "You Better Believe This," by Dan Carlinsky, *Modern Maturity,* 1974; "In Search of the (Nearly) Miraculous," by Susan Lydon, *Village Voice,* October 22, 1979; "Believe It or Not," by William Allen, *Saturday Review,* February 1973; "Believe It or Not," by Kenneth Turan, *Washington Post,* April 1, 1973; DHS (letters, notes).

Goes to Hell: "Ripley Goes to Hell," *The Troy Times,* May 7, 1928; SCRAP (untitled, *Time,* March 26, 1928).

CHAPTER 12

Simon & Schuster and book reviews: *Only Yesterday: An Informal History of the 1920s,* by Frederick Lewis Allen, Harper Perennial, 2000, pp. 144–45; Simon & Schuster, simonandschuster.net [accessed October 1, 2012]; "Simon & Schuster Inc. History," www.fundinguniverse.com/company-histories/Simon-amp;-Schuster-Inc-Company-History.html [accessed October 1, 2012]; RE (Schuster letter to Ripley, October 31, 1927); DHS (Ripley's contract with Simon & Schuster); SCRAP (untitled, by Harry Hansen, *The First Reader;* "Behind the Backs of Books and Authors," by Mary Rennels, *New York Telegram,* day unknown, 1929).

Lawsuit: NYT ("Sue Ripley," May 20, 1930).

Travel to Central America: SCRAP (untitled, *Peddie News,* date unknown; untitled, *San Antonio Light,* date unknown; "Believe It or Not, but Ripley Is Home," unknown publication and date); NYT (Cass Baer's obituary, May 11, 1929); RE (October 23, 1933 journal entry).

Signing on with Hearst, working with Connolly: "Notes on an American Phenomenon," by John K. Winkler, *The New Yorker,* April–May 1927 (5 parts); *The Chief: The Life of William Randolph Hearst,* by David Nasaw, Mariner Books, 2001, pp. 237, 322–23, 379–80, 387); *The Uncrowned King: The Sensational Rise of William Randolph Hearst,* by Kenneth Whyte, Counterpoint, 2009; MMP, pp. 15, 37; SID (letter to Bradley Kelley, October 29, 1964); author interview with Tom Quinn, NYAC historian; DHS (contracts); *Winchell: Gossip, Power, and the Culture of Celebrity,* by Neal Gabler, Vintage, 1995, p. 104; kingfeatures.com/about-us/king-features-history; NYT (Connolly obituary, April 18, 1945); SCRAP (assorted undated clips, including "Robert L. Ripley Is Guest of Honor"); "The Press: Average Man," *Time,* November 26, 1945; RE (Connolly letter to Ripley, October 29, 1929).

Living at the NYAC: SCRAP (assorted undated clips, including "Ripgrams," 1930); author interview with Tom Smith; *Terrible Honesty: Mongrel Manhattan in the 1920s,* by Ann Douglas, Farrar Straus and Giroux, 1996; DHS (notes by Hazel Storer).

Believe It! sidebar (plane crash): *The Chief: The Life of William Randolph Hearst,* by David Nasaw, Mariner Books, 2001, p. 380.

Early King Features cartoons . . . and controversies: SCRAP (including "Catholic Father Declares Ripley Shows His 'Tremendous Ignorance,'" *Honolulu Star-Bulletin,* undated; "Believe It or Not," *The Northwest Review,* edited by Rev. SJ Ryan, 1929; "Ripley Contest Has 7 More Days," *San Francisco Examiner,* 1929; and "Best Sellers of Year Reported by Publishers," by Fanny Butcher, *Chicago Tribune,* December 21, 1929).

CHAPTER 13

Hyman working for Ripley: DHS (Hyman letter to Considine, 1959).

Fans and fan mail: NYP (untitled story, by Norman Klein, 1929); SCRAP (untitled *Boston Daily Record* story January 11, 1930); MMP, pp. 10, 15, 37. "Odd Man," by Geoffrey T. Hellman, *New Yorker,* 1940; part 2, p. 27; "Strange Things Under the Sun," by Hugh Leamy, *The American,* October 1929; RE (original letter).

Fame, radio, and movie offers: SCRAP ("Ripley, True Pioneer," *Kansas City Star,* 1929); "Believe It or Not," by Sylvia Covino, *The Bluebird,* Julia Richman High School, 1930); "Strange Things Under the Sun," by Hugh Leamy, *The*

American, October 1929; "Ripley Target of Circuit Bids," *Billboard*, February 22, 1930; "Odd Man," by Geoffrey T. Hellman, *New Yorker*, 1940, part I, p. 22; "The Most Unforgettable Character I've Met—Robert Ripley," by Douglas F. Storer, *Reader's Digest*, June 1959, Vol. 74, No. 44623.

Elmer Fudd and Vitaphone films: *Winchell: Gossip, Power, and the Culture of Celebrity*, by Neal Gabler, Vintage, 1995, p. 112; SCRAP (untitled *Variety* story, June 25, 1930, and untitled *Chicago Herald Examiner* story, June 8, 1930); *Believe It or Else*, directed by Tex Avery, written by Dave Monahan, Warner Bros. Pictures, 1939; NYT ("Cartoons of a Racist Past Lurk on YouTube," by Daniel Slotnik, April 28, 2008).

Hearst and radio: *The Chief: The Life of William Randolph Hearst*, by David Nasaw, Mariner Books, 2001, pp. 389–90, 405, 437; SCRAP ("Ripley to Lecture for Radio Fans at Roselle Tonight," publication unknown, undated, 1922).

Letters and Pearlroth: DHS (Hazel Storer notes); *Dear Mr. Ripley: A Compendium of Curiosities from the Believe It or Not! Archives*, by Mark Sloan, Roger Manley, Michelle Van Parys, and Robert Ripley, Bulfinch Press, 1993; SCRAP ("Ripley's Career Began When He Was Fourteen," *New York American*, 1929, exact date unknown); "Believe It or Not," by Kenneth Turan, *Washington Post*, April 1, 1973; "You Better Believe This," by Dan Carlinsky, *Modern Maturity*, 1974.

Travels: "Telephone Remarks to the National Automobile Chamber of Commerce," January 6, 1931, by Herbert Hoover, The American Presidency Project, www.presidency.ucsb.edu/ws/index.php?pid=22999 [accessed October 1, 2012]; Sideshow World, sideshowworld.com [accessed October 1, 2012]; SCRAP (unnamed article, "Ripley's Home by Sea and Air," *Memphis Press Scimitar*, May 27, 1930, and uncredited *International News* photos March 6, 1931 and May 22, 1931); MMP, pp. 74–76.

Lawsuit and Doug Ripley: NYT (May 20, 1930); author interviews with Robert and Rebecca Ripley.

CHAPTER 14

Onuki and women: "No One Would Believe It," by Ruth Biery, *Radio Stars* magazine, May 1936; DHS (Hyman letter to Considine); NYT (September 19, 1926 and February 25, 1932); MMP, p. 76; *Time*, March 7, 1932; *Los Angeles Times*, May 5, 1918 and February 25, 1932; www.strippersguide.com.

Details of *Mariposa* trip: RE (Ripley's travel journal); KFS (assorted cartoons and essays); original travel brochure; assorted NYT clips; *Los Angeles Times* (February 4, 1932); "Fiji's Cannibal History," www.fijiancustomculture .com/2009/10/fijis-cannibal-history.html [accessed October 1, 2012]; SCRAP (untitled article, *Daily Democrat News*, May 29, 1939); *Pearl Buck in China: Journey to the Good Earth*, by Hilary Spurling, Simon & Schuster, 2011, p. 201; Zhenjiang Pearl S. Buck Research Association, www.pearlsbcn.org/e/ (Buck's speech at Nobel Prize Award Ceremony) [accessed October 1, 2012].

Introduction to Ruth "Oakie" Ross: DHS (Hazel Storer notes, and Bill Mac-Donald letter to Doug Storer, 1962); RE (interviews with Edward Meyer); TBS interviews with Li Ling-Ai; MMP, pp. 72–3.

Santa Rosa visit: SRD (Ripley obituary, May 28, 1949); SCRAP (assorted clips).

CHAPTER 15

Charles "Cash and Carry" Pyle: SRD (February 5, 1995); *Chicago Daily Tribune* obituary, February 4, 1939; SH; *Sports Illustrated*, May 2, 1955; SCRAP (untitled columns by Westbrook Pegler, *Chicago Tribune*, July 29, 1933 and November 7, 1933).

Odditorium and Chicago World's Fair: RE (letters and contracts); "Chicago's World's Fair Remembered," by Ray Weiss, *Chicago Tribune*, May 7, 1984; "Baseball's First All-Star Game," by Jennie Cohen, June 13, 2010, www.history.com/ news/baseballs-first-all-star-game [accessed October 1, 2012]; Sideshow World, www.sideshowworld.com [accessed October 1, 2012]; "Masters of the Midway," by A. J. Liebling, two-part series, *The New Yorker*, 1939.

Travels to Iraq and Persia: RE (Ripley's personal travel journal); KFS (cartoons and articles); SCRAP ("The Name Believe It or Not Is Familiar," by Mary Morris, unknown New York newspaper, unknown date); "Bob Ripley Writes This Week's Guest Column," *Will Rogers Field News*, March 5, 1943; DHS (Hazel Storer notes).

Odditorium performers, sideshows, and P. T. Barnum: Sideshow World, www.sideshowworld.com; *American Sideshow*, by Marc Hartzman, Tarcher, 2006; "1934 World's Fair," Sideshow Ephemera Gallery, http://missioncreep. com/mundie/gallery/gallery8.htm [accessed October 1, 2012]; "Frieda Pushnick: Armless and Legless Wonder Girl," http://missioncreep.com/mundie/ gallery/gallery21.htm [accessed October 1, 2012]; The Human Marvels, www .thehumanmarvels.com [accessed October 1, 2012]; "Masters of the Midway," by A. J. Liebling, two-part series, *The New Yorker*, 1939; *Freak Show: Presenting Human Oddities for Amusement and Profit*, by Robert Bogdan, University of Chicago Press, 1990.

CHAPTER 16

Decision to move to Mamaroneck: SCRAP (undated "News and Views" and "Ripgrams" clips; Ripley profile in *Hobbies: The Magazine for Collectors*, July 1940); interviews with Greg Daugherty; NYT (Ripley obituary, 1949); DHS (notes and letters by Hazel Storer and Bob Considine); SCRAP ("Ripley's Life a Believe It or Not," by Gladys Baker, *Birmingham News-Age-Herald*, May 12, 1936); MMP, pp. 41–43.

Odditorium, continued: RE (telegrams and letters, press releases and brochures); SCRAP ("Barnum Was Wrong, Says Ripley," *Boston Advertiser*, 1930, day unknown); "Which Is the Real Masakichi?" www.anomalies-unlimited .com/Death/Masakichi.html [accessed October 1, 2012]; "Century of Progress Exposition," *Encyclopedia of Chicago*, www.encyclopedia.chicagohistory.org [accessed October 1, 2012].

Doug Storer and radio: RE (publicity press releases); DHS (assorted notes, letters, and articles); "The Most Unforgettable Character I've Met—Robert Ripley," by Douglas F. Storer, *Reader's Digest*, June 1959; "To Be or Not to Be Like Bing," by Alton Cook, *World Telegram*, October 17, 1935; MMP, pp. 114, 120.

Ripley and Russia: RE (telegram, Hearst to Ripley, June 15, 1935; copies of letters to legislators; undated memo from Joe Simpson to Ripley, "RE: Anti-Communist Broadcast"; Ripley telegram to Hearst, March 18, 1936; Ripley letter, March 10, 1936; John F. Royal letter to Storer, March 14, 1936); DHS (Hazel Storer notes on Ripley's "politics"); SCRAP (untitled *Daily Worker* article, April 6, 1935; *New York American* clip, March 3, 1936); *The Chief: The Life of William Randolph Hearst*, by David Nasaw, Mariner Books, 2001, pp. 484, 493–94); "Russia Afraid of Ripley, say Legislators," Associated Press, March 4, 1936; "Appeal for Religion," *New York American*, June 5, 1936.

Ripley's income and popularity: NYT ("Highest Salaries Paid in the Nation Are Listed by House Committee," January 9, 1936); "How Comic Cartoons Make Fortunes," by Alfred Albelli, *Modern Mechanix and Inventions*, November 1933; SCRAP ("A Laugh with Rube Goldberg," April 19, 1936; "Believe It or Not," column by O. B. Keeler, date unknown); DHS (Hazel Storer notes on "travel").

CHAPTER 17

Female relationships, especially Oakie: SCRAP ("New York, Day by Day," by O. O. McIntyre, June 16, 1937; "Ripley Discovers a New Republic," *Sunday Republican*, Waterbury, CT, June 30, 1935; "Ripley Pins His Faith in Future on Aviation," by Frances Wayne, *Denver Post*, January 14, 1943; "Search for Oddities Leads Robert Ripley to Visit 181 Countries," by Harriet Mencken, unknown publication, 1936; "Mr Ripley Visits Shetland," *The Shetland Times*, September 15, 1934; "The Name Believe It or Not Is Familiar," by Mary Morris, unknown New York newspaper, unknown date; "No One Would Believe It," by Ruth Biery, *Radio Stars* magazine, May 1936); ships' passenger logs, including the SS *Ile de France,* September 28, 1934; MMP, pp. 72–3, 41–3; RE (1962 letter from Bill McDonald to Doug Storer); DHS (extensive notes by Hazel Storer about Ripley's "women"); according to the US Census, Ross was born July 11, 1899, and lived at 112 W. 59th Street, also Park Avenue, Central Park South, and Beekman Place.

Details about life at BION Island: *1001 Curious Things: Ye Olde Curiosity Shop and Native American Art,* by Kate C. Duncan, University of Washington Press, 2001; MMP, pp. 41–43, 72–73, 169; *Just a minute, Mrs. Gulliver,* by Millie Considine, Prentice-Hall, 1967, reprint edition; RE (unpublished memoir by Ripley's housekeeper, Almuth Seabeck); DHS (Hazel Storer notes); "Ripley's Boat Draws Visitors," by O. O. McIntyre, unnamed newspaper, New Castle, PA, June 25, 1937; "Ripley Was Crazy About Dogs," by Greg Daugherty, *Bark,* Nov/Dec 2007); SCRAP (undated "News and Views" clips, 1933–36); author interviews with Robert and Rebecca Ripley; RE (Cygna Conly memos to KFS; Joseph Connolly memo to Robert Ripley, March 3, 1938).

Hix and other competitors: "How Comic Cartoons Make Fortunes," by Alfred Albelli, *Modern Mechanix and Inventions,* November 1933; *Everything Was Better in America: Print Culture in the Great Depression,* by David Welky, University of Illinois Press, 2008, pp. 93–4; www.bernarrmacfadden.com/macfadden5.html; *Men of Tomorrow: Geeks, Gangsters, and the Birth of the Comic Book,* by Gerard Jones, Basic Books, 1995, pp. 29–33; DHS (copies of lawsuit filings); SCRAP ("Believe It or Not," column by O. B. Keeler, date unknown); *Schulz and Peanuts: A Biography,* by David Michaelis, Harper Perennial, 2008, p. 93.

Radio shows with Storer: RE (assorted Storer/Ripley letters and contracts; BION radio script, August 2, 1938; Kuda Bux film footage); DHS (assorted Storer/Ripley letters and contracts); MMP, pp. 84, 112–113; SCRAP ("Search for Oddities Leads Robert Ripley to Visit 181 Countries," by Harriet Mencken, unknown publication, 1936; "New York, Day by Day," by O. O. McIntyre, 1934; "Fire on Air," *Time,* August 15, 1938; undated Crossley ratings clip, 1936);

Daily Life in the United States, 1920–1940: How Americans Lived Through the Roaring Twenties and the Great Depression, by David E. Kyvig, Ivan R. Dee, 2004, p. 90; *Everything Was Better in America: Print Culture in the Great Depression,* by David Welky, University of Illinois Press, 2008, p. 67; SID (letters: December 2, 1938 and December 15, 1938).

CHAPTER 18

Prewar radio and travel: MMP, p. 114; DHS (legal contracts from 1930s; Hazel Storer "chronology" notes); SCRAP (untitled *Daily Democrat News* clip, May 29, 1939; "Ripley Broadcast Carries Cavern Publicity to Entire World," *Eddy County News,* June 9, 1939); NYT ("14,000 See Ruth Smash Soft Ball as Celebrities Play in Garden," by Louis Effrat, May 10, 1939).

Note on female performers: Betty Lou went on to have a successful sideshow career, earning enough money to send her twelve siblings to college. She died in 1955 at age twenty-two. Frieda Pushnik spent six years with Ripley and in 1943 joined the "Congress of Freaks." She entered semi-retirement in the 1950s, but appeared occasionally in films, including 1963's *The House of the Damned.* Frieda died in 2000 at the age of seventy-seven. (Sources include *American Sideshow,* by Marc Hartzman, Tarcher, 2006, p. 230; "1934 World's Fair," Sideshow Ephemera Gallery, http://missioncreep.com/mundie/gallery/gallery8.htm [accessed October 1, 2012]; "Frieda Pushnick: Armless and Legless Wonder Girl," http://missioncreep.com/mundie/gallery/gallery21.htm [accessed October 1, 2012]; The Human Marvels, www.thehumanmarvels.com [accessed October 1, 2012]).

Odditoriums (San Fransisco and NYC), Lou Dufour, and Doug Ripley: Virtual Museum of the City of San Francisco, www.sfmuseum.net/hist1/index0.1.html [accessed October 1, 2012]; "CC Pyle Dies," *Chicago Daily Tribune,* February 4, 1939; www.sideshowworld.com/SSNL-Spring-2008-P5.html; "Masters of the Midway," Liebling, *New Yorker*; DHS (Hazel Storer notes, and assorted letters and documents); author interview with Robert Ripley (nephew).

Traveling radio shows: SCRAP (International Newsreel photo, January 1, 1940; "Words and Music," by Sid Weiss, *Radio Daily*, February 8, 1940; "Bob Ripley Program at Grand Canyon," by Kenneth Webb and Charles Speer, *Santa Fe Magazine*, unknown date); MMP, pp. 124–126; RE (radio scripts).

Believe It! sidebar (Goldwater): RE (letter from Ripley to Goldwater, October 7, 1940); Joan Nevills Staveley and Sandra Nevills Reiff interview, Cline Library, Northern Arizona University, September 12, 1994.

Odditorium flop: "Odd Man," by Geoffrey T. Hellman, *New Yorker*, 1940; DHS (Hazel Storer notes, and Odditorium documents and court files).

Believe It! sidebar (Widdicombe and Tapscott): "The Log of the SS *Anglo Saxon*'s Jolly Boat," Imperial War Museum, www.iwm.org.uk/upload/package/7/anglosaxon/log.htm and "Landfall," Imperial War Museum, www.iwm.org.uk/upload/package/7/anglosaxon/landfall.htm [accessed October 1, 2012]; DHS (Hazel Storer notes and letters); MMP, p. 130.

CHAPTER 19

Ripley's parties and life at BION: SCRAP ("America's Catch of the Season," by E. V. Durling, *Boston Evening American*, March 3, 1942; "Where a Globetrotter Hangs His Hat," *Liberty Magazine*, May 11, 1946); "If You Were Housekeeper to Mr. Ripley," by Nanete Kutner, *Good Housekeeping*, 1942; *You're Right Mr. Ripley*, unpublished manuscript, by Almuth Seabeck (Ripley's housekeeper); DHS (Hazel Storer notes on "parties"); "Life Goes to a Party," *LIFE*, July 8, 1940; "Odd Man," by Geoffrey T. Hellman, *New Yorker*, 1940; MMP, pp. 101, 104, 108; "Believe It or Not," by Jack Banner, *Radio Guide*, November 9, 1935.

Note: One of the more revealing articles I came across was an undated clip found in the Ripley archives—"The Name Believe It or Not is Familiar"—written by Mary Morris for an unnamed New York newspaper. Morris describes the day she spent with Ripley, at one point asking him what he liked most about the East. "Love, marriage, romance," he said. "In the Mohammaden countries there are no fights between husband and wife, no divorces. Men are left to enjoy themselves. Women aren't making noise all the time with court litigation like they do here." In the United States, he added, "Our moral codes, or standards, are all wrong."

TBS: I managed to review the unedited interview that TBS conducted with Li Ling-Ai, during which Li mentions Ripley's relationships with Fannie Hurst, Babe Murray, and others, including Oakie. (In the same interview, Li declined to say whether she and Ripley had been lovers.) TBS also interviewed Hazel Storer, who also discussed Ripley's love affair with Oakie. (Li died in 2003, and Storer died in 2005.)

Losing Oakie; other women: RE (interviews with Edward Meyer; Ripley's will); SCRAP ("Ripley Returns with Brand New Believe It Or Nots," International News Service, September 25, 1936; "The Name Believe It or Not Is Familiar," by Mary Morris); DHS (detailed handwritten notes by Hazel Storer on "women"); TBS (unedited interview footage, Hazel Storer); MMP, p. 72; "Tosia Mori," Canadian Ken, http://canadianken.blogspot.com/2008/06/toshia-mori .html; *Just a Minute, Mrs. Gulliver,* by Millie Considine, Prentice-Hall, 1967, reprint edition; *You're Right Mr. Ripley,* by Almuth Seabeck (unpublished manuscript); *Liberty Magazine,* May 11, 1946; "Believe It or Not Ripley," by Jack Stone, *The American Weekly,* June 22, 1947.

Believe It! sidebar (Wong and Mori): *Anna May Wong: From Laundryman's Daughter to Hollywood Legend,* by Graham Russell Hodges, Hong Kong University Press, 2004.

Wartime: RE (Hoover letter to Ripley, May 1941; Taft letter to Ripley, September 19, 1941); *Liberty Magazine,* May 11, 1946; MMP, pp. 92, 104, 108; passenger list for the SS *President Cleveland,* 1927.

CHAPTER 20

Li Ling-Ai and China Relief efforts: Charles Pearson press releases (from Robin Lung); TBS interview; SCRAP (*New York Journal* article, date unknown);

Liberty Magazine, May 11, 1946; "The Name Believe It or Not Is Familiar," by Mary Morris; author interviews with Robin Lung.

WWII radio shows . . . and CIAA spies: RE (contract, January 10, 1939; BION radio show scripts); "The Most Unforgettable Character I've Met—Robert Ripley," by Douglas F. Storer, *Reader's Digest*, June 1959; DHS (assorted letters and contracts, 1941–43); *Walt Disney: The Triumph of the American Imagination*, by Neal Gabler, Vintage, 2007, pp. 372, 394–95; www.waltandelgrupo.com; "Ripley Pins His Faith in Future on Aviation," by Frances Wayne, *Denver Post*, January 14, 1943); "Nelson A. Rockefeller's Office of Inter-American Affairs (1940–1946) and Record Group 229," by Gisela Cramer and Ursula Prutsch, *Hispanic American Historical Review*, 2006; "Coordinator of Inter-American Affairs," http://en.wikipedia.org/wiki/Coordinator_of_Inter-American_Affairs (external references and links); The Venona Project, http://sovietspies.blogspot .com.

Deaths: "Seven Story Fall Kills Linda Lee, Radio Singer," *New York Evening Journal*, August 25, 1942; DHS (letters and Hazel Storer notes); *You're Right Mr. Ripley*, by Almuth Seabeck (unpublished manuscript); "Where a Globetrotter Hangs His Hat," *Liberty Magazine*, 1946.

Radio, parties, and troubles: "Ripley Finds Aviation Way to Brotherhood," *St. Louis Post Dispatch*, February 11, 1943; SCRAP (NYT, May 25, 1943); "Big Town Heartbeat," *Atlanta Journal*, January 30, 1944; "Father Carves Name in Engine," *Herald Advance*, Milbank, SD, February 17, 1944; "The Voice of Broadway," Dorothy Kilgallen column, February 28, 1944; "In Hollywood," by Louella Parsons, *Pittsburgh Sun-Telegraph*, February 10, 1944; "Does His Own," *Radio Life*, February 20, 1944; "Believe It or Not," *Time*, January 29, 1945; "Believe It or Not Here's Ripley," by Lee Bevins, *Pageant*, October 1948; "On the Side," by E. V. Durling, *Boston Evening American*, March 3, 1942; "Ripley to Sail Chinese Junk," by Priscilla Endicott, *Westchester Times*, July 31, 1947; RE (assorted letters and memos, 1942–44); TBS interview with Li Ling-Ai; NYT ("JV Connolly Dies," April 18, 1945); DHS; MMP, p. 101.

CHAPTER 21

The *Mon Lei:* DHS (letters, Hazel Storer notes); *You're Right Mr. Ripley,* by Almuth Seabeck (unpublished manuscript); RE (Bill McDonald letter to Doug Storer, 1962; Cygna Conly letter to Joe Willicombe, March 18, 1966; Willicombe itinerary, 1947); SCRAP ("Ripley Arrived Today," by Sidney Epstein, December I, 1947, publication unknown; "Ripley to Spend Vacation Here," by SW Matthews, *Miami Daily News,* date unknown; "I Found the Lost Weekend," by Louise Baer, *DAC News,* date unknown; *Key West Citizen* article, February 14, 1947; "Ripley to Sail Chinese Junk," by Priscilla Endicott, *Westchester Times;* "Planes and Yachts Greet Ripley Today," by Jack Leary, *Albany Times-Union,* August 8, 1947); MMP, pp. 176–77.

CHAPTER 22

Most of the details of Ripley's final trip to China come from a detailed journal written by George McMillin, found at the Ripley archives. Other sources include: RE (letters, 1947–1949, including Ripley to Storer, February 27, 1948, Ripley to Ward Greene, October II, 1948, and Storer to Ripley, July 25, 1948; also 1949 BION show scripts); MMP, pp. 193, 197; DHS ("Partnership Leads to Believe It or Not," by Hazel Geissler, *St. Petersburg Evening Independent,* March 29, 1979; Hazel Storer notes and letters); "Ina E. Ohnick, Magnate's Widow Who Survived a Wartime Prison," by Peyton Whitely, *Seattle Times,* September 18, 1992); *The Man Who Loved China,* by Simon Winchester, Harper, 2008, pp. 46–7, 50–I; SCRAP ("Ripley Aboard President Cleveland," *Honolulu Star-Bulletin,* date unknown); TBS interviews with Hazel Storer and Li Ling-Ai.

CHAPTER 23

Ripley's volatility, declining health, disputes with brother: RE (numerous letters to and from Ripley, 1947–1949; Cygna Conly memo, January 20, 1947; KFS inneroffice memos); interviews with Robert and Rebecca Ripley; MMP, pp. 193, 206; *Just a Minute, Mrs. Gulliver,* Millie Considine, Prentice-Hall, 1967, reprint edition; SRD ("Robert Ripley Will Be Buried in City of Roses," May 28, 1949); DHS (Hazel Storer notes and letters; Doug Storer business letters and memos); "Believe It or Not Ripley," by Jack Stone, *The American Weekly,* June 22, 1947; SFC ("When Fights Were Fights," by Harry B. Smith, February 13, 1935); TBS interviews with Hazel Storer and Li Ling-Ai; SID (notes on Ming Jung).

CHAPTER 24

Ripley's final days and death: RE (Doug Storer letters; BION show scripts; BION film footage); NYT ("The Battle for Shanghai Ended Today," May 27, 1949; Ripley funeral, June 1, 1949); DHS (Hazel Storer notes); TBS interviews with Hazel Storer and Li Ling-Ai; MMP, pp. 210–211; author interviews with Robert and Rebecca Ripley; "One Man's Junk Is Another Base's Treasure," by Andy Stephens, *Air Force Print News Today,* December 7, 2006; "The Most Unforgettable Character I've Met—Robert Ripley," by Douglas F. Storer, *Reader's Digest,* June 1959; SRD ("Robert Ripley Will Be Buried in City of Roses," May 28, 1949).

Note: According to an essay written by Ripley employee Kay Lawrence (which I found in the Ripley archives), Ripley was dictating something to Liese Wisse when he started to convulse. Lawrence arrived at the hospital soon after he was pronounced dead, and found Wisse hysterical and sobbing. A doctor told them it was a heart attack. They were soon joined by Cygna Conly, Robert Hyland, and Doug Ripley. Lawrence writes that all of them except Doug Storer were grief stricken. Storer, she said, was "nonchalantly twirling his watch chain . . . talking about what he planned to do in the future regarding the business."

EPILOGUE

The aftermath and the legacy: SCRAP ("Ripley to Sail Chinese Junk," by Priscilla Endicott, *The Westchester Times,* July 31, 1947); author interview with Allan Holtz; RE (undated essay by Kay Lawrence); author interviews with Robert and Rebecca Ripley; "Ripley Auction," *LIFE,* September 12, 1949;

"With or Without Dragons," *The New Yorker*, September 1949; author interviews with Edward Meyer; "Believe It or Not," by Kenneth Turan, *Washington Post*, April 1, 1973; "Believe It or Not Going Strong at 33," *Editor & Publisher*, December 15, 1951; SRD ("A Big Tree, A Little Church, A Restoration," by Gaye LeBaron, December 25, 2010); "Would You Believe Louis XIV Never Took a Bath?" by Jill Millikin, *Wall Street Journal*, February 1, 1972; "In Search of the (Nearly) Miraculous," by Susan Lydon, *Village Voice*, October 22, 1979; TBS interviews with Hazel Storer and Li Ling-Ai; "Li Ling Ai," *Village Care News*, Spring 2003.

Note: Other *Believe It or Not* writers and artists included Lester Byck; Paul and Walter Frehm (Paul would win a National Cartoonist Society award in 1976); Don Wimmer; Joe Campbell; Art Sloggatt; Clemens Gretter; Carl Dorese; Bob Clarke; Clarence Thorpe; and Stan Randall.

ACKNOWLEDGMENTS

Supreme gratitude to Norm Deska and Edward Meyer at the Ripley Entertainment company for opening your doors to me, allowing me inside the archives, entrusting me with your treasures, and for giving me a chance to tell the full story of LeRoy Robert Ripley. Without your help, this book could not have been written.

Also at Ripley Entertainment, I'm thankful for the support of Jim Pattison Jr., Amanda Dula, and Anne Marshall, as well as Anthony, Viviana, Amy, Natasha, Angela, and Todd, and everyone who made me feel so welcome during my many visits to your Orlando HQ.

I'm deeply indebted to Sidney Kirkpatrick, who mined portions of Ripley's story before me and, in an act of humbling graciousness, agreed to share with me his research. Thank you, Sidney (and Nancy).

To the Ripley family—Ripley's grandniece, Rebecca; her father, Robert; and her uncle, Doug (Ripley's nephews)—thanks for putting up with my phone calls and letters, and for speaking with me so graciously and openly about your memories of the Ripley brothers.

Acknowledgments

Many thanks to Greg Daugherty, for the Mamaroneck tour; Tom Van Pelt, for sharing his Ripley collection; and to both men, for welcoming me into their homes. In Santa Rosa, I'm grateful for the assistance of the wonderfully gracious and funny Lee Torliatt and the rest of the crew at the Sonoma Historical Society, and Santa Rosa's longtime columnist and semi-official historian, Gaye LeBaron. Thanks to John Hacku, who oversaw Santa Rosa's sadly short-lived Ripley museum.

At the New York Public Library, I count myself once again among the fortunate writer-researchers to have benefited from the skills and generosity of Dave Smith—thanks! And though I may not remember all the names (nor you mine), my humble thanks go out to the sixth-floor microfilm crew and others at the Seattle Public Library. I'm also thankful for the time I was able to spend at the library's Scandiuzzi Writers' Room—thank you, Chris Higashi.

Robin Lung, I appreciate the help you offered with the story of Li Ling-Ai and her relationship with Ripley. (Best of luck with your film, *Finding Kukan*—nestedeggproductions.com.) For assistance with the history of comics, my thanks to Allan Holtz, Cole Johnson, and the excellent website Stripper's Guide (www.strippersguide.com). To the Pearlroth family, Jeff and Jonathan, thanks for speaking with me. And to Tom Quinn, thanks for sharing bits of the history of the NYAC.

With each of my books, I've been fortunate to have friends and family willingly read and critique sloppy drafts; thanks to Katherine Reed, Pauline Trimarco, and Brian Klam. I'm grateful to New Jersey records sleuth John Mooney for tracking down Ripley's marriage license. And, since writing is often such a solitary pursuit, I'm thankful to those who made the job less solitary or offered advice or support, a well-timed cocktail, or a bed: Jack and Deirdre Timmons, for the loan of the Vashon

Island retreat; Lisa Loop, for coaching and editorial input; Andrew Chapman, for moral support and lunches; Reid and Lucas Adams, for bourbon and a bed while researching at UNC; Joe D'Agnese, Denise Kiernan, and Tom and Rebecca Gholson, for being there from the start; Spencer and Man Cohen, for Chinese translations; and Phil Thompson, for loaning me the Mini during my Florida visits, and for much more.

To William Langewiesche, thank you for taking a look at an early draft and offering advice. And my gratitude to Richard Florest, for providing outstanding editorial input at a crucial stage.

Heartfelt thanks to Michael Carlisle for getting this project rolling and, especially, to my agent, Rob Weisbach, thank you for believing in and championing the project. I look forward to many more.

At Crown, I'm incredibly grateful to my editor, Rick Horgan, and his assistant, Nathan Roberson, for their diligent, smart, and relentless efforts in shaping and elevating this story, as well as to copy editor Rachelle Mandik for regularly saving me from myself. And my sincere thanks to everyone at Crown— designers Jaclyn Reyes and Nupoor Gordon, production editor Robert Siek, and especially Tina Constable, Christina Foxley, Ellen Folan, and Kristen Fleming—for believing in Ripley's story.

Finally, to Mary, Sean, and Leo, my unbelievable believe-it-or-not family.

Index

Index

Index

Index

Mandy, James, 234

Manila (Philippines), 329

Manning, John J., 339

Mao Zedong, 350, 361, 364

Marco Polo, 200

Marineland (Fla.), 268–69

Mariposa (SS), 190, 194–96, 198, 199

Markoff, Gypsy, 279

Masakichi, Hananuma, 230

Massey, Ilona, 335

McClure, H. H., 165

McCormack, John, 237

McDonald, Bill, 337

McGraw, John, 49, 50

McIntyre, O. O., 243, 249

McMillin, George, 324–28, 332, 335–36

McNamee, Graham, 259

Mencken, H. L., 134, 142

Meyer, Edward, 376

Miller, Clyde, 156

Missouri (USS), 318

Missouri Valley College, 263

Mon Lei, 315–21, 330, 344, 366–69

monogamy, 290

Moore, Thomas, 154

Mori, Toshia, 291, 292

Morris, Mary, 399

movies. *See* Films; *specific movies*

Mukden (China), 198

Munsey, Frank A., 107–8, III, II4, II6, 134, 234

museums, 370, 372

Muslims. *See* Islam

Nairobi (Kenya), 203, 204

National Aeronautic Association, 307

National Air Races, 273

national anthem, 168–69

National Broadcasting Company (NBC), 176, 191, 193, 233, 234, 238–39, 255, 256, 258, 302, 324, 351–54

Nehi Corporation, 263, 302

Nelson, Ozzie, 233, 260

New Deal, 235, 237, 333

newspapers, 10, 22, 134

   See also specific papers

New York American, 75, 165, 167, 182, 185

New York Athletic Club, 72–75, 79–80, 83, 87, 135, 166–67, 188, 224

New York Daily Mirror, 139

New Yorker magazine, 160, 167, 277, 368

New York Evening Post, 136–38, 142, 145, 147, 152, 156

New York Herald, 107, 108

New York Journal-American, 361

New York Sun, 107, 108, III, 134

New York Times, 373

New York World, 45

New York Yankees, 49

Index

ABOUT THE AUTHOR

Neal Thompson (www.nealthompson.com) is a veteran journalist and author of three previous books: *Light This Candle: The Life & Times of Alan Shepard, America's First Spaceman; Driving with the Devil: Southern Moonshine, Detroit Wheels, and the Birth of NASCAR;* and *Hurricane Season: A Coach, His Team, and Their Triumph in the Time of Katrina.* Thompson and his books have been featured on NPR, ESPN, the History Channel, Fox, and TNT, and his stories have appeared in *Outside, Esquire, Sports Illustrated,* and the *Washington Post Magazine.* He lives in Seattle with his wife and two skateboarding sons.